Theology and Discovery:

Essays in honor of
Karl Rahner, S.J.

Theology and Discovery:

Essays in honor of Karl Rahner, S.J.

Edited by
William J. Kelly, S.J.

Marquette University Press
Milwaukee, Wisconsin

Library of Congress Catalog Card Number: 80-82361

© Copyright 1980
Marquette University Press
Printed in the United States of America

ISBN 0-87462-521-1

Editor's Preface

The Rev. Karl Rahner, S.J., was awarded the Pere Marquette Discovery Medal March 28, 1979. The medal was offered in honor of Father's 75th birthday and in celebration of his achievements in theology both for the Church and for the world. The graphic of the medal is reproduced on the cover of this volume. The three days following the presentation of the medal were given over to a symposium featuring major papers by outstanding theologians and responses to these papers. After the presentation of the Discovery Medal, Fr. Rahner gave a touching acceptance speech. This speech serves beautifully as a *Foreword* to this volume.

Not all of the major papers touch directly on Rahnerian themes, but an overall theological order, headed by Fr. Dulles' reflection on "Discovery," was decided upon. However, to assist the reader to a better understanding of spatio-temporal references in both the papers and the responses, the original chronological order is given in an appendix.

All who collaborated in the activities of the Discovery Award and the symposium are deserving of thanks, for those efforts led to the publication of this volume. A special debt of gratitude is due to Mr. Mark Lowery for his invaluable and indefatigable editorial assistance. The undersigned, however, takes editorial responsibility for the final version of this volume.

Rev. William J. Kelly, S.J.
Chairman, Theology Department
Marquette University
Milwaukee, Wisconsin
March 1980

Foreword

by Rev. Karl Rahner, S.J.

As I express my warm gratitude to Marquette University, to all its officers and representatives and, in a special way to its Theology Department, and as I give you wonderful people my warm thanks for the great honor I was granted, this tribute is not directed, I would like to think, neither at the beginning nor the end toward my person or toward my merits. Those are minimal and insignificant, and they are more keenly felt as such by me in my old age which is close to death. It is my preference that both the tribute and my thanks be directed toward the contemporary theology in its entirety—that theology shaped in the last thirty years and recognized somewhat officially by the Second Vatican Council.

Of course, I have in mind an orthodox Catholic theology. That goes without saying. A theology which would not be obedient and docile under the word of God as it is proclaimed in the Church would not be Catholic theology. But I am envisaging a Catholic theology that is courageous and does not shun relative and restricted conflicts with Church authorities. I am thinking of a theology which can no longer be uniform in a Neo-Scholastic approach. I call this the Pius epoch, but this era of the Popes who bore the name ''Pius'' has after all come to an end. I envisage a theology which is in dialogue with its time and lives courageously with it and in it.

This is all the more possible because it is characteristic of this time to be at a critical distance from itself, something *God makes possible.* It is a special grace to this age to be able now to have a critical distance from ourselves given us from the Cross for Christ. In this more critical distance, I envisage a theology which in the Church at large must be the theology of a worldwide Church. That means a theology which does not only recite its own medieval history but, one that can listen to the wisdom of the East, to the longing for freedom in Latin America, and also to the sound of African drums. I envisage a systematic theology that is an inner unity and what Trinitarian Theologians call (literally a dancing around together) *perichoresis* of fundamental and dogmatic theology. I envisage a theology that enables human beings of our time to have a real grasp on the message of freedom and redemption, a theology that courageously abandons external stanchions of seemingly self-evident truths and things, something which does not stem necessarily from what is Christian, but rather from the changing historical situation structured by its intellectual and social elements. I envisage a theology that does not only move along the numbers in our familiar friend

"Denzinger" interpreting old ecclesiastical pronouncements, but a theology which breaks new ground for *new* pronouncements of the Church.

It would be a theology which takes seriously the hierarchy of truths, a theology which lives by the ecumenical hope that baptized Christians should be able to communicate in that which they all live in their faith. Such a communication should be possible without losing sight of the multiplicity of charisms of life and thought. I envisage a theology which comprehends itself as an interpretation of the reality which through grace is present in every human being; a reality which is not only given to man by external indoctrination. It would be a theology through which this reality would find itself, and which would not pride itself upon its clear concepts but would force them to open over and over again into the incomprehensibility of God himself. Such a theology would not secretly seek to understand itself as *the* theoretical underpinning of a life of middle-class ethics supervised by God.

One could continue in this vein for a long time. But my purpose is not to degrade the old theology whose grateful children we are and remain. It has been rather to hint from afar that our time calls also us theologians sleeping under the broom tree of orthodoxy like Elijah in old days: *Surge, grandis tibi restat via*—Arise, a long journey lies ahead of you.

It has been my intention to serve that theology a little with my poor spirit, my very limited strength and my short life. I feel that that theology is being honored today and is being encouraged to continue so that the Word of God may hurry along and bear fruit.

I thank you.

Table of Contents

Revelation and Discovery

by Rev. Avery Dulles, S.J.

I. Statement of the Problem

The problem of faith and reason is not merely a pastime for theologians. It is a matter of pressing importance for the culture in which we live. Western society, since the end of classical antiquity, has been built upon faith—in part the philosophical faith inherited from classical culture, and in part also the religious faith derived from the Judeo-Christian tradition. Beginning with the sixteenth century, critical reason asserted the claim to be the final arbiter of every faith. With the Enlightenment of the eighteenth century and the Positivism of the nineteenth, critical reason achieved a certain supremacy. Our own nation, like a number of others, is heir to the assumptions that reason can be a sufficient support for public life and that faith belongs to a private sphere in which people are allowed to indulge their private tastes. But as the decades pass, it becomes increasingly evident that critical reason is incapable by itself of legitimizing any intellectual commitments of spiritual values. We must therefore find a way of reintroducing a certain kind of faith into the sphere of public life.

To draw up guidelines for this enterprise is an immensely difficult task, lying far beyond the purview of the present paper. I would hope, however, that the remarks I shall be making on faith and reason may be somewhat relevant to this larger enterprise.

Directly, however, I shall here address a strictly theological problem. I have chosen to speak of revelation and discovery, and thereby to show my esteem for the scholar who is being honored at this convocation with the Père Marquette Discovery Award. The award is appropriate because of Rahner's many creative discoveries in the theological field. It is also appropriate, I shall contend, because his theology gives an opening for considering revelation under the rubric of discovery. This proposal, whether or not it can rightly be ascribed to Rahner, is a challenging and revolutionary one.

We have grown accustomed to dividing human knowledge rather neatly into two compartments. On one side of the divide is acquired, or natural knowledge; on the other side, revealed or supernatural knowledge. Acquired knowledge is that which one gains by the free and deliberate exercise of one's own powers. Revealed knowledge, according to this schematization, is freely bestowed by God. It lies over and above what the human intellect can achieve without assistance from on high. God can be known through either channel, reason or revelation. We know him by reason when we ascend to him by reflection on creatures. We know him by faith when we submit humbly to his revelation concerning himself.[1]

On which side of this divide is discovery? According to the common view it is acquired knowledge. Karl Barth and his followers frequently impugned Friedrich Schleiermacher for having, as one author expresses it, "put discovery in place of revelation, the religious consciousness in the place of the Word of God."[2] If our religious knowledge is discovery, many would hold, it cannot be revelation, and if revelation, it cannot be discovery.

According to the theory just outlined, discovery and revelation are distinct in their source, their content, their method, and their warrants. The source of discovery is the discoverer, whereas the source of revelation is an external revealer. The content of discovery is something relatively difficult of access, but still within the capacities of the discoverer, whereas the content of revelation is, characteristically, that which lies beyond the knower's investigating powers. The method in discovery is an intense application of the subject's own cognitive faculties, whereas in revelation the recipient, laying aside the canons of personal judgment, submits trustingly to what the other is saying. In discovery the contents are warranted by the discoverer's own competence, whereas in revelation the warrant is, at least primarily, the authority of the person who reveals.

The popular contrast between discovery and revelation, however, overlooks certain resemblances pointed out in the work of many contemporary thinkers, such as Michael Polanyi and Karl Rahner. Relying on major authors such as these, I should like to propose, as my thesis for this paper, that revelation can be brought within the category of discovery, and that it may even be defined as a gifted religious discovery.

As a preliminary observation, it might be worth noting the resemblance between the two terms. Discovery means uncovering and thus laying bare. Revelation is commonly traced to the Latin root which means the removal of a veil, an unveiling. The two terms, etymologically, are practically synonymous. Both indicate the manifestation of something previously hidden.

The resemblance between discovery and revelation is brought out by Michael Polanyi, who as a philosopher of science spent many decades probing the genesis of scientific theories. According to Polanyi,

---

[1] Thomas Aquinas, *Summa Contra Gentiles,* Bk. IV, chap. 4, no. 11.

[2] H. R. Mackintosh, *Types of Modern Theology* (New York: Scribner's, 1937), p. 100.

> Discovery is defined as an advancement of knowledge that can-
> not be achieved by any, however diligent, application of explicit
> modes of inference. Yet the discoverer must labor night and
> day. For though no labor can make a discovery, no discovery
> can be made without intense, absorbing, devoted labor. Here
> we have a paradigm of the Pauline scheme of faith, works, and
> grace. The discoverer works in the belief that his labors will
> prepare his mind for receiving a truth from sources over which
> he has no control.[3]

The category of discovery is one that bridges all the disciplines,
and hence is not peculiarly religious. One can speak, for instance, of
a scientific discovery, a philosophical discovery, a discovery leading
to artistic creation, or a religious discovery. Among all these types of
discovery there is a certain isomorphism or analogous unity.

John Henry Newman, I suspect, was one of the first thinkers who
carefully reflected on the peculiar nature of discovery. In his *Grammar of Assent* he analyzed at some length, with many illustrations
from a variety of disciplines, the distinction between proof and
discovery, between formal and informal inference. He attributed
discovery to a mysterious power which he designated, not too
helpfully, as the "illative sense." In line with Newman's distinctions, a contemporary theologian, Thomas F. Torrance, contrasts
two forms of inquiry, which he calls the problematic and the interrogative. Torrance himself notes the importance of this distinction
for the theology of revelation:

> The problematic form of inquiry seeks to order the
> knowledge we have already attained so that no distortion in the
> framework of what we know may hinder or misdirect the ac-
> quisition of further knowledge. The interrogative form of in-
> quiry is a means of opening up the way to apprehend what is
> new, and therefore is not a procedure that can altogether be for-
> mally anticipated, just because it must always involve the leap
> forward to be obedient to the new as it is allowed to disclose
> itself. The interrogative form of inquiry must always reckon
> with the fact that in the last analysis it cannot say just how it has
> come to learn the truth. In natural science this is spoken of as
> *discovery,* in theology this is spoken of as *revelation;* the difference
> between discovery and revelation being determined by the
> nature of the object with which each has to do.[4]

II. The Concept of Discovery

Before we seek to measure how far the concept of discovery may

---

[3] M. Polanyi, "Faith and Reason," *Journal of Religion* 41 (1961): 246-47.

[4] T. F. Torrance, *Theological Science* (London: Oxford U. Press, 1969), pp.
130-31.

be applicable to revelation, it will be helpful to analyze this concept in itself. By a discovery we mean a genuinely new advance in knowledge which is no mere deduction from, or application of, what was previously known in an explicit way. Discovery is an insight that changes the knower's outlook or horizons. To this extent it requires what Polanyi calls "a heuristic process, a self-modifying act, and to this extent a conversion."[5] Placing the discoverer in a new intellectual sphere, it causes him to "think differently, speak a different language, live in a different world."[6]

Modern historians of science, such as M. Polanyi, A. Koestler, and T.S. Kuhn, have pointed out that science progresses not so much through routine application of formal methods of proof and inference as through feats of the creative imagination. The French mathematician, Henri Poincarè, distinguished four stages in the typical discovery process: preparation, incubation, illumination, and confirmation.[7] Before I say anything about religion or revelation, I should like to indicate what these four stages are.

Discovery begins with a state of mind called wonder. The mind contemplates a certain set of data which arouse curiosity. The first phase of discovery, therefore, is to see the question. To perceive a problem, as Polanyi remarks, is to see something that is hidden. "It is to have an intimation of the coherence of hitherto not comprehended particulars."[8] To see a problem is itself an act of tacit knowledge—a knowledge going beyond what we can put in words. For the questioner is convinced that there is a meaning or explanation waiting to be found. Without this uncanny awareness of what is not yet manifest, there is no real problem, and hence there will be no search and no discovery.

The history of science gives innumerable instances of curiosity being aroused by facts in which the investigator or genius, thanks to a favorable preparation, will be able to discern a problem, and hints of a solution, in routine everyday events. Think of the stories, apocryphal or not, of Toscanelli watching the hull of a distant ship sinking over the horizon, of Galileo observing the regular swinging of a lantern in his local church, of Newton being struck by a falling apple while resting under a tree. These common, repeated experiences were uncommon and unique for these particular observers, for they were gifted with a curiosity that prompted them to seek meaning where others had been content simply to acknowledge facts.

---

[5] M. Polanyi, *Personal Knowledge* (New York: Harper Torchbooks, 1964), p. 151.
[6] Ibid.
[7] Cf. ibid., pp. 121-31.
[8] M. Polanyi, *The Tacit Dimension* (Garden City: Doubleday Anchor, 1967), p.21.

The second stage in the process of discovery is incubation—a mysterious stage in which ideas hatch without our being able to control them. According to Polanyi's analysis, which I find especially cogent, this stage involves activity on two levels, the conscious and the unconscious. On the conscious level we allow ourselves to become obsessed with the problem. It becomes a consuming passion that preoccupies us day and night. Passionately concentrating on the desired solution, the inquirer intently focuses on that which has not yet appeared. The mental act is similar to that by which, in a muscular performance, we focus our attention on the intended action—for example: playing a tune, jumping over a fence, or getting a bicycle to turn a corner. If we took our attention off the result and concentrated on the muscular movement, we would become confused and would fail in our objective. So too, in scientific inquiry, the discoverer has vague intimations of the kind of solution being sought, and must keep his attention focused on the point where the meaning may be expected to emerge. George Polya gave the young mathematician the paradoxical advice: "Look at the end. Remember your aim. . . . Do not lose sight of what is required. Keep in mind what you are working for. *Look at the unknown. Look at the conclusion.*"[9]

When we are on the way to discovery, our imagination fixes on the intended solution and coaxes the mind to deliver from its unconscious the appropriate ideas. The tacit dimension in this "maieutic" phase is vividly brought out by Polanyi's description:

> We say then that we are racking our brain or ransacking our brain; that we are cudgeling or cracking it, or beating our brain trying to get it to work.
> And the action induced in us by this ransacking is felt as something that is happening to us. We say that we tumble to an idea; or that an idea crosses our mind; or that it comes into our head, or that it strikes us, or dawns on us, or just presents itself to us. We are actually surprised and exclaim 'Aha' when we suddenly produce an idea. Ideas may come to us unbidden, hours or even days after we have ceased to rack our brain.[10]

All of us have experienced this mysterious process many times; for example, when we are trying to recall a forgotten name. In such cases we both know and do not know what we are looking for. If we knew it, we would not have to search, but if we did not know it, we

[9] G. Polya, *How to Solve It: A New Aspect of Mathematical Method* (Princeton N.J.: Princeton U. Press, 1948), p. 112; cf. M. Polanyi, *Personal Knowledge*, p. 127.

[10] M. Polanyi, "The Creative Imagination," *Chemical and Engineering News* 44 (April 25, 1966): 85-92; quotation from p. 91.

would not be able to recognize the right answer when it came. While searching, we have to wait almost passively for the imagination to come up with a fruitful suggestion. As various suggestions pass in review, we begin to find ourselves moving along what Polanyi describes as a "gradient of deepening convergence."[11] We sometimes have the exciting feeling that we are on the verge of the discovery we are seeking. So, too, in trying to recall a name or a fact, we can sometimes feel it, so to speak, rising toward the surface of our consciousness. We say, "I shall remember it in a minute," "It is almost on the tip of my tongue."

The third and climactic moment of the process is called illumination. The new idea comes into our mind unbidden, often at a moment when we do not expect it. This is a common experience familiar to every historian of science. We have all heard the legend of Archimedes, who allegedly discovered the principle of specific gravity when he was relaxing at the baths.[12] Particularly interesting to the theologian is the language in which Johann Gutenberg spoke of his own invention. While preoccupied with the task of obtaining multiple copies of the Bible in time for an impending pilgrimage to Aachen, he took part in a wine-harvesting festival. Seeing a wine press at work, he suddenly realized that lead in a fluid state could be pressed and molded into type. To describe this illumination, Gutenberg has recourse to mystical and religious language: "A simple substitution which is a ray of light," he wrote; ". . .To work then! God has revealed to me the secret that I demanded of him. . . . I have had a large quantity of lead brought to my house, and that is the pen with which I shall write."[13]

The German physicist, Hermann von Helmholtz, observed that in his experience "happy ideas came unexpectedly without effort like an inspiration."[14] According to W. I. B. Beveridge, von Helmholtz "found that ideas did not come to him when his mind was fatigued or when at the working table, but often in the morning after a night's rest or during the slow ascent of wooded hills on a sunny day."[15] At such times the mind is apparently better disposed to profit from casual hints that come along the way. The period of incubation, according to Arthur Koestler, liberates the mind from the restraints of conventional thinking and thus favors the creative

---

[11] Ibid., p. 88.

[12] For a popular account see Arthur Koestler, *The Act of Creation* (New York: Dell Publ. Co., 1967), pp. 105-109.

[13] Ibid., pp. 121-23.

[14] W. I. B. Beveridge, *The Art of Scientific Investigation* (New York: Vintage Books, 1961), p. 93.

[15] Ibid.

leap which is symptomatic of genius.[16] Examples of sudden and unexpected discoveries are dramatically reported in the lives of René Descartes, Henri Poincarè, Albert Einstein, and others.[17]

Occasionally the key to the solution is furnished by imagery in a dream. The nineteenth century organic chemist, Friedrich von Kekule, made one of the most brilliant discoveries in the history of his specialty—namely that the molecules of certain important organic compounds are closed chains or rings—as a result of a dream in which he saw a snake catch hold of its own tail and whirl before his eyes.[18]

In this connection one is inevitably reminded of poetic inspiration. The Greek poets invoked the Muses—and this may have originally been something more than a literary fiction. Plato, in the *Ion* and the *Phaedrus,* maintained that poets, like prophets, are out of their senses when they compose. This does not seem to be regularly the case with modern poets, but one reads in the lives of a William Blake[19] or a Rainer Maria Rilke that certain of their lines came to them in a state of hallucination. Samuel Taylor Coleridge testified that the entire text of his *Kubla Khan,* amounting to two or three hundred lines, was given to him in an opium trance, although some of the original lines were lost because a visitor, who came unexpectedly on a matter of business, disturbed his recollection. The lost lines then had to be supplied by more laborious methods of composition.[20]

The fourth and final step in the process is confirmation. In every supposed discovery there is a certain risk of illusion. As already observed, the discovery, being separated by a logical gap from what was previously known, could not have been achieved by formal reasoning. As John Henry Newman observed, "The great discoverers of religious principles do not reason. . . . It is the second-rate men, though most useful in their place, who prove, reconcile, finish, explain."[21] The mathematician Polya said much the same thing when he wrote, "When you have satisfied yourself that the theorem is true, you start proving it."[22] Norwood Hanson, in his

---

[16] Koestler, *The Act of Creation,* pp. 209-10.

[17] Ibid., pp. 210-11.

[18] Ibid., pp. 118, 169-70.

[19] William Blake asserted concerning his poem, *Milton:* "I have written this poem from immediate Dictation, twelve or sometimes twenty or thirty lines at a time, without Premeditation, and even against my Will; the time it has taken was thus rendered Non Existent," *The Letters of William Blake,* ed. G. Keynes (London: Hart-Davis, 1956), p. 85.

[20] Koestler, *The Act of Creation,* pp. 166-69.

[21] J. H. Newman, *Grammar of Assent* (Garden City: Doubleday Image, 1953), pp. 296-97.

[22] G. Polya, *Mathematics and Plausible Reasoning* 2:76; quoted by Polanyi, *Personal Knowledge,* p. 131.

Patterns of Discovery, illustrates at length that new theories in physics are not achieved either by deduction or by any controlled process of induction, but rather by a mysterious process which Hanson, following C. S. Peirce, calls "abduction" or "retroduction." A theory, says Hanson, is not a conclusion from explicitly known premises but rather a conclusion in search of its own premises.[23]

As historians of science well know (and here again the application to religion is obvious), new discoveries do not easily win recognition. Frequently they encounter fierce opposition, even ridicule. The English surgeon, Wilfred Trotter, is quoted as saying:

> The mind likes a strange idea as little as the body likes a strange protein and resists it with similar energy. It would not perhaps be too fanciful to say that a new idea is the most quickly acting antigen known to science. If we watch ourselves honestly we shall often find that we have begun to argue against a new idea even before it is completely stated.[24]

How, then, can the innovator clear up his own doubts and overcome the opposition of others? To begin with, one may say that the more original the discovery, the less cogently can it be demonstrated. We demonstrate by reduction to the already known. Discovery, however, means grasping the not-yet-known. It is a leap forward, the seizure of something radically new. The new cannot be established within the old categories or by the old methods, for they were incapable of generating the new insight. In fact, the new insight challenges the whole framework of thought that sustained the theory it rejects.

The discoverer therefore finds himself confronted by a dilemma. As Polanyi puts it, "To the extent to which it represents a new way of reasoning, we cannot convince others by formal argument, for so long as we argue within their framework, we can never induce them to abandon it."[25] According to Thomas S. Kuhn, "the transfer of allegiance from paradigm to paradigm is a conversion experience that cannot be forced."[26] In discovery, as already stated, the clues cannot be explicitly attended to, or the solution will disappear. It is necessary for the clues to be perceived only in a subsidiary way. For this reason, they cannot serve as the basis of formal argument.

How, then, does the discoverer know that the new solution is acceptable? First, the discovery is often practically self-validating.

---

[23] N. R. Hanson, *Patterns of Discovery,* chap. 4, "Theories," (Cambridge: Cambridge U. Press, 1958), esp. pp. 85-90.

[24] Quoted by Beveridge, *Art of Scientific Investigation,* pp. 146-47.

[25] Polanyi, *Personal Knowledge,* p. 151.

[26] T. S. Kuhn, *The Structure of Scientific Revolutions,* 2d ed. (Chicago: U. of Chicago Press, 1970), p. 151.

As we approach the solution we have the sensation of moving down what I have called, following Polanyi, the "gradient of deepening coherence." As the clues begin to coalesce into an unexpected pattern, corresponding to the goal of our tacit orientation, our anticipations direct our approach toward what we eventually light upon as the solution. The discovery, when it appears, corresponds to what, in the search, we already felt must be there. "It arrives accredited in advance by the heuristic craving which evoked it."[27] The perception of the answer arouses spontaneous joy and satisfaction. It gives a sudden release of heuristic tension as expressed in the famous "eureka" of Archimedes.[28]

Further confirmation is provided by the ability of the new discovery to account for data that were not envisaged during the search. The wider the range of data it explains, the stronger will be the reality-index for the theory. Newtonian physics prevailed over Aristotelian, I would suspect, largely because it gave a simple unitary account of heavenly as well as earthly bodies, thus overcoming the split between the sublunary and the celestial worlds. Heisenberg's quantum mechanics and Einstein's theory of relativity had the further advantage of applying to the subatomic and supragalactic worlds, which proved to be beyond the grasp of Newtonian physics. Science is still in search of a unified field theory in which all the forces of particle physics and astrophysics can be successfully integrated into a single science. Each new theory is pregnant with a multitude of unforeseen implications. The more capable it proves of resolving problems not even contemplated when the theory was first devised, the more likely we are to believe that the theory is an accurate account of the way things actually are.

Thirdly, the acceptability of a discovery to others is a powerful index of its validity, especially if those who accept it are serious, discriminating, and concerned with truth. Polanyi speaks of a persuasive passion that is the inevitable concomitant of the heuristic passion.[29] When we believe, everyone who is converted to our way of seeing things reinforces our own conviction, and everyone who fails to accept our views is a living threat to our own faith. No doubt a true believer will be able to endure a great deal of opposition, but such a person will not cease to give testimony with the hope of converting others. The general acceptance of the new theory by acknowledged experts is practically tantamount to proof.

On the basis of this analysis of discovery, we may now sum-

---

[27] Polanyi, *Personal Knowledge,* p. 130.
[28] Ibid., p. 122.
[29] Ibid., pp. 150-60.

marize. Discovery is a self-transcending act of reason wherein an inquirer, driven by a passionate desire to learn a hidden truth, which he trusts is waiting to be found, allows his imagination to suggest ways of synthesizing the data, until he strikes upon an insight that arrives accredited in advance by the heuristic craving that evoked it. Further confirmation of the truth of the insight is provided by the unexpected fruitfulness of the insight in accounting for new data and by its power to satisfy other inquirers in their search for truth.

III. Religious Discovery and the Dialectic of Conversion

Transferring this concept of discovery to the religious sphere, I should like to suggest that the analysis just given applies with striking accuracy to the process of religious conversion and to the genesis of religious faith. It would be possible to parallel the experiences of the scientific explorers and poets almost point for point with those of religious seekers. This is eloquently attested by the classical authors who have described their own conversion, such as Justin Martyr, Augustine, Pascal, and Newman. Additional confirmation could be found from the testimonies collected in William James' *Varieties of Religious Experience,* even though James is perhaps overinclined to concentrate on highly emotional crises in which the intellectual ingredient is minimal.

The religious quest, like the scientific, begins with passionate questioning. Persons sensitive to the dimension of ultimacy in human experience, unwilling to rest in merely proximate explanations that might satisfy more superficial minds, persistently ask whether life and the world, in the final analysis, issue into a meaningless void, or whether the proximate meanings disclosed in everyday experience point to an ultimate and abiding significance. In their search they are driven by a primordial faith that the world as a whole cannot be meaningless and that the enigmas of life, dark as they may be, are not ultimately absurd. The religious inquirer is existentially involved in the search, for the questions are of ultimate concern to the subject as a person.[30]

Religious discoveries, therefore, demand a certain spiritual preparation. They do not come to persons totally caught up in the day-to-day practicalities of life. They demand that the seeker have a sense of the inadequacy of all that is not God—a perception gained, very often, by crises in one's personal life. At such times we begin to sense what is meant by Paul's statement in Acts that all peoples have been fashioned so "that they should seek God, in the hope that they might feel after him and find him" (Acts 17:27). Our search for

---

[30] Cf. P. Tillich, *The Courage to Be* (New Haven: Yale U. Press, 1952), p. 123.

God, viewed retrospectively after the finding, was accompanied by a certain prior awareness which directed the entire quest. We were already on the lookout for him whom Paul speaks of, in his Areopagus sermon, as the "unknown God" (Acts 17:23). For this reason the religious seeker can quite literally carry out the precept of Polya, "Look at the unknown; look at the conclusion." If we take our eyes off the God for whom we are looking the whole quest collapses.

Dominated by the search for the God who is loved, the religious inquiry unfolds prayerfully. Conscious of our inability to unravel the meaning of life, we confidently turn to him whom we seek, and beg him to illumine the darkness of our minds. While concentrating on the unknown God, we mull over the whole range of our experience for hints of his reality and presence. We interrogate the order of nature, the entire span of recorded history, and the personal events that have shaped our own lives, hoping that, as we do so, we shall stumble upon clues. We cannot force the evidence to speak to us. The process is not under our control. If a favorable environment is maintained, the tacit awareness which set our quest in motion will bear fruit of its own accord. Creatures will answer us as they answered Augustine in a famous passage of the *Confessions:*

> And what is this God? I asked the earth and it answered: 'I am not he,' and all things that are on the earth confessed the same. I asked the sea and the deeps and the creeping things with living souls, and they replied: 'We are not your God, look above us.' I asked the blowing breezes, and the universal air with all its inhabitants answered: 'Anaximenes was wrong, I am not God.' I asked the heaven, the sun, the moon, the stars, and 'No,' they said, 'we are not the God for whom you are looking.' And I said to all those things which stand about the gates of my senses: 'Tell me about my God, you who are not He. Tell me something about Him.' And they cried out in a loud voice: 'He made us.' My question was in my contemplation of them and their answer was in their beauty.[31]

The third moment, that of illumination, is the climax of the search. At a certain point the spirit is caught up in the blessed vision of peace. A light invades our hearts so that we may see God's glory reflected in his creation and especially, St. Paul assures us, in the face of Christ Jesus (2 Cor 4:6). In rapturous joy the soul exclaims, as did Augustine in his *Confessions:* "Late have I loved you, O beauty ever ancient and ever new! Late have I loved you!"[32]

The disclosure of God in Jesus Christ comes as the "solution" to

---

[31] Augustine, *Confessions,* Bk. X, chap. 6, trans. Rex Warner (New York: Mentor-Omega Books, 1963), p. 215.

[32] Ibid., Bk. X, chap. 27.

the Christian convert. The solution, like a scientific discovery, arrives "accredited in advance by the heuristic craving which evoked it." As Henri de Lubac asserts in his *The Discovery of God,* we never encounter God as a complete stranger. We meet him as one with whom we were already somehow familiar. When God reveals himself, we experience a shock of recognition—as though we had known all along that this is what he must be like.[33] Augustine, Pascal, and others have argued that the search for God presupposes God's active presence to the mind that seeks him.[34]

Even after the discovery is made, however, the process of confirmation goes on. Religious faith, like a scientific theory, pays off by providing intelligibility to events that would otherwise appear meaningless or absurd. It provides ideals by which one can live and which, indeed, challenge people to become what they sense to be their own best selves. Those who have been themselves converted are driven by a passion to convert others, partly in order to share the riches they have found, but partly also to reinforce their own conviction. But missionary success is not essential to belief. Those who have had an intense experience of personal conversion are in a position to stand within a cognitive minority. They do not cherish the illusion that the majority is always right.

At no point within the present life does religious discovery provide a complete and satisfying answer to all our religious questions. As Augustine profoundly observed, "God is both sought in being found and found in being sought."[35] Ultimate reality is essentially incomprehensible to the human mind, and for this reason every religious disclosure terminates in what Viktor Frankl has happily called a "meaning beyond meaning," a "suprameaning," one that exceeds the finite intellectual capacities of man.[36] The paradox of the "known unknown" is illuminated to some extent by a recognition of the polar structure of the process of discovery. The quest, as we have said, is dominated by a tacit awareness of its goal. But the goal in the case of religious knowledge is never fully attained in the present life, and hence the awareness of it remains in some measure tacit. Unlike

---

[33] H. de Lubac, *The Discovery of God* (Chicago: Regnery, 1967), pp. 78-80. The same point has been made on various occasions by K. Rahner, e.g., in "Atheism and Implicit Christianity," *Theological Investigations* 9, trans. Graham Harrison (New York: Herder and Herder, 1972): 158.

[34] Augustine, *Soliloquies,* Bk. I, chap. 2 (New York: Cosmopolitan Science and Art Service Co., 1943), p. 17; B. Pascal, *Pensées,* no. 554 (New York: E. P. Dutton, 1940), p. 151.

[35] Augustine, *On the Trinity,* Bk. XV, chap. 2 (CC, series latina, vol. 50A), p. 461.

[36] V. E. Frankl, *Man's Search for Meaning* (New York: Washington Square Press, 1963), pp. 187-88.

conceptual or objectivizing knowledge, knowledge through participation leaves intact the mystery of that which is known. We know
God, most of all, through an involvement in the passionate search
for him. In the language of Ian Ramsey, one may say that every
disclosure of the divine takes place through a combination of
discernment and commitment.[37] In order to perceive what is disclosed, one must have an existential affinity for it, an affinity which
achieves itself in love.

IV. Biblical Faith as Discovery

Thus far I have used as my examples of religious disclosure the
acts of discovery by which great converts, such as Augustine and
Newman, have found God in the biblical writings and in the faith of
the Christian Church. Although these conversions were discoveries
to the converts themselves, they were not basically new discoveries
for the community of faith. These converts, at the end of their personal search, accepted the faith of a community which was already
in being. We must therefore now put a further question: Does the
phenomenology of discovery apply also to those great foundational
disclosures by which the deposit of biblical and Christian faith was
originally built up? Is it correct to say that Abraham and Moses,
Isaiah and Jeremiah, Jesus, Paul and John discovered the truths
which they proclaimed and which became constitutive of the community of biblical and Christian faith? Theology does not generally
speak of these disclosures as discoveries but rather as revelation.

On closer examination, however, the prophets and apostles of
biblical times do not differ markedly as individuals from the converts
of subsequent centuries. We think of them as innovators, but,
generally speaking, they had a very different image of themselves.
They felt called to adhere faithfully to the tradition that had been
handed to them by others. The prophets were urging the rulers of
Israel and Judah to return to the God of the Sinai Covenant.
Apostles such as Paul and John were seeking to maintain intact the
revelation already given—a revelation shared by them with the
entire apostolic Church.

To assess the biblical evidence is no easy task, for the accounts are
often figurative and rarely circumstantial. What does it mean when
an Old Testament text affirms that the word of God came to a given
prophet at a certain time and place? How did the mind of Joseph
function when he interpreted the dreams of the Pharaoh (Gen
49-51)? By what mental process did Daniel (if he was an actual
historical figure) unravel the meaning of Nebuchadnessar's dream

---

[37] I. T. Ramsey, *Religious Language*, chap. 1 (New York: Macmillan Paperbacks,
1963), pp. 11-54.

(Dan 4)? What really happened when Moses looked at the back of the Lord (Ex 33:23)? And in the New Testament: how did Peter discern that Jesus was the Messiah and Son of God (Mt 16:16 par; Jn 6:69)? What were Paul's intellectual processes when he was raised to the "third heaven" (2 Cor 12:1-4)? How historical and how literal is each of the passages in question? We are often compelled to rely on tenuous conjectures.

To the extent that any generalization is warranted by the biblical texts, one would have to say that the prophets and apostles received their messages in what Alan Richardson describes as "disclosure situations."[38] Through some unusual combination of natural phenomena or historical occurrences, their heuristic passions were aroused, their imaginations were stimulated, and they became possessed by powerful insights which cast a whole new light on the meaning of life—insights which they then sought to pass on to others by testimony.

In primitive times, it would seem, the reception of religious knowledge was more passively experienced than is common in literate cultures. The ecstatic prophets of the eleventh through the ninth centuries apparently underwent hallucinatory experiences, as did various pagan shamans such as the Canaanite prophets of Baal. In the words of W. F. Albright,

> . . . the prophetic movement takes root in group-ecstaticism, i.e., in dances and other physical motions repeated so often by members of a group that they finally succumb to a kind of hypnotic suggestion, under the influence of which they remain unconscious for hours. In this state the subconscious may remain abnormally active, and persons of a certain psychological type may have visions and mystic experiences which thereafter control, or at least affect, their entire life. This phenomenon is universal among mankind, being found among savages, in antiquity, and among the highest religions of today.[39]

To what extent this type of visual and auditory hallucination was still a factor in the great literary prophets of the later Old Testament period, it is not easy for us to say. Rabbi Abraham Heschel offers wise cautions on this point:

> It is not within our power to decide about the nature of the visions and voices received by the prophets: whether they were real or merely subjective phenomena; whether the voice was perceived in trance or in a waking state. It is vain to speculate

---

[38] A. Richardson, *History Sacred and Profane* (Philadelphia: Westminster Press, 1964), p. 103

[39] W. F. Albright, *From the Stone Age to Christianity,* 2d ed. (Garden City: Doubleday Anchor, 1957), pp. 303-4.

how the divine mind coalesces with the human, or to ask at
what point the divine begins to operate; whether the formula
'thus says the Lord' introduced a verbally inspired message; or
whether only the thought was revealed, the language being the
prophet's own.[40]

In the great prophets to whom biblical books are ascribed, such as
Amos and Hosea, Isaiah, Jeremiah, and Ezekiel, it would be
fallacious to surmise that inspiration was equivalent to passivity. Far
from being solitary mystics absorbed in divine contemplation, they
were men deeply involved in the history of their times, actively taken
up with urgent problems in the spheres of politics, economics, social
and military affairs. Their sudden inspirations were no doubt often
the fruits of unconscious gestation of ideas such as we have noted in
many of the great inventors and poets.

Even where ecstatic phenomena occurred, we need not assume
that God simply by-passed the mechanisms of the human psyche.
On the empirical plane there was no clear distinction between the
true and the false prophets. Visions and auditions are not self-
authenticating as means of knowledge, but God can use them in
imparting divine truth, for they represent ways in which authentic
religious discoveries may arise.

Already in the later prophets, one begins to note an increasing
reliance on critical and reflective thought. The prophets of the exilic
and post-exilic period think long and deeply about how the reverses
of Israel are to be reconciled with God's faithfulness to his covenant.
Of Jeremiah it has been well said by Gerhard von Rad:

> As the child of his age, it was no longer possible for Jeremiah to
> resign himself to the will of Jahweh; he had to question, and to
> understand. In his sensitiveness and vulnerability, his feeling
> for the problems of religion, he was certainly at one with many
> of his contemporaries. . . . And the seriousness with which he
> took this intellectual state, which of course lay outside his pro-
> phetic calling proper, is shown precisely by the wide range of his
> reflection on theological problems.[41]

If prophecy tends to deviate from the paradigm of discovery by
virtue of the predominance of the passive over the reflective element
(a predominance which becomes even more acute in the apocalyptic
period), the reverse is true of biblical wisdom, which seems almost
too reflective to merit the title of discovery. Some of the early
examples of wisdom, it may be conceded, are cosmopolitan, prac-

---

[40] A. J. Heschel, *The Prophets,* 2 vols. (New York: Harper Torchbooks, 1971): 2:
209.

[41] G. von Rad, *Old Testament Theology,* 2 vols. (New York: Harper and Row,
1965), 2:205.

tical, and hardly original. But in the more religious and specifically biblical wisdom writers, the heuristic element is prominent. These writers, though they never claim to be recipients of God's word, regard their instruction as a gift of God and thus as revelation (Pvb 2:6f, Qoh 2:26). They remind us that the discoveries of the reflective mind, when it prayerfully ponders the meaning of Scripture, of nature, and of history, deserve in their own way to be called revelation (Sir 1:6, 24:33, 39:6-8). Solomon, as portrayed in the Book of Wisdom, prays for wisdom as a divine gift (7:7) and confesses: "I could not win wisdom unless God gave it" (8:21). Whatever we may make of these passages theologically, they suggest to us that the wisdom of the Hebrew sages often came from sources over which they felt that they had no control, and may in the phenomenological sense be called discovery.

In no book of the Bible is originality more closely intertwined with theological reflection than in Job. In a dramatic form that vividly mirrors the dialectical progress of the author's own musings, this book sets forth a devastating critique of the conventional theology of history. Convinced of the utter transcendence of the divine wisdom (28), Job rebels against a God-talk that has become too glib. The conclusion of the book, to the effect that God deserves to be trusted even when we can discern no order or justice in the events that shape our lives, deserves to be called one of the high points of religious discovery in the history of human thought. An undue bias toward the prophetic form of revelation has perhaps prevented Christians from appreciating the wisdom of Job as deeply as they might.

So far as the Old Testament is concerned, therefore, the category of discovery would seem as adequate as any to describe the process by which the legacy of Israel was built up. Discovery can be stretched to include ecstatic phenomena, for as we have seen, some poets and scientists made their discoveries through dreams and hallucinations. Discovery can also include the rational processes by which the Hebrew sages found the attributes of God reflected in the beauty and order of creation, those by which the prophets meditated on the meaning of history, and those by which a critical thinker such as Job was inspired to construct his "negative theology."

The contribution of the New Testament follows, in general, the same forms we have encountered in the Old. We cannot accurately reconstruct the psychology of Jesus, but he would seem to have been in certain respects a prophet (cf. Lk 7:16, 24:19, etc.). It is not unlikely that he, like the Old Testament prophets, experienced occasional visions and locutions, and that he was conscious of being in a special way led by the divine Spirit.

The Christian faith, to the extent that it offers a content clearly distinct from the Old Testament, relies not so much on the teaching of Jesus as on his career, including especially his death and resurrection. Jesus himself is seen as the manifestation of the living God. Does the process by which the disciples perceived Jesus in this light correspond to what we have described as discovery? Does Jesus fulfill for his followers a religious quest in which they were existentially involved?

We know so little of the genesis of New Testament faith that it is difficult to answer these questions with assurance. But the vocabulary of the writers suggests that Jesus came to them as the resolution of a tension and the fulfillment of a hope. Luke's repeated emphasis on spiritual joy as a response to the Good News indicates the same kind of heuristic resolution we have noted in the excitement of scientists and poets. So likewise, the doxologies which punctuate Paul's letter to the Romans permit us to surmise that Paul himself had gone through an agonizing search and that his encounter with the risen Jesus brought an overpowering consolation somewhat similar to that which Luther was later to find in the Pauline doctrine of justification through faith instead of works. Generally speaking, we may say that the eloquent manner in which the New Testament writers were able to present the Christ-event as an answer to the deepest and most universal religious aspirations attests that they themselves had participated in the religious quest to which their writings speak.

As we seek to apply the phenomenology of discovery to the New Testament, we cannot but be struck by the pervasive concept of a higher wisdom—a wisdom not of this world. Already in the Gospels, Jesus is portrayed as thanking his Father for having hidden his secrets from the wise and bestowed them upon the little ones (Mt 11:25 par). This theme is extensively developed in the Pauline and Deutero-Pauline letters. The world did not know God through wisdom, says Paul, but the foolishness of God is wiser than the wisdom of men (1 Cor 1:17-2:16). God has made Christ the wisdom of the Christians (1 Cor 1:30), a "secret and hidden wisdom of God" (1 Cor 2:6-7), imparted by the Holy Spirit, which has been bestowed by the risen Christ (1 Cor 2:10-15). In modern terminology we might say that the Holy Spirit functions for Paul as constituting a new horizon whereby reason is enabled to transcend itself and achieve a discovery beyond its normal capacity.

The Pauline Captivity Epistles likewise portray Christ as a superabundant fulfillment of a legitimate human aspiration for wisdom—an aspiration which without the help of the Holy Spirit leads only to vain philosophy and deceit (Col 2:8). The gratuitous element in the discovery, which Paul attributes to the Holy Spirit, corresponds to the sense of of giftedness which, as we have already seen, is a constant of the heuristic process.

Can we detect in the New Testament anything resembling the confirmation process which we have described as the fourth stage of the experience of discovery? The revelation of God in Jesus, like other discoveries, came to the disciples as unexpected and yet somehow anticipated. Scandalized by Jesus' freedom from the Law, they soon discovered in him a paradoxical fulfillment of the true meaning of the Jewish Law. As they meditated on his teaching and life they found in him everything that the Hebrew Scriptures had been pointing to under designations such as the Son of Man, the Son of David, the Messiah, and other similar titles. He it was, for the Christians, whom the Law and the Prophets had foretold. In the light of Jesus as the Christ, the Scriptures spoke to them with new power and depth. Jesus therefore arrived accredited in advance by the heuristic craving that opened the hearts of the disciples to him.

A further confirmation was provided by the persuasive power of the gospel. Originally perceived as a message of salvation to the Jews, it unexpectedly showed itself as the answer to the religious longings of the Gentiles. As Wolfhart Pannenberg remarks:

> In the proclamation of the Christian mission it was possible for a Hellenistic man to recognize in a surprising and unforeseen shape that God about whose true nature he had been inquiring. . . . Not until he was presented in the form of the Christian message did the Biblical God convince the gentile world of his claim to be the one true God.[42]

Elsewhere Pannenberg observes: "It is from this perspective, namely, the explication of the Christ event as an event for all peoples, that it becomes clear that the father of Jesus Christ had always been the one God from the very beginning of Israel and, indeed, from the beginning of the world."[43]

The confirmation process continues to occur throughout the course of church history. The personal revelation of God in Jesus Christ has proved in every generation to be an unfailing source of light. Thus Vatican II can still claim that in him is to be found "the key, the focal point, and the goal of all human history"[44] and that "through him and in him the riddles of sorrow and death grow

---

[42] W. Pannenberg, "The Revelation of God in Jesus of Nazareth," *Theology as History,* ed. James M. Robinson and John R. Cobb, Jr. (New York: Harper and Row, 1967), pp. 108-9.

[43] W. Pannenberg, "Dogmatic Theses on the Doctrine of Revelation," *Revelation as History* (New York: Macmillan, 1968), p. 135.

[44] Vatican II, *Pastoral Constitution on the Church in the Modern World,* art. 10, ed. Walter M. Abbot, p. 208.

meaningful.''[45] The inexhaustible fruitfulness of this revelation has-been for Christian believers an abiding confirmation of their faith.

V. Christian Faith as Revelation

Our survey of the biblical data indicates, therefore, that the category of discovery may be an acceptable one for analyzing, in its human and phenomenological aspects, what has been traditionally called ''revelation.'' This conclusion gives rise to yet another problem to which we must now turn our attention. Is revelation an appropriate term by which to describe those fundamental religious disclosures which occurred in the biblical times which have furnished the primary themes of Christian belief and preaching down through the centuries?

In a wide sense of the word revelation may be taken as a virtual synonym for what we have been calling disclosure. Schleiermacher, for example, sometimes used the term in a merely phenomenological sense, without explicit reference to God as revealer. In his *Speeches on Religion,* for instance, he wrote: ''Every original and new communication of the Universe to man is a revelation.''[46] In a somewhat similar vein a contemporary American theologian writes:

> Revelation I define as that event which changes—enlarges, enhances—a person's or community's capacity for perception. Revelation does not just deliver information (although it may do that). It does not simply add a little or even a lot to what was known before. Instead it disrupts a world of meaning, requires a new outlook, a new *gestalt.* Because of this, all else fits together differently. . . . The contemporary phrase, 'mind-blowing,' is an apt one to describe the effect of revelation. It shakes, creates, liberates.[47]

If we wish to use the term ''revelation'' in this sense, there is no difficulty in saying that the biblical disclosures are revelation, but we shall have to face the further question whether revelation should be ascribed to God as its source, and if so why. Since ''revelation'' has commonly been used to mean a communication specially attributable to God as its source, it would perhaps be better not to use the term in this ''neutral'' sense, but to speak rather, in this context, of disclosures. Ian Ramsey and Alan Richardson, in their apologetical writing, refer frequently to disclosures, and even of cosmic dis-

---

[45] Ibid., art. 22, p. 222.

[46] F. Schleiermacher, *On religion: Speeches to Its Cultured Despisers* (New York: Harper Torchbooks, 1958), p. 89.

[47] R. L. Shinn, ''Perception and Belief,'' unpublished Presidential Address to American Theological Society, New York, N.Y., April 9, 1976.

closures, but shy away from the term revelation, for, as Richardson puts it, revelation "is an interpretative concept used by dogmatic theologians and apologists."[48] If Christian theologians could point to nothing more than disclosure experiences, there would be little to distinguish them from those who reject the concept of revelation, such as Karl Jaspers,[49] who writes simply of "limit experiences," and Abraham Maslow, who prefers the term "peak experiences."[50] Why do Christian theologians insist on speaking of the disclosures on which their faith is founded as revelation?

As a first approach to an answer we may say that it is quite conceivable that one and the same disclosure might be, under different aspects, both discovery and revelation. It would be discovery insofar as it was a fulfillment of a human heuristic craving and revelation insofar as the fulfillment was a gift of God. It is quite conceivable that God might implant in the human spirit a longing for revelation and then himself, by the bestowal, enable man to fulfill that longing. There is no reason for asserting, then, that if a given disclosure is a discovery, it cannot, therefore, be revelation.

With the help of Karl Rahner we may take this line of thought somewhat further. What we have been describing as discovery or disclosure is a particular instance of a more general phenomenon—that of a self-transcending movement. In a certain sense every becoming involves a certain element of novelty in which the effect is something more than the cause. But the novelty and self-transcendence are most apparent when the agent rises above itself and becomes ontologically richer than it was before acting. Wherever any such action occurs, according to Rahner, we are warranted in saying that the advance has taken place because of the Absolute Being which is the cause and ground of the activity of the creature which transcends itself.

Rahner applies these principles, in the first place, to the process of evolution by which material creation develops towards that kind of free, self-reflexive being which we call spirit.[51] Self-transcendence in the direction of spirit can occur, Rahner maintains, because the Absolute Being is spirit. The fact that hominization, seen from below, is the product of evolutionary striving does not preclude but rather requires that, seen from above, the same process should be the creative intervention of God.

---

[48] Richardson, *History Sacred and Profane*, p. 224, note 1.

[49] K. Jaspers, *Philosophical Faith and Revelation* (New York: Harper and Row, 1967).

[50] A. H. Maslow, *Religions, Values, and Peak-Experiences* (Columbus: Ohio State U. Press, 1964).

[51] K. Rahner, *Hominisation* (New York: Herder and Herder, 1965), pp. 87-93.

The term "intervention" should in this case be cautiously used. It seems to imply that God first exists somewhere outside the universe, which he then has to invade, as it were, from beyond its borders. Properly understood, the transcendence of God implies that God is omnipresent and hence that he is always immanent to his creation. As Rahner puts it, he is "the living, permanent transcendent ground of the self-movement of the world itself."[52] To assert this intimate presence of God at the heart of the world is to reassert a commonplace of the Christian tradition. The Bible repeatedly alludes to the indwelling of God in his creation, and the indwelling of creation in God. It proclaims that in God we live and move and have our being (Acts 17:28), that all things were created in the divine Word (Jn 1:3; cf. Col 1:16), and that in him everything continues in being (Col 1:17).

A second instance of the principle of gifted self-transcendence is furnished by Christology. Salvation history, according to the biblical view, reaches its climax in the person of Jesus. Jesus may be seen from either of two points of view. From above, so to speak, he appears as God's supreme self-bestowal—as the Incarnation by which the Word of God personally unites itself to a human nature. From below, this same Jesus appears as the supreme flowering of a creation in quest of union with its divine maker. In point of fact, Jesus is both. He is Son of God and Son of Mary. In him God fulfills and crowns a tendency that he himself has implanted within his own creation—and especially within the religious strivings of the Israelite people. The history of Jesus Christ, therefore, is both a transcendent self-fulfillment of the inner thrust of salvation history and the radically new self-gift of the divine. Except for the divine self-gift history could not ultimately fulfill its own inner dynamism.

The logical distinction and the real unity of these two aspects of Christology—Christology from below and from above—can serve to illuminate the two aspects of revelation. According to the view I am here proposing, with considerable dependence on Karl Rahner, revelation should not be understood as an insertion of fully formulated divine truths into the continuum of human knowledge but rather as the process by which God, working within human history and human tradition, enables his spiritual creatures to discern more profoundly the true meaning of their existence. Like evolution and Christology, revelation has two aspects. Seen from above, it is God's free act of self-communication; seen from below, it is the self-unfolding of the human spirit in its quest for transcendent truth and meaning. This upward movement, insofar as it is borne by the

---

[52] K. Rahner, "Observations on the Concept of Revelation," in K. Rahner and J. Ratzinger, *Revelation and Tradition* (New York: Herder and Herder, 1966), p. 12.

power of grace, has a divine or supernatural component. A radically discontinuous breakthrough in our perception of religious meaning, resulting from the immanent activity of the transcendent God, may be fittingly called revelation.

When are we justified in asserting that such a divinely given breakthrough in the human religious quest has in fact occurred? The course of history is strewn with many miscellaneous insights, some of them sudden and unexpected. Are all of them to be called revelations or just some? If some, what is the criterion of selection? How can any given utterance be identified as a communication from the divine mind, so that it may be truly called the word of God? In our day it would take considerable boldness for anyone to affirm that Gutenberg's printing press or Coleridge's *Kubla Khan* were revealed by God. Why then should we assign God as the source of the insights of a religious prophet or mystic? In view of all that has been learned about the tacit dimension of knowing, the "bicameral mind," and the complex workings of the unconscious, we are reluctant to ascribe the deliverances of ecstatics, however dramatic, to God's action within their minds.

Real as these difficulties are, Christian theology is not helpless before them. What we have in biblical history is not a miscellaneous bundle of individual discoveries, but a cumulative series of disclosures building upon one another and converging toward a common meaning. To Christian eyes the entire series culminates in Jesus Christ, who, as the fulfillment, unlocks the hidden meaning of all that leads up to himself. Vatican II in its Constitution on Divine Revelation can speak of a single plan (*oeconomia*), the meaning of which is ultimately manifested in Christ, "who is the Mediator and at the same time the fullness of all revelation."[53] Thus the books of the Old Testament, according to the Council, acquire and show forth their full significance when "caught up into the proclamation of the gospel."[54]

Christians, therefore, are not left in the dilemma of having to pick and choose among a miscellany of ostensible revelations. They are committed, in the final analysis, to one revelation and only one—the revelation of God in Jesus Christ. The unity of the plan of revelation, as it converges toward this one center, is an indication that the human speakers on the stage of history are directed by a higher mind that manifests itself through them. As we say in the Constantinopolitan Creed, it is the Spirit of Christ who already spoke by the prophets.

---

[53] Vatican II, *Constitution on Divine Revelation,* art. 2, ed. Walter M. Abbott, p. 112.
[54] Ibid., art. 16, p. 122.

Within the biblical tradition the inspired prophets and writers do not rely exclusively on their own personal lights. They are conscious of participating in the stream of salvation history. They therefore interpret current events, and discern the signs of their own times, with the help of the memories and interpretative categories handed down to them in the tradition. Allowing their imagination to be stimulated by the prophetic texts, and submitting to the guidance of the same prophetic Spirit, the first Christians were empowered to recognize in Jesus the Christ, the Son of God.

Although in a wide sense any religious discovery could be called "revelation" insofar as it proceeds from a divinely inspired dynamism in the psyche, Christian theology insists that the name "revelation" belongs by an altogether special title to God's self-manifestation in Jesus Christ. For anyone who accepts the Christology of the New Testament and the classical creeds, it is evident that Jesus represents the advent of the Absolute within history, and that in him the divine appears personally on earth. Through the altruistic love exhibited in the Incarnation itself, and in the Crucifixion as the consummation of the same movement of kenotic self-bestowal, we have the full manifestation within history of that which is distinctively and properly divine. As an inseparable complement to this self-gift we have the resurrection of Jesus from the dead, which shows forth the redemptive power of that absolute love, bringing creation to its definitive goal. As Pannenberg correctly asserts, the goal of all creation is proleptically realized in the resurrection of Jesus.

The Christ-event, therefore, is the decisive and climactic breakthrough of creation into the sphere of the ultimate. Jesus is the first fruits of a divinized humanity and of a divinized world.

For those who in faith accept the Christian self-understanding, therefore, it is undeniable that Jesus is the appearance of the divine itself within history. The dogmas of Christian faith—such as the Incarnation, the atoning death of Jesus, and his resurrection—articulate what the community of the disciples discerned as taking place in the event of Jesus Christ. The mere fact of Christ, taken as an objectively certifiable occurrence, is not yet revelation, but when met by a believing interpretation which captures its true significance, it becomes revelation in a special and altogether unique sense. God's self-revelation in Jesus therefore comes to fulfillment only in the human discovery whereby it is received.

To accept Jesus as the unsurpassable self-communication of God demands that one be caught up in the dynamism of the event itself. The discovery cannot come to those who simply look at the facts as disinterested spectators. To be involved in the divinization process, as it radiates from Jesus, requires an existential affinity with the meaning of the events themselves. In biblical terminology, no one comes to Jesus without being drawn by the grace of the Father (cf. Jn 6:44). Without a heart touched by divine love we would be incapable of apprehending that love in Jesus. But if God's love shines in our hearts it may be given to us to recognize what Paul describes as "the glory of God shining in the face of Christ Jesus" (2 Cor 4:6).

The revelation which reaches its fullness in Jesus does not begin with his historical appearance in the history of Israel, nor does it end with the Easter occurrences. The Spirit of the risen Christ, poured out "upon all flesh" (Acts 2:17), prompts people of every age and land to ask—at times with passionate intensity—the question of God, the question to which Christ becomes the definitive answer. Thanks to the Holy Spirit all can be attuned to the God of revelation, so that when they hear of him they can exclaim, in the words of the Canticle, "I have found him whom my soul loves" (Ct 3:4). The revelation can be recognized as authentic inasmuch as those who come to believe already knew the God of Jesus, in a tacit way, through their inner religious orientation.

VI.   Christian Faith as Discipleship

In the final section of this talk I should like to deal with a possible objection to what I have been saying thus far. Revelation, according to the common view, is the objective correlative of faith. What does it mean to have Christian faith if not to accept the Christian revelation? Discovery, however, is the achievement of those who arrive at solutions to problems in which they have been personally involved. Christianity may indeed come as a sort of discovery to an adult convert who embraces it as the answer to a prolonged and arduous quest. But if revelation were necessarily discovery, faith would seem to be the privilege of a few intellectuals and would hardly be accessible to the simple believer, who submits to the teaching of the Bible and the Church without ever claiming to have made any real discovery. Must we not respect the unquestioning faith of those who gratefully accept the teaching given to them without ever having to undergo a religious conversion?

The objection merits examination because it provides an occasion for me to make some necessary qualifications to what I have been saying. I have been using as my primary paradigm the individual—whether prophet, apostle, or adult convert—who makes a personal religious discovery. But I have tried also to indicate that biblical and Christian faith is a cumulative patrimony, in which new insights are given only to those who dwell within the tradition.

Further, God always remains, for his pilgrim people, veiled in mystery. Even the most outstanding pioneers must be content to "see through a glass darkly." Because the fullness of vision remains a distant hope, the revelation given in this life falls short of clarity. It is not the vision, but stands in place of that vision. In other words, it is pro-visional.

To complete this line of thought it would be necessary to speak more fully of faith than it has been possible to do in these pages. Faith is not the same as revelation. It is not even directly correlated with revelation, as I have been using the term. For revelation, in the sense of discovery, is an insight in which the mind rests satisfied. Faith, however, is a stretching forth toward an insight not yet given. Faith animates the quest for revelation; it sustains the process of discovery; but to the extent that discovery or revelation is given, faith is supplanted. Faith, therefore, stands in dialectical tension with discovery, and hence also with revelation. The completeness of revelation, if it were ever given (as the asymptotic goal of revelation within our pilgrim condition), would do away with the very possibility of faith.

Christianity, then, should not be seen simply as discovery or revelation. Under the conditions of this life it is constituted more prominently by faith. The first Christians were well advised when they spoke of their movement as "the Way" (*he hodós* - Acts 9:2; 18:26; 19:9, 23; 24:22). They were convinced that under the guidance of Jesus they were on the path to truth and life (cf. Jn 14:6). They were conscious of not yet having the final vision but of having in Jesus the guide and promise of that vision.

It is questionable whether we ought to speak of Christians as having revelation. Significantly, the authors of the New Testament, like those of the Hebrew Bible, rarely speak of revelation as something that has been given. They prefer to use terms designating revelation with verbs in the future tense (e.g., Rom 2:5, 8:18-19, 1 Cor 1:17, 3:13, 4:5, 2 Cor 5:10, Col 3:4, 2 Thess 1:7). They are conscious of having received in Jesus sufficient light and guidance to know how they ought to walk, but not sufficient light to dispel the surrounding darkness.

In replying to the objection, however, I may seem to have destroyed my thesis. Using the category of discovery, I have been arguing for an isomorphism between Christianity and human disciplines such as science and philosophy. In admitting now that discovery is given more in hope than in actual achievement, I may seem to have destroyed the parallelism and to have reduced Christianity, once again, to an arbitrary commitment without a firm intellectual basis. What could be more unscientific, it may be asked, than to commit oneself to what one does not understand?

This would indeed be unacceptable by scientific standards if science were what the Enlightenment conceived it to be. But the Enlightenment concepts of reason and science themselves need to be challenged. The post-critical philosophy of Michael Polanyi sets forth a different and more realistic concept of science. To be a scientist, Polanyi contends, is not primarily a matter of accepting assured and demonstrable conclusions. A scientist is defined as a member of the scientific community—a community which is identified not by what it presently holds but by the way in which it goes about making discoveries. The process of exploration and the discoveries themselves are always sustained by a whole network of beliefs, any one of which could conceivably be false.

To become a scientist, therefore, is an act of faith—one that involves trust in the community, its leaders, and its processes. The neophyte affiliates himself to the community, apprenticing himself to those already accredited as masters. Under the guidance of the master the neophyte is led through a series of guided discoveries. These discoveries, although they may not be original so far as the community is concerned, are educative for the apprentice. By directed experiments of this kind one learns what it is to discover and thus becomes qualified to enter the ranks of those who move the community itself forward to new discoveries.

Apprenticeship, of course, is not peculiar to the scientific community. It is crucial to all disciplines, especially those which depend most heavily on tacit or implicit knowledge. To become a violinist, an actor, or a painter is possible only through a prolonged period of apprenticeship in which the master imparts to the disciple the techniques and methods of creative performance.

Polanyi has many important reflections on the collapse of the notions of tradition and apprenticeship in modern Western society. While the articulate contents of science are successfully taught all over the world in hundreds of universities—he remarks—the unspecifiable art of scientific research is in danger of being lost, to the great detriment of science itself, which depends to a large extent on the implicit and the inarticulate. Personal example, he maintains, is the principal carrier of tradition.

> To learn by example is to submit to authority. You follow your master because you trust his manner of doing things even when you cannot analyse and account in detail for its effectiveness. By watching the master and emulating his efforts in the presence of his example, the apprentice unconsciously picks up the rules of the art, including those which are not explicitly

> known to the master himself. These hidden rules can be
> assimilated only by a person who surrenders himself to that
> extent uncritically to the imitation of another. A society which
> wants to preserve a fund of personal knowledge must submit to
> tradition.[55]

The kind of deformation which Polanyi detects in the Enlightenment concept of science has actually affected the interpretation of
religion as well. Influenced by the Cartesian ideal of clear and
distinct ideas, theologians of the seventeenth and eighteenth centuries sought to formulate Christianity in terms of necessary articles
of faith or other explicit beliefs. Even today, many think of Christianity primarily as a matter of professing certain tenets expressly
taught by the Bible or by the Church.

While convictions unquestionably have a place in any committed
life, the more vital dimension of Christian faith, according to my
view, is the tacit. The Christian is defined as being a person on the
way to discovery, on the way to a revelation not yet given, or at least
not yet given in final form. Identified less by explicit than by implicit
faith, the Christian trusts that, in following the crucified and risen
Christ, he is on the route to the one disclosure that will fully satisfy
the yearning of the human spirit. This confidence is sustained by a
series of lesser disclosures which occur on the way, and are tokens or
promises of the revelation yet to come.

Christianity, then, is essentially a matter of discipleship. This is
what it has been from the beginning, and what it remains except
where people think that faith can be communicated by scholarly
instruction in the university classroom. Christian instruction, even
more than science, is a matter of personal discipleship, or *disciplina*
in the original sense of the term. By returning to the New Testament
matrix we can retrieve the concept of discipleship.

Initially, the followers of Jesus were attracted, it would seem, by
blind admiration for his wonderful power in word and deed. But
Jesus was not content to win admirers. He selected a group of
disciples, formed them into a community, and subjected them to
prolonged training under his supervision. By progressive exercises
in discovery he led them to grasp—or rather to be grasped by—the
realities which he knew at first hand, in order that they might be able
to read the "signs of the times" and replicate Jesus' own feats of
discovery. This ability required rigorous schooling under personal
direction. For the assimilation of Jesus' teaching the disciples had to
be prepared through moral dispositions, an appropriate way of life,
and a fitting style of prayer and worship.

---

[55] Polayni, *Personal Knowledge*, p. 53.

These points have been persuasively made by Aaron Milavec, a contemporary theologian who has thoroughly immersed himself in the thinking of Polanyi. Milavec writes:

> The Synoptic Gospels retain some of the character of Jesus' practice in teaching his disciples. He frequently takes them aside, he responds to their questions, he exposes the deeper meanings of his public deeds, he corrects their false expectations, he sends them out in pairs to do on their own what he had successfully demonstrated in his own practice. Their independent successes demonstrated to him the extent to which they had come to share his own personal powers as a result of their reverential self-giving into his hands. Jesus thereby was assured that they would not be blind messengers passing on riddles which they do not understand, but, on the contrary, would have the necessary responsibilities to adapt and innovate their own teaching and practice in accordance with their own openness to their listeners and to God's Spirit (which now guided and befriended them independent of Jesus' presence).[56]

As Dr. Milavec then goes on to explain, Christianity down through the centuries must retain its shape as a religion of discipleship. Faith cannot be passed down as a mere thing—as a set of propositional truths. Faith is something we must grow into, and the normal way of growing into it is through nurture in a community of faith. The mature Christian is one who can discern the signs of God at work in his or her own life, and reach Christian decisions without being able to offer cogent objective proof that they are the right ones. Christianity, then, is not so much a system of doctrine as a set of skills acquired through long practice under the guidance of the community and its leaders. In every generation the adult members must accept responsibility for transmitting the delicate art of being a Christian to the younger members of the community. One cannot expect the young to accept Christian doctrines unless they are prepared for these by participation in the life of the community, with its prayer, its worship, and its standards of behavior.

The Christian Church, under the aspect we have been considering, has strong traits of similarity with the political and scientific communities, which are likewise communities of faith and discovery. As a religious community the Church lives by a transcendental faith—a faith that reaches out to ultimate meaning and unconditioned value. It places its trust in the guidance of Jesus Christ, who uniquely manifests, as its paramount symbolic embodiment, the goal of the religious quest. Under the leadership of Christ

---

[56] A. Milavec, "Modern Exegesis, Doctrinal Innovations, and the Dynamics of Discipleship," *Anglican Theological Review* 60 (January 1978): 64.

and his Spirit the Church tends forward to a goal beyond anything this world can hope to achieve in historical time. Straining toward that goal, the Church leads its members continually forward, preparing them for the great revelation which is yet to be given—the vision of God mediated through the glorified humanity of his eternal Son. That vision will be a transcendent fulfillment of every human striving and at the same time a gift immeasurably surpassing all that we can merit or achieve. On that day, faith as we have known it on earth will fall away, and in its place we shall enjoy the fullness of discovery. By the light of God we shall see him in whom there is no darkness. *In lumine tuo videbimus lumen* (Ps 35:10 Vg).

A Response to Fr. Dulles

by Rev. Joseph T. Lienhard, S.J.

With the thoughtfullness and graciousness we have come to expect of him, Fr. Dulles has used the occasion of his paper to compliment Fr. Rahner on his receiving Marquette University's Discovery Award Medal. He has taken the term "discovery" and shown us, in a paper admirable for its clarity and richness, how reflection on this term, derived from an experiential description of the process of discovery, can enhance our understanding of some more traditional theological categories. Fr. Dulles has built his paper around six terms: faith, reason, revelation, discovery, disclosure, and discipleship. Of the six, the one which was to me both the most striking and the most provocative was the last, discipleship; but a little more about this later.

Fr. Dulles defines revelation as "the process by which God, working within human history and human tradition, enables his spiritual creatures to discern more profoundly the true meaning of their existence."

Of discovery he says the following: "[it] is a self-transcending act of reason wherein an inquirer, driven by a passionate desire to learn a hidden truth, which he trusts is waiting to be found, allows his imagination to suggest ways of synthesizing the data, until he strikes upon an insight that arrives accredited in advance by the heuristic craving that evoked it."

Of the two statements, it is clearly the second which is expressed in language that is both richer and more thought-provoking. Fr. Dulles speaks of discovery with such words as "passionate desire," "hidden truth," "trust," "imagination," "insight," and "craving."

He has been able to show that discovery and revelation are two aspects of the same phenomenon, and that both are necessary; the language of "discovery" concentrates our attention on the subject, just as Fr. Rahner, some forty years ago in *Hörer des Wortes,* drew attention to the hearer, without whom the Word would go unheard.

At the beginning of his paper, with a reference to St. Thomas' *Summa contra gentiles,* Fr. Dulles draws attention to a traditional scholastic understanding of faith and reason as two discreet ways of knowing and kinds of knowledge, a view that he is, I think, dissatisfied with. According to this view, reason is acquired, or natural knowledge, gained by the free and deliberate exercise of one's own powers. God is known by reason when we ascend to him by reflection on creatures. Faith is revealed, or supernatural, knowledge, freely bestowed by God. God is known by faith when we submit humbly to his revelation concerning himself.

Before continuing this line of thought, I would like to insert a personal note. Perhaps if a mathematician were to read Fr. Dulles's paper, he would be most attentive to the references to George Polya. But I am no mathematician. As I read the first twelve or thirteen pages of the paper, I was continually reminded of phrases and thoughts from St. Augustine. The suspense was resolved at the beginning of the third part, where Fr. Dulles mentions St. Augustine, and then quotes him extensively. In what follows, I would like to supply some reflections derived from St. Augustine which seem to me to complement what Fr. Dulles has said.

The first concerns the topic I just mentioned, faith and reason. In the body of his paper, Fr. Dulles explains fully and richly the complementarity and mutuality of discovery and revelation. Another chapter might have included a similar discussion of faith and reason. We are all, I think, aware of the difficulties of looking at faith and reason as two discreet ways of knowing and two discreet kinds of knowledge, as in the traditional scholastic understanding of these terms. We are also familiar with Augustine's very different approach to this pair of terms. Reason, for Augustine, is not discursive thinking or ratiocination, but—at least in its psychological usage—the gaze of the mind, *aspectus mentis*. As is well known, the keystone of Augustine's thought on this is the mistranslation of Isaiah 7:9 which he read in his Latin Bible, namely: "nisi credideritis, non intellegetis"—"unless you shall have believed, you will not understand." Reason, therefore, is that by which the vision of the Truth is seen; and faith is the necessary way to that vision (cf. Jn 14:6). In the *Enchiridion* address to Laurentius, Augustine writes (ch. 5):

> . . . once the mind has been endowed with the beginning of faith "which works through love" (Gal 5:6), it tends through right living to attain to sight where dwells for the holy and perfect of heart that ineffable beauty, the full vision of which constitutes supreme happiness. Surely, this is the answer to your question: What is the beginning and what the end of human endeavor? We begin in faith and are made perfect by sight.[1]

One of the questions asked by Laurentius (ch. 4) had been, "to what extent religion is supported by reason."

I would suggest that this Augustinian understanding of faith and

---

[1] St. Augsutine, *Faith, Hope and Charity*, trans. Louis A. Arand; Ancient Christian Writers, vol. 3 (Westminster, Md.: Newman Bookshop, 1947): 13.

reason or vision corresponds a good deal more closely to what Fr. Dulles has said of discovery and revelation than the later, scholastic view does.[2]

Another point of close contact is in the tenth book of the *Confessions,* where Augustine meditates on memory. The importance of memory for Augustine is well known; R. A. Markus goes so far as to suggest that memory ultimately has the same function in Augustine's thought as divine illumination does.[3] In any case, Augustine speaks of memory, and of forgetfulness as somehow standing between memory or knowledge and ignorance. He speaks beautifully of the experience of remembering what we have forgotten, whether it is a name—or the happy life.[4] This remembering could well be described as discovering; Fr. Dulles speaks of the role of illumination in the process of discovery, and writes: "the discovery, when it appears, corresponds to what, in the search, we already felt must be there."

A third point, and this concerning discipleship, which I mentioned earlier: Augustine is clear on the fact that there is some knowledge which is possible only after commitment. What is known cannot be divorced from what is loved; and nothing is fully known to which the consent of the will has not been given. In the same sense, Dr. Tallon has spoken of "affective intentionality as access to reason." In Book 7 of the *Confessions,* Augustine's knowledge of God's spiritual nature, his acceptance of the Scriptures as explained by Ambrose, and the explanation of evil which he took over from Plotinus, all remained ineffective until he was willing to live out the implications of those intellectual convictions. Only after his experience in the garden, in which he reads the verse from St. Paul's letter to the Romans, can he write: "instantly, in truth, at the end of this sentence, as if before a peaceful light streaming into my heart, all the dark shadows of doubt fled away" (*Confessions* 8, 12, 29 trans. Ryan). In the same vein, I suggest, "discipleship" is—or should

---

[2] It might even be fruitful to consider a dialectic between faith and reason parallel to that proposed by Fr. Dulles for discovery and revelation. Fr. Dulles writes that "the completeness of revelation . . . would do away with the very possibility of faith." But cf. 1 Cor 13: 13, and the understanding of *epektasis* or eternal progress in Gregory of Nyssa, especially as treated by Jean Daniélou. The similarities between Gregory of Nyssa's thought and Augustine's are provocative. See J. F. Callahan, *Augustine and the Greek Philosophers* (Villanova, 1967).

[3] "*Memoria* and divine illumination are alternative ways of expressing the basis of Augustine's theory of knowledge": R. A. Markus, "Augustine, St.," *Encyclopedia of Philosophy,* 8 vols. (New York: Macmillan and Free Press, 1967) 1:20.

[4] Cf. *Confessions* 10, 19, 28, and 10, 20, 29. See also R. J. O'Connell, *St. Augustine's Early Theory of Man, A.D. 386-391* (Cambridge, Mass.: Belknap Press of Harvard University Press, 1968), and *St. Augustine's Confessions: The Odyssey of Soul* (Cambridge, Mass.: Belknap Press, 1969).

be—very much at home alongside such words as reason, discovery, and disclosure.

By way of conclusion: three themes, among many others in Fr. Dulles's paper, seem to me to have distinct resonances in Augustine's thought: the relation of faith and reason, the philosophy of memory, and his insistence on the inseparability of knowledge and love. Both authors have been, for me, a source of "illumination."[5]

---

[5] Fr. Dulles has discussed faith and reason in *The Survival of Dogma* (Garden City, N.Y.: Doubleday, 1971), and this theme in Augustine in his book *A History of Apologetics* (New York: Corpus, 1971).

A Response to Fr. Dulles

by Dr. Andrew Tallon

Commentators, like speakers, are invited to talk. They have to come up with something to say, in less time than that allowed the speakers, and *on* time. But first of all, a profound phenomenology of the commentator, in himself as well as in relation to being in general *(das Sein im Ganzen),* would show that the commentator must *listen*—at least long enough, but not longer than necessary—before he speaks. Blessed be the commentators, therefore I say, for they shall be called Hearers of the Word.

I am happy to accept the role, resisted yesterday morning by the biblicists, of handmaid (or rather butler, as Fr. John Sheehan changed the name) of Theology. Philosophy is old enough to feel parental about all discipline. What parent has not felt, often and deeply, like maid, butler, cook and everything else for his or her much loved children?

This is at least our third paper on method in this symposium. Fr. William Dych's also emphasized and quite explicitly focused on the non-verbal as pre-conceptual cognition involving affectivity, a position Fr. Rahner first stated in *Hearers of the Word* and developed over the next twenty-five years until it was stated in the general theory of experience Fr. Dych was able to use. Fr. Sheehan's paper, for me in Philosophy, was also on method. Like Fr. Dych's (and again for me from my perspective within Philosophy) it finds its solution in the idea of discipleship, as Fr. Dulles presents it. Only the disciple who walks in Jesus' footsteps, as Scheler puts it, can be more than a dial-a-dogma recorded message, repeated verbatim, unchanged for centuries. This is the beauty of St. Ignatius' *Exercises,* in the full thirty-day form at least, because that experience begins to provide something close to enough to make real disciples; only such persons, and only if they follow up that encounter with daily prayer, can then discern spirits on their own and transcend the letter because they have received the spirit. So I suspect that Fr. Dulles's is not the last paper on method in this symposium, and I look forward to Fr. Egan's with anticipation, and to Fr. McCool's, and even to Dr. Ommen's, because I believe I am not deluded in saying that we are at last at a point in evolving human consciousness when *positive* relations, not male, exploitive ones (if I may name them such) are becoming our way with the earth.

This is the theme of my brief remarks, and I hope my brief incubation of them yields to illumination. I said that the role of handmaid is gladly accepted. Philosophy is used to it, trying to get down to the ground and foundation of everything, including all science—physical, human, and divine. Yet the ultimate "ground," as Levinas says, is not so much "underfoot" as "overhead," i.e., in the face of the other person in whom I meet a word and law higher than my autonomy, a commandment "Thou shalt not kill—Thou shalt love!" The theme—the old yet new theme—of calling logical, verbal reason into question and rejecting it as the only method has, since Husserl, Heidegger, Buber and others in our day, been called the question of non-representational intentionality. Some want to throw out intentionality altogether, but they have in mind only the dominant representational intentionality. They seem, to put it in Thomist terms, to take phantasma in the Aristotelian and Thomist phrase *conversio ad phantasma* always to mean images of a representational sort, perhaps also betraying a visual bias very much in need of correction by a dialogic—listening and speaking—philosophy.

As we all know, reaction against the reason enthroned by Descartes began right after the coronation, and Descartes' methodic doubt became Kant's real critiques. Thus the opening to and recognition for another access to meaning has come late, not never, and that other tradition has, in character, always been waiting off-stage, in the wings. It is very significant to me that the names mentioned by Fr. Dulles to identify his rapprochement of revelation to discovery were Augustine, Pascal, Newman (and he could have mentioned Bernard, Francis, Bonaventure and others, of course), the philosophers and theologians of the heart, as Pascal's familiar *logique du coeur* and Newman's *cor ad cor loquitur* make manifest. The theme of the heart as cognitive, in fact as *the* cognitive power of man, is, of course, central to the Hebrew Bible, and also to the New Testament. *Affective intentionality as access to meaning,* as cognitive, has begun to receive serious scholarly attention. (Bob Wood's excellent translation, published last year, of Strasser's *Phenomenology of Feeling, An Essay on the Phenomenon of the Heart,* written twenty-five years ago, is evidence.) In apologetics (if I may still use that term), the proper scope of the paper under discussion this morning, the form this general consciousness of the inadequacy of old methods takes is to call into question the primacy of the active, reasoning, logical, verbal agent and—beyond this negative moment—to consider his positive *complement* (the *whole* is the true cognitive and affective person), the receptive, feeling, loving, non-verbal agent-as-patient.

Thus I personally locate Fr. Dulles's paper within the general challenge to univocal reason of which we are all aware and, further, within the most promising response to that challenge which is put, philosophically, in terms of affective intentionality as access to meaning.

After such a sweeping statement as I have just made I may be expected to justify my considering Fr. Dulles's thesis as a contribution to that movement. Last night, in the spoken form of his paper, he used a phrase not present in the written form I had read just the day before. He spoke of "the bicameral mind," and I knew I was not off the mark. The context was the following; he wrote: "In view of all that we have come to hold about the tacit dimension of knowing and the complex workings of the unconscious, we are. . . ." After "the unconscious" he inserted the new words. Today, as we know, neurologists and psychologists are offering physiological bases to confirm the universal experience of a dual mode of knowing, fully accrediting the non-verbal complement of the verbal, the mystical brother—or better, sister—of the logical. Robert Ornstein's *Psychology of Consciousness* some time ago showed that evidence from split-brain surgery (Merleau-Ponty had access to some similar evidence from war victims in *Phenomenology of Perception*) can translate into the traditional complementary pairs of yin and yang, west and east, animus and anima, eros and agape, male and female (all due caution observed). More recently the Canadian psychologist Sandra Witelson found herself able to draw the conclusion that the combination of heredity and culture were not enough to explain that women less than men were able to resist or reject the influence of the right side of the brain in face to face personal encounters, the result being a more affective, non-verbal, and intuitive response because *both* sides of the brain are involved. Women are more "cordial" in such situations, but so can men be, whose response is also allowed to come from both sides. Both men and women can learn the value of such repressions. A fortiori, when alone in the quiet of one's study, when the absence of the face of the other makes it so much easier, how marked the tendency toward left-side dominance. In the recent book *Le fait féminin* Witelson makes provocative applications of this new information and offers bibliography.

Just how far can we go in speculating on male-dominated philosophy, theology, science, and business, much less in the arts, creative and healing? I for one was, if not overwhelmed, certainly struck by the unmistakably affective language of Fr. Dulles's paper. He speaks, and often, of reason driven by passion, of opening to the mysterious, implicit, unconscious, tacit. He has constant recourse to the ideas of the heart, arduous quest, passion, tension, desire, feeling, and my favorites (and, I think, his), "passionate desire" and, especially, "heuristic craving."

All this culminates in the vision of Jesus as given, apprenticing his disciples in Eastern fashion, leading them to grasp, or better (as Fr. Dulles puts it so well) to be grasped by the love and person He is.

This reminds me of one of my favorite quotations from Levinas, a saying Nygren would dearly love. He said, "There is only one thing better than being God, and that is being God's beloved." Only a creature could say that, a creature of a God who is love. As finite beings, as Fr. Phil Donnelly said and lived, we are created to receive.

This leads to my conclusion. The metaphysical ground of finite spirit, found in Karl Rahner's early works and developed with unity and consistency over the years, provides the ground of what Fr. Dulles says and of what is going on in the general recognition of the inadequacy of living without a heart, with half a brain. Finite spirit is created person that can know and love only in radical dependence on otherness, the first otherness of its own embodiment and the second otherness of another person. Expressed cognitively this is the *conversio ad phantasma;* expressed affectively it is the concept of the heart.

Method in Theology According to Karl Rahner

by Rev. William V. Dych, S.J.

We have with us this week not one, but two famous theologians who are celebrating their seventy-fifth birthday this year. The one you know, and the other's name has become practically synonymous with the question of "Method in Theology," Fr. Bernard Lonergan. I remember Fr. Lonergan saying to me last year when I was with him at Boston College that writing is no problem. It is rewriting that is the problem. I never doubted his word, but came to appreciate its truth in a special way during the past several weeks. For when I found out that he was going to be with us here this morning, it seemed appropriate to do a bit of rewriting and take advantage of his presence. To do that I have made a few changes in my approach to the question of method in the theology of Karl Rahner.

Instead of a straightforward presentation of what I consider to be some of his basic methodological principles, it seemed to me that the best way we could spend our time would be to initiate something of a comparison or contrast between the two of them. In doing that, however, three reservations are in order here at the outset. First, we have nothing of the size and scope of Bernard Lonergan's *Method in Theology* by Karl Rahner to serve as the basis of comparison. To make the comparison I have selected from the *Grundkurs,* for example, some remarks on method which seem to present fairly close points of contact. But they are a selection, and hence, secondly, no attempt will be made to give a comprehensive or systematic summary of what either has said on method. Finally, for the sake of making the comparison statements will be taken out of their logical habitat in the midst of many other statements by the respective authors, and this runs the risk of distorting them. Should I not succeed in my efforts to avoid this, however, corrections should be readily available straight from the horses' mouth.

I. Existence and Reflection

In his *Grundkurs des Glaubens,* Karl Rahner has a section entitled, "Some Basic Epistemological Problems," and the first of these problems to be mentioned concerns the relationship between "reality and concept," or between one's "original self-possesion and reflection upon it.''[1] The ''reality'' in question is that of a person actually living a life of Christian faith, and the ''concept'' or ''reflection'' refers to the process of theological reflection upon such a life, conceptual reflection upon either of the two basic questions posed by the *Grundkurs:* What does it mean to be a Christian, and what is the logic or what are the grounds upon which one bases a decision to be one.[2] The point of making the distinction is to stress that the *Grundkurs* moves on the second of the two levels. As an introduction to the *idea* of Christianity, it is a theological and/or philosophical reflection upon the reality itself in an attempt to reach this idea or concept. Hence the question: what is the relationship between reality and concept?

The answer begins by asserting that there is in human life a necessary ''unity in distinction'' between conscious and free human existence itself and reflection upon it. This differentiated unity is asserted in order to avoid the opposite extremes of ''theological rationalism'' and ''classical modernism.'' The former would maintain that we really know something only when we have objectified it in a concept, and this process reaches its full reality in scientific knowledge. The latter, on the other hand, maintains that conceptual reflection is an altogether secondary and dispensable process in relation to the original self-possession of one's existence in consciousness and freedom. To avoid both extremes there is asserted a dialectical relationship of mutual dependence between the two levels of the one knowledge. What is the nature of the two poles in this dialectical relationship?

There is, first of all, in the actual process of existing consciously and freely as a human being a conscious relation to or union with or knowledge of reality which is more than and qualitatively different from the kind of knowledge mediated by a concept or a ''clear and distinct idea'' of this reality. For example, when a person experiences the reality of loving or being loved, of trusting or being trusted, of being tormented by questions or moved by compassion, there is through the very self-presence of conscious existence a knowledge of reality which can be pointed to, but never completely recaptured by or expressed in concepts which objectify this reality. This knowledge is called ''original'' knowledge in the sense that it is knowledge which wells up from the origins or depths of one's own existence in the actual process of being in existence as a conscious and free subject. There is, secondly, in this knowledge itself an ele-

---

[1] Karl Rahner, *Grundkurs des Glaubens. Einführung in den Begriff des Christentums* (Freiburg: Herder, 1976), pp. 26-28 (14-17). Numbers in parentheses refer to the English translation: *Foundations of Christian Faith. Introduction to the Idea of Christianity* (New York: Seabury Press, 1978).

2 Ibid., p. 14 (2).

ment of reflection. For there is not only the experience, but the self-presence or self-possession of the conscious subject in the experience which grounds the movement toward reflection, conceptualization, expression and communication.

The relation between these two poles of the one knowledge is not static, but dynamic, and the movement is in both directions. There is the movement of original knowledge gained through actually being in existence towards further and fuller objectification in concepts, towards understanding and judgment, towards expression, language and communication. There is, secondly, the need to relate the concepts back to the original experience from which they have been derived and towards which they point. Through this second movement we discover the "real" meaning of words and concepts which we have learned from the common language in which we have been formed and which we have perhaps been using for a long time. Without it we can have a perfectly clear and distinct understanding of what we are saying and yet not really "know" what we are talking about. If the original, experiential knowledge without reflection, conceptualization and expression would be "blind" and "mute," the words and concepts without experience would be empty.

Insofar as our knowledge of religious realities manifests this same dialectical and irresolvable tension between original knowledge and its objectification in concepts and words, in this instance theological concepts and words, there is within theology the necessary and ongoing process of this two-fold movement. There is the need to grasp and express more fully and clearly what we have aleady experienced and come to know prior to such "clear and distinct ideas," and there is the need to show that the religious or theological concepts do not introduce the hearer for the first time to the realities spoken about, but rather conceive and express realities already present and known in the actual process of conscious human existence. The very function of a *Grundkurs* is not primarily to gather data for or develop conceptually any of the various disciplines which are involved in theological knowledge, but to use as much of this as is necessary to show the relationship between theological knowledge and human existence as already known through the experience of actually living it, that original experience in which, as Fr. Rahner says, "what is meant and the experience of what is meant are still one."[3]

It is this last phrase which might provide a point of contact and a basis for comparison with Fr. Lonergan. The third chapter of his *Method in Theology* is entitled "Meaning," and in the seventh section

---

[3] Ibid., p. 28 (17).

he analyzes the various "elements" of meaning.[4] These elements are distinguished into the sources, the acts and the terms of meaning. The sources of meaning are all conscious acts and all the intended contents of these acts, and they can be divided into "transcendental" and "categorical" sources. Transcendental sources of meaning are the very dynamism of intentional consciousness itself, while the categorical sources are the determinations of this consciousness through experiencing, understanding, judging and deciding. The transcendental dynamism of consciousness grounds the questioning which leads to the answers which are its categorical determinations.

Acts of meaning are then divided into "potential," "formal," "full," "constitutive" and "instrumental," and it is in connection with the first that a phrase occurs which is similar to the one just quoted from the *Grundkurs*. In the potential act of meaning, meaning is still "elemental," and there has not yet been reached "the distinction between meaning and meant."[5] Examples of potential acts of meaning would include intersubjective acts of meaning such as a smile, and the meaning which a work of art has prior to its interpretation by a critic. Both of these embodiments or carriers of meaning have been explained in detail earlier.[6] It is not until one arrives at a "formal" act of meaning that there emerges the "distinction between meaning and meant."[7] Formal acts of meaning include conceiving, thinking, defining, supposing or formulating, and the "meant" is what is conceived or thought or defined and so on. However, the precise nature of the distinction between meaning and meant has not yet been clarified, for one has not yet determined whether the object of one's thought is just an object of thought, or something more than that. For this determination there is needed a "full" act of meaning, and this occurs in the act of judging. This leads to "constitutive" acts of meaning which come with judgments of value and decisions, and finally to "instrumental" acts which give expression to the foregoing process.

Looking at the two analyses, I do not suppose that either Fr. Rahner or Fr. Lonergan would disagree with any of the details that the other mentions. There does seem, however, to be a difference of emphasis or a different evaluation of the relative importance of various moments in the process of theological method. Whereas Lonergan stresses that acts of meaning prior to the process of con-

---

[4] Bernard Lonergan, *Method in Theology* (New York: Herder and Herder, 1972), pp. 73-76.

[5] Ibid., p. 74

[6] Ibid., for "intersubjective meaning" see pp. 59-61, and for "art" see pp. 61-64.

[7] Lonergan, *Method in Theology,* p. 74.

ceiving and defining are "potential," Rahner, while noting the need for and the dynamism towards "fuller" meaning, stresses that there already is a "fullness" of another kind in the "original" knowledge of experience itself, a fullness which is left behind when one begins to objectify the experience in concepts. This is not true, he says, in any and every kind of knowledge, for example, when a scientist or an historian is organizing his data, but it is true in reflecting on the actual process of living out a human existence, in reflecting on what he calls "human, existential realities." Here "original knowledge," where "what is meant and the experience of what is meant are still one," is the "fuller" knowledge. Perhaps the difference can be explained by the fact that a book on theological method would be concerned primarily with what theological reflection has in common with other kinds of human reflection, or what characterizes human reflection as such, whereas a *Grundkurs des Glaubens* would be concerned primarily with what makes it different because of the uniqueness of its subject matter, namely, human existence precisely in relation to God. In any case, it might be worthwhile to look more closely at the nature of this "pre-conceptual" fullness.

II. Pre-Conceptual Knowledge

In the same chapter of *Method in Theology* that we have been considering there is a section entitled, "Linguistic Meaning,"[8] and it deals with the "embodiment" of meaning in language:

> By its embodiment in language, in a set of conventional signs, meaning finds its greatest liberation. For conventional signs can be multiplied almost indefinitely. They can be differentiated and specialized to the utmost refinement. They can be used reflexively in the analysis and control of linguistic meaning itself. In contrast intersubjective and symbolic meanings seem restricted to the spontaneities of people living together, and, while the visual and aural arts can develop conventions, still the conventions themselves are limited by the materials in which colors and shapes, solid forms and structures, sounds and movements are embodied.[9]

This is then applied later to the question of the expression of religious experience and the clarification of religion. Fr. Lonergan uses the term "word" to refer to any expression of religious meaning or religious value, whether the carrier of this religious meaning or value be intersubjectivity, art, symbol, language or the lives and deeds of individuals or groups which have been remembered and

---

[8] Ibid., pp. 70-73
[9] Ibid., p. 70.

portrayed. All of these modes of expression have their uses, "but, since language is the vehicle in which meaning becomes most fully articulated, the spoken and written word are of special importance in the development and clarification of religion."[10]

What attracted my attention in this passage was the phrase "fully articulated," and it reminded me of Rahner's insistence that "original knowledge" has a natural drive towards objectification, expression, language and communication. Once again, however, there is the reminder that language cannot "completely" recapture the original knowledge nor express it "fully."[11] There is no mention of the various kinds of "words" in Lonergan's sense, nor any hierarchy of lesser and fuller modes of articulation. But it seems that there is a "fullness" in original knowledge which escapes any and all language, however fully articulated or clarified. My point, once again, is not to indicate a disagreement by the two about this, but simply to point out where the emphasis is placed when the question of method is treated. Rahner seems to me to emphasize that there is a "more" or a "fullness" in experience which is intrinsically "inconceivable" on the level of reflection, and intrinsically "ineffable" on the level of expression, and that this "more" or this "fullness" must be constantly returned to as an intrinsic moment in theological method. As coming prior to conceptualization it is pre-conceptual knowledge, but the "pre" does not indicate an initial stage which at least in principle could be "raised" to the level of conceptual knowledge. The principle is rather the opposite, for it points out the inherent and permanent inadequacy of conceptual knowledge vis-à-vis the original knowledge embodied in experience. The nature of this "pre-conceptual knowledge" is not developed in any great detail in the *Grundkurs,* nor elsewhere to my knowledge, so I would like to consider a simple example in order to clarify it, an example perhaps not unlike Fr. Lonergan's "phenomenology of a smile" in his treatment of intersubjective meaning.[12]

At the very beginning of conscious life when a child is born into the world, it finds itself in the midst of a kaleidoscope of colors, sounds and other sensible stimuli which it learns only gradually to organize and unify into a world of distinguishable and recognizable objects. Moreover, in learning to distinguish and "objectify" the outside world, the child is also learning to distinguish himself from it. The emergence of a world of objects is simultaneously and identically the emergence of a conscious subject within this world, a

---

[10] Ibid., p. 112.

[11] Rahner, *Grundkurs des Glaubens,* p. 27 (16).

[12] Lonergan, *Method in Theology,* pp. 59-61.

center of consciousness which is not only aware of other things, but also aware of itself as different from them. All human knowledge includes this element of self-awareness or self-knowledge, even when our attention is focused on something else. This point is emphasized very strongly in both *Method in Theology* and the *Grundkurs* and is an important methodological principle in both.[13] All human knowledge, then, is "two-directional," it encompasses both subject and object, both knower and known in the single act of knowledge. This is not meant in the sense that all knowledge has two "objects," but that in focusing on or attending to something else, the subject is aware of itself in the process, and this self-awareness is a constitutive element in being a human knower, a conscious human subject in the world.

In learning that the world is different from himself, however, the child is also learning that it is by no means indifferent. The world of persons and things of which the child is becoming aware is in one way or another affecting it. Awareness is accompanied by affectivity, indeed, more than just accompanied by it, for the two are not separate and disparate operations. The child is becoming aware not of a world of objects *and* a self as two separate things, but rather of a relationship, the self and the world as related in some affective way. Initially our knowledge is not a disinterested "observation" of objects "out there," but a knowledge of relationship, the relationship between the knower and the known which is grasped through both awareness and affectivity. Awareness and affectivity together in their mutual interrelationship are the way in which we become conscious of the real world and the real self, and together they constitute the single pathway into conscious, human existence in the world. We do not begin, then, as neutral, impartial observers or spectators of a world "outside" us, a passing scene in which we have no part. Human life is not lived at such a distance. We begin, rather, already *within* this world and *within* this scene, very much a part of it as it is of us, being affected by it as well as affecting it, and it is *this* relationship that comes to conscious awareness in human knowledge.

There are two points I want to call attention to in this simple example, two points of unity which, to use the term which William Lynch uses in his *Christ and Apollo,* we could call the "unity of sensibility." First, there is the unity between knower and known or subject and object in all knowledge. The two are known not in isolation, but in relationship. Being "in touch" with a world is simultaneously and identically being "in touch" with one's self. Secondly, there is

---

[13] Lonergan, *Method in Theology,* pp. 8-9; Rahner, *Grundkurs des Glaubens,* pp. 28-30 (17-19).

the unity of awareness and affectivity in which this relationship is grasped. It is through both in their interaction and interdependence that we become aware of the reality and "objectivity" of the world and the reality and "objectivity" of ourselves. This lived unity in the conscious existence of the knower can only subsequently and secondarily be analyzed into separate faculties such as intellect and will, or separate operations such as knowing and desiring. In concrete life they are interwoven, so that it is not an isolated "reason" or "mind" which thinks and knows, but the whole person from out of the concrete totality of the self and within the concrete totality of the situation in which it exists. To assert this unity is not to assert an identity, nor to deny any distinctions among these various elements, but rather to assert their mutual interaction and interdependence in the concrete life of the knower and the concrete process of his knowing. Perhaps this simple example can serve as an illustration on the individual level of the same point being made on the social level by such contemporary studies as that of Jürgen Habermas on the intrinsic relationship between knowledge and human interest in the process of knowing in his book by the same title,[14] or that of Berger and Luckmann in their work entitled, "The Social Construction of Reality."[15]

In addition to this "unity of sensibility" in and through which we are related to and interact with the real world and it is related to us, the example of the child can perhaps serve to bring out another aspect of human knowledge which touches more directly on the question of expression and language. For here in the early stages of learning it is obvious that we know the meaning of things before we know the meaning of words. Words are not the initial medium of our knowledge of and communication with the real world. Learning, knowledge and communication take place long before we can read and write, and even long before we can understand words or use them ourselves. Anyone who has ever seen a child in the early weeks and months of life has witnessed such non-verbal learning and communication, and probably even engaged in it. The child's emerging world of persons and things speaks to it in a variety of non-verbal languages, a variety of actions, movements, signs and gestures. For example, when the child is held or when it is touched gently or roughly, when it sees a smile, the example which Fr. Lonergan used in his analysis of intersubjective meaning, or when it receives a sign of affection, in all these instances very particular things and very

---

[14] Jürgen Habermas, *Knowledge and Human Interest* (Boston: Beacon Press, 1971).

[15] Peter Berger and Thomas Luckmann, *Social Construction of Reality. A Treatise on the Sociology of Knowledge* (New York: Irvington Press, 1966).

important things are being "said" to it, and when the child has learned what these movements, actions and gestures mean, it has entered into communication with its world. It is learning through these signs and gestures not only that reality is there, but that it has a face. If it is lucky, it is learning that it has a human face, but it could also be learning the opposite.

Eventually another process begins as the child learns words or names for all of the realities which it already knows about from its own experience of them, words which refer to and identify realities which it knows, but are not the source of its knowledge. Existence itself and the real world which has touched this existence are the source. When education in a more formal sense begins, the child will learn about all sorts of other realities which may never have entered the world of its own experience, and, if this education continues far enough, it can learn ever more sophisticated and specialized names for things, and discover ever more sophisticated relationships between things in a variety of scientific and academic disciplines. For each of these disciplines represents a particular way of generalizing, conceptualizing, categorizing and naming things and their interrelationships.

But precisely because they are abstract and general, neither the everyday names for things such as mother or father or water, nor their scientific names, should the child learn in one science that mothers belong to the category of mammals, or in another that through a particular kind of analysis water can also be called H_2O, none of these names ever express what may have been his concrete and quite wordless and nameless experience of these realities. In order to exist as social beings we have to acquire a vast arsenal of such words and concepts, and in order to function as a general language which everyone can share, our words and concepts have to prescind or abstract from the particularities of individual experience. But that does not mean that we, even when using these words, can abstract from the particularities of our own individual experience, for the world we live in and interact with is a world of the concrete and the particular. Hence we can all use the same words with a very general and very precise conceptual content, but they can be weighted with a very different experiential content and have a very different experiential meaning for different individuals. This is not true, of course, for any and every reality which we name, but it is true of those realities which have made up our concrete world and have more directly and immediately touched our lives.

There is, then, a kind of knowledge which we all have and which is acquired not "from without" by learning from teachers or books, but is acquired "from within," by being in existence, by being in touch with and being touched by a world of real persons and real things. It is communicated not by words or concepts, but by life itself, by our experience of human existence as an existence in conscious relationship with particular persons and particular things. It is not only "pre-conceptual" knowledge, but in principle it is to some extent non-conceptualizable. This "pre" or this "non" indicates not a deficiency, but a "fullness," the fullness which resides in the particularities of individual experience. To express the positive nature of this knowledge we can once again borrow a phrase from William Lynch and distinguish the knowledge which we have in concepts and its kind of fullness, and the knowledge which we have in "images" and its kind of fullness. These images can come to expression in "images" in a second sense, but in themselves and in the first instance they are not "things" inside us, but are reality itself in the concrete modalities and tonalities in which it has spoken to us. It is in our images of reality that we grasp the real self and the real world together in the unity of their lived and experienced relationship, and in the unity of awareness and affectivity in which we grasp this relationship.

This non-conceptual and non-conceptualizable knowledge through images, then, constitutes not only our initial knowledge of the real world and the real self, but also our most concrete and most "objective" knowledge: this is, indeed, the way reality has been, this is what my experience of existence has been like, and nothing is more real and more objective for a human knower than this. At this most basic and most concrete level of what Rahner calls "original" knowledge, what is most objective *is* what is most subjective, and what is most subjective *is* what is most objective, for it is precisely the actual, lived relationship between the two which is known. Because human existence cannot be lived in the abstract or "at a distance," but is a conscious and affective relationship with concrete realities, we form and cannot help but form such images of the real. For at this level we have no other access to the real world except through our experience of it. Our images of the real differ from our concepts of the real, then, not because one is subjective and the other is at least potentially objective, but because images contain the real, objective particularity and concreteness of the objective world, and concepts abstract from this. I can attach false ideas to my images by thinking that everyone's experience is just like my own, or by thinking that human existence is nothing more than or different from what I have already experienced. But these false generalizations simply mean that my images must grow and develop just as conceptual knowledge must, grow through contact with the experience of other people and develop with the growth of my own experience.

We shall not have time to look at this growth process in any detail, for example, the movement from an early stage of being dependent and "being shaped" by the world towards a more independent and mature "shaping" of a world and a self, or from an early stage of being largely "dispersed" in a manifold of disparate and disconnected experiences towards the active process of "shaping" one's world and one's self into a unity, a world and a self with form, movement, coherence and direction. But this non-conceptual knowledge in images is the kind of knowledge which is called "original" knowledge because it has its origins in or wells up from the depths of existence and constitutes not just an initial stage of knowledge which can be gotten beyond, but a permanent element in our knowledge of human existence. Hence the irreducible nature of the tension between original or experiential knowledge and its objectification in concepts, and the need for the ongoing, two-directional movement between the two. Hence also the irreducible nature of the various languages in which the two kinds of knowledge reach their most adequate expression and the tension between them. For there is no one, single, univocal kind of "fullness" in language and articulation, but the same kind of analogy which characterizes reality itself and our knowledge of reality. The fullness which one kind of language achieves might entail the loss of another kind of fullness, a loss which can be offset only by another kind of language.

III. Unthematic Knowledge of God

A final example of the differences of emphasis which we have been considering can be found, I think, in the two authors' treatment of the knowledge of God. In both, the notion of self-transcendence and the experience of transcendence is central. Fr. Rahner defines transcendental experience as follows:

> We shall call *transcendental experience* the subjective, unthematic, necessary and unfailing consciousness of the knowing subject that is co-present in every spiritual act of knowledge, and the subject's openness to the unlimited expanse of all possible reality.[16]

It is an *experience* because this unthematic knowledge is an element in and a condition of possibility for every concrete experience of any object whatsoever. It is transcendental in two senses: it belongs to the necessary and constitutive structures of a knowing subject, and in this experience the subject transcends all categories and all possible objects. Transcendental experience, in other words, is the expe-

---

[16] Rahner, *Grundkurs des Glaubens,* p. 31 (20).

rience of the subject's own self-transcendence. Fr. Rahner remarks further that such an experience occurs not just in knowledge, but also in the experience of freedom. The question about the source and the ultimate term of human self-transcendence arises in the subject both as conscious and as free. A final remark hearkens back to what we have already considered with regard to knowledge and language. Transcendence occurs not in the abstract, objectifying concept which we need in order to talk about it, nor in the talk itself which is equally necessary, but in the experience of human existence which precedes both.

It is on the basis of this analysis that Rahner introduces the question of an "anonymous and unthematic knowledge of God."[17] Our original knowledge of God, he says, is not the kind of knowledge in which we grasp an object which appears directly or indirectly within the horizon of our experience. Rather, it has the character of a transcendental experience:

> Insofar as this subjective, non-objective luminosity of the subject in its transcendence is always orientated towards the holy mystery, the knowledge of God is always present unthematically and without name, and not just when we begin to speak of it. All talk about it, which necessarily goes on, always only points to this transcendental experience as such, an experience in which he whom we call "God" encounters man in silence, encounters him as the absolute and the incomprehensible, as the term of his transcendence which cannot really be incorporated into any system of coordinates. When this transcendence is the transcendence of *love*, it also experiences this term as the *holy* mystery.[18]

Since this transcendental experience occurs whenever the subject is functioning as a knowing and free subject, this unthematic, experiential knowledge pervades all human experience properly as such.

The relationship between the two moments in this transcendental experience, namely, knowledge and love, is considered in more detail in a later article which we shall look at briefly. How, first of all, must knowledge or intellect itself be understood if it is to be seen as the capacity to know God precisely as the "holy mystery?" If, Rahner says, the intellect is understood primarily and exclusively in an a posteriori and positivistic way as the capacity to know individual objects and their causal or functional relationships, then the knowledge of God as mystery is ruled out from the outset. For then the experience of God as mystery can only appear as a still unsolved problem, or, if it is insoluable, as a contradiction, as something

---

[17] Ibid., p. 32 (21).
[18] Ibid.

which goes counter to the very nature of knowledge. To avoid this, Rahner says:

> The intellect must be understood more fundamentally as the capacity to encounter the incomprehensible, as the capacity to be grasped by that which lies always beyond our control, and not originally as the capacity to grasp something, and to master and control it.[19]

If we examine the nature of human intellectual activity, we find that this is, indeed, the basic character of our knowledge. For we situate and define individual objects within frameworks which themselves are not so situated and defined, and all of our understanding of "clear and distinct ideas" is based on presuppositions which themselves have not been clearly understood and definitively established. All of our knowledge is conscious of its provisional and tentative nature, is aware that it takes place within an infinite, unending process, a process which cannot be ended by ourselves. We can, indeed, must define knowledge or intellect, then, as "the capacity for entering into the presence of the incomprehensible."[20] This occurs, moreover, not at the end of the process of knowledge, but from the very beginning and as the very essence of knowledge.

What, then, can we call the act by which man knows God as incomprehensible mystery, and yet finds in this knowledge not a limit and a barrier to his search, but its fulfillment?

> This act is the act of abandonning and entrusting oneself to this very incomprehensibility as such, an act in which knowledge goes beyond its own essence and becomes fully itself by becoming love.[21]

If the experience of God as mystery is not to be the experience of meaninglessness or absurdity, the experience of a final and impregnable barrier to man's quest for knowledge, truth and love, a barrier which shows the futility of the quest, then the acceptance of this mystery must not be seen as an impassable limit to knowledge, but as its deepest content, and such an acceptance is the acceptance of love. Such an understanding of knowledge is available to us within the realm of finite experience, for interpersonal love is precisely the acceptance of another whom we cannot comprehend, master or control, and the letting go of self in trust for the good of another when we cannot calculate the result. Here we find an

---

[19] Karl Rahner, "Die menschliche Sinnfrage vor dem absoluten Geheimnis Gottes," *Geist und Leben* (June, 1977): 444.

[20] Ibid., p. 445.

[21] Ibid., p. 446.

analogy, but only an analogy, for understanding the knowledge of God as being at its deepest level the risk of love.[22]

The similarity of Fr. Lonergan's treatment of these same topics is for me, at any rate, quite striking. In his chapter on "Religion," he speaks of the inevitability of the question of God in human experience:

> The question of God, then, lies within man's horizon. Man's transcendental subjectivity is mutilated or abolished, unless he is stretching forth towards the intelligible, the unconditioned, the good of value. The reach, not of his attainment, but of his intending is unrestricted. There lies within his horizon a region for the divine, a shrine for ultimate holiness. It cannot be ignored. The atheist may pronounce it empty. The agnostic may urge that he finds his investigation has been inconclusive. The contemporary humanist will refuse to allow the question to arise. But their negations presuppose the spark in our clod, our native orientation to the divine.[23]

In his treatment of human self-transcendence, he says that it is the only way that man can achieve "authenticity," and that this self-transcendence is not only cognitive, but also must become "moral."[24] Moreover, our questions for intelligence, for reflection and for deliberation constitute only our capacity for self-transcendence. "That capacity becomes an actuality when one falls in love."[25] There is, further, the insistence that all love is a process of "self-surrender," and that loving God "is being in love without limits or qualifications or conditions or reservations."[26] The fulfillment which one finds in such love is not something which we can produce by our knowledge of choice, but rather it abolishes our horizon and sets up a new horizon in which the love of God transforms both our knowledge and our values.[27] Finally, Lonergan defines faith as "the knowledge born of religious love."[28]

If one were to develop any of these notions in either author, there are certainly differences to be found. The one difference that I want to mention is, once again, not so much a question of disagreement in the sense that the one denies what the other asserts, but a difference of emphasis which is parallel and analogous to similar differences we have already considered. Fr. Rahner places his primary emphasis on

---

[22] Ibid., pp. 447-48.
[23] Lonergan, Method in Theology, p. 103.
[24] Ibid., p. 104.
[25] Ibid., p. 105.
[26] Ibid., p. 106.
[27] Ibid., p. 106.
[28] Ibid., p. 115.

the "unthematic" knowledge of God, that experience of God as a question which is had throughout all of human experience and whenever a human subject is functioning as conscious and free. It would, then, be part of what was called in our first section "original knowledge," and is never able to be completely conceptualized or verbalized as we considered in our second section. This methodological principle, of course, would explain the predominance in Rahner's theology of such thematic topics as the "supernatural existential" and the "anonymous Christian." It would also explain, I think, the centrality of the experience of mystery in his theology, and that for him this is the prototypical name for God. The basic focus of Fr. Lonergan, on the other hand, seems to me to be the explicit, thematic experience of God, the level which Rahner would call the objectification and thematization of the original experience. In these latter processes the human mind functions in quite the same way that it functions in objectifying and verbalizing other elements of experience, and hence the concern with these operations or processes in themselves and as a universal method applicable to all scientific knowledge.

IV. Conclusion

This brings us to what is perhaps not so much a conclusion as an observation. I find in Fr. Rahner's *Grundkurs* a drive towards unity, an attempt to get back to that basic level of experience where "what is meant and the experience of what is meant are still one." Fr. Lonergan's "drive" on the other hand, seems to go mainly in the opposite direction, towards ever greater differentiation and clarification of this unity. I suppose that that is why one wrote a *Grundkurs des Glaubens* in an effort to relate the "Idea of Christianity" back to the reality itself, and the other wrote a *Method in Theology.* In any case, we are the richer for both.

A Response to Fr. Dych

by Rev. Bernard J. F. Lonergan, S.J.

In the eleventh volume of his *Theological Investigations* Fr. Rahner published a 68-page paper setting forth his *Reflections on Methodology in Theology*. He began by expressing his embarrassment when asked to treat this topic for, while over the years he had touched upon methodological aspects of particular questions, he had never attempted to tackle the issue in its full range.[1] I think one has to accept some such a view of Rahner's work. Dr. Anne Carr of the University of Chicago Divinity School did a doctoral dissertation on Fr. Rahner's views on method and found it necessary to reach them by inference from his writings on more particular topics. And Fr. Dych, to whose address I am to offer an appendage, reviewed Dr. Carr's work favorably in *Theological Studies*. But if Fr. Rahner has not tackled the problem of method in a general fashion, he has given us an extremely penetrating account of the difficulties of that task at the present time. The work of a contemporary theologian, he has said, has to find a niche in the midst of an uncontrollable pluralism of theologies. This pluralism emerges out of an ongoing and incalculable development of human thought. His task can hardly be the contribution of a collaborator working on a common site on which a single building is being erected according to a settled plan that is known to all. On the contrary, he finds himself an alien, alone, isolated. He may work on the basis of a world of ideas, from certain premises, with certain philosophical preconceptions as his tools. But he can hardly fail to be aware that all such suppositions are subject to historical conditions and to the limitations of particular epochs. Yet such awareness does not make him capable of eliminating these limitations. For the first time in the history of theological thought theology not only is conditioned by history but also is aware of being unable to overcome this conditioning.[2]

Such sentiments are not peculiar to Fr. Rahner. Well before Vatican II, while I was teaching at the Gregorian, Fr. Eduard Dhanis, who held a succession of high offices at the Gregorian and in the Roman Congregations, expressed to me his firm conviction that, while Catholic theologians agreed on the dogmas of the Church, they agreed on little else. Finally, while Vatican II brought many blessings, it remains that Fr. Rahner's paper on methodology in

---

[1] Karl Rahner, "Reflections on Methodology in Theology," *Theological Investigations* 11, trans. and ed. David Bourke (London: Darton, Longman & Todd; New York: Seabury Press, 1974): 68f.

[2] Ibid., p. 74.

theology was begun in 1969 and that Fr. Dhanis' contention that theologians were unanimous in their acceptance of the dogmas of faith only with difficulty can any longer be maintained.

It remains that Fr. Rahner himself has very clear ideas on a particular method. He names it indirect method. He has given us a large sample of it in his *Foundations of Christian Faith*. It is a method that can be backed by appeals to the rules for the discernment of spirits for the second week of St. Ignatius' *Spiritual Exercises*, to Newman's *Grammar of Assent*, to Polanyi's tacit knowledge, to articles by Eric Voegelin, and to my own account of *Natural Right and Historical Mindedness.*[3]

Nor is his contribution limited to such an indirect method. For if one understands by method, not something like *The New Method Laundry* or a book of recipes for a cook, but rather a framework for collaboration in creativity and, more particularly, a normative pattern of related and repeated operations with ongoing and cumulative results, then I believe one will find ways to control the present uncontrollable pluralism of theologies, one will cease to work alien, alone, isolated, one will become aware of a common site with an edifice to be erected, not in accord with a static blueprint, but under the leadership of an emergent probability that yields results proportionate to human diligence and intelligence. In brief, I should say that Fr. Rahner has laid down the conditions and expounded the need for a radical development in theological method. Such insight into the needs of contemporary theology are, to my mind, a remarkable confirmation of the widely held view that Fr. Rahner has been among the foremost doctrinal theologians of his age.

It remains that my own concern has been less with developing doctrines than with discovering how one develops them with method. A first point, of course, is that "method" means different things in different historical contexts. Perhaps the most celebrated was Descartes' proposal that we begin from indubitable truth and proceed by deduction even to the point of deducing the conservation of momentum from the immutability of God. In contrast, Hans-Georg Gadamer's great work on *Wahrheit und Methode,* Truth and Method, has been understood to take "method" in a Cartesian sense and to contend that the search for truth was what counted

---

[3] Ibid., pp. 76-84. See also: Karl Rahner, *Foundations of Christian Faith,* trans. and ed. William Dych (New York: Seabury Press, 1978), pp. 8 f.; pp. 346 f; Eric Voegelin, "Reason: The Classic Experience," *The Southern Review* 10 (1974): 237-64; Eric Voegelin, "The Gospel and Culture," *Jesus and Man's Hope,* ed. D. G. Miller and D. Y. Hadidian (Pittsburgh: Pittsburgh Theological Seminary, 1971), pp. 59-101; Bernard Lonergan, "Natural Right and Historical Mindedness," *Proceedings: American Catholic Philosophical Association* 51 (1977): 132-43.

while "method" was an obstacle.

My own thought on method began in England where I studied philosophy. H. B. W. Joseph's *Introduction to Logic* not only grounded one thoroughly in the Aristotelian syllogism but also offered an instructive introduction to scientific procedures, an account that was broadened by some knowledge of the calculus and of the logical inadequacy of Euclid's argumentation. Then Newman's *Grammar of Assent* charmed me with its convincing account that common sense does not develop in accord with the rules of syllogism. From Newman I went to Plato and from Plato to Augustine's early dialogues at Cassiacum. I studied theology in Rome where among my companions was an Athenian who had studied philosophy at Louvain, was at home with Maréchal and taught me what was meant by the statement that human knowledge was discursive, not a matter of taking a look with the eyes of the mind, but of asking questions and coming to know when one chanced upon satisfactory answers. Doctoral work on Aquinas' development of the concept of actual grace and on the dependence of concepts on understanding helped me towards a rounded view.

So by 1949 I began to work out my notion of method as a Generalized Empirical Method. A first stage was the book, *Insight,* which found common features in mathematics, physics, common sense, and philosophy, and later with help from Hans-Georg Gadamer, in interpretation and history.

I recount these strange *faits divers* because they throw some light on my perhaps stranger opinions. I list them with some attempt at order.

First, metaphysics is first in itself but it is not first for us. What is first for us on a reflective level is our own conscious and intentional activities. Such reflection must not presuppose metaphysics, else the metaphysics will not be critical, and so it does not speak of potencies and habits, however implicit, but only of conscious and intentional events and their experienced interrelations.

Second, as Vernon Gregson has remarked, such reflection is like a therapy. Just as Carl Rogers' client-centered therapy aims at having the client discover in himself the feelings he cannot name or identify so reflection on one's interior operations is a matter of coming to name, recognize, and identify operations that recur continuously but commonly are thought to be very mysterious. Insights are a dime a dozen, most of them are inadequate when taken singly, but far too many people are certain either that they do not exist or at least are excessively obscure.

Third, the omission of talk about potencies and habits and concentration on events and their experienced relations, pulls thought out of the realm of faculty psychology into that of intentionality analysis. That yields a psychology of data, questions, and answers, with the questions on the three levels of questions for intelligence, questions for sufficient reason for factual judgments, and questions for evaluation and decision.

Fourth, this makes the precedence of intellect on will like the precedence of sense on intellect. It makes it just what normally happens. It does not exclude divine operation directly on the fourth level. As St. Paul instructed the Romans: God's love has flooded our inmost hearts by the Holy Spirit he has given us. Such flooding hardly can be due to some intellectual apprehension in this life, especially since the mystics are given to celebrating their cloud of unknowing.

Fifth, at this point Generalized Empirical Method becomes theological. The transition may be illustrated by the words of our Lord to St. Peter, "Blessed are thou Simon Bar Jonah for flesh and blood has not revealed this to thee but my Father who is in heaven" (Matt 16:17). Words, that Eric Voegelin contrasts with the words to the other disciples, tell no man that I am the Christ (cf. Matt 16:20). The two, Voegelin contrasts as *revelation,* the Father to Peter, and *information,* the words of the disciples to every Tom, Dick and Harry. A similar doctrine is to be had from John 6:44f, and John 12:32. Besides the inner gift of the spirit, there is the sensible spectacle of Christ on the cross. With those steps we are already into Christian Theology.

A Response to Fr. Dych

by Rev. Walter J. Stohrer, S.J.

As Rector of the Jesuit Community at Marquette University, I would like to preface my remarks on Fr. Dych's paper with my own personal words of greeting. I extend a warm welcome to all who are visiting our campus for this celebration of Fr. Karl Rahner's past and continuing achievements in theology. It is my hope that our symposium at Marquette will be an occasion for lasting personal enrichment for all.

In choosing to discuss the problem of method, Fr. Dych has, of course, identified a pivotal aspect of Karl Rahner's theology. He has elected to offer a brief discussion of this question within the context of a comparison and contrast with Fr. Lonergan's own method in theology. Fr. Lonergan and I agreed over our burnt toast this morning in the Jesuit Residence dining room that he was in the best position to speak about the relative merits of this approach. In my own brief remarks I have chosen to identify some of the operative themes from Fr. Rahner's earlier philosophical anthropology which might enable us to achieve a better understanding of Fr. Dych's present perspective.

Fr. Dych has noted that a serious concern in the development of any methodology is expressed in the need to grasp and express more fully that which we have already experienced and come to know. He has alerted us to the broader purpose of the *Introduction* of Fr. Rahner's *Grundkurs,* which is to draw attention to the relationship between theological knowledge and human existence as already known through the experience of actually living it. This primary experience is that experience which, as Fr. Rahner has noted, expresses an unthematic unity. It is that experience in which "what is meant and the experience of what is meant are still one."[1]

It is widely recognized by students of Rahner's thought that his theological work is distinctive not only for its speculative power, but also for its pastoral and practical quality as well. I vividly recall the comment of one of my fellow students in my Innsbruck seminary days some twenty years ago. After we had heard a particularly exciting lecture by Fr. Rahner, my friend suggested in words similar to these: "He has something for everyone—for the highly gifted and those not so gifted, for the speculatively inclined, as well as for those with a more practical temperament or immediate pastoral concern. That range of appeal is a testimony to the genius of the man."

[1] Karl Rahner, *Grundkurs des Glaubens. Einführung in den Begriff des Christentums* (Freiburg: Herder, 1976), p. 28.

Perhaps I can best focus my remarks today by posing a question: What is the secret of Rahner's broad appeal? And what does our answer to this question tell us about the manner in which Rahner himself has personally embodied and implemented his amazingly fruitful theological method?

In his early seminal works, *Spirit in the World* and *Hearers of the Word,* which first appeared in 1939 and 1941 respectively, Fr. Rahner chose to make explicit two key terms in his working definition of man. He noted that "Spirit *(Geist)* is used as the name of a power that reaches beyond the world to grasp the metaphysical; world *(Welt)* is the name of the reality accessible to man's immediate experience."[2] In these descriptions Rahner made explicit his view that the proper object of his enquiry is the human person who is at one and the same time in the world and oriented beyond the world. Thus, world immediacy and world transcendence are intertwined in human existence. In this context, Rahner specified the existential conditions for human knowing and willing. In doing so he laid the epistemological and metaphysical foundations for that basic insight to which Fr. Dych has directed our attention this morning, namely, that man takes full possession of himself in consciousness only through his relationship with the world.

It is interesting to note that the original title of Fr. Dych's paper was "Method in Theology according to Karl Rahner." His revised title is "The Role of Experience in the Theology of Karl Rahner." It is evident that to understand the intimate relationship between personal experience and theological method is, in Fr. Dych's opinion, to be well on the way to understanding Karl Rahner's foundational theological perspective.

Rahner's position draws attention to the fact that man is a being who unites opposites. As spirit man is self-presence, the primeval unit and source of being and knowledge. But man is also in the world, for he lives in a direct, immediate, and usually unthematized relationship with the world. The immediate co-presence of man's spiritual orientation toward being in dynamic interaction with his world constitutes the continuing point of departure of a theological method grounded in Rahner's philosophical anthropology.

Several other pieces in the Rahner mosaic of the human person serve to illumine the "original knowledge" identified by Fr. Rahner, and alluded to by Fr. Dych. One of these themes is Rahner's insistence that "the development of the question is the first and most difficult business of the philosopher."[3] Here we are

---

[2] Karl Rahner, *Geist in Welt,* 2d ed. rev. (Munich: Kösel-Verlag, 1957), p. 14.
[3] Ibid., p. 37.

reminded that there is an intimate connection between man and the being-question which characterizes him. Man questions being: this is the first observation about man which Rahner finds fundamentally significant. But man is more than an active questioner of being. He is the questioned as well. The being-question, or *Seinsfrage,* is part of man's continuing experience. It is constitutive of him in his existential condition, and Rahner never lets us forget this.

Indeed, it is Rahner's contention that man reaches his full human potential precisely to the extent that he is faithful to his vocation of questioning. "Man questions being in general in order to become himself," he notes.[4] Rahner nuances this point by noting that man is "the necessarily questioning questioner of being."[5] Hence, in virtue of the primacy of the question in Rahner's anthropology, the problem of being and the problem of man are reductively one and the same. Man is spirit in matter, not pure transcendence. And long before man reflects on himself as questioner in any thematic or scientific way, he is actually living the question as well as partial answers to it. I would submit that this perspective on man has been especially significant for the development of Rahner's theological method, a method distinguished by vigorous and relentless questioning. Conceptualization and language have a necessary orientation to man's original experience.

In establishing the primacy of the question for theological and self-integration, Rahner also emphasized that questioning man is a being "already in the world."[6] The world of man's everyday experience is pre-given, or at least co-given with existential man. It is the background and horizon of his questioning, and it is always there. The world is man's primitive element, his milieu, a fact which leads Rahner to suggest that the only knowledge man can have is his knowledge as a dweller at home in and on intimate terms with this world.[7]

Spirit in the World demonstrated that man is the finite questioner of being in the world. This implies that man realizes and fulfills himself by applying himself to the phenomena which his presence in the world makes possible. The more rich and varied man's experiences are, the more there is revealed through them the goal of the human spirit, "being as such,"[8] which also extends beyond this world. But man is himself a phenomenon, and indeed the most spiritual of all,

---

Ibid., p. 71.

Ibid., p. 72.

Ibid., p. 75.

Ibid., p. 76.

Karl Rahner, *Hörer des Wortes,* 2d ed. rev. (Munich: Kösel-Verlag, 1963), p. 199.

for in him existence in the world reaches its most sublime finite expression. In a philosophy of religion developed in *Hearers of the Word,* Rahner suggests that it is in the immediate human world of time and history that God, if He speaks at all, reveals Himself to man. Man listens in his history to the word of God or awaits God's self-disclosure. Says Rahner: "Only one who hears in this way is what he really has to be: man."[9] Man's attentiveness to God's possible revelation is constitutive of man himself. This reflection moves toward a descriptive definition of man as "the being of receptive spirituality standing in freedom before God, Who is free in regard to a possible revelation, a revelation which, if it occurs, takes place in the form of a word spoken in man's history."[10]

It is clear that Rahner's earlier work provided a program for further elaboration and reflection. This was developed by Rahner as a theologian, where his central concern has remained the same: It is the vocation of man to make his relatedness to the world explicit, and in so doing, to define himself by thematizing his relatedness to his self-revealing God. The development of this level of consciousness necessarily implicates the elaboration of a theological methodology.

I would submit, then, that at the outset of his explicitly theological reflection Rahner exercised a fundamental epistemological option. He established as a fundamental methodological component the supremacy of the "sum" over the "cogito." In doing so he secured the total inadequacy and unacceptability of phenomenalism in all its forms, either its Rationalist expression associated with Descartes' "clear and distinct ideas," or the Empiricist inspired expression of phenomenalism classically expressed in Hume's subjective preoccupation with "perceptions." For if we begin in the mind, rather than in a reflective interdependence with the world of our immediate experience, we are condemned to end in the mind. In his discussion of method in his *Grundkurs,* Rahner has articulated the concrete unity of lived experience, the experience of Christian faith in its foundations, that is, in the structure of operative human consciousness, and in the operative self-understanding within the human person. His theory of human knowledge has aptly been characterized as a "concrete speculation."[11]

Man's vocation as a world dweller opens to him the riches of the historical Christ Who pitched His tent in our midst. With Jesus of Nazareth men share an encounter with the world. It is precisely this

---

9. Ibid., p. 199
10. Ibid., p. 200.
[11] Otto Muck, "A priori, Evidenz und Erfahrung," in *Festgabe für Karl Rahner,* 2 vols., ed. Johannes B. Metz (Freiburg: Herder, 1964), 1:94-96.

intimate contact which man has with the world which prepares him for the actuality of God's historically revealed Word. This is the point of departure for all theology. It is significant that Ignatius of Loyola concludes his *Spiritual Exercises* with the "Contemplation for Obtaining Love," which suggests that this sacramental universe is graced, a trysting place with God. The Lord of History is not only the end of man's earthly journey; He is the journey itself. I would submit that Karl Rahner's theological method, grounded in his earlier epistemological and metaphysical positions regarding human existence, has done much to enhance our appreciation of this sublime aspect of our pilgrim condition.

Karl Rahner and the Christian Philosophy of Saint Thomas Aquinas

by Rev. Gerald McCool, S.J.

It is interesting that the year of our symposium devoted to the philosophy and theology of Karl Rahner is also the centenary year of *Aeterni Patris*. *Aeterni Patris* was the *magna charta* of the Neo-Scholastic revival. While he was still Cardinal Archbishop of Perugia, Leo XIII had been one of the group of Italian Neo-Thomists whose suspicion of German philosophy and its influence on Catholic theology had made itself felt in the debates and decrees of Vatican I. *Aeterni Patris,* which appeared quite early in Leo XIII's pontificate, restricted its scope to the education of Roman Catholic priests. Nevertheless it set the tone for the whole pontificate of that great Pope. Leo's hopes for a Catholic intellectual revival and his confidence that Catholic influence could be restored in social and political life rested in great part on the conviction which he expressed in *Aeterni Patris* that the Christian Philosophy of St. Thomas could regain its rightful place as the directing and integrating source of Catholic thought and Catholic action.[1]

A decade and a half ago Vatican II followed upon Vatican I. Vatican II's *Decree on Priestly Formation* placed much less weight on the Christian Philosophy of St. Thomas than *Aeterni Patris* had done. Whereas *Aeterni Patris* had recommended the philosophical and theological method of the Angelic Doctor as the one method truly suited for the education of Catholic priests, *The Decree on Priestly Formation* preferred to accept the contributions of several philosophical systems.[2] Furthermore, the *Decree* sets down as the first objective in the reform of ecclesiastical studies a better integration of philosophy and theology. At least by implication, it would appear that the integration of philosophy and theology proposed in *Aeterni Patris* had not proved satisfactory and that the Council Fathers thought that the time had come for the Church to experiment with another model. Karl Rahner's *Foundations of Christian Faith*[3] is the best known and, in my opinion, the most successful attempt to show what the new model of priestly education would look like. Thus, in the centenary year of Leo XIII's encyclical, *Aeterni Patris* and *Foundations of Chris-*

---

[1] Gerald A. McCool, *Catholic Theology in the Nineteenth Century; The Quest for a Unitary Method* (New York: Seabury, 1977) pp. 216-40.

[2] *Decree on Priestly Formation (Optatum Totius),* Nos. 14-15. See *Documents of Vatican II,* ed. Walter M. Abbot (New York: America Press, 1966).

[3] Karl Rahner, *Foundations of Christian Faith,* trans. William Dych (New York: Seabury, 1978).

tian Faith confront each other as two models of priestly education, the old and the new.

I. Christian Philosophy and the Ideal of *Aeterni Patris*

The opposition between the two is real and significant. *Foundations of Christian Faith* represents the mature thought of a great theologian who began his career as a Maréchalian Thomist still convinced that the philosophical and theological ideal of *Aeterni Patris* was a valid one. As a result of his own intellectual evolution the Rahner of *Foundations of Christian Faith* has been forced to reject that ideal as unrealizable. Nevertheless the new concept of philosophy and theology which undergirds *Foundations of Christian Faith* has emerged in the course of Rahner's progressive development as an independent philosopher and theologian who is still willing to accept the Angelic Doctor as a Father of the Church.[4] Thus the contrast between the relation between philosophy and theology in *Aeterni Patris* and in *Foundations of Christian Faith* is important not only for the history of Catholic thought but for the understanding of Rahner's own major work.

"Christian Philosophy," as it was used in *Aeterni Patris,* had definite historical connotations. The phrase was directed against the "separated" Post-Cartesian philosophy which, whether it was rationalist or empiricist in tone, adamantly opposed the slightest influence of Revelation upon its reflections on the grounds of its philosophical method and its stringently rational norms of philosophical evidence. The phrase was also used to specify the relation between philosophy and theology in the synthesis of the Angelic Doctor and to distinguish it from the different relation between them which structured a number of nineteenth century Catholic theologies. Not only the fideists and traditionalists, who fell into Roman disfavor, but the theologians of the Catholic Tübingen School, who were never the object of ecclesiastical censure, defined Christian philosophy as an intellectual reflection carried on inside theology itself as an integral part of a single complete intellectual reflection illuminated by the light of faith.[5] The Neo-Scholastics did not deny that, as a concrete activity, Christian Philosophy was carried on by a believing mind elevated by supernatural grace. Nevertheless, as an intellectual discipline, philosophy was distinct from theology. Philosophy, Christian or not, had its own formal object, its own distinct method, its own purely rational norms of evidence.

---

[4] Karl Rahner, "On Recognizing the Importance of Thomas Aquinas," *Theological Investigations* 9, trans. Graham Harrison (New York: Seabury, 1975): 3-12.

[5] McCool, *Catholic Theology in the Nineteenth Century,* pp. 129-44.

Philosophy, as such, did not require the light of faith; it was an activity of natural reason which, by its own unaided power, was capable of judging the truth or falsity of philosophical propositions.[6]

In nineteenth century Catholic theology the proper understanding of "Christian Philosophy" was not a peripheral issue. The controversy over the proper relation between faith and reason, nature and grace dominated Catholic theology in the years before Vatican I.

The Neo-Scholastics insisted that their philosophy and theology were the only ones which could do justice to the authentic Catholic position on faith and reason, nature and grace. In the Scholastic philosophy of the Angelic Doctor a clear distinction was made between natural knowledge of God, the infinite creator of the universe, and supernatural knowledge of the Trinity and of the Incarnate Word, the redemptive source of sanating and elevating grace. Likewise, in the Aristotelian metaphysics of the Angelic Doctor, the distinction between substance and accident grounded a metaphysics of nature and grace in which the distinction between the natural and the supernatural orders was clear and unequivocal.

Before the Neo-Scholastic revival Catholic theology had turned its back on St. Thomas' philosophy of knowledge. In the tradition of Aristotle, St. Thomas had staunchly maintained that the entire objective content of human intellectual knowledge was derived from sense experience. In that case, even the fundamental ideas on which the first principles of metaphysics' necessary knowledge depend must be acquired from sense experience through the Aristotelian process of abstraction. On the other hand, the more recent theories of knowledge favored by Catholic theologians in the first half of the nineteenth century followed the subjective starting point of Descartes, the Post-Kantian idealists or Saint Augustine. According to these theories of knowledge the abstractive intellect's grasp of the contingent objects of sense experience could never ground the necessary truths of metaphysics. The fundamental ideas on which the first principles of metaphysics rested must be derived from the mind's intuitive grasp of God or of the Infinite Idea of Being. Absolute Being was the first in the order of knowledge as it was first in the order of reality. Without some intuitive grasp of Absolute Being itself the intellectual activity of the human mind would be impossible.[7]

To put the distinction in its nineteenth century context, the philosophy of knowledge of the Angelic Doctor was a philosophy

---

[6] Ibid., pp. 173-83.

[7] For an account of the ontologism of Gioberti, Rosmini and the Louvain School, see McCool, *Catholic Theology in the Nineteenth Century,* pp. 113-28.

confined to discursive reason, at least as the Non-Scholastic theologians saw it, whereas the philosophies of knowledge favored by the traditionalists, the ontologists and the theologians of the Catholic Tübingen School derived their first principles from the intuitive intellect.[8] In the nineteenth century theological context this distinction was taken to mean that there was an unbridgeable gap between the theology of the Neo-Scholastics and the theologies of the opposing schools. In the opinion of their opponents the Neo-Scholastics were saved from the explicit profession of empiricism only by their own philosophical naiveté. An intuitive grasp of God or Being was required to ground the necessary first principles of metaphysics and Scholastic epistemology denied the existence of this a priori grasp of Being. Its starting point in sense experience and its reliance on the abstractive intellect could ground neither the necessary knowledge of metaphysics nor a philosophical proof of God's existence. If the Neo-Scholastics were less muddle-headed, they would profess agnosticism. No other course was open to them.

The Neo-Scholastics, naturally enough, saw things differently. In their opinion once a theologian was unwary enough to admit that an a priori intuitive grasp of God or Absolute Being was required to ground the necessary first principles of human reason, he could no longer defend the essential distinction between natural and supernatural knowledge of God which his Catholic faith required. According to orthodox Catholic teaching God can be grasped directly only through the supernatural knowledge elicited by a mind elevated by grace. The strict mysteries of divine revelation transcend the grasp of natural reason. They are the object of supernatural faith. Philosophy is an intellectual activity carried on under the light of natural reason. Theology, whose object is divine revelation, is an intellectual activity performed under the supernatural light of faith.

Yet, if a theologian were to hold that an intuitive grasp of God or Infinite Being were required to ground the first principles of metaphysics, he could no longer claim that there was and must be an essential difference between philosophy and theology. This was the precise point which confirmed the Neo-Scholastics in their conviction that an epistemology of intuitive reason and its a priori grasp of God or Absolute Being was the philosophical source of the seemingly opposed evils which plagued nineteenth century Catholic theology: rationalism and traditionalism. Rationalism reduced theology to philosophy. On the other side, by requiring an a priori grasp of the Divine Being through a primitive revelation to ground the necessary

---

[8] See McCool, *Catholic Theology in the Nineteenth Century*, pp. 37-58; 67-81.

first principles of human reason, traditionalism reduced philosophy to theology. Neither of these opposed systems could preserve the proper balance between faith and reason and distinguish super-natural from natural knowledge of God. Only an abstractive theory of knowledge could do that. In the interest of orthodoxy therefore Catholic theology should abandon the subjective starting point of Post-Cartesian philosophical systems and return to the metaphysics of the Angelic Doctor grounded upon sense experience and the abstractive intellect.[9]

History showed that philosophy of knowledge and metaphysics went together. When Descartes abandoned the epistemology of St. Thomas in favor of his own epistemology of the intuitive thinking subject, he not only severed the immediate intentional bond between thought and material reality, he also shattered the ontological unity of man. For the Cartesian revolution in philosophy severed the unitary sensitivo-intellectual knower into an angelic intuitive mind juxtaposed to an inert machine. Moveover, in Descartes' philosophy of nature Aristotelian final causality was displaced by a deterministic physics of inert atoms and constantly created local motion. In the Aristotelian universe of active being thought, will, sense and inani-mate nature were bound together in an intelligible dynamic whole through the links of Aristotle's four-fold causality. Because of its subjective starting point Post-Cartesian philosophy had proven itself incapable of reconstituting man's lost unity of thought and action. It was equally incapable of restoring the human knower's bond with inanimate nature.

Nothing less than a return to the Scholastic philosophy of knowledge and being could restore man's shattered unity. In St. Thomas' philosophy of knowledge the cognitive act which began with sense experience and culminated in the judgment was a single unified act of sense and intellect. Furthermore, the unified act of knowledge cooperated in its turn with the will in the performance of man's concrete act of free choice. The condition of possibility for the dynamic unity of sense, intellect and will in thought and action was an Aristotelian metaphysics of form and matter, faculty and act. For only through these metaphysical principles could man's operations be unified through their dynamic source, a sensitivo-intellectual human nature operating through its proper faculties.

The same metaphysics of matter, form and goal-directed natural action was required to link the human knower to the dynamic universe with which he interacts. The Aristotelian metaphysics of

---

[9] This was the line which Joseph Kleutgen took in his critique of the Non-Scholastic philosophers and theologians. See McCool, *Catholic Theology in the Nineteenth Century,* pp. 167-87.

efficient causality explained how the objects of sense as agents produce in the human knower an intentional participation in their own
ontological reality. It also showed how man, as a sensitivo-
intellectual nature, could move from potency to act by objectivizing
these intentional forms through the affirmation of the judgment. For
in Aristotle's metaphysics of knowledge the knowable in act and the
knower in act are identical.

Clearly then, the Neo-Scholastics believed, a return to the
metaphysics of matter, form, nature, activity and finality was
needed to restore the unity of will, mind, sense and animate nature
which Post-Cartesian philosophy had lost. The Christian Philosophy
of the Angelic Doctor was a Christian Aristotelianism. Precisely
because it was an Aristotelian philosophy of knowledge, man and
being, it could dispel the confusion between intellect and will which
ran through Post-Cartesian idealism and prevent the reduction of
intellect to sense which characterized Post-Cartesian empiricism.[10]

II. *Aeterni Patris* and the Structure of Theology

The Christian Philosophy of the Angelic Doctor would not only
restore the lost unity of man and nature, it would also assure the
proper unification of the natural and the supernatural orders
without the danger of reducing one order to the other. The key to the
successful distinction and unification of the natural and supernatural
orders, the Neo-Scholastics held, was the Aristotelian metaphysics of
substance and accident which Post-Cartesian philosophy had abandoned. In St. Thomas' Aristotelian metaphysics of grace and nature
grace was a supernatural accident through whose formal causality
man's Aristotelian nature was elevated to the supernatural order
and thus rendered capable of attaining a supernatural end. The
theological virtues were distinct supernatural accidents which
informed the faculties of the intellect and will. Both grace and the
theological virtues were accidents in the Aristotelian category of
habit. Grace was an entitative habit informing the soul whereas the
theological virtues were operative habits informing the faculties of
intellect and will.

Thus in St. Thomas' metaphysics of grace and nature, the
Aristotelian metaphysics of substance and accident, habit, act and
faculty were required to ground the ontological distinction between
the capacities of man's unaided intellect and will in the natural order
and the essentially higher capacities of the same faculties once they

---

[10] This was the burden of Matteo Liberatore's argument for the restoration of St.
Thomas' philosophy to the Schools. See McCool, *Catholic Theology in the Nineteenth
Century,* pp. 145-66.

have been elevated to the supernatural order through the influence of sanctifying grace and the infused virtues of faith, hope and charity. It was not surprising then, the Neo-Scholastics believed, that the Catholic theologians who had abandoned the Aristotelian metaphysics of substance and accident under the influence of Post-Cartesian philosophy had proved incapable of producing a satisfactory theology of grace and nature.

This was the position defended by leading Neo-Scholastics like Matteo Liberatore and Joseph Kleutgen whose approach to philosophy and theology underlay the conception of Christian Philosophy proposed in *Aeterni Patris*.[11] In Leo XIII's encyclical the Christian Philosophy of the Angelic Doctor was intended to serve as a corrective to the Christian philosophy of the nineteenth century Catholic theologians whose epistemology, metaphysics and theological method had been influenced by Post-Cartesian philosophy and its subjective starting point. A return to the Christian philosophy of St. Thomas in the education of the Catholic clergy was expected to have very definite consequences upon the structure and method of Catholic theology as it was taught in the Church's seminaries and in her approved higher faculties of theology. Joseph Kleutgen had already indicated what these would be in his critical evaluation of Non-Scholastic theology in his celebrated *Theologie der Vorzeit.*

A proper regard for the distinction between faith and reason required a clear distinction between philosophy and fundamental theology on the one hand and dogmatic theology on the other. Although Post-Cartesian epistemology and metaphysics were incapable of preserving this distinction, the epistemology and metaphysics of the Angelic Doctor had no difficulty in doing so. St. Thomas' epistemology of the abstractive intellect was capable of grounding a sound philosophical proof for God's existence from the data of sense experience. St. Thomas had no need of any a priori grasp of God or Absolute Being to ground the necessary principles required for metaphysical reasoning. Therefore his metaphysics could not only ground God's existence but establish the naturally knowable truths concerning God through which the possibility and credibility of revelation could be vindicated from our objective knowledge of the physical world. Furthermore, as Matteo Liberatore pointed out, man's natural reason could also establish the principles of a sound natural law ethics of man and society.[12] Drawing upon the contributions of philosophy, fundamental theology could vindicate the

---

[11] For the influence of Liberatore and Kleutgen on the composition of *Aeterni Patris* see McCool, *Catholic Theology in the Nineteenth Century,* pp. 226-28.

[12] This was the theme of Liberatore's *Istituzioni di Etica e Diretto naturale* which was published in 1865.

reasonableness of the assent of faith. Apologetics did not require the supernatural light of faith to establish the evidence of its conclusions. Therefore it was not a part of theology, as Drey, Hirscher and the Catholic Tübingen theologians had taught.[13]

A clear understanding of the Aristotelian speculative and practical intellect showed that there was no need to recur to the a priori philosophical methods of Post-Cartesian philosophy to ground the necessary principles of speculative and practical philosophy. Furthermore, a return to Aristotelian method in both speculative philosophy and ethics would assure the proper distinction between these disciplines and reestablish the proper relation between them which Descartes had destroyed and which had never been successfully restored. Indeed, as Liberatore emphasized, one of the major contributions which the Christian Philosophy of St. Thomas could make to the reform of the social order would be a return to Aristotelian ethical reasoning in social ethics and political theory.

Kleutgen harbored equally high hopes for the beneficial consequences of a return to the Aristotelian method in positive and speculative theology. Thus, in the intellectual movement represented by *Aeterni Patris,* the Christian Philosophy of the Angelic Doctor was considered to be not only the only suitable propaedeutic to theology but the structuring element of an Aristotelian science of positive, speculative and moral theology which was clearly distinguished from apologetics or fundamental theology.

Precisely as an Aristotelian science, supported by an Aristotelian epistemology and metaphysics, this restored Scholastic theology would be a *Theologie der Vorzeit* in which the theological method, the relation between fundamental and dogmatic theology, and the structuring philosophical armature would be radically different from what they had been in the nineteenth century *Theologie der Neuzeit* which Leo XIII evidently considered unsuitable for the intellectual formation of future priests.

III. Consequences of Rahner's Rejection of *Aeterni Patris*

Aeterni Patris, as we have already mentioned, confined its specific recommendations to the education of the Catholic clergy. Nevertheless, in the mind of Leo XIII, the revival of the Christian Philosophy of the Angelic Doctor advocated in his Encyclical was the essential intellectual element in a broad and vigorous campaign both to regain for Christian Revelation its rightful role in the integration of modern culture and to restore Catholic morality to its proper place in the political life and social organization of the modern

---

[13] Kleutgen made this point at great length in his attack on Hirscher's apologetics. See McCool, *Catholic Theology in the Nineteenth Century,* pp. 188-203.

world. This two-fold goal determined the intellectual direction taken by the Neo-Scholastic revival. Serious study of medieval philosophy and honest debate with contemporary philosophy characterized the internal development of Neo-Scholastic philosophy, at least from the beginning of the twentieth century. The integration of the arts and sciences by contemporary scholastic philosophy subalternated to the theology of the Angelic Doctor became the defining ideal of Catholic education. Scholastic individual and social ethics, subalternated to moral theology, inspired the vigorous Catholic social and political movements which marked the pontificates of Leo XIII, Pius XI and Pius XII. Catholic Action, the Christian Socialist parties in Europe and Latin America, the Labor School movement in the United States are historical monuments to the intellectual, social and pastoral movements directed by the Neo-Scholastic philosophy inspired by *Aeterni Patris*.

The intellectual, social and pastoral consequences which follow from Rahner's definitive rejection of the ideal proposed by *Aeterni Patris* cannot be properly estimated until we realize that, on the basis of his own experience with the Christian Philosophy of the Angelic Doctor in its developed form, Rahner is convinced that it cannot and never could have performed the cultural and social function which the Church and her authorities expected it to play from the pontificate of Leo XII until practically the eve of the Second Vatican Council.[14] Rahner has not only challenged the theologian to provide a new ideal of Catholic culture. He has invited the theologian to enter upon a new era of Political Theology.

IV. Development Beyond the Ideal of *Aeterni Patris*

At the beginning of Rahner's career the Neo-Thomist revival stimulated by *Aeterni Patris* was approaching its high point. Thomist historians of philosophy, like Etienne Gilson, were convinced that they could identify the authentic Christian Philosophy of the Angelic Doctor and determine its proper relation to theology.[15] Maréchalian Thomists still believed that, by using the transcendental method, they could "go beyond Kant" and overcome Kantian idealism from within.[16] By doing so, they could vindicate the Angelic Doctor's metaphysics of being, potency and act as the genuine metaphysics of man and being.[17] Once that had been done, St. Thomas' meta-

---

[14] Karl Rahner, "Pluralism in Theology and the Unity of the Creed in the Church," *Theological Investigations* 11, trans. David Bourke (New York: Seabury, 1974): 3-23, esp. 4-12.

[15] Etienne Gilson, *The Philosopher and Theology* (New York: Random House, 1962), pp. 174-214.

[16] See *A Maréchal Reader,* ed. Joseph Donceel (New York: Seabury, 1970).

[17] See Emerich Coreth, *Metaphysics* (New York: Seabury, 1968).

physics had established its right to serve as the norm through whose use the plurality of other philosophical systems could be judged. A Maréchalian Thomist therefore could integrate both philosophy and its history into his personal synthesis. More than that, Blondel's Christian Philosophy[18] could be transformed into a Transcendental Thomist apologetics of exigence in which the Infinite Pure Act of Being, the Intelligent and Free Creator of the world could manifest Himself to the human spirit as the goal of its inborn intellectual and volitional dynamism and the question of historical Revelation's possibility could no longer be ignored.

The influence of this conception of the Christian Philosophy of the Angelic Doctor in its Maréchalian form upon the composition of *Hearers of the Word*[19] and *Spirit in the World*[20] is obvious. And Rahner himself confesses that, as a young man, he was thoroughly devoted to philosophy and that his confidence in the power of Thomism to integrate the contributions of other philosophical systems into its own structuring of experience had not been undermined.[21]

Although Rahner was never a Thomist in the school of Cajetan and John of St. Thomas, as was Jacques Maritain, at the beginning of his career he would not have rejected out of hand the brilliant integration of the arts and sciences, ethics and politics which Maritain accomplished through a dazzling exploitation of St. Thomas' metaphysics of knowledge, man and being. For the Rahner of *Hearers of the Word* and *Spirit in the World* made use of the same Thomistic distinction between unobjective self-awareness and objective knowledge of the other through the cognitional sign which Maritain exploited brilliantly in *The Degrees of Knowledge*[22] and *Creative Intuition in Art and Poetry*.[23] Again, although Rahner disagreed with Maritain in his understanding of their nature and role, he too employed the abstraction of the concept from the phantasm by the agent intellect, the position of the object by the judgment, the

---

[18] For an excellent summary of Blondel's own philosophy, see James M. Somerville, *Total Commitment: Blondel's L'Action* (Washington: Corpus Books, 1968). See also Maurice Nédoncelle, *Is There A Christian Philosophy?* (New York: Hawthorne Books, 1960), pp. 85-114.

[19] Karl Rahner, *Hearers of the Word* (New York: Seabury, 1969). For a selection of texts from *Hearers of the Word,* see Gerald A. McCool, *A Rahner Reader* (New York: Seabury, 1975), pp. 1-65.

[20] Karl Rahner, *Spirit in the World* (New York: Seabury, 1968).

[21] Karl Rahner, "On the Current Relationship Between Philosophy and Theology," *Theological Investigations* 13, trans. David Bourke (New York: Seabury, 1975): 61-79, esp. 70-71.

[22] Jacques Maritain, *The Degrees of Knowledge* (New York: Charles Scribner's Sons, 1959).

[23] Jacques Maritain, *Creative Intuition in Art and Poetry* (Princeton, N.J.: Princeton University Press, 1953).

analogy of being and the metaphysics of *esse,* form and matter as the backbone of his own philosophical synthesis. Nor would Rahner have been unwilling in principle to accept the subalternation of both speculative and practical philosophy to theology which was the keystone not only of Maritain's Thomistic integration of culture but—perhaps even more importantly—of Maritain's Christian Political Philosophy of the Angelic Doctor from which the Christian Democratic parties of Europe and Latin America derived a great deal of their inspiration.[24] Today, however, without mentioning Maritain by name, Rahner rejects in principle this type of integration of contemporary culture and political theory by a Scholastic philosophy subalternated to theology as *de facto* impossible.[25] Instead of promoting the further development of the philosophical and theological ideal of *Aeterni Patris* through his own intellectual reflection Rahner has shown that the ideal was a mistaken one from the beginning.

Rahner is now convinced that the Neo-Scholastic movement represented by *Aeterni Patris* was the last great effort by the Church to integrate Christian experience through a single philosophico-theological system.[26] His *Foundations of Christian Faith* cannot be read, as were *Hearers of the Word* and *Spirit in the World,* as a contribution to the further development of a Thomistic synthesis. Neither is it the foundational work of a new philosophico-theological synthesis. *Foundations of Christian Faith* is a radically different type of philosophico-theological reflection in the more modest style demanded by the present state of contemporary culture.

Foundations of Christian Faith is a fascinating book for many reasons. To an historian of the Neo-Scholastic Revival it would be fascinating simply as the culminating stage of an initially Thomistic reflection which led its author, in dialogue with history, modern philosophy and science, and contemporary exegesis and theology, progressively to abandon *Aeterni Patris's* understanding of the Christian Philosophy of the Angelic Doctor, the theology of grace and faith which underpinned that conception, the relation between philosophy, theology and contemporary culture proposed in the Encyclical, and finally the Encyclical's conception of the nature and divisions of theology as an intellectual discipline. A consideration of the historical development of Rahner's thought is even more significant for a critical evaluation of *Foundations of Christian Faith.* Rahner's most recent work is neither a purely philosophical treatise

---

[24] Gerald A. McCool, ''Jacques Maritain: A Neo-Thomist Classic,'' *The Journal of Religion* 58 (1978): 380-404.

[25] See n. 21.

[26] Again see n. 21, esp. p. 71 in the article cited.

nor a book of traditional apologetics. Its aim is to guide its reader through a first intellectual reflection carried on under the light of faith. The goal of this reflection is to convince the believer that, once the Christian mysteries are properly understood, his assent to them is reasonable even though he is incapable of responding to the multitude of serious difficulties brought against his faith from history, philosophy, the social and natural sciences.

Foundations of Christian Faith is a work in an entirely new theological genre. Many questions can be asked about the understanding of philosophy and theology which structures the work. Questions also arise about the interrelation of these disciplines and their respective relation to the social and natural sciences. Other questions come up concerning the connection of the philosophy employed in *Foundations of Christian Faith* to the Transcendental Thomism developed in Rahner's early works. Finally the question arises concerning the promise of *Foundations of Christian Faith* as a lasting contribution to Post-Vatican II theology.

These later questions, however, will have to be postponed until after our account of Rahner's progressive rejection of the philosophy and theology presupposed in *Aeterni Patris*. The historical origin of Rahner's new fundamental theology conditions the interpreter's effort to understand it and to appreciate it properly.

V. Rahner's Progressive Rejection of *Aeterni Patris*

Reflecting the viewpoint of the nineteenth century Scholastics, *Aeterni Patris* considered Scholastic philosophy to be a single philosophical system, common to all the Scholastic Doctors, whose starting point and method distinguished it irreducibly from Post-Cartesian philosophy. In the Christian Philosophy of the Angelic Doctor the epistemological starting point, far from being a transcendental reflection on the activity of the thinking subject, was a direct grasp of the extramental real through sense experience. As a direct realism of sense experience, St. Thomas' Scholastic philosophy rejected the Kantian transcendental method. St. Thomas' metaphysics of the agent intellect relieved him of the necessity of postulating an a priori grasp of the Infinite Absolute to ground the activity of the thinking mind and the necessary content of its thought. The pluralism which characterized Post-Cartesian philosophy could not be attributed to the sound development either of philosophy or of the positive sciences. It was due to the subjective starting point of Post-Cartesian philosophy and to its intrinsically defective method.[27]

---

[27] This negative attitude toward Post-Cartesian philosophy characterized the approach of Jacques Maritain. See *Three Reformers: Luther, Descartes, Rousseau* (New York: Charles Scribner's Sons, 1929). Etienne Gilson was also firmly convinced of the incompatibility between the Kantian transcendental method and the realism of St. Thomas' epistemology. See *Elements of Christian Philosophy* (New York: Doubleday, 1960), pp. 220-40.

Even at the beginning of his career, Rahner had already abandoned the position that there was an intrinsic incompatibility between the starting point and method of an authentic Thomism and the starting point and method of Kantian and Post-Kantian philosophy. In the tradition of Maréchal the starting point of *Hearers of the Word* was a reflection upon the conscious activity of the thinking subject and the method employed was a transcendental reflection on the dynamism of the thinking subject as being-present-to itself. In the tradition of Post-Kantian philosophy the Infinite Absolute manifested itself to the moving mind as the cognitive Horizon whose conscious presence was the necessary condition for the activity of thought and its necessary content. Since the conscious presence of the Absolute Horizon was unobjective, Rahner believed that his philosophy was in the tradition of Aristotle, Thomas and Kant and not in the ontologistic tradition of Malbranche, Plato, Augustine and Descartes.[28] The union of thought and being in the Infinite Horizon revealed itself to be the ontological condition of possibility for the necessary relation of the known object to the knowing mind prior to the act of knowledge. Thus, in clear opposition to the epistemology of Kleutgen and Liberatore (and of Gilson and Maritain as well), and in the tradition of the great Post-Kantian systems, the Absolute manifested itself, albeit unobjectively, as first in the order of thought as it was first in the order of being and as the ground of the ontological relation between them.

In *Hearers of the Word* and *Spirit in the World* Rahner's transcendental reflection on the knowing subject grounded an Aristotelico-Thomistic metaphysics of man and being. The human knower who "went over to the other" in sense knowledge "returned to himself" in self-awareness through the abstraction of the concept under the influence of the agent intellect and the objective affirmation of the judgment. The subject's return to himself in self-awareness simultaneously with his performance of the unitary act of sensitivo-intellectual knowledge required as its condition of possibility a composition of matter and form in the cognitive agent and the emanation of the intellectual and sensitive faculties from the knower's soul.[29] As a composite of matter and form the free cognitive subject was an essentially historical being and, as a member of a species in virtue of his hylomorphic composition, the knower was also an essentially social being.

The knower's unobjective grasp of the Absolute Horizon through the *Vorgriff* was the condition of possibility for the intellect's abstrac-

---

[28] Karl Rahner, "St. Thomas on Truth," *Theological Investigations* 13:13-31, esp. pp. 14-15.

[29] Rahner, *Spirit in the World,* pp. 279-80.

tion of the concept and the conversion to the phantasm required for every act of objective knowledge. Thus there occurred in the human knower a necessary interplay between his unobjective knowledge of his own being and God and his objective knowledge of extra-mental reality through the conceptual judgment. This interplay made possible the analogy of being through which the human knower's discursive intellect could possess indirect and imperfect knowledge of the Infinite Pure Act through objective judgments whose objective content had been derived by abstraction from sense experience.[30]

In *Hearers of the Word* and *Spirit in the World* the Infinite Unity of Thought and Being related the intelligible object to the human intelligence prior to its first act of knowledge.[31] Ontologically therefore the intelligible in act and the intelligence in act were identical. The condition of possibility for this identity achieved in the act of human knowledge was the ontological bond of efficient and final causality which linked the hylomorphic knower and the hylomorphic agents of the material world.

Thus the epistemology and the metaphysics of man and being presented in *Hearers of the Word* and *Spirit in the World* were considered to be authentically Thomistic even though the philosophical method through which they had been critically vindicated was the transcendental method associated with the philosophy of Kant. This point will be of considerable importance in our later effort to interpret the philosophy and theology of *Foundations of Christian Faith* correctly. To what extent are the epistemology and metaphysics of this latter work still to be considered Thomistic?

From the very beginning of his career then, Rahner embraced a philosophical starting point and method which the nineteenth century Scholastics and their successors, Gilson and Maritain for example, had rejected as incompatible with the Christian Philosophy of the Angelic Doctor. Later in his career, Rahner went further and argued that the Post-Kantian systems were genuine developments of St. Thomas' Christian philosophy.[32] The very turn to the subject, historically attributed to Descartes, which is the hallmark of modern philosophy, can be traced back to the Angelic Doctor himself. In fact, this turn to the subject, as the defining characteristic of a philosophical orientation, was St. Thomas' great contribution to western philosophy which his successors unfortunately overlooked. In the logic of this line of argument it would follow that the Post-Cartesian systems which the nineteenth century Scholastics rejected

---

[30] Rahner, *Hearers of the Word,* pp. 45-53.

[31] Ibid., pp. 31-44.

[32] See Rahner's introduction to Johannes B. Metz, *Christliche Anthropozentrik* (Munich: Kosel, 1962).

were closer to St. Thomas' philosophical form of thought than the "best way of philosophising" advocated by the nineteenth century Scholastics themselves.[33] It would also follow that the understanding of the Christian Philosophy of the Angelic Doctor presented in *Aeterni Patris* was historically false.

VI. Rahner's Correction of the Nineteenth Century Theology of Grace and Faith

In *Hearers of the Word* and *Spirit in the World* the subject's unobjective knowledge of his own spirit as being present to itself and the subject's unobjective *Vorgriff* of Infinite Being as the condition of possibility of all objective thought emerged as essential elements of Rahner's philosophical anthropology. In *Spirit in the World* the Thomistic metaphysics of the emanation of the faculties from the soul disclosed the metaphysics of man which Rahner later generalized to the entire realm of being with great success. This was the metaphysics of the "real symbol."[34] In the metaphysics of the real symbol being expresses itself and reaches its proper perfection in the "other" or its "real symbol." This, as is well known, is the metaphysics which Rahner exploited brilliantly in his theology of the Trinity, the Incarnation and Uncreated Grace.[35] It structures Rahner's "proper understanding" of the Christian mysteries. This is a point of some importance for the interpretation of *Foundations of Christian Faith*. For in that work the correspondence between the dynamic exigencies of the human spirit and the proper understanding of the Christian Mysteries is the key to its whole development. The influence of Blondel's Christian Philosophy of exigence in its Maréchalian form is still at work; and the effect of the metaphysics of the real symbol, which first appeared in Rahner's exegesis of Thomas' metaphysics of man, can still be felt. The Neo-Thomistic tradition of the connection between a Thomistic epistemology of concomitant conscious and abstractive intellect, a Thomistic metaphysics of man, and a corresponding metaphysics of being has been carried on, albeit in very modified form, from Rahner's early works to his latest masterpiece.

Rahner's transcendental theology, however, and his own historical research brought him to see in the course of his own

---

[33] *Optima ratio philosophandi* was the term of praise used to designate the Christian Philosophy of the Angelic Doctor in *Aeterni Patris*. Gilson applies it to his own understanding of St. Thomas' Christian Philosophy. See *The Philosopher and Theology*, pp. 174-99.

[34] Karl Rahner, "The Theology of the Symbol," *Theological Investigations* 4, trans. Kevin Smith (Baltimore: Helicon, 1966): 221-52. See McCool, *A Rahner Reader*, pp. 120-30.

[35] See McCool, *A Rahner Reader*, pp. 132-204.

theological evolution that the nineteenth century Scholastic theology of grace and faith reflected in *Aeterni Patris* was mistaken. Rahner came to see that the distinction between the order of grace and the natural order could no longer be understood in the sense in which the nineteenth century Scholastics understood it. The Post-Tridentine theologoumenon of the state of pure nature had lost its intrinsic plausibility.[36] Reacting to the thought of Henri de Lubac, Rahner then worked out his own theology of the supernatural existential.[37]

In Rahner's philosophical anthropology, as we have seen, the mind's unobjective grasp of the Infinite God was the condition of possibility for every act of objective thought. As the ontological effect of the Triune God's offer of His self-communication to the soul in Uncreated Grace the knower's spiritual dynamism was elevated by the supernatural existential. A distinction between the supernatural and the natural orders was still demanded in Rahner's theology of grace and nature, since his metaphysics of the real symbol required that the Triune God who communicated Himself in Uncreated Grace express Himself in his "other." Nevertheless the same metaphysics required that, in the concrete order in which God's offer of self-communication challenges every man to accept it or reject it, at least implicitly, the order of creation must be included in the historical order of salvation as a necessary moment.[38]

Rahner's philosophical anthropology forced him to reject the nineteenth century extrinsecism in which the order of grace was excluded from the grasp of even implicit self-awareness. In the concrete subject whose spiritual dynamism had been elevated by the supernatural existential the Absolute Horizon of that dynamism was the Triune God. Consequently the human spirit had to be aware, at least implicitly, of its own elevated dynamism and of the dynamism's supernatural goal. In man's deepest experiences therefore, in which man responds to the call of that Absolute Horizon, there is an experience of grace, even though the human respondent may not be explicitly aware that what he is experiencing is grace.[39]

---

[36] See Karl Rahner, *Nature and Grace* (New York: Sheed and Ward, 1964), esp. pp. 114-43. Also McCool, *A Rahner Reader,* pp. 173-84.

[37] Karl Rahner, "Concerning the Relationship Between Nature and Grace," *Theological Investigations* 1, trans. Cornelius Ernst (Baltimore: Helicon, 1961): 297-317, esp. pp. 300-02; 310-15. Also McCool, *A Rahner Reader,* pp. 185-90.

[38] Karl Rahner, *The Christian Commitment* (New York: Sheed and Ward, 1963), esp. pp. 44-53. Also *A Rahner Reader,* pp. 190-96.

[39] Karl Rahner, "Reflections on the Experience of Grace," *Theological Investigations* 3, trans. Karl-H. Kruger and Boniface Kruger (Baltimore: Helicon, 1967): 86-90. Also McCool, *A Rahner Reader,* pp. 196-99.

This theology of experienced grace, and its corrollaries, the theologies of implicit faith, hope and love and of the Anonymous Christian, is the key to the distinction between philosophy and theology in *Foundations of Christian Faith*. A theology of experienced grace would have scandalized the nineteenth century Scholastics whose thought is reflected in *Aeterni Patris*. For one of their strongest arguments in favor of a return to the Christian Philosophy of the Angelic Doctor was their conviction that any a priori grasp of God's triune reality undermined the distinction between the natural and the supernatural orders which orthodox Catholic theology must preserve.

Moreover, Rahner's transcendental theology, combined with his own historical research, led him to reject the nineteenth century theology of faith which is reflected in *Aeterni Patris*. This, as we have already seen, was evident in Rahner's theology of the Anonymous Christian's implicit faith. It is even more obvious in Rahner's theology of the Christian Mystery.[40]

Rahner's research into the notion of Mystery in Catholic theology convinced him that the correct notion of the Christian Mystery could not be the nineteenth century Scholastic conception of the revealed mystery as a series of propositions which, although they cannot be understood in this life, could be understood in the after-life. On the contrary, the correct understanding of the revealed mystery is the One Holy Mystery in its threefold manifestation as Triune God, Incarnate Word, and Uncreated Grace. As the Absolute Horizon of the elevated mind, the Holy Mystery is the Infinite Being whose unobjective grasp is the condition of possibility for every act of objective understanding but which, as the Absolute Horizon of its dynamism, must elude the mind's objective understanding even in the Beatific Vision.

Thus in the Anonymous Christian's concrete response of implicit faith and love to the Absolute Horizon of the world encountered through his spiritual dynamism we find his supernatural response to the Holy Mystery.[41] The elevated human spirit's drive to the Infinite Triune God makes man a mystery; and the solution to the mystery which man is in the concrete order of salvation can come only from the Revelation which is the self-communication of the Holy Mystery.

Rahner's theology of the Holy Mystery is combined with his

---

[40] Karl Rahner, "The Theology of Mystery in Catholic Theology," *Theological Investigations* 4:36-73. Also McCool, *A Rahner Reader,* pp. 108-20.

[41] Karl Rahner, "Anonymous Christians," *Theological Investigations* 6, trans. Karl-H. Kruger and Boniface Kruger (Baltimore: Helicon, 1969): 390-98. Also McCool, *A Rahner Reader,* pp. 211-14.

Maréchalian adaptation of Blondel's philosophy of exigence in *Foundations of Christian Faith*. That point is not without significance for the understanding of Rahner's new fundamental theology. It helps to explain why *Foundations of Christian Faith* is not a Blondelian apologetics of immanence but a new type of fundamental theology in which the exigences of man's elevated dynamism are shown to be fulfilled through the threefold self-communication whose central moment is the Incarnation of the Word. Rahner's theological anthropology becomes a Christology when the metaphysics of the real symbol manifests that the Incarnate Word represents the perfect fulfillment of the incarnate spirit's possibilities; and, for the proper understanding of the Holy Mystery, Christology is all important.

VII. Rahner's Definite Rejection of the Ideal of *Aeterni Patris*

From the beginning of his career, Rahner, as a Maréchalian Thomist, had refused to accept the nineteenth century belief that rejection of a subjective starting point and the use of the transcendental method was a defining characteristic of Thomism. Rahner's theology of grace and nature undermined the nineteenth century Scholastic theology which determined the relation between philosophy, apologetics and dogmatic theology in Catholic seminaries after the publication of *Aeterni Patris*. Further contact with contemporary philosophy, science and exegesis finally led him to abandon completely the conviction shared, in principle at least, by Neo-Scholastic philosophers and theologians that St. Thomas' philosophy of knowledge, man and being could structure a common Catholic theology and philosophy and, in doing so, become the integrating element of Catholic culture and education and provide the directive principles of Catholic political and social action.[42]

Two forces in Rahner's thought moved him toward this radical break with the Neo-Scholastic tradition. The first was his growing emphasis upon man as the mystery who is ordered to the Holy Mystery. Mystagogy and the return to the mystery in prayerful silence were given a growing emphasis in Rahner's theology. Rahner's own spirituality and the interplay between unobjective and objective knowledge of God which had marked his thought from the beginning undoubtedly influenced this development in his theological anthropology.[43]

---

[42] Karl Rahner, "Christian Humanism," *Theological Investigations* 9:187-204.

[43] Karl Rahner, "Intellectual Honesty and the Christian Faith," *Theological Investigations* 7 (New York: Herder and Herder, 1971): 47-71. Also "Experience of Self and Experience of God," *Theological Investigations* 13:122-32.

The second force which moved Rahner in this direction was his increasing awareness of the vast expansion of scientific knowledge and the extent and profundity of contemporary philosophical pluralism. Man was a mystery to himself, not only because he was ordered to the Holy Mystery by his spiritual dynamism, but because, on the level of his objective knowledge, he could never master the vast sum of historical and scientific knowledge required for him to understand himself, to say nothing of his relation to inanimate nature and to his fellow men. Concupiscence did not exist simply as the free human subject's moral inability to bring every aspect of his human activity under the mastery of his free decision. Concupiscence existed on the level of speculative thought as well. This sort of gnoseological concupiscence was the human knower's abiding inability to master himself and his world on the level of objective speculative thought.[44]

In our contemporary world gnoseological concupiscence must be the *de facto* condition of every man. This meant that the age of the Renaissance man was over. Gnoseological concupiscence, as an unavoidable condition of contemporary man, made any attempt at speculative unification of science and culture a practical impossibility. Although Rahner, to my knowledge, has never mentioned Maritain by name, it is clear that in Rahner's opinion, gnoseological concupiscence has rendered obsolete any Thomistic unification of science and culture on the model of *The Degrees of Knowledge* or *Creative Intuition in Art and Poetry*.

The impossibility of such a synthesis did not arise simply from the speculative philosopher's inability to master the vast range of contemporary historical and scientific knowledge. It came from the vast diversity and extreme complexity of philosophy itself. Rahner was quite aware that, at the time of the *Nouvelle Théologie* movement, his Maréchalian colleagues had come to terms with philosophical pluralism. On the basis of their Maréchalian distinction between the objective content of the concept and the affirmation of the judgment, grounded on the mind's dynamic orientation to Absolute Being, they had defended the possibility of several metaphysical systems against traditional Dominican Thomists like Garrigou-Lagrange. Diversity in the objective content of the concept permitted the possibility of several fundamental conceptual frameworks and consequently of several distinct metaphysical systems. The mind's dynamic reference to Absolute Being, on the other hand, gave the human knower a firm grip on the intelligible realm of being and the transcendentals. Pluralism therefore need not degenerate into

---

[44] Karl Rahner, "On the Current Relationship Between Philosophy and Theology," *Theological Investigations* 13:61-79; esp. 68-70.

relativism and Maréchalian Thomism could still defend its right to be considered a normative system on the basis of which the contributions of other philosophical systems could be integrated into a coherent vision.[45]

For Rahner, however, hopes of this sort had become illusory. No single mind could hope to master the vast complexity of philosophical systems. No single mind could hope to understand them all, and what cannot be understood cannot be integrated. Gnoseological concupiscence meant that the vast array of the sciences and the multitude of philosophical systems must be allowed to exist, side by side, unintegrated, in individual minds. A Maréchalian synthesis of philosophical pluralism was as illusory as a Maritainian synthesis had proven to be. The Maréchalians might have become more open to philosophical pluralism than Maritain was willing to be but they had not become open enough.

VIII. The New Situation of Catholic Theology

The Church's recognition of the death of the Neo-Scholasticism proposed in *Aeterni Patris* has come late. The state of gnoseological concupiscence in which contemporary man must live can no longer be ignored, and Rahner believes that the Church is not yet prepared to cope with it. Catholics could still believe that a unification of culture through a Scholastic philosophy subalternated to Scholastic theology was possible as long as the "ghetto mentality" of the pre-Vatican II Church still existed. Contact with secular science, history, non-Catholic theology and the pervasive influence of the contemporary secularized culture dominated by the mind-set of the positive sciences have confronted contemporary Catholics with a host of problems whose solution requires a radically new orientation in Catholic theology.

The theology of the future can never cease to have its source in Scripture. It must be an ecclesial theology which remains in contact with the teaching office of the Church. It must be at once positive, historical and genuinely speculative. As a theology of the whole Church, it must be ecumenical. Catholic theology can never again be the theology of a single culture and, as a theology of the diaspora Church, it must be open to and respectful of the diverse cultures in which the dispersed Christian community must live. As a theology of hope and charity, in which love of God can never be separated from love of man, it must be a practical theology, and, as a relentless critic of ideologies, perhaps even a political theology. It might well be that

---

[45] Jean Marie LeBlond, "L'Analogie de la Vérité," *Recherches de Science Religieuse* 34 (1947): 129-41. See also Robert F. Harvanek, "The Unity of Metaphysics," *Thought* 25 (1950): 21-52.

in the theology of the future practical theology will play a defining role.[46]

Above all, the theology of the future must be pluralistic. An unbridgeable plurality of philosophies means that the theologies which they structure must also constitute a plurality. Furthermore, the vast range of scientific knowledge and the diversity of secular cultures means that the practitioners of the diverse future theologies will not be able to really understand each other. The Church will have to allow the plurality of theologies to exist side by side, unintegrated, in the minds of the diverse theologians.

To preserve the unity of the Church's faith amid the unintegrated plurality of diverse theologies will be a difficult, even a dangerous, task. Nevertheless, the Church now knows that, in intellectual honesty, her magisterium can no longer impose theological conformity by requiring a single philosophical system and the classical culture which it reflects as the structuring norm of Catholic theology. The age of *Aeterni Patris* has passed. It is impossible for the Church to return to it, and the implications of that realization for her educational policy and her social and political action are enormous.

The theologian of the future can no longer theologize on the basis of a pre-given philosophical system. Since God's self-communication in Revelation presupposes natural reason as the "other" in which it expresses itself, there must always be a distinction between faith and natural reason. The Council Fathers of Vatican I committed themselves to the possibility of a knowledge of the Absolute Horizon of man's spiritual dynamism independently of historical Revelation. Consequently the distinction between faith and reason is an essential one, and, as a reflection in faith on the historical word of Revelation, theology must always include philosophy within itself as an intrinsic moment in its process of reflection.[47]

Nevertheless, the theologian is now compelled to do his philosophizing within his own theology.[48] Philosophy has now become an intrinsic element within theology itself. It is no longer a subalternated discipline with its own formal object as the nineteenth century Scholastics held. Furthermore, the contemporary natural and social sciences have won their autonomy in respect to philosophy. Therefore the theologian must deal with them directly. He can no longer attempt to integrate their data into his theological

---

[46] Karl Rahner, "Possible Courses for the Theology of the Future," *Theological Investigations* 13:32-60.

[47] Karl Rahner, "Philosophy and Theology," *Theological Investigations* 6:74-81. Also McCool, *A Rahner Reader*, pp. 75-80.

[48] Karl Rahner, "Philosophy and Philosophizing in Theology," *Theological Investigations* 9:46-63. Also McCool, *A Rahner Reader*, pp. 80-89.

synthesis through the mediation of a pre-given philosophical system into which the data of the sciences has already been integrated. In other words, philosophy has ceased to be the exclusive dialogue partner of theology.[49]

At the end of his intellectual evolution therefore Rahner has completely abandoned the speculative unification of science and culture proposed in *Aeterni Patris*. Philosophy no longer integrates the sciences as an independent discipline subalternated to theology. Rahner's theology of grace and nature has undermined the Neo-Scholastic distinction between philosophy, apologetics, speculative and moral theology. An unbridgeable plurality of theologies, each of which is structured by its intrinsic philosophical moment, confronts directly the vast diversity of sciences and the multitude of secular cultures which co-exist, side by side, unintegrated, in our contemporary world. It is no wonder that Rahner has come to believe that the relation of theology to philosophy and the sciences in the pluralistic theology of the future will be complex and very difficult to specify.

IX. Transcendental Theology and *Foundations of Christian Faith*

Within the complexity of pluralistic theology Rahner believes that there is still a place for transcendental theology.[50] Transcendental theology is not all of theology. Indeed it is only one aspect of theology. A transcendental reflection upon the conditions of possibility of human knowledge can ground a metaphysics of man and being capable of serving as the philosophical moment inside a theological reflection. In this way Rahner has worked out his own transcendental theology of the Trinity, the Incarnation, Uncreated Grace, the Church and the Sacraments and his transcendental Eschatology. This, in fact, is the transcendental theology employed in *Foundations of Christian Faith*.

The inevitable state of gnoseological concupiscence in which modern man exists precludes the possibility that the believing Christian, even the beginning student of theology, can either master the vast array of the natural and social sciences which exist in the modern world or comprehend the multitude of theological systems in which the Church's faith can be expressed. No single theologian can master the whole of theology or answer the multitude of difficulties

---

[49] Karl Rahner, "Theology as Engaged in an Interdisciplinary Dialogue with the Sciences," *Theological Investigations* 13:80-93. Also "On the Relationship Between Theology and the Contemporary Sciences," *Theological Investigations* 13:94-102.

[50] Karl Rahner, "Reflections on Methodology in Theology," *Theological Investigations* 11:68-114, 84-101.

which can be brought against the Church's faith. Specialists in theology can only hope to master their own narrow field; and, often enough, specialists cannot communicate with one another. Even for the specialist in theology, once he begins to operate outside his own delimited domain, gnoseological concupiscence is unavoidable.

The distinction between unobjective and objective knowledge, which Rahner had used since *Hearers of the Word,* suggested the possibility of a new type of fundamental theology which would help the believing Christian to overcome the difficulties which arise from his state of gnoseological concupiscence. The vast array of the sciences and scientific history operate on the level of objective knowledge. No individual can master these today. On the other hand, every human knower has unobjective knowledge of his own spiritual dynamism and the Absolute Mystery to which it is ordered as its Horizon. When the Christian Mysteries, which in reality are the One Holy Mystery of God's self-communication, are properly understood through the instrumentality of a transcendental philosophy derived from a reflection upon the conditions of possibility of man's knowledge and love, it is possible to show how the Christian Mysteries make sense out of the believer's concrete experience. Thus, drawing upon dogmatic theology, Rahner's new transcendental fundamental theology manifests the reasonableness of assent to the Church's faith even though gnoseological concupiscence prevents the believer from comprehending the variety of theologies through which that faith can be expressed or from answering the multitude of difficulties which history, exegesis and the sciences can raise against it.

X. *Foundations of Christian Faith* and the Philosophy of the Angelic Doctor

Yet, even though Rahner has abandoned his faith in the conception of the Christian Philosophy of the Angelic Doctor proposed in *Aeterni Patris* and has shown that it cannot perform the role in the integration of science and culture which Leo XIII assigned to it, can the philosophy of knowledge, man and being which structures *Foundations of Christian Faith* still be called, in any significant sense, Thomistic? This is hardly a question which would deeply interest Rahner himself. He is well aware that the pluralism of Neo-Thomism itself has shown that Leo XIII's hope of rejuvenating the "common philosophy of the Angelic Doctor" has proven to be unfounded. Neo-Thomism never was a single philosophical system.

Philosophizing within his theology, Rahner has endeavored to ground his metaphysics of man and being through his transcendental reflection on the human subject's spiritual dynamism. Rahner is not interested in parading as an anti-Thomist. He has never lost his reverence for the Angelic Doctor as a Doctor of the Church and the Maréchalian Thomism of his early works is a matter of record. Nevertheless, *Foundations of Christian Faith* is Rahner's fundamental theology and Rahner's transcendental theology stands on its own. Thomistic *limpieza de sangre* has long ceased to be a matter of moment to Rahner. For Rahner, the interesting question about *Foundations of Christian Faith* would not be "is the book Thomistic?" Rather the interesting question would be "is it sound?" or "is what it proposes to do really feasible?"

Nevertheless the Thomistic character of Rahner's transcendental philosophy is of interest not only to the historian of the Neo-Scholastic Revival who is concerned with the movement's lasting influence on Catholic thought. It also concerns the philosopher or theologian who is interested in locating Rahner's philosophy in the spectrum of contemporary systems, evaluating it and forming some estimate of its on-going influence. The Thomism of Rahner's thought, if we can call it that, can be significant in our evaluation of it.

One can argue that, although the pluralism of irreducible philosophies in the Neo-Scholastic movement is clear evidence that there never was and could not be a single Thomistic system, there has been a "family resemblance" among the plurality of systems which have existed in the Neo-Scholastic Revival. The source of this "family resemblance," I have argued elsewhere, is their common inspiration in the works of the Angelic Doctor and the connection which the Neo-Scholastics have made between St. Thomas' philosophy of knowledge and his metaphysics of man and being since the time of Liberatore and Kleutgen.[51]

In each of these systems the philosophy of knowledge is built upon the dynamic interrelation between the phantasm and the agent intellect in the unitary act of sensitivo-intellectual knowledge. Therefore in all these systems the human knower is an incarnate spirit, a unitary sensitivo-intellectual agent whose cognitive and volitional activity is directed toward an inborn natural end. In all of these systems the knower's implicit awareness of his own activity is concomitant with his grasp of extramental reality through the conceptual judgment. In the act of knowledge the intelligible object is united to the knower in the intentional *species*. As their common perfection, knowledge is the actuation of both knower and known. The intelligible object is ontologically ordered to the intelligence prior to the act of knowledge and the ground of the intrinsic relation

---

[51] Gerald A. McCool, "The Centenary of *Aeterni Patris*," *Homeletic and Pastoral Review* 4 (January 1979): 8-15.

between being and knowledge is found in God, the Supreme Truth, in whom thought and being are identical.

As a result, each one of the great twentieth century Thomistic systems was marked by its realistic epistemology and its metaphysics of *esse*. In every one of them consciousness was defined in terms of being. Being was not defined in terms of consciousness. In their realistic epistemology of knowledge the human knower was defined as a dynamic nature whose characteristic movement of knowledge and love was explained through the interplay of the four Aristotelian causes. In their metaphysics the contingency of the moving mind and its finite objects grounds an argument for the existence of God as the Infinite, Changeless Act of Being in which Being and Knowledge are identical. In its highest form knowledge is being present to itself.

In all the twentieth century Thomistic systems the epistemology of the concept and the judgment enabled the human knower to mount from his experience of himself and his world to a true, albeit indirect and imperfect knowledge of the divine attributes grounded upon the analogy of being.

Within the "family relationship" of all the twentieth century Thomistic systems, a more limited "family relationship" can be established among the Thomists in the Maréchalian tradition. Despite the diversity among the systems inspired by Maréchal, their authors, taking their cue from St. Thomas' *De Veritate,* have made a transcendental reflection upon the act of knowledge their philosophical starting point. Epistemology, or in Lonergan's case, cognitional theory, has become the *point de départ* of their metaphysics. The philosophy of knowledge and love which was peculiar to St. Thomas among the medieval doctors has been made the inspiration of a contemporary transcendental philosophy of the knowing subject whose spiritual dynamism confronts him with a call to moral conversion originating from the Pure Identity of Knowledge and Being toward which his mind and will are directed in their striving. The knowing and loving subject, the a priori conditions of whose spiritual dynamism are disclosed through a transcendental reflection on his spiritual activity, is the invariant reviser of every scientific, philosophical, moral and social system. Consequently a transcendental reflection upon the conditions of possibility of knowledge and love as such should yield a metaphysics of man and being, limited in its scope, but perennial in its basic structure. A Thomistic metaphysics of man and being grounded in this manner would constitute the basic structure of a Transcendental Thomism.

In this sense the metaphysics of man and being presented in

Hearers of the Word and *Spirit in the World* was a Transcendental Thomism. The act of human knowledge proceeded from the cooperation of sense and intellect in the abstraction of the concept and the affirmation of the judgment. As a sensitivo-intellectual knower, a spirit in the world, man was an agent, composed of matter and form, whose activity was directed by the Pure Act of Being as its final cause. Since the act of knowledge was the act of both knower and known, the sensible objects of human knowledge were also agents whose activity was directed to its end by a natural appetite.

Unobjective knowledge of the self was another expression for Thomistic concomitant consciousness. Unobjective knowledge of God was required for God's final causality to influence the active intellect in its abstraction of the concept.

From this metaphysics emerged Rahner's philosophical anthropology of man as spirit in the world, open to transcendence, yet essentially historical and social. From this metaphysics also emerged Rahner's metaphysics of God as the Pure Infinite Act of Being-Present-to-Itself which could "go over into its other." And from Rahner's epistemology emerged his distinction between the human knower's unobjective grasp of God in the *Vorgriff* and his objective knowledge of God through the analogy of being.

In his subsequent theological writings Rahner has paid little attention to Thomistic terminology. His emphasis has been more on man's experience of himself as a transcendent historical spirit in the world and on man's experience of God in His self-communication. Nevertheless Rahner's epistemology remains the epistemology of a knower whose knowledge requires a receptive sensibility and the activity of a goal directed intellect. Something of the nature of matter, form, activity and finality are still required to account for man's unity as a knower and his ontological bond with the other beings in his world. Although God is the Absolute Mystery, enough can be said about Him through the analogy of being to establish that he is the Pure Act of Being-Present-to-Itself and the free creator of the world. Enough can also be known about the Free Personal God to work out the metaphysics of His self-communication.

XI. Thomism and the Reaction to *Foundations of Christian Faith*

The question of Rahner's Thomism, even in the weakened sense in which I have used the word, is important in considering the reaction to *Foundations of Christian Faith,* especially in the United States. For Rahner's transcendental theology structures the entire work, and the philosophical moment inside that theology is close enough to the Transcendental Thomism from which Rahner has emerged to differ notably from the philosophical systems which enjoy popular favor in our country and toward which American theologians are inclined to turn.

The partisans of linguistic analysis will not take kindly to Rahner's unobjective knowledge of the subject. Unobjective knowledge of the subject is unlikely to strike them as a fruitful source from which to derive a critically grounded metaphysics. Furthermore, the interplay between unobjective and objective knowledge on which Rahner's whole system depends, implies that the subject's perduring intentionality runs through the objective world of knowledge and constitutes it under the influence of an a priori Horizon. We can anticipate therefore that the linguistic philosophers will raise the same sort of difficulties against Rahner's transcendental philosophy which they are accustomed to raise against the phenomenologists. Transcendental subjects, intentionality and Horizons are conceded no epistemological validity in tough-minded analytic philosophy.

Phenomenologists are also likely to have difficulty with *Foundations of Christian Faith*. For, although phenomenologists are not opposed in principle to transcendental subjects, intentionality and Horizons, it does not follow that they will be receptive to Rahner's transcendental philosophy. Rahner's philosophy interprets consciousness in terms of being. Being is not interpreted in terms of consciousness. Rahner's spirit in the world is a metaphysical subject. The subject's acts of knowledge and love are not just modifications of consciousness. They are metaphysical activities. The Absolute Horizon of consciousness is the Infinite Pure Act of Being, and, as such, is the metaphysical final cause of the human subject's spiritual dynamism. In Rahner's philosophical anthropology the conceptual judgment can vindicate an analogous knowledge of the transcendent abiding God and go on to ground a metaphysics of God's self-communication in the order of being. Therefore, for most phenomenologists, Rahner's transcendental anthropology will appear to be another form of Thomistic cognitional theory and epistemology; and they will be inclined to question the metaphysics which he has derived from it.

Whiteheadian process philosophers will also have their problems with *Foundations of Christian Faith*.[52] Rahner's Absolute Horizon, they will object, is the Infinite Pure Act of Being, who, although he can "change in his other," remains changeless in Himself. As the pure identity of Being and Knowledge, Rahner's Absolute Mystery is still "the great exception to the system" which Whiteheadian meta-

---

[52] For an excellent introduction to Whitehead's process metaphysics see Ivor Leclerc, *Whitehead's Metaphysics* (New York: Macmillan, 1958).

physics excludes. Furthermore Rahner does not solve the problem of internal relations, as Whitehead did, through the "revised subjectivist principle." Rahner solves the problem on the level of being. In Rahner's metaphysics, God, as the Pure Identity of Knowledge and Being, is the ontological ground for the intrinsic relation of intelligible objects to human intelligences prior to the act of knowledge. To put it in other words, Rahner, in the tradition of St. Thomas, interprets intentionality fundamentally in terms of being. He does not interpret it on the model of knowledge, as I would argue that Whitehead does in his "revised subjectivist principle."

Even more fundamentally, Rahner differs from Whitehead because he solves the problem of internal relations on the basis of a metaphysics of creation which Whitehead rejects. For it is precisely because God is the Transcendent Creative One that, as the Identity of Thought of Being, He can relate the multitude of finite beings to each other through an intelligible network of causal relations. In fine, Rahner's metaphysics remains a metaphysics of being, creation and analogy. Because it does, Rahner's metaphysics of the human subject, of God and of the ontological bond between the two, cannot be reconciled with Whiteheadian process metaphysics.

XII. The On-Going Influence of *Foundations of Christian Faith*

It would seem then that, even on the level of transcendental reflection, Rahner has not overcome philosophical pluralism. A transcendental anthropology presupposes that there is an abiding human subject and that the a priori structure of his spiritual dynamism can be disclosed through a transcendental reflection on the a priori conditions of possibility of his conscious activity. Hardnosed empiricist linguistic philosophy would deny the validity both of the transcendental method and of its presupposition that any knowledge of a transcendental a priori subject is possible. Rahner's transcendental anthropology brings him to knowledge of the Infinite Free Creator. Few phenomenologists would be ready to accept a transcendental reflection on the cognitive subject which opened out into a metaphysics of being. On the basis of its own reflection on human experience Whiteheadian process philosophy would deny that its condition of possibility could be a metaphysics of being and creation like the metaphysics which structures *Foundations of Christian Faith.*

Transcendental anthropology therefore is no guarantee of an "instant common fundamental theology." The theologian who decides to adopt Rahner's transcendental approach will have to vindicate his right to do so, and, in the pluralistic philosophical community of the United States, that right will not be conceded easily. The future of transcendental fundamental theology will depend on the ability of the theologian who employs it to justify its epistemological and metaphysical presuppositions by hard philosophical argument. The fact that a theologian declares that he is philosophizing inside theology will not excuse him from the necessity of being a sound and knowledgeable philosopher. If he is not, he may soon find that he is talking to himself, and that the philosophical community has ceased to take him seriously.

Rahner, who is a superbly trained philosopher, is perfectly well aware that philosophical pluralism exists even in respect to the possibility of a transcendental reflection upon the intellectual and volitional dynamism of the human subject and to the results which can be derived from it. But this philosophical pluralism is not the unbridgeable philosophical pluralism which has arisen from the vast proliferation of objective knowledge in contemporary science and culture. For the human spirit is unobjectively present to itself, and transcendental reflection confines its attention to the fundamental structure of thought and love itself.

Nevertheless, transcendental reflection is not easy. It requires a solid philosophical education and a disciplined attention to the knower's personal experience. Yet Rahner is confident that his transcendental philosophy can vindicate its metaphysics of man and being by pointing to the unobjective awareness which every man possesses of his own thinking and volition and to the invariant structure of its a priori conditions of possibility. As a philosophy, transcendental anthropology is no better than the philosophical evidence which it can educe in support of its assertions. But Rahner, I am convinced, has done a very good job of educing the evidence which he requires.

An important pastoral advantage which Rahner has discovered in his transcendental theology is that it directs the believer's attention away from the vast amount of objective knowledge about which no agreement is possible and focuses it on his own fundamental experience of himself and God. This, after all, is where the action is in human life. This is the personal realm of faith, hope and love, and of silent return in prayer to the Absolute Mystery. God is not found in idle talk about many things. God is found in the heart's surrender to the Darkness Who is Light. This echo of the silence of St. Thomas is one of the most attractive features of Rahner's fundamental theology. It can also be one of its most significant messages to the American philosophers who are more inclined to talk about many things than to know themselves or to pray to God.

Although it will be only one theology among many, Rahner's

transcendental theology strikes me as one of the most fruitful approaches which Catholic theologians could employ in an age of gnoseological concupiscence. Rahner's concern with the return to the Mystery in Catholic theology may have distracted his attention from the further possibilities which transcendental theology holds out for establishing a bond between fundamental theology and the other theological disciplines and for the integration of the data of the sciences into theology. Even though it is true, as Rahner asserts, that the theologian must frequently today dialogue directly with history and the sciences and not depend on their prior integration by a pregiven philosophical system, direct integration of scientific data into theology is not free from problems. History, the positive sciences and scientific exegesis, in the concrete form in which they are presented today, are often intertwined with epistemological and metaphysical presuppositions which are badly in need of philosophical criticism. In *Insight*[53] and *Method in Theology*[54] Bernard Lonergan has provided a brilliant illustration of how a cognitional theory, epistemology and metaphysics originally inspired by the Angelic Doctor's philosophy of knowledge can be used for such a critical integration of the data of the sciences into a scientific theology. It would be fascinating to see to what extent the two transcendental approaches to theology could be used to complement each other without doing violence to their own authentic character.

XIII. Conclusion

In our study of Rahner's changing relation to the Christian Philosophy of the Angelic Doctor we have seen how a Transcendental Thomist, in the course of his intellectual evolution, was brought to abandon the approach to philosophy advocated in *Aeterni Patris* and to move away from the theology of grace and faith and the structure of theology contained in Leo XIII's Encyclical. We have also seen the collapse of Rahner's faith in Thomism as a unitary system capable of structuring a Catholic culture and directing Catholic political and social action. The contemporary condition of gnoseological concupiscence and the unbridgeable pluralism of contemporary philosophy convinced Rahner that the ideal of a unitary system of philosophy and theology proposed in *Aeterni Patris* was unrealizable. Rahner now believes that Neo-Thomism was the last great effort of the Church to build her theology on a single philosophical system.

As a contribution to the Church's effort to cope with gnoseological

---

[53] Bernard J. F. Lonergan, *Insight* (New York: Philosophical Library, 1957).

[54] Bernard J. F. Lonergan, *Method in Theology* (New York: Seabury, 1972).

concupiscence, Rahner has employed his transcendental theology to construct the new fundamental theology presented in *Foundations of Christian Faith*. Although the philosophy of knowledge, man and being which undergirds that work is Rahner's own, they reveal that Rahner can still be called a philosopher in the tradition of the Angelic Doctor. For that reason, Rahner's philosophy will be severely criticized by the partisans of opposing epistemological and metaphysical positions.

Consequently *Foundations of Christian Faith* will not become an "instant common fundamental theology." Despite that fact, it is clearly a great book, and its lasting influence should be another sign that the inspiration of the Angelic Doctor is still fruitful enough to warrant Rahner's esteem for St. Thomas as a Doctor of the Church.

A Response to Fr. McCool

by Rev. Robert Kress

My remarks are less a direct commentary on specific points made by Fr. McCool, more a complementary expansion of certain key insights in his explanation of Karl Rahner's relationship to Thomism and St. Thomas Aquinas himself. My own observations will emphasize certain similarities between Karl Rahner and Thomas Aquinas, similarities which persist in spite of, even better, because of Rahner's departure from what had come to be identified as "Scholasticism" in general, Neo-Thomism in particular.

I. Personal and Existential Similarities

Although Karl Rahner is justly judged to be extraordinarily well versed in what he often calls textbook scholastic and Thomistic philosophy and theology, he himself went beyond them and the classic commentators to the works and thought of St. Thomas himself. This is evident from *Geist im Welt* up to the latest volume of *Schriften zur Theologie*. Such fondness and affinity is rooted, first of all, in a similarity of historical situations for both thinkers.

For both a fact of life was a "knowledge explosion"—for Thomas Aquinas in the rise and flourishing of the medieval universities with the concomitant expansion of method and content in knowledge in general; for Karl Rahner in the rapid expansion of method and content in not only the humanistic, but also the physical sciences. More specifically, both have been challenged by a new philosophy, Aristotelian for Aquinas; Kantian, Hegelian, Transcendental Thomist, Heideggerian for Rahner. Similarity between Aquinas and Rahner is not limited only to the situation. It extends also to the response. For they neither capitulated nor fled. Rather, both met the challenge of the "new thought" by relatively integrating it into the Christian tradition which each had inherited. Thus Aristotelian philosophers have a notoriously difficult time in finding Aristotle in the writings of St. Thomas, and certain kinds of Thomists as well as Kantians, Hegelians and Heideggerians have an equally difficult time locating their mentors in the writings of Karl Rahner. This should not be surprising, since, for example, Rahner has repeatedly disavowed the Heideggerian entitlement. Of both Rahner and Aquinas, it seems to me, can be aptly paid what Ammonius said of Aristotle, "Amicus quidem Plato (Socrates), sed magis amica Veritas." For both Aquinas and Rahner affinity with the famous is not the issue—rather the truth is.

Other affinities of Aquinas and Rahner are discernible in what Fr. McCool emphasizes under the rubric "philosophizing within theology." This implies an explicit affirmative acceptance of and reverence for the secular, the worldly, the, as we shall see later, inherent and "autonomous" value of the creation.

As a consequence of this attitude, both thinkers are willing to find theology's "partner-in-dialogue" (thus does Rahner's own term allow us to escape the agitation associated with "handmaid," which agitation the suggested replacement of "butler" has not been able to allay at this symposium) wherever it is to be found. Not only do they not impose ab extra the solution; more importantly, perhaps, they do not impose ab extra the *status quaestionis*.

> In the future, theology's key partner-in-dialogue, to which it will have to relate its 'philosophising' in the sense we have adumbrated, will no longer be philosophy in the traditional sense at all, but the 'unphilosophical' pluralistic sciences and the kind of understanding of existence which they promote either directly or indirectly. At least in the concrete situation determined by the cultural, intellectual, social and natural sciences, it is science, no longer mediated by philosophy, which constitutes theology's partner-in-dialogue.[1]

This has led both Aquinas and Rahner to develop new literary forms for theology—the former's *Summa Theologiae* and the latter's *Grundkurs des Glaubens*. Interestingly enough, these works are proclaimed by both authors to be for beginners (*incipientes* and *Einführung* or *erste Reflexionsstufe*), although I must admit that I don't know exactly what kind of beginners they had in mind—certainly not the beginners whom I encounter daily. Perhaps, though, the solution lies ready at hand—in Rahner's contention that we are all "rudes," and hence in an insuperable, but not negatively valued, beginner's state.[2]

In the achievement of both Aquinas and Rahner there is discernible both a balance and respect for the tradition that enables them to transcend their contemporaries in the disclosure of the truth of being. This I take to be the import of the comments of George Lindbeck that Rahner is a "man who in comprehensiveness and sheer intellectual quality can, alone among contemporary Catholics, be ranged alongside of Barth and Tillich, and who in terms of balance is perhaps the greatest of the three."[3] And the Anglican John Mac-

---

[1] Karl Rahner, "Philosophy and Philosophising in Theology," *Theological Investigations* 9, trans. Graham Harrison (New York: Seabury, 1972): 61-62.

[2] Karl Rahner, *Grundkurs des Glaubens* (Freiburg: Herder, 1976), p. 20. In this context Rahner also suggests that "man muss eine höhere Naivität erkämpfen und erleiden. . . ." See *Wagnis des Christen* (Freiburg: Herder, 1974), p. 73.

[3] George Lindbeck, "The Thought of Karl Rahner," *Christianity and Crisis* 25 (October 18, 1965): 211-15.

quarrie: "Among contemporary theologians, I have found Karl Rahner the most helpful. . . . Karl is outstanding. He handles in a masterful way those tensions which constitute the peculiar dialectic of theology mentioned above: faith and reason, tradition and novelty, authority and freedom, and so on."[4]

Thus, both Aquinas and Rahner have been able to avoid those two extremes in theology/philosophy which are restricted to no single age, but which recur in different guises throughout the history of Christianity and which J. Pieper has described as medieval Augustinism, Angelism, biblicism, excessive other-worldism on the one hand, and philosophism, Latin Averroism, heterodox Aristotelianism, excessive this-worldism on the other.[5] During the lifetime of St. Thomas the first group was associated with Augustinianism and the Secular Clergy, the second with the revolutionary secularists and Siger of Brabant, as well as the devotees (whatever their de facto identity and status may have been) of the so-called double truth. In our own age Rahner has been able to avoid what "Bartley diagnoses contemporary Protestant theology of all tendencies as suffering from a 'retreat to commitment.' "[6] as well as the neofundamentalism and simple secularism to which not a few contemporary Catholic authors have succumbed.

Finally, perhaps, I should merely recall what Fr. Egan mentioned in regard to the coinciding of life and theology for Karl Rahner— certainly a parallel between him and St. Thomas. A confirmation of which is, perhaps, the personal, calm *Sachlichkeit*—"a certain monotony, a regularity, a homogeneity that comes from a person's turning toward the final theme of theology . . . God" as Rahner describes it—which both thinkers have been able to achieve in undeniably turbulent times.

II. Philosophical and Theological Similarities

Not only, however, in regard to their lives and times do significant similarities and parallels exist between Thomas Aquinas and Karl Rahner, but also in the content of their thought. As Fr. McCool has so clearly shown, Rahner had to grow away from and out of that approach to and interpretation of St. Thomas which was prevalent during the first half of this century. In his return to the original

---

[4] John Macquarrie, *Principles of Christian Theology* (New York: Scribner's, 1977), p. vii.

[5] Joseph Pieper, *Scholasticism* (New York: McGraw-Hill, 1960), pp. 118-35. Also, his *Guide to Thomas Aquinas* (New York: Pantheon, 1962), pp. 63-74, 103-17.

[6] See Wolfhart Pannenberg, *Theology and the Philosophy of Science* (Philadelphia: Westminster, 1973), p. 76, citing W. Bartley, *Retreat to Commitment* (New York, 1962).

thought of Thomas Aquinas, Karl Rahner was able to find better problems and insights for the development of his own proper thought, which has culminated, as Fr. McCool pointed out, in the new theological literary genus and insights of *Foundations of Christian Faith.* Although Rahner's "Summa" (as it has been widely hailed) may not greatly resemble those "summas" of scholastic and Thomistic philosophy and theology which dominated Catholic theology during his student days, it is my contention that it does considerably resemble the insights of Thomas Aquinas, who was and has remained an inspiration and source to Rahner throughout his entire career.

In both, a prime desideratum is the organic unity of what is commonly denominated the natural and supernatural. In Rahner this concern is reflected in his key ideas, namely the ontology of the real symbol, the supernatural existential, created and uncreated grace, reason and faith, anonymous Christianity, which Fr. McCool has mentioned, and also negative theology and the incomprehensibility of God. I propose that one root of these key Rahnerian ideas is the "creation-ontology"[7] of Thomas Aquinas. And I do not think it fanciful to suggest that one way of regarding Rahner's thought is as a creative meditation on such prototypical texts of Thomas as the following.

1. The perfection of the effect manifests the perfection of the cause. To denigrate the perfection of creatures is, therefore, to denigrate the perfection of the divine power. (C.G. III, 69).

2. Nothing can satisfy the will of the human being except the universal good. (S.T. I-II, q.2, a.8).

3. All things, by desiring their proper perfections, desire God himself, insofar as the perfections of all things are certain likenesses of the divine being (esse). (S.T. I, q.6, a.1, ad 2).

4. God turns (converts; convertit) all things to himself insofar as he is the principle of being (essendi), for all things, insofar as they are at all, tend (have an inner dynamism) into the likeness of God, who is being itself (ipsum esse). (S.T. II-II, q.34, a.1, ad 3).

5. It is clearly not a convincing argument to say that what is derived from nothing tends of itself to nothingness and thus the potency to not-being resides in all created things. . . . Hence the potency to not-being does not dwell in creatures, but God has the power either to give them being or to allow the inflow of being into them to dry up. (C.G. II, 30).

---

[7] See especially Josef Pieper, "Kreatürlichkeit. Bemerkungen über die Elemente eines Grundbegriffes," in *Thomas von Aquin 1274-1974,* ed. Ludger Oeing-Hanhoff (Munich: Kosel, 1974), and Leo Dimpelmann, *Kreation als ontischontologisches verhältnis* (Munich: Karl Alber, 1969).

6. It is impossible for the good of our nature to be destroyed completely by sin. (De Malo q.2, a.12).

7. Our intellect in knowing anything is extended to infinity. This ordering of the intellect to infinity would be vain and senseless if there were no infinite object of knowledge. (C.G. I, 30).

8. The desire of the last end is not among those things over which we have mastery. (S.T. I, q.32, a.3, ad 1).

9. Each being naturally loves God more than itself. (S.T. I, q.60, a.5, ad 1).

10. Every rational being knows God implicitly in every act of knowledge. For, just as nothing has the nature of desirability except through its likeness to the first goodness, so nothing is knowable except through its likeness to the first truth (De Ver q.22, a.2, ad 1).

11. Created things in themselves do not lead away from God but towards him; for "the invisible things of God are clearly seen, being understood by the things that are made" (Rom 1:20) (S.T. I, q.65, a.1, ad 3).

12. This is the final human knowledge of God: to know that we do not know God (De Pot q.7, a.5, ad 1).

13. God is honoured by silence, not because we may say or know nothing about him, but because we know that we are unable to comprehend him (In Trin q.2, a.1, ad 6).

14. The least insight that one can obtain into sublime things is more desirable than the most certain knowledge of lower things (S.T. I, q.1, a.5, ad 1).

In making this suggestion I do not, of course, want to suggest that Rahner is interested in merely repeating or liturgically reciting what Thomas Aquinas said. Rather, in Rahner's search for the truth, the meaning of being, fundamental ontological insights and approaches of St. Thomas are clearly discernible and efficacious, however diverse the language and the style. For Rahner the *Seinsfrage* is the *Gottesfrage,* and *Der Mensch ist die Seinsfrage.* This perichoresis of theology, ontology and anthropology is clearly faithful to the most original and proper insights of St. Thomas, as J. B. Metz has pointed out in what remains his most significant book, *Christliche Anthropozentrik.* [8]

Two brief remarks will conclude this section. In his recent interview with Fr. Leo O'Donovan, Rahner mentions his interest in apocatastasis. [9] His "Christian Philosophy of and from St. Thomas," especially as this is manifested in Aquinas' interest in the statement

---

[8] J. B. Metz, *Christliche Anthropozentrik* (Munich: Kosel, 1962), along with the introduction by Karl Rahner.

[9] Leo J. O'Donovan, "Living Into Mystery," *America,* March 10, 1979, pp. 177-80.

of Wisdom 1:13 that "Death was not God's doing, he takes no pleasure in the extinction of the living. To be—for this he created all" would certainly make it not implausible for Rahner to develop what he calls a non-heretical theory of apocatastasis. (For St. Thomas' interest in this text, the following references can be proffered: In Sent 1, d. 8,3,2. In Sent III, d. 11, 1, ad 7. In Sent IV, d. 46, I, 3, ad 6. In Meta 10, 12(#2145): De. Pot 5, 4, ad 6. De Car 1. Quaes Quodlibet 4,4. C.G. II, 30. S.T.I, q.75, a.6, ad 2. S.T.I-II, q.10, a.1. S.T.III, q.13, a.2.)

Finally, it is always said that "the blatant consequence of Rahner's Christology is his proclamation of anonymous Christianity."[10] Such statements are, of course, not unacceptable, but a highly articulated reading of Rahner would also indicate that such an explicit Christology would not be available in the first place, were it not for what might be called the "anonymously Christian ontology of creation," to which Rahner could certainly have been inspired by Thomas Aquinas. Hence, like Aquinas, Rahner has been able to avoid the pitfalls of both Christomonism and revelational positivism on the one hand, and the reductionism of "liberal Protestantism" and secular humanism on the other.

Thus, one may suspect, has Rahner's theology and philosophy been rewarded by his familiarity with the "Christian Philosophy of/from St. Thomas Aquinas."

III. Similarity in Significance

In this third and last point I would like merely to point out one more similarity between Karl Rahner and Thomas Aquinas, in the spirit of both point number two above and Fr. Egan's comment about the coinciding of life and theology in Karl Rahner. In regard to St. Thomas, G. K. Chesterton remarks "There is a certain private audacity in his communion, by which men add to their private names the tremendous titles of the Trinity and the Redemption; so that some nun may be called 'of the Holy Ghost'; or a man bear such a burden as the title of St. John of the Cross. In this sense, the man we study (Aquinas) may specially be called St. Thomas of the Creator."[11]

I do not wish to canonize Father Rahner already, although personally I wouldn't have any serious objections, and his own theology of grace would certainly allow for such without presumption, however embarrassing that might be for him personally. His can-

---

[10] Otto Hentz, "The Idea of Christianity," *Thought,* December, 1978, pp. 440.

[11] G. K. Chesterton, *St. Thomas Aquinas* (New York: Sheed & Ward, 1933), p. 141.

onization we shall remit to God and Church. However, nevertheless we can legitimately look ahead and plan in case such a blessed event should eventuate, in which case a title would be needed. In accord with that communion in life and thought that I think can be discerned between St. Thomas Aquinas and our honored guest today, and playing upon Chesterton's suggestion of "Sanctus Thomas Creatoris Dei," I would like to suggest "Sanctus Carolus Creaturae Dei," and as an equivalent alternate "Defensor Hominis." For I know of no theologian who has labored so well to save the human being from the nihilism and insignificance inherent in atheism, pantheism and even that excessively rationalistic theism so roundly (and basically justly) berated during this symposium.

As Rahner has labored so diligently to show, and so successfully too it seems to me, God is neither the negation nor the limitation of human being. Rather than the demoter, God is the promoter of human being and dignity—their very possibilizer as well as actualizer. Thus, even the divine incomprehensibility of God is not primarily a divine attribute. It is, rather, an anthropological insight and statement, disclosing the ontological and epistemological congeniality of the divine and human, which, since it cannot exist on its own, is by its very nature pointed to some beyond. According to St. Thomas and Karl Rahner, this *apeiron,* which has preoccupied philosophy and theology from the very beginning, is not an empty, hollow, annihilating *(néant)* abyss,[12] but has been discovered and revealed to be the Holy Mystery into which

> . . . a Christian allows himself to fall into the mystery which we call God; that he is convinced in faith and in hope that in falling into the incomprehensible and nameless mystery of God he is really falling into a blessed and forgiving mystery which divinizes us; and that he also knows this on the level of reflexive consciousness and of his explicit faith, and he hopes for it explicitly, and does not just live it out in the anonymity of his actual existence. And to this extent to be a Christian is simply to be a human being, and one who also knows that this life which he is living, and which he is consciously living can also be lived even by a person who is not a Christian explicitly and does not know in a reflexive way that he is a Christian.[13]

---

[12] See Karl Rahner, *Schriften zur Theologie* 12 (Einsiedeln: Benziger, 1975), especially p. 316, but also pp. 290, 300, 308. See also his *Everyday Faith* (New York: Herder & Herder, 1967), p. 186: "It is the maturity of the Christian relation to God. For that maturity is aware that the creature does not disappear in the abyss of God when it abandons itself to him, but only then becomes truly living and established. It can find the creature in God because that creature has entered into him but has not been swallowed up in him."

[13] Karl Rahner, *Foundations of Christian Faith,* trans. William Dych (New York: Seabury, 1978), p. 430.

In a word, the Abyss, the Beyond, is literally, as Jesus himself addressed it, "Abba, Father" (Mark 14:36).

Conclusion and Colloquy

Since, in keeping with many years of Jesuit meditation points at Innsbruck, I have structured these comments into three points, we have now come to the conclusion and colloquy. Like St. Thomas in his own day and way, Karl Rahner in his own has been able to help us understand philosophically and theologically what W. H. Auden[14] intuited poetically, namely

> That after today
> The children of men
> May be certain that
> The Father Abyss
> Is affectionate
> To all Its creatures,
> All, all, all of them.
> Run to Bethlehem.

---

[14] W. H. Auden, *For the Time Being* (New York: Random House, 1944), p. 103.

A Response to Fr. McCool

by Rev. Patrick J. Burns, S.J.

Fr. McCool has contrasted the place of Christian philosophy in the Neo-Scholastic reform movement that lay behind Leo XIII's *Aeterni Patris* with the place of philosophy in Karl Rahner's *Foundations of Christian Faith,* published almost a century later. Fr. McCool is admirably equipped to undertake such a study. His *Catholic Theology in the Nineteenth Century* has recently established him as an authority on the history of Catholic theology at the time of *Aeterni Patris,* just as his *Rahner Reader* earlier established him as an authority on the thought of Karl Rahner. I am particularly impressed by Fr. McCool's summary of the complex historical background behind *Aeterni Patris* and its position on Christian philosophy.

At the close of this Marquette University symposium on the thought of Karl Rahner, I would like to make just two comments on how Fr. McCool describes the development of Rahner's own theology and then note one area for further investigation.

First, I would simply observe that most, if not all, of the positions which Fr. McCool cites to document what he calls Rahner's correction of nineteenth-century theology are really not peculiar to Rahner himself. The Catholic community's intellectual milieu has changed immensely since 1879. While Rahner has often taken the lead in acknowledging such change, it is still true that Rahner himself is also the product of the Church and culture and theological world in which he has lived and worked. For all its profundity, there is also a certain topicality about Rahner's work, as he tries to respond to the questions and experienced salvation needs of his fellow believers. Therefore I would be inclined to describe Rahner's long theological career more in terms of Rahner moving *with* his faith community and his theological colleagues than in terms of Rahner, as an individual theologian, reacting *against* the nineteenth-century Neo-Scholasticism of *Aeterni Patris.* I think this is particularly true of Rahner's position on pluralism in philosophy and theology, a position which accurately reflects a vastly different world from the relatively limited Catholic environment which gave rise to *Aeterni Patris.*

My second comment concerns Fr. McCool's description of stages of development within Rahner's own thought. Fr. McCool speaks of "development beyond the ideal of *Aeterni Patris,*" "progressive rejection of *Aeterni Patris,*" and finally "definitive rejection of *Aeterni Patris.*" Such language, I suspect, tends to overemphasize the difference between the early and the later Rahner. I myself am impressed by the *continuity* of Rahner's basic philosophical orientation. I would be inclined to say that the decisive break with nineteenth-century Neo-Scholasticism came with Maréchal, whom Rahner read privately as a young Jesuit during his first philosophical studies in Pullach. Maréchal had already broken with Neo-Scholasticism, and Rahner from the beginning was committed to another type of philosophizing. Obviously, there has been an enormous amount of theological development in Rahner's thought from the late thirties and forties, when he first published *Spirit in the World* and *Hearers of the Word,* through the fruitful post-war years in Innsbruck and Munich and Münster, to the appearance of *Foundations of Christian Faith* several years ago. Central categories and themes like the supernatural existential, the theology of symbol, the unity of love of God and love of neighbor, anonymous Christianity, the experience of grace, and the mystical dimension of Christian everyday life have emerged during these years to make explicit what was at best implicit in Rahner's first publications. But I would tend to think that Rahner's basic philosophical orientation has remained rather constant throughout all these theological developments. It is true that Rahner's thought on the relationship of nature and grace, the order of creation and the order of redemption, the supernatural existential and anonymous Christianity have all tended to challenge any neat distinction between philosophy and theology, to integrate apologetics as a dimension of theology itself, and to lead to the kind of philosophizing-within-theology that characterizes *Foundations of Christian Faith.* Fr. McCool quite properly points this out. But I would regard most of these developments as already implicit in the younger Rahner, with his concentration as a transcendental Thomist on analysis of the concrete operations of the knowing and believing subject in the world. It is also true that in his earlier writings (and throughout his long years of lecturing at Innsbruck) Rahner spent a good deal of his time trying explicitly to relate his emerging systematic positions to Christian tradition as expressed in the categories of Neo-Scholastic philosophy and theology. However, I would attribute this in part to the simple demands of communication with an audience still overwhelmingly committed to doing theology in such Neo-Scholastic categories and in part to Rahner's honest respect for a system he knew so well even though he had in principle already moved beyond it. Thus I would explain the relative absence of explicit dialogue with the Neo-Scholastic position in Rahner's more recent work not so much in terms of any change in his personal philosophical allegiance as in terms of broader changes in the Christian community for whom Rahner writes and whose openness to contemporary categories has increased enormously in the years since Rahner first began to publish. In other words, I believe that Rahner himself *began* his professional career already committed to a transcendental Thomism that differed quite substantially from the Thomism of late nineteenth-century Neo-Scholasticism. His thought developed, of course, but I would prefer to describe this as a development of Rahner's original commitment to transcendental Thomism, not as a series of breaks with nineteenth-century Neo-Scholasticism.

Finally, allow me to indicate one area which Fr. McCool did not have an opportunity to investigate and which strikes me as a fruitful area for further investigation. That is the question of the relationship of Rahner's *Spirit in the World* not to nineteenth-century Neo-Scholasticism but to the thought of Thomas Aquinas himself. Rahner presents his position in *Spirit in the World* as an interpretation of Thomas. It is certainly a creative interpretation. Is it also a valid or legitimate interpretation? As we know, this has been a question ever since Rahner first proposed the main lines of his interpretation as a young doctoral student in Freiburg in the mid-thirties. I believe that both Martin Heidegger and Rahner's own director, Martin Honecker, had their own opinion at the time. I simply suggest here that it would be a very interesting project now, forty years later, to re-examine Rahner's interpretation of Thomas as a work of creative historical retrieval—perhaps by using some of the new hermeneutic categories developed in the intervening years by men like Hans-Georg Gadamer and Paul Ricoeur.

The Impasse of Ultimate Reassurance and Christian Certitude

by Rev. Prof. George Muschalek, S.J.

I. Man's All-Pervading Quest for Stability and Reliability of Life

In the Spring of 1929, John Dewey delivered at the University of Edinburgh the Gifford Lectures on "The Quest for Certainty."[1] It was one of those intellectual events which gives rise to heated debate, a long series of publications, advocating his basic thesis or rejecting it, hailing this new philosophy or condemning it. In fact, Dewey had uncovered a question which seemed to be a question for everyone and every age and which nonetheless has found surprisingly little continuing interest, except for Dewey's book and the ensuing debate. There are few investigations that deal directly with the problem of human certainty. This is an astonishing fact considering that the problem of certainty so much pervades everything we do or think that it seems to be connected with man's entire life and with the whole range of human activities. It therefore arouses our sympathetic interest when we see in what context Dewey formulates his question. "Man who lives in a world of hazards is compelled to seek for security." This is Dewey's opening statement, and it is the motif which will characterize all of his thinking on certainty.

In fact, man is extremely vulnerable, more than any other living being. To be sure, only part of his activities are overt attempts to make his life secure. Such was the often mentioned struggle for survival of primitive humanity, where everybody's hands and minds were kept busy from childhood to old age protecting themselves from cold, from wild beasts, from hunger, from bellicose tribes. Life was indeed a search for security; life in its stark needs demanded that.

The transition to a sedentary life was one of the deepest caesuras the history of humanity has ever experienced. It seems to have found only one parallel in our time, in humanity's orientation towards the future.[2] This new attitude has turned everybody's hopes to that stage of the evolution of the human race where life would be definitively secured by scientific and social progress. These two deep caesuras in human history have to do, in different ways, with stability and security of life. The transition to sedentary life enabled man

---

[1] J. Dewey, *The Quest for Certainty* (New York: G. P. Putnam's Sons, 1960).

[2] H. Freyer, *Theorie des gegenwärtigen Zeitalters* (Stuttgart: Deutsche Verlagsanstalt, 1967; reprint of the first edition 1955). In this paper, translations from foreign works are mine unless otherwise noted.

to be concerned with other things than external protection, food and shelter. He tended to stabilize his existence in a new way by building a house, creating a stable family, and by looking for continuity in his work and purposes. The outlook on stability had changed, but stability of life remained a pivotal issue.

With relative freedom from external threats to his mere survival, man became engaged in questions which had to do with stability and certainty on a deeper level. He felt that human life lacked certainty and security if its origin and end were unknown. Life appeared shaky and exposed to chance if not seen as stretching from a defined origin to a corresponding end. Unless life was perceived as built-in between such an origin and such an end (both consonant with the peculiar value of human life) deep uncertainty prevailed.

This is not to say that we have to conceive this quest for certainty as merely a transition from external to internal forms of security. Even the hunters of 20,000 B.C. had found ways to portray animals in dusky stone caves, selected for sacred purposes. On those cave walls, in today's France and Spain, pictures of animals in dazzling beauty can be found, intended to conjure mysterious powers. Magic was a very early form of the struggle for survival and for security or certainty.

Nonetheless, the quest for stability of life, for a clear view of human existence, for orientation in a chance world, took on a new form when basic biological needs receded and human life came to new questions about itself. Human life amidst non-human reality, amidst nature as opposed to man and one with him, awakened to questions which, in a new way, were in search of orientation, explanation, and understanding of human life. Man tried to find the possibility of living by knowing the truth and overcoming fallacies. It was a new quest for certainty. This human drive so pervades every fiber of a person's physical and mental life that even reaching out for the beautiful has to do with the human need for a total view of reality. Poetry can arise when the human mind contemplates reality and exposes itself to it without demanding the fulfillment of any practical needs. Philosophy will find its expression when favored by the same freedom from immediate penury. Seen this way, philosophy is in fact akin to poetry, because both are forms of encompassing experience of reality, and both are reactions to it.[3]

It is important to see that, on this higher level of human existence, the concern for certainty has not disappeared; it has only been transformed. Attention to external reality was vital for the security

---

[3] E. Heller, *The Disinherited Mind* (New York and London: Harcourt, Brace and Jovanovich, 1975) p. XIV f., speaks of the link Thomas Aquinas saw "between poets and philosophers in their preoccupation with the marvellous."

of primitive man in the midst of countless dangers from animals, hostile tribes, and from nature. Attention to external reality has become something different in the age of civilization. But is it altogether different? Our interest need not be fixed upon the *variety* of forms of reality, but rather upon the *one basic human need* to see and hear and know more about reality in order to be able to live. In this case, two apparently very different ways of attending to reality are seen as stemming from one and the same source. It is life's unquenchable drive to secure everything that is necessary to live. Various as these undertakings may be, they are all concerned with protecting, stabilizing, enlarging, in brief, securing human life. Man, to put it differently, must have a clear and reliable relationship to reality, so as to be able to live. That can and must take place on the level of physical security, and it can and must take place on the level of "meaning." We grope toward those connections with "reality," be it nature, other humans, or God, which provide us with meaning while we maintain connections with those realities which provide us with the means for physical survival.

If at this point we return to John Dewey, we might be even more sympathetic to the universal role he attributes to the search for security. He sees two main ways for humanity to seek security or certainty. One is to *propitiate* the powers which surround man and determine his destiny. Magical cults, ceremonial rites, sacrifice and supplication were the means of that propitiation. Its end was the change of the self "in emotion and idea," which allowed man to ally himself with a destiny he could not conquer, to surrender to the powers, "even in sore affliction," to find security, even amidst misfortune and destruction.[4] For Dewey, not only all forms of religious attitude, magical as well as highly spiritual, are steps on this road to security, but also traditional philosophy insofar as it aspires towards the security of absolute truth.

The approach to security, as Dewey portrays it, is radically different. Here it is not *changing the self* to ally with fortune, but it is *changing the world through action* which would lead the human race to security.[5] Dewey's contribution is a genuinely philosophical approach because it tries to retrace complex human activities to basic attitudes. In fact, if the human race is to come to terms with a basically hostile fate, there are only two ways to do it: man can yield to fate on all levels of his existence, or he can spend all his efforts subjecting fate so that it would no longer threaten his life, and this again on all levels of his existence. Dewey has in fact formulated one

---

[4] Dewey, *Certainty*, p. 3.

[5] Ibid.

of the most crucial alternatives: surrendering to reality (understood most comprehensively) or subjecting it.

He opts clearly for the second alternative. What is needed now is activity instead of passive contemplation, risk and insecurity of action instead of the (in his view fallacious) security of absolute truth. Summarizing his investigation into the history of man's attitude towards security or certainty, Dewey writes: "We have seen how cognitive quest for absolute certainty by purely mental means has been surrendered in behalf of search for a security, having a high degree of probability, by means of preliminary active regulation of conditions."[6] Connected with this is the shift from "inert dependence upon the past to intentional construction of the future."[7]

Dewey is thinking in a tradition, upon which he is more dependent than he cares to admit, that orients human activity to activeness in a specific sense. Activity has come to mean creating instead of receiving, making instead of contemplating. It has a long history, reaching back to the eighteenth century with Giambattista Vico, and its first beginnings might be found at the dawn of the modern era in the fifteenth century.[8] Dewey shares with his predecessors great optimism in the human potential. Today, we read his lines of 1929 with mixed feelings:

> We have attained, at least subconsciously, a certain feeling of confidence; a feeling that control of the main conditions of fortune is to an appreciable degree passing into our hands. . . . Barring the fears which war leaves in its train, it is perhaps a safe speculation that if contemporary western man were completely deprived of all the old beliefs about knowledge and actions he would assume, with a fair degree of confidence, that it lies within his power to achieve a reasonable degree of security in life.[9]

As for the degree of "certainty" or "security" (terms which are often used by Dewey indiscriminately), it is surprising to see him abandon the hope for full certainty and make us face the fact that only some degree of "securing certainty" (as we could call it) can be reached. This, however, is consistent with his view of certainty and man's activities. Protecting security can only be reached to a limited degree. Today we, with fifty years of additional experience of

---

[6] Ibid., p. 290.

[7] Ibid.

[8] K. Löwith, *Meaning in History* (Chicago and London: The University of Chicago Press, 1949, ninth impression 1967), on Vico pp. 115-36; G. Muschalek, *Tat Gottes und Selbstverwirklichung des Menschen* (Freiburg-Basel-Wien: Herder. 1974), especially pp. 59-101.

[9] Dewey, *Certainty,* p. 9.

human affairs, know this even better than Dewey.

Thus we are left with the question: is Dewey's "Quest for Certainty" still a challenging task, or has it been reduced to a quest for security, which is meant to protect us from hazards as best it can, which means (practically) to a very modest degree? It would mean, at the same time, that we should join in the huge operation to create security by scientific and technical means—a task necessary for our survival—and abandon all questioning about any other forms of certainty. In this case, Dewey's book on certainty would justly have been the last one on this subject.

Before we draw such a conclusion, let us take a brief look at the history and the fate of that new form of certainty we could term "securing certainty."

II. The Quest for Securing Certainty in the New Age

In this brief description of a new attitude toward our stabilizing and insuring human life on all levels, I should like to focus on two major forms in which this new quest can be found. The first form is the boundless faith in science as the final cure of all human ills. That faith has not yet ceased, although confidence in it has considerably lessened since the late nineteenth century. But other layers of hope and struggle have superimposed themselves upon that original faith. The other form in which this changed attitude towards certainty finds its expression is our contemporary experience of the world. This includes the vexing question concerning the way this new experience of the world allows for, or even demands, an experience of a God beyond the world.

1. The History of the Boundless Faith in Science

Human life has no doubt deeply changed during the centuries in which modern science has developed and transposed itself into technology. But often those changes are most mentioned which are least significant. It is not the external transformation of our lifestyle which matters so much, but incomparably more the changed human attitude towards the reality surrounding us, towards our self-assessment and the ways in which we hope to be able to ground our own life firmly. Our modern scientific era has brought about a distinct understanding of certainty.

At the origin of the modern empirical attitude towards reality we find Francis Bacon's idea that the right empirical knowledge will bestow power on man. "Knowledge and human power come to the same thing," for "nature cannot be conquered except by obeying her."[10] Scientific thinking was born in the seventeenth century out

---

[10] Francis Bacon, *De augmentis scientiarum* 1, 3.

of a state of deep uncertainty. When the medieval world dissolved, the human world view and human self-understanding found at first a new form in Renaissance and Humanism. But the religious and political order had been deeply unsettled. The sixteenth and seventeenth centuries revealed that loss of orientation, or at least the extreme need for re-orientation. The religious movements of the Reformation evidence that struggle for a new certitude in God. Skepticism like that of Montaigne was the subdued species of the quest for certainty, a quest that had, to a large extent, resigned hope of attaining absolute certainty and was seeking the human balance in skeptical distance from any position.

It was in this climate that Descartes set out to find what was later called the rock-bed of knowledge, so firm that no doubt should ever shake human certainty. It was no chance coincidence that Descartes was a mathematician and physicist. His certitude can be called ultimate reassurance. By returning into the self, the human spirit sought the absolutely firm basis which all preceding reflection upon world and God had not given to mankind. Descartes, the father of modern philosophy as he is commonly called, and, as we could add, a father of the modern quest for reassurance, had reversed the direction of the search for certitude. It was no longer by exposing oneself to the given world, to nature, to cosmos, and to God that the human spirit should find its place in the world and its self-assessment, but by returning to the inmost process of thinking or affirming or doubting. Starting from this new center everything, including especially God's existence, was to be assured. Later, we shall reflect upon the significance of the direction the search for certainty takes, returning to the questioning subject or surrendering to the reality outside oneself.

Galileo, greatly admired by Descartes, does not seem to fit into the scheme of the new search. His investigations were precisely directed to the outside world, and into remote regions which before had not been accessible to mankind. And yet, he adopted clearly enough the new direction leading back into the reassuring subject, and of course set a new pattern and a new dimension to this search. The origin of the new quest for certitude—and it was such a quest not only in Descartes' work but also in beginning modern science—was the hope of finding a new and more reliable foundation of human thinking and existence. For Galileo, mathematics was the expression of truth "which to him had become the revelation of God that could not be surpassed or refuted by any other revelation and by no 'verbal inspiration.' "[11]

---

[11] E. Cassirer, *Philosophie und exakte Wissenschaft* (Frankfurt: Vittorio Klostermann, 1969), p. 54.

The revolutionary force did not lie in the discovery and application of new methods but in the reformulation of mankind's question about certitude. From now on, man's place in the world and in human society, his internal and external organization was to be found by the strict and doubt-free method developed by Descartes and modern science. The driving force behind the progress of scientific thinking is usually overlooked, forgotten, or perhaps repressed. The history of science and astronomy in the modern era is not a straightforward ascent, as it is still represented by some, but a history proceeding in waves, each of which has its great expectations at the beginning, its triumphant ascent, and its (usually muted) decline.[12] The early stage of science was enthusiastic about the possibility of discovering God's presence in the world and His providence governing the world by strictly scientific methods. From now on, it seemed that the agonizing state of uncertainty about God and man had gone, and the human spirit had established a new, infallible way to insure this crucial knowledge.

But after a while, the sobering discovery was that progress had been made in discovery of data, but that the hoped-for new and unshakable discovery of God, and with it, of man's place in the world had not taken place. Therefore, the interest of scientific exploration shifted, from mechanics to inorganic nature, from there to organic nature, then to human existence directly by exploring history, culture, and society. Different disciplines developed with their extraordinary results. But looking at the guiding faith behind those movements, we must say that new areas of scientific research were entered not as a victorious general subjects one country after the other, but as people move onto other grounds because of the failure of the drilling to find the hidden, wildly needed riches.

As late as the nineteenth century, faith in scientific truth as the key to all human problems appeared to be boundless. It was the power of the new scientific method—new, because it was the form scientific thinking had taken in that century—"to reveal the secret of nature and history and make known to man the law of his individual and social destiny."[13] It was only from 1870 on that the vigorous optimism slackened. "The spirit tired of searching an imaginary object turned back upon itself in order to observe the inner laws of its functioning."[14]

---

[12] As for the brief history of faith as the driving force in the history of science, I am much indebted to F. H. Tenbruck, "Die Glaubensgeschichte der Moderne," *Zeitschrift für Politik* 23 (1967): 1-15.

[13] D. G. Charlton, *Secular Religions in France* (London-New York-Melbourn: Oxford University Press, 1963), p. 2, who quotes E. Bréhier, *Histoire de la philosophie*, tome II (Alcan, n.d.).

[14] Bréhier, *Histoire*, p. 910, as quoted by Charlton, *Secular Religions in France*, p. 3.

Faith in a strictly scientific solution to all human problems including the most basic and encompassing ones, has had a colorful history, with many new beginnings and many disappointments. Despite the "slackening" which we mentioned in describing the mood after 1870, the history of this faith is still going on, as represented by the subdued but strong conviction that basically all human problems can be solved scientifically.

To understand better the hope and disillusionment of that history, we have to turn to a contemporary form of reassurance which has to do with a new experience of reality.

2. The Two Opposite Forms of World Experience

We have seen that the question of certitude has to be solved on a level deeper than that of scientific method or scientific theory. In fact, the scientists of the nineteenth century, for instance in France, in their boundless optimism constantly overstepped, without admitting it, the limits of verifiable science and of strict positivism in order to create a philosophy of science which would solve all human problems.

We have, therefore, to turn to the question, or to a segment of it, as to what kind of basic relationship to world-reality is required to arrive finally at a certitude that would answer the tenacious questions about that reality.

On February 10, 1944, a Norwegian political prisoner in his solitary confinement began to write a diary. "Was interrogated twice. Was flogged. Betrayed Victor. Am weak. Am terribly frightened by pain, But no fear of death."

It is not correct to say that he "wrote" the diary. Under the extreme conditions of his isolation, all he had were sheets of brown toilet paper and a wire tack he had found. That was all he had—that and his life that he carried around in this bare cell in the hollow of his hand, as the editor of this diary puts it.[15] With an unbelievable patience he punched letter after letter in the paper, hardly readable to himself, rolled them into scrolls and squeezed them into a ventilating shaft on the floor. There they were discovered after the war. That diary, more than a hundred pages in print, is one of the most moving documents of that terrible period. The prisoner, Peter Moen, was an insurance actuary, a highly cultured person. He had been the organizer of the underground press; that was enough to arrest him.

The six months in prison before his death saw the dramatic struggle of two worlds in one man: the modern, enlightened, scien-

---

[15] *Peter Moens Tagebuch,* ed. E. Schaper (Frankfurt a.M.-Hamburg: Fischer Bücherei, 1959), p. 7.

tific mind of an autonomous man, and that other ego which was in a desperate search for God, a search which was one long outcry of a man, who thought and wrote down that he would be "done for" if he did not receive an answer.

He wrote in his diary on the 10th of August, 1944:

> I have while here in prison frequently pointed out in speech and in writing what all history and psychology show, that religion is man's creation and nothing else. Its 'truths' are devoid of all signs of objectivity: causality, measureability and experimental repetition. So it is with the 'truth' of the basic religious phenomenon: the working of God in man. This is not carried out according to some law, its effects cannot be measured, and it cannot be made the object of verifying experimentation. . . .
> Even if the firing squad awaited me, I cannot force any kind of a 'creed' for myself. I tried that in the extreme distress of solitary confinement. It was all in vain![16]

"In vain"—these words come back several times. This seems to be the outcome of this desperate struggle, on the surface of things, and as far as *we* can tell.

With immense respect for this man, and with all possible reverence for his individual fate, which is never a "case," we might be tempted to see in this prisoner in solitary confinement, torn between two experiences, *modern man,* existing in so many men and women today, most of them nameless and voiceless. These two opposite experiences may, in the extreme, tear man apart. It is, on the one hand, the experience of a closed world, rational, perfectly coherent in its causality, leaving no room for a god; on the other hand, a world which, at times, drives man out of himself and of this closed world, in an elementary hunger for the "totally other," obviously beyond and even against this world.

Experience against experience—this is our situation. The atheism of the nineteenth century is gone, one could say. It had been an atheism which very often was a new religion with a new quest for the Supreme Being. The new atheism does not seem to be capable of raising or answering any question about a Supreme Being. But this atheism is now, in turn, itself violently questioned by a new experience. That man who had set everything upon the straightforward and unequivocal experience of the world and himself, finds himself imprisoned, imprisoned in his own world. Today the biggest problem is how mankind can survive, how man can regain his personal freedom in a world controlled by technology and totally administered; how he can find the society which is human and not rendered lifeless by isolating individuals from each other,

---

[16] Ibid., p. 104f.

disintegrating in deadly passivity, or in deadly violence.

These are not unconnected problems of today's life. Rather one can find a common trait in this new situation: the loss of what had been so triumphantly affirmed, namely the closeness of world and man to the human experience. World and fellow man have become so remote that, at times, a comparison with solitary confinement is not hyperbolic. Out of this situation, atheism is again questioned, now in a completely new way.

Here in this short reflection we are not going to broach the difficult question as to what the causes of that development are, and, of course not, how the different ailments can be cured, one by one. We should also be careful not to assign causes to these various problems too lightly. But *in* these symptoms we can try to find a major line, a thread which runs through these symptoms. I would assume that this thread is man's experience of the world which has changed so much. By "world" we understand the other human beings, all that given reality around us, living and lifeless, and finally that reality which has been constructed by man. Man made the world habitable, and used it for his purpose by transforming it more and more into a realization of his own idea about world and man. It is the experience of that complex phenomenon "world" that we are going to examine, and to contrast it with the other experience we call the experience of God.

We have to admit that by posing the problem this way we could seem to *presuppose* that there is a real difference between world-experience and God-experience. But this is not the case. We simply start from the *question,* raised not only by Peter Moen, but by so many others, *whether* there can be and must be a difference between these two; and if so how that difference must be understood.

a. We need experience of the world.

From the end of the Middle Ages, the interest in and the quest for *experience* came to the fore. Nominalism turned away from the abstract and concerned itself with the concrete which is present here and now and can be experienced. Luther gave that movement a religious and reformatory (in a way revolutionary) turn: How can *I* find a merciful God—I, this human being here and now, in this situation,—a God who is not a remote God, a "universal God," so to speak, but *my* God, a God who is concerned with me as if I were the only person in the world. *Experience* from then on became a theme. What was conceived as, and expected from, experience, changed considerably in the course of modern history. Publications on experience in the last decade have stressed this fact, and rightly so. But we should not overlook the common trait, the enduring basic attitude in all those different forms of experience as a method of discovery, a means of controlling reality, an avenue to philosophical certitude, a way to life, human life and religious life. In all those different forms we find the need for *immediacy of reality*. Man needs the world which surrounds him. World is nothing else but the extension of one's own existence, the outer parts of it as it were. As far as "world" contains other human beings, it is even an essential part of one's *inner* existence. It is, therefore, understandable that the human spirit has to find ways to be in close contact with that—his—reality, and that it has to reach some sort of immediacy of reality, an immediacy which would guarantee the access to *truth*—we would then *know* what things are, and thereby what we ourselves are,—and we could *live* because we would be in immediate contact with the conditions of our own life. World is that which offers food, for body and mind, shelter, room for creativity, and so on. British empiricism had a concept of experience different from that of Descartes or Kant, from that of the modern empirical sciences, and from that experience which is being claimed today by religious groups. But in all these different forms one can detect a common quest for an immediacy of the world, for a nearness of reality, however that nearness may be conceived. In all these forms, it will be the immediate contact with reality which fascinates man and promises numerous possibilities for him to realize his life, to make his life real in the full sense.

When we reflect for a moment upon our contemporary expectations and needs, we must say that today, in a totally new form, we need our world badly, experience of it, and immediate access to it. We know that this is no longer a matter of individual decision only, of a philosophical decision whether one should—yes or no—turn to the world in the immediacy of experience. For complex reasons, we are in a situation which does not allow unrestricted access to the world and its reality. For many people it has become difficult to reach nature, to gaze at forests and lakes. They experience themselves as if stored in huge containers, houses in which an anonymous crowd lives, surrounded by similar housing containers. It has become a familiar pattern to point out the fact that we have no longer simple, unlimited access to the air we breathe. Nothing can summarize better to what degree our vital relationship to the surrounding world has been disturbed.

We should not forget disturbances at a higher level, which are not so clearly seen, because not willingly admitted. It is the relationship of one human being to the other. We *seem* to live in an epoch of social consciousness, if we look at the thousands of books which are flooding the market dealing with human relationship at the level of the individual and of society. Never before has everything so clearly been related to society, and never before have there been so many theories on communication, offered as training in high schools, universities, and in continuing education. One might think that, for the first time in history, we have discovered both the nature and the high value of inter-personal communication. And in a way, this is correct. But often we only discover the value of something when it is gone. Taking a closer look we have to say that this is the case here. The tremendous interest in social responsibility and communication and the tremendous efforts to study and promote them are often necessary, but not so much because we have made so much progress in discovering the world of man, but because we have fallen behind so terribly in what our human existence would require. Of course, we have been forced to make conscious what previously had been unknown, only lived. That in itself is real progress. We must not, however, overlook the frightening loss of experience, of natural, even if unreflected, experience at this level: the experience of the closeness of the given world, and especially that of our fellow human beings. That is what we need to live by, not the scientific analyses *as such,* on the abstract level of their reflections. What we can observe today is another form of crude alienation of one human being from another. It might be found in the seemingly innocent form of every-day isolation and disinterestedness, in the lack of sensitivity. But it is also registered more and more in the extraordinary form of violence. Seen in our perspective we must say that violence is loss of experience in its extreme form. Of course, violence is also experienced, and very painfully at that. But if we persist in our understanding of experience, we must say that precisely here we do not have a rich and enriching access to reality but are barred from it. If we do not use the term "experience" in an abstract, formalized way, so that it can be applied to any form of immediate awareness, then we have to say that experience in its proper sense is immediate access to and contact with reality, not a loss of it; that it means enjoying one's world, and first of all the world of human beings, and not the absence of it, the loss of it. Primary experience is not the experience of solitude, but rather experience of world and community.

In short, we need the experience of the world as that which is the integral part of all life. We need that reality and *experience.* That means, we cannot live just by reflecting, reasoning, by making decisions, by acting. All that is necessary, but it will be *our* expression of life only if it is imbedded in and permeated by experience, experience of *our* reality, which makes that reasoning, deciding, and acting not something foreign, imposed upon ourselves, or extracted from us—not even communicated by an encompassing history, in which the individuals drift like chips of wood in a stream. Action must be the manifestation of one's own life, acquired and expanded by experience.

And we need the experience of God. Can there be such a thing? In the realm of the unverifiable? Will that not necessarily be finite experience reduced to finite dimensions, so that it must be called a delusion? But it would be so good to have one: the immediacy of God's reality. It would change everything. We are caught in the dilemma: we postulate, like Peter Moen, the experience of God, and we do not believe in such a thing seriously. Thus, a second step is necessary. We need the experience of God in the experience of the world.

b. The experience of God in the experience of the world.

It might appear to be a solution to our dilemma to locate the experience of God *in* our experience of the world. But then the question arises whether world experience is being piously draped, but would not give access to the experience of God who is the infinitely other in the world—if at all it is God we are talking about. The question is what it means to search for the experience of God in the world. Given the fact that God is infinitely different from the world and uniquely above it, it is not self-evident that there is some identity between God-experience and world-experience. But it is true that God can only be found in the world. We need, however, the right perspective in which we can place this statement. We would have to say that God is too great to be found only outside the world. It would be quite a different perspective if we thought, without saying it, that the world is so great that God must have his place within it. Here, we are saying explicitly the opposite: God is too great to be found only outside the world. If we conceive of God as the Holy Being that is completely separated from the world then we would think of Him in terms of a Being that, however great it may be, can and must be opposed to the reality of the world, and can and must be compared with it. There is a deep tendency in man to dethrone God—a tendency that is in constant struggle with the even deeper tendency to acknowledge him unconditionally. The tendency to dethrone Him may cloak itself in seemingly devout motives. Is it not thinking most highly of God if one contrasts Him as sharply as possible with the non-divine reality, called world? One could think here of the problem of Christian love for one's fellow man, so often dethroned for the benefit of a seemingly "holier" obligation vis-à-vis God, pictured outside the world—"religion" as an excuse for love; faith, understood here as correct faith, as prime concern instead of love which is the prime concern of the New Testament.

God's *real* transcendence means that, at the same time, He is above and in the world, both for the same reason: His transcendence. To put it less technically, His incomparability is such as not to allow us to place Him within the world and outside of it. If He were to be found only outside the world, He would necessarily be comparable to other realities. The location, or the undialectical description, of His sphere of existence, namely that He is "outside the world," would make it clear that we have made God comparable to other realities. God is too great for being within a finite framework of comparison. Seen from this angle, the claim that God must be found in the world has nothing to do with reducing God to finite dimensions. On the contrary; only this understanding of transcendence opens up infinite dimensions.

It is remarkable that in the Christian tradition, mysticism has always retained its special and privileged closeness to the world, whatever the many misunderstandings of mysticism may be. According to the great mystics, mystical experience is certainly an extreme form of God-experience, the form in which man is transported beyond the sphere of everyday things. He has an experience which is totally different from everyday experiences, frightening as night can be, in which all things disappear, and blissful as the full force of blinding sunlight which may strike us, in which we close our eyes so as to be able to enjoy it. Mystical experience abandons the world, but Christian mystical experience is only a true one if it, by itself, opens up the person to a new, more profound experience of the world. The principle of the God-world relationship in Christian theology can be found there. World is disclosed fully in and through the at times even ecstatic experience of *God*. Because of God's being both beyond and in the world, human experience, as long as it is undistorted, will reach God and the world in one and the same act. This is at least what we can deduce from this principle of Christian experience at this point of our reflection: the unity of God-experience and world-experience. Now we have to determine more precisely this twofold experience.

3. The Need for the Experience of God as God in the Experience of the World.

What does that mean? How else can God be experienced if not as God? But it is not hairsplitting if put that way. Since God has that unique relationship to the world, so difficult to grasp, by which He is co-extensive, so to speak, with the world, and at the same time totally different from it, He can easily be confused with or separated from the world. In either way, we could experience God—how could we escape it?—but our experience would misunderstand itself.

To make this clearer we have to think for a moment of another misunderstood experience, that of the world. In many religions outside the Judeo-Christian tradition, the dividing line between the finite world and the infinite deity was not sharply drawn. The divine realm was understood differently. World became permeated by divine powers, worldly realities were identified with them, world was divinized to a certain degree. It is a theme of contemporary Christian theology to point out that under the influence of Judeo-Christian faith world has become "de-divinized," free from divine powers, reinstated in its character of a finite created world. From now on, world could be *entered* by man; it had lost its sacred, forbidding character. Man had no longer to remove his shoes and to worship the world. He could without hesitation walk right into this world, take full possession of it, move around freely in it, not only as in his garden, but more and more as in his own workshop. World had become the "worldly world," as it is often said. This theory is correct at first sight, but not when we see all its ramifications. At this stage we can notice that in our thinking about world and God, the same rules do not apply to both. It could be shown in detail that the more man has become aware of the "worldliness" of the world, the more he has freed it from all intermingling with divine powers and from all too clear reference to the divine realm, the more world itself has grown beyond its limitations. It has begun to fascinate man anew, in a different way now, to be sure, but to fascinate him, to attract his expectations and to rivet them to it, so that finally we see today the phenomenon of a re-divinized world, a world which has become again, unintentionally, a somewhat numinous reality, before which man stands in awe and, time and again, in horror. By either attitude, awe or horror, we may be fixed to something, riveted to it to the point of becoming lifeless. One might ask whether that is the case in *any* form of misunderstood religiosity.

The starting point had been correct: world is world and nothing else. Or maybe not quite correct. What if world can only remain real world if it is constantly referred and attached to what is not world, to God? What if world cannot retain for man its richness of being world, and nothing else, unless its reference to God is clearly seen, decidedly affirmed, and experienced as such? World cannot remain world by itself; God can. That makes the whole difference. Therefore we must say that the seemingly innocuous and reasonable formula of the "worldly world" was, in a hidden way, misleading from the beginning.

A world which is clearly seen as related to God is more "world" than it is without that reference. On the one hand, it really remains the finite realm of things, the extension of man's existence, so to speak, without growing unexpectedly into divine fascination. On the other hand, it is more than just finite material man could use as he pleases: it is more than just a quarry than man would be allowed to exploit unscrupulously to build his city. We have learned, bitterly reminded by a mistreated world, that the biblical command "fill the earth and subdue it" (Gen 1:28) had not been said by a God who was to retire and leave the world to man, but by a God who had placed man and woman as his representatives so that they may act in *His* name. This means a different attitude towards world. Today we are beginning to appreciate it anew. Dealing with the world in the function of God's representatives means to use it for one's own needs, certainly, but also to affirm it and to preserve it as God's work—difficult as it may sometimes be to determine exactly what that means in a concrete situation.

Let us return to our statement: we have to experience God as God. Only then we can experience world as world. The logical sequence of it cannot be reversed. But what does it mean to experience God as God? We said before, in our second step, that God cannot be experienced outside the world. That is true. But He must be experienced *as God*. Otherwise God is dissolved into world-experience, even if we do not want it. There are indications enough today that it is precisely God as God who is sought in experience. Any one-dimensional formula of, or approach to, God-experience must be wrong. It means forgetting about God's transcendence, which is his being in and beyond the world.

To escape the suspicion that this is just playing with words I will point out three areas in which God can and must be experienced precisely *as God*.

The first one could be described as the experience of God as *the active subject of history,* of world history and of the history of the individual human being. Can God still be experienced as active in history? God as Governing Providence has been dethroned, as openly stated by Voltaire in the eighteenth century. Since then, man experiences all sorts of causes acting in and upon this world, but no longer God. One cannot help wondering whether that has been the right direction. Of course there are wrong avenues that must be avoided. God cannot be pictured as a being maintaining His place and role in history *among* many other factors. God does not have to "maintain" His role over against other causes. He is in all of them and above all. Yet we have not seen God *in* all causes if we are simply *exposed* to them all, and if the deep conviction has faded away that those innumerable events take their shape by God's might, and that in this way they represent the reality of God's government over the world and the individual. This dimension is open only to a certitude which is that of religious faith. That does by no means say that we look at the bewildering multiplicity of causes *as if* God were acting through them. It is rather the discovery of the real design in a multitude of incoherent causes. It is transition from the many unconnected sounds to a tune, a transition which is due to the ability of this ear to hear music. Nobody can say that this tune is not *in* that sequence of sounds. It is there but as something that is incomparably more than the sounds themselves. And yet, on the level of acoustics, there is nothing to be found but sounds.

The real experience of an acting and governing God would have an immense meaning for individual existence. Let us name just one dimension which is strangely forgotten today. It is the question whether the human individual can reach full human value only as a member of an endless human history, as a member of mankind progressing towards its fulfillment, or whether any human being achieves fulfillment in his or her own existence. Could the second aspect be maintained without that specific God-experience in our world-experience? I do not think it could. World would be necessarily experienced as mercilessly spread out in time and history, without having the non-worldly foothold which would allow the human persons in it to be more than relative, and more than practically expendable elements. But we cannot go into that within the limits of this presentation.

Another form in which God can and must be experienced as God is the experience that there is only one thing really necessary in human life. This reminds us of the New Testament, where Mary and Martha adopt a different attitude towards the necessary in life. But we also find it in the writings of someone who is certainly not interested in preserving a biblical axiom. Ludwig Feuerbach claimed that at this point of history we have to concentrate on the one thing which is really necessary. The hansom of history is small. One will not find a seat if one is late; by the same token, one can carry only the necessary and essential, that which is one's own, not however one's furniture. Similarly, but against a Christian background, Kierkegaard claimed that we had to make our decision, yes or no, about the one thing really necessary. This line of tradition could be traced back to Israel and her experience that she had been confronted with the question: do you accept the fact, in your confession and in your life, that there is only one God, Yahweh, and that there is no other? It seems that throughout history man had to face the question whether and how he acknowledged the fact that the endless multiplicity of things must be structured, must be subordinated to one principle, one idea or reality. This seems to have been the case especially at turning points in human history. It is certainly not too much to say that today we are at such a turning point. One of the most painful experiences can be the impression that the immense multitude of things—problems, tasks, opportunities, technical and cultural means, the bewildering and confusing richness of the modern world—that this immense multitude is crushing us to death. The search for the one necessary task seems to have been the hope for those times. The decisive question is whether the elected idea or reality can stand the test. At any rate, it is not difficult to see how human life is freed to be itself again by such a structuring of reality. World can then become world again, a truly rich possibility.

Finally, the third aspect of "God as God in our experience" should be mentioned. It is the reality of the Holy. Here too, the fact that the idea of the Holy has been banned from our consciousness can be indicative of its being needed today. This suspicion is confirmed when we watch different forms of the "secular Holy" sprout up everywhere.[17] What we just said about the Holy—that it had been banned from our consciousness—was not quite correct. The Holy has rather been dissolved into what we call world. Through Christ (a common theological interpretation goes) everything has become holy. By His incarnation all of reality has been sanctified. That is certainly true. The negative second part of this thought, which is then added, is less obvious and gives rise to doubt: since then, it is said, there is no experience of the Holy possible and distinct from what we could call profane reality. The truth of that statement is debatable, not only in view of the continuing search for the experience of the Holy, be it in modest and fragmented form. It is also debatable because the Holy ceases to be a possible experience if it is coextensive with all reality. It does not, however, seem to be possible for a human being to remain human for long without a centering and liberating experience of the Holy.

It might seem as if we had lost sight of our initial question. We had asked whether today there is still room for an unrestricted question about certitude. The question is, having surpassed the primitive stage of searching for absolute reliance upon divine powers and absolute truth, whether we would have to turn resolutely to creating and making a world which would then be safe and controlled by us, rather than relying upon some given stability and receiving it. We have seen, in the first answer to this question, that these hopes have a long history, and that the boundless faith in science and progress has at least been muted towards the end of the course of its two hundred year history. We added that those eschatological hopes had

---

[17] It might be helpful to think of the beginning of a pronounced and pervading secularism in the nineteenth century. As for that phenomenon in France, we see the surprising combination of a totally secular thinking with a deep concern about the religious center of human activity, a concern about the "secular holy" that is. Cf. n. 13, D. G. Charlton, *Secular Religions in France*.

their corresponding faiths upon which the scientific attitude did not reflect, and in fact could not.

The brief examination of the history of the faith underlying scientism showed us that those hopes were not fulfilled, not because of a defect in method but because of a profoundly changed attitude vis-à-vis the world. The experience of the world has so much changed as to alter totally the question of certitude and faith in God. These most recent discussions, still in full swing, have as their focus, whether they know it or not, the kind of relationship to reality the modern human mind has adopted. It is crucial for human certitude in what way reality displays itself to human experience: what range reality has—segments only or totality of being—and whether it is basically positive so that it can be affirmed and even loved, or negative, hostile and dangerous. If its "substance," so to speak, is experienced as positive, trust and surrender are possible; if it is forbidding and threatening, protecting and securing oneself is called for. Thus we have, for a while, abandoned ourselves to the question: what closeness to the "world" and what trust in it is accessible to us today. This question has led us to the answer that the modern era's search for certitude through experience forfeits its hopes if it clutches world-reality imperiously to satisfy its need for immediate reliability. World-reality reveals its closeness to man only if it is left in its founding relationship to God, a relationship which, as we have seen, must be realized in experience and as an attitude, and not only accepted theoretically. Only such a lived closeness to world-reality is the sphere in which trusting certitude can arise, which seems similar and yet is diametrically opposed to protecting security. A brief analysis of these two attitudes must be undertaken in this last part.

III. At the Crossroads of Self-Reassurance and Surrendering Certitude

Most of what should be said positively about the meaning and scope of certitude must be postponed to an appropriate discussion.[18] Here we can only mention some viewpoints which, in our view, must be respected if the question about a certitude which surpasses self-assurance is to be satisfactorily answered.

1. Security versus Certitude.

Security and certitude are not only concepts with some difference in meaning, but they are even opposites. That is not to say that there is no common source which feeds these attitudes. It is the common

---

[18] I have to refer the reader to my forthcoming book, *Power and Impotence of Certitude*.

drive for stability, reliability, and (described still more generally) for that permanence for which life by its own nature is striving. It is thus one of the most elementary strivings that unites the human concern for both security and certitude. But as soon as this vital drive emerges in the realm of personal decision, security and certitude settle at opposite ends. The concern for security is warding off dangers, and if experience of reality has come to see that reality primarily as antagonistic, warding off dangers will unwittingly transform itself into warding off reality. A rift opens between a person who is chiefly bent on securing certainty on the one side and the reality surrounding him or her on the other. As for the person's own situation, the pervading concern for security will concentrate his interest on protection and self-preservation. One cannot help but think of the characteristics of early childhood where those preoccupations with the self are appropriate in view of the child's helplessness. We are confronted with the curious fact that the allegedly mature attitude of humanity that has shed its dependency on superior powers and is relying more and more on constructing the world for its own fulfillment and security is in danger of being reduced to an early stage of human development due to its preoccupation with its own security. To be sure, concern for security has to play an important role in human life. Humanity could not survive if it, and every individual in it, did not protect itself against dangers. What is under discussion here is only the imperceptible substitution of security for certitude.

It might seem that there is no other way of reaching reliability and permanence of life than by protecting it. But we only have to formulate the question to become aware that an immense human potential has been blotted out if we reduce human life's quest for permanence and reliability to the concern about self-preservation in security. We know that human life is scorched by the predominance of self-secluding protection, and that on the other hand it grows, and "finds itself" by committing itself to others. It is not so clearly seen that life in its quest for *knowing* is equally dependent on commitment. It is known that interest in a subject is the condition of understanding it. Turning to a given reality is necessary to see and to discover it. Mostly, however, this is understood as an external prerequisite like the turning of a camera in the direction of its object to take a picture of it. Human understanding is different in that it presents an *internal* unity of turning to an object or a person, in interest or love, and the insight that accompanies it. Another person cannot be understood without a positive, open, and benevolent interest, or even love, spent on him or her. "Love is blind," yes, but only when it overrides the perception of reality. It is in that case, strictly speaking, no longer love in the proper sense but grasping, or even greedy, self-interest which shapes reality, the other person for instance, in a way to fit one's own needs. Love that deserves its name is clear-sighted and not blind. It is the inner opening force that allows a person to become aware of the encountered reality, be it a person or a thing.

It is not that a decision would *precede* human knowledge—a succession of willing and knowing which is all too human and means obscuring, instead of clarifying, reality. Nor does the decision, in all vital affairs, *follow* human knowledge. A subtle balance between the will to see and seeing itself is required without allowing either one to take clear priority. Only this delicate balance allows for knowing in all those cases in which the human person is directly affected. Tilting the balance to one side accounts for the known deformations of knowledge. We find wishful thinking, ideologies, dogmatism, fanaticism, if the balance is tipped in favor of wishes and decisions; we have extreme forms of rationalism, an abstractness which is alienated from reality, and a real blindness vis-à-vis decisive truths concerning human existence, if the volitional element in knowing is discarded, for whatever reasons that might be. These things, however, can no longer be pursued in this context.

We have come to mention decisive truths. Naturally, the intimate union between the human option concerning a problem or a reality and a corresponding knowledge takes place there where the human being is personally affected by those issues, and therefore must commit himself to them. The more we leave the realm of factual questions which do not directly interest the human being, and rise to issues which have a clear impact on human existence, the less human knowledge can be factual, purely theoretical information, and the more it can grow and unfold only in the symbiosis of will, interest, and even love.

That leaves us with a last step of our reflections, the question of what this means with regard to our knowledge of God that we call faith.

2. Certitude vis-à-vis a God Who is Both Within and Outside the World.

"There is no greater pestilence than security," Luther writes with regard to man's attitude towards God.[19] Why that emphatic, almost furious rejection? Security and certitude seem to be least reconcilable there where the human person is before God. The concern for security, so often necessary, and most of all when external threats have to be staved off, loses its sense when it is used with regard to God. First, it is so much out of place to try to secure oneself over

---

[19] Martin Luther, *Scholia zu Isaias* (1532-1534) (*Weimarer Ausgabe* vol. 25), p. 330f.

against a Being that, according to one's own confession, cannot be staved off, or prevented in any way from carrying out His purpose. This attitude would be a strange mixture of acknowledgement of God's power on the one hand, and of discounting it on the other hand. A God against Whom one could secure oneself would be a God of very limited power. We get a first idea why being bent on security before God is irreligious. It reduces God to the dimensions of *a* god, of a pagan deity, or of a demon. Nonetheless, it is a frequent attitude, and many fearful practices in Christian life, revealing more compulsive habits than religious decisions, will be born of that security-seeking spirit before God.

The same attitude can be described in still another way. If being concerned about one's own security means turning back upon oneself and shoving away whatever appears as threatening, then securing oneself vis-à-vis God is tantamount to loving oneself, and rejecting—in a real way hating—God. From this point of view, it becomes more understandable why the Old Testament prophets did not tire of warning Israel against securing herself by all sorts of machinations and alliances instead of relying on Yahweh. Isaiah's attempt to turn away Ahaz, king of Judah, from an alliance with Assyria when Judah was threatened by Syria and Ephraim (Isaiah 7:1-9) stands out as an example.

Looking at God's unique relationship to the world, we might be able to give another reason for the fact that the only appropriate attitude before God is a certitude which is not intent on securing but on surrendering. We have said that God is, so to speak, co-extensive with the world and at the same time totally different from it. He is present in everything and operative in any of the processes of nature and activities of humans and history. A different idea of God would simply be an artifact and an abstraction. It thus means that He is, in a way, within our reach. He is in that world we are acting in and upon, and, in a certain sense, He is identical with it. It could therefore seem that the totality of our life-work, which is building up a habitable house for ourselves and a human city for our society and for mankind, would include whatever we do in our relationship to God. It is a continual question whether and in what way we need God to build our city, and in what way we can obtain God's help, use His help, and maybe use Himself. Religious concern and striving are tempted to bring God into the endless net of our schemes and actions to make life safe and the earth habitable.

If God were simply seen as being in the world, this solution might appear the only acceptable one. A being that is not, in the proper sense, standing before us as another person distinct from everything else around him, inevitably slides into something which is the *context* of our life and world, "worldly world" in the manipulative sense. The human person too remains fully a person that cannot be manipulated only if that person does not dissolve into the world surrounding us to become the material for our life. In the fullest sense this holds true with God. He is accepted and revered as God only if He is seen and experienced as the One Who is totally other than the world. Such a God, however, deserves surrender on the part of man. That would mean that the ultimate human attitude before reality is characterized by loosening one's grip and giving oneself up. It is a resignation of commitment and love, a resignation that surpasses and takes away all self-affirmation and self-assurance, attitudes that ultimately fail, if not embedded in surrender. It is a resignation that is ultimate human fulfillment. Of course, a specific view of human existence is presupposed in this description, or seen differently, is the result of it. Stabilizing life, or, as we said, making it liveable by knowing about its beginning and end, in short, certitude, is ultimately not achieved by securing reassurance but by surrendering certitude. The profoundest reason for it is the human being's greatness.

A Response to Fr. Muschalek

by Rev. Joseph A. Bracken, S.J.

In his paper, George Muschalek has argued that the human quest for certainty cannot be satisfied by resolutely "creating and making a world which would then be safe and controlled by us,"[1] as John Dewey in his book *The Quest for Certainty,* would have us believe, but only by a new positive experience of the world as God's dwelling-place as well as our own. Hence, rather than vainly seek security against a basically hostile world through our own efforts, we should surrender the direction both of our individual lives and of our corporate world to God, understood as "the active subject of history."[2] With this hypothesis I am fundamentally in agreement. Accordingly, in my own comments this afternoon, I will offer, not so much a criticism of Muschalek's hypothesis, as rather an extension of it in a new direction not explicitly handled in his paper. I will try, namely, to set up a model or paradigm for the God-world relationship along the lines implied by Muschalek in his paper. Whether he himself will agree that this is indeed an appropriate model for his understanding of the God-world relationship will, of course, become evident only later in the general discussion.

I begin with the following quotation from Muschalek's paper: "World is disclosed fully in and through the at times even ecstatic experience of *God.* Because of God's being both beyond and in the world, human experience, as long as it is undistorted, will reach God and the world in one and the same act."[3] One is immediately reminded here of the efforts both of Karl Rahner and of Bernard Lonergan to ground human intentionality in God, understood as the implicit horizon of all acts of knowing and willing. God, in other words, is for Lonergan the object of the pure, unrestricted desire to know.[4] For Rahner, he is the ontological unity of being and knowing presupposed in all human questions about the meaning of existence.[5] All three thinkers then, Lonergan, Rahner and Muschalek, agree that human existence is somehow contained within or bounded by the even greater reality of God. As Muschalek remarks, "God is too great to be found only outside the world."[6]

---

[1] George Muschalek, "The Impasse of Ultimate Reassurance and Christian Certitude," p. 122.

[2] Ibid., p. 120.

[3] Ibid., p. 118.

[4] Bernard J. F. Lonergan, S.J., *Insight: A Study of Human Understanding,* 3d ed. (New York: Philosophical Library, 1970), pp. 634-77.

[5] Karl Rahner, *Hearers of the Word,* trans. Michael Richards (New York: Herder & Herder, 1969), pp. 31-68.

[6] Muschalek, p. 117.

As noted above, Muschalek also believes that God is the active subject of human history. This poses some initial problems as to the nature of our human co-operation with God in the day-to-day events of ordinary life; but these problems are, in my judgment, not insoluble. Muschalek himself explains the matter as follows. God works in and through the "bewildering multiplicity" of secondary causes in this world so as to bring them into a unified harmony, much as a composer combines disparate sounds into a melody.[7] This analogy has, of course, its limitations. Musical notes cannot think and act for themselves, as presumably human beings can. Hence the composer has a much easier job in ordering the different notes into a harmony than God has in protecting, on the one hand, the basic freedom of his rational creatures and yet, on the other hand, coordinating their separate activities into a broader plan of his own choosing. I myself believe that these speculative difficulties about the interrelation of human and divine causality cannot be satisfactorily solved, unless one accepts a much more radical hypothesis: namely, that God is the author of all my positive, i.e., non-sinful, actions just as much as I am, and conversely that through my actions I affect the inner life of God, or more specifically, the relations of the three divine persons to one another within the divine being. In other words, God's life and my life overlap, so that all of my life and indeed all of creation is contained within God, and part of God's life is exercised within me and the rest of creation.

Diagrammatically, this idea, together with the earlier notion that God is the horizon of all human intentionality, can be expressed in the following manner. Imagine three concentric circles, A, B & C, with a common center. Everything within B and C is contained

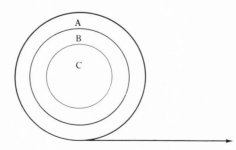

within A but not vice-versa. Likewise, everything within C is contained within B but not vice-versa. Hence the transcendence of the Trinity (circle A) to creation as a whole (circle B) and to each individual creature (circle C) is assured. Similarly, the relative

---

[7] Ibid., pp. 120-21.

transcendence of creation as a whole to the individual creature is assured. Yet, by reason of their common center, the three circles function as a single comprehensive reality. They are, in other words, very much like a wheel made up of three layers, all of which move together in a clockwise circular direction and at the same time move forward in a horizontal direction. What happens to me, and indeed to every other individual creature as represented by circle C, ultimately affects creation as a whole (circle B) and the three divine persons in their intratrinitarian life (circle C). The arrow on the diagram thus represents the unidirectionality of history, both human and divine.

What is presupposed here, of course, is a process understanding of reality, including the reality of God. That is, the three divine persons in their dynamic interrelation with one another within the Trinity constitute a strictly interpersonal process which is their nature or being as one God. Ceation is to be understood as a material reproduction of this divine life. Hence it too is a process or, better said, an interrelated series of processes, chief among them being the interpersonal process which is the human race. Finally, every individual creature but, above all, every human being is itself a dynamic unity of various organic and inorganic processes. Hence everything that exists (apart from God) is part of a process bigger than itself. Only the three divine persons in their relations with one another are a strictly subsistent reality, i.e., not part of a process greater than themselves as God.

Pantheism might well seem the logical consequence of such a worldview, were it not for the fact that process, not substance, is the key concept here. A process may be defined as a dynamic unity in totality of functioning parts or members. Within a process, accordingly, the parts retain their own integrity as parts, and yet they are subsumed into the higher dynamic unity which is the process.[8] A substance, on the other hand, as that which exists in itself, cannot become part of something else without ceasing to be a substance. If it becomes, for example, subordinated to a substance of a higher order, then it becomes an accident, ontologically speaking, in relation to the other substance. Precisely for this reason, it is important to describe the God-world relationship in terms of processes, not substances. For, if God is the one divine substance encompassing all of reality, as in Spinoza's *Ethics,* then pantheism is the inevitable consequence. All creatures are simply accidental modifications of God's infinite being. On the contrary, if God is by nature a process,

---

[8] Cf. Erwin Laszlo, *The Systems View of the World* (New York: Braziller, 1972), pp. 19-75. Laszlo's concept of "natural system" as a dynamic unity of autonomous (or quasi-autonomous) parts closely resembles what I mean by process.

not a substance, then the process which is the infinite being of God can comprehend the process of creation without danger of pantheism. For, as a functioning part in a larger process, creation remains itself even as it contributes to the larger reality which is the being of God. Similarly, you and I as individual entities can both be ourselves and yet be "parts" or members within the broader processes of creation and the triune life of God.

If more time were at my disposal, I would elaborate on the reality of sin, how this malfunctioning within human beings necessitates certain adjustments both within creation and even among the three divine persons in their intratrinitarian relations. But, since this is not possible, I hope that I have in any case made clear how a process understanding of reality such as I have suggested above can unexpectedly illuminate Muschalek's proposal for a new experience of God, self and the world in our present generation. For, if human beings see God, self and the world as realities which are indeed distinct, yet are dynamically related to one another within a single comprehensive process, then they should have no trouble feeling at home in the modern world.

A Response to Fr. Muschalek

by Rev. Ladislas Orsy, S.J.

Professor Muschalek speaks from an immensely rich background. To understand the meaning of his sentences, it is not enough to listen to what he says. It is necessary, also, to enter into the world from which he speaks. This is the world where our human nature, our heart, reason, and all, meets the luminous presence of God and responds with fear and joy.

The initial question of Professor Muschalek is prompted by Dewey: "Is man, who lives in a world of hazards, compelled to seek for security?" But his concluding answer, that the "ultimate human attitude before reality is characterized by loosening one's grip and giving oneself up," comes from elsewhere. It is reminiscent of the evangelical rule,

> For whoever would save his life will lose it, and whoever loses
> his life for my sake will find it (Mt 16:25).

Professor Muschalek acknowledges the legitimacy of the question. As we discover a world of hazards around us, we raise questions about security. But the ultimate answer is not in surrounding ourselves with protective barriers. Rather, it is in moving beyond hazards and protective devices into that luminous presence of God where surrender is what brings life.

Precisely because the content of the paper is so rich, I am compelled to comment on only some parts of it. Thus, I shall discourse on three themes present in it, and I shall expand somewhat beyond the thoughts of Professor Muschalek. However, I believe that I shall move in much the same direction, since I find that I am very much in agreement with the fundamental trend of his ideas. The three themes are: experience, experience of God in the world, and surrender to God. Briefly, I shall make three points: experience has always been a foundational value in the Christian tradition; the experience of God in the world is part of our life of faith; surrender to God is an ongoing process, and to be a Christian has always meant both insecurity on the road and certainty of a point of arrival.

I. The experience of a transcendental reality has always been, and remains, a foundational value in Christian life

Professor Muschalek's account of the role of experience in human life can be expanded by speaking specifically of the role of experience in Christian life. Indeed, the role of experience in proclaiming and accepting the Christian mysteries has been stressed right from the beginning, in the earliest Christian literature. I can do no more here than to point to some well-known events and teachings that bear out, with overwhelming force, the truth of this view.

Christianity was born from the experience of the Risen One. That event was so new and stupendous that, to this day, our mind looks at the risen Christ and raises question after question about him; about the empty tomb, and the empty sky after he was taken away from his disciples. But, besides the resurrection, another event took place. The disciples were transformed by the experience. They received a new capacity to see; they discovered a new presence to contemplate; they became aware of a new power to speak—a transforming experience, if ever there was one!

The early Christian literature speaks, certainly, of the external events of the life of Jesus as they were preserved in the memory of the community. They speak with some down-to-earth freshness about the life of the growing communities. Experience is always there. In reality, all of the Scriptures should be quoted, but let me confine myself to two specific documents.

The letter of Paul to the Romans is the first. I simply suggest that you read it from the solemn greeting in the beginning to the end of chapter eight. Seemingly, it is a discussion about the Law. In reality, it is the proclamation of a new life built on experience, on the experience of the Spirit of God:

> . . . it is the Spirit himself bearing witness with our spirit that we are children of God (Rm 8:16).

The impact of this experience is that the hazards of this life count for little or nothing when compared to the certainty that is in the heart of Christians:

> For I am sure that neither death, nor life, nor angels, nor principalities, nor things present, nor things to come, nor powers, nor height, nor depth, nor anything else in all creation, will be able to separate us from the love of God in Christ Jesus our Lord (Rm 8:38-39).

Another document, a later one, is the first letter of John. Experience is indeed a foundational value there. Its first paragraph is nothing else than a recounting of an experience that came to the disciples in every way that man can experience something, and it overwhelmed them:

> That which was from the beginning, which we have heard, which we have seen with our eyes, which we have looked upon and touched with our hands, concerning the word of life—the life was made manifest and we saw it, and testify to it, and proclaim to you the eternal life which was with the Father and was

made manifest to us—that which we have seen and heard we proclaim also to you, so that you may have fellowship with us; and our fellowship is with the Father and with his Son Jesus Christ. And we are writing this that our joy may be complete (Jn 1:1-4).

The text speaks of hearing, seeing, looking, touching—all sense perceptions. But, beyond them, it refers also to a deeper spiritual experience of an ineffable presence that was made manifest to the disciples, and that now must be proclaimed.

If we turn to the great personalities of Christian history, we find that the wellspring of their lives and actions, of their thoughts and words, was in a mysterious, lasting encounter with God. The field for investigation would be immense. We can do no more here than to offer some pointers. Those who are familiar with Christian literature through the centuries will, no doubt, know immediately what we are hinting at.

Underlying the instructions that Ignatius of Antioch gave to the churches of Asia Minor, and prompting his plea to the Church of Rome, was the experience of God the Father who powerfully upheld him so that he could be the wheat of God destined to become the pure bread of Christ. The *Confessions* of Saint Augustine are a powerful monument to the foundational value of experience in Christian life; indeed, from that experience, much of the articulation of Augustinian theology was born. Bernard of Clairvaux moved the Christian world in so many ways, but virtually every piece that he wrote, every sermon that he uttered, testified that he was moved by an experience much more than by conceptual considerations. Francis of Assisi was not a learned man. He did not leave behind monumental works in theology. Yet, from the time of his first conversion, he lived and acted as someone fascinated by an ever-present internal vision. Thomas Aquinas left behind a monumental creation in theological science; yet, at one point late in his life, he put down his pen because his experience of the ineffable was so overwhelming that all conceptual work appeared to be straw in comparison to it. Then, there is Teresa of Avila, recent Doctor of the Church, whose works are no more and no less than delightful reports of her experience of God. John of the Cross offers, in his prose, a cool-headed, systematic, scholastic explanation of the same experience; but in his poems, he celebrates the same experience with the rhythm of words which speak of fiery symbols.

And we could go on and on. We omitted many more than we named. Yet, at this point, a caution should be sounded. While we quote mystics, we should stress that Christians always believed that internal experience is the foundation of external professions of faith—no one can say that Jesus is Lord without the experienced testimony of the Spirit. This experience is subtle and simple. It is not the privilege of a few, but rather, the gift of many.

II. The experience of God in the world is part of our life of faith

When Professor Muschalek speaks of the experience of God in the world, he points to our experience of the contingency of this created universe. Contingency indicates to our intelligence an insufficiency. The whole creation is unable to account for itself. It is so fragile and limited in its existence that, to grasp its meaning, we must go beyond it. Thus, the experience of the contingency of this world leads to a perception of a Being who knows no frailty, no beginning and no end. Thus, we perceive God through the world, in the world.

Analogies to illustrate our encounter with God in the world can be found, imperfect as they must remain. A person can sit on the bank of a river, delight in the sight of its majestic flow, and yet he can perceive, in the very same act, that the river cannot account for its own existence. There must be a source somewhere; there the waters break to the surface. There must be an ocean somewhere; there the river terminates its course. In the contingency of the river, the necessity of a source and an outlet is perceived.

Or, let us take a person who contemplates that masterpiece of Michelangelo, the statue of Moses. The inert marble had become so powerfully alive through the work of the master that, according to the legend, when he was ready, Michelangelo hit the statue with a hammer and cried at it, ''Speak.'' Yet, that Moses did not speak. If we look at it, after the first overwhelming impression, we know there is no life in it, and then our intuition goes beyond the marble, which is contingent, and we think of the artist who gave life to it. The perception of the contingency of a marble statue leads to the knowledge of a creative artist.

A dialectical process is always there. Fragility postulates strength. Limits in time and space postulate eternity and immensity. Thus, in the contingency of this world, the necessity of a living God is perceived. The same caution we sounded a little while ago should be noted again. The striking analogies we use should not deter our attention from the fact that the perception of God in the world is the privilege of men and women of good will seeking the light to guide them. In a more restful age than ours, it may have been easier for the farmer or the wanderer to discover God in this created world. Granted that the world has changed, as long as there are stars in the sky and flowers on the earth, it should be, and is, possible for man to pause and perceive both the fragility of this created world and the permanence of the One who holds it all in existence.

III. Surrender to God is an ongoing process; to be a Christian has always meant both insecurity on the road and certainty of the point of arrival

Professor Muschalek concludes his paper in striking paradoxes: "It is resignation that is ultimate human fulfillment." Also, "certitude is ultimately not achieved by securing reassurance but by surrendering certitude." Then, he concludes, "the profoundest reason for it [for fulfillment in resignation] is the human being's greatness." That is, in the greatness of one's being is the reason for such paradoxical existence. But, where precisely is this greatness to be found in a human being?

It must be in the human mind, in that restless mind that has the capacity to move from the knowledge of one small thing to that of another, and yet can never be satisfied. It can never rest in such an ongoing, but fragmented, process. Beyond all things and all details, it reaches out restlessly for what cannot be circumscribed by any definition, what knows no limits. The greatness of a human being is in the fact that even when he looks at finite objects, his mind is seeking an infinite Being.

Greatness is found in the heart of man that inspires him to reach out for what is good, for what appears to bring happiness. And yet, again, his heart cannot rest in any one object, cannot find full satisfaction in values that succeed each other rapidly and exist only in time and space. No matter how intensely we taste the goodness of this creation, our heart is longing for uncreated goodness.

There is the greatness of man. Not only is he open to receive all that is true, but he is moved by a restless desire to find what is Truth. He is not only open to what is good, but he is moved constantly by a longing for goodness itself.

Surrender means, then, to give in to our deepest longing, to anchor ourselves in the source of our being, which is also the goal of our pilgrimage through this life. Man's greatness consists in the fact that he has an innate capacity to transcend himself.

But this act of transcending ourselves takes place in the depth of our beings. While it may delight our mind, while it may nourish our heart as nothing else can, much of our humanity, in the very same act, can remain without tangible security or logically-grounded certainty.

The result is, then, a living paradox right in a human being. As he surrenders, he attaches himself to an infinite Being. In the very same movement, he detaches himself from the assurance of solid ground under his feet and the convincing certainty of a logical operation. Thus, his life becomes an existing paradox. He is fulfilled, and he lives in resignation. He experiences certainty in clinging to the One-who-is, and he experiences lack of assurance in his humanity arising from the fact that he is not clinging to fractional truth, to morsels of goodness.

The pattern we describe is really the pattern of the beatitudes. Each of them is saying forcefully that it is possible for a human being to experience fulfillment in the midst of frustration; there can be blessedness in emptiness. Thus, different as the eight beatitudes can be, they are variations on the same theme. They speak of the greatness of the human being who is blessed many times over, no matter what his miseries are.

We began with a pertinent philosophical question: "Is man, who lives in a world of hazards, compelled to seek for security?" We conclude by affirming that man can see beyond all hazards, can reach beyond all dangers, into a world where his mind and heart come to rest in the One-who-is.

"The Devout Christian of the Future Will . . . be a 'Mystic'."[1] Mysticism and Karl Rahner's Theology

by Rev. Harvey Egan, S.J.

Prophesying that Western theology in the twenty-first century will center upon the dialogue with the great religions of the East, William Johnston, S.J., a noted scholar of mysticism, urges that Western theology be rethought in the light of mystical experience so that mysticism can be the very heart of the theology of the future.[2] I would maintain, however, that the mystical theology of the future has already had an auspicious beginning because of the theological method and explicit mystical theology of Karl Rahner. He stands, moreover, as one of the first theologians of this century to take seriously the mystics and their writings as valid *theological* sources.

One of his very early writings focuses upon the mystical riches of the Fathers and stresses the importance of critical reflection in the areas of asceticism and mysticism.[3] His detailed work on the "spiritual senses" which immersed him deeply in the mystical doctrine of Origen and Bonaventure,[4] his interest in the mystical side of Thomas Aquinas,[5] his appreciation of John of the Cross,[6] Teresa of Avila,[7] and Ignatius of Loyola, his detailed work on the sacrament of penance,[8] and, finally, his understanding of the empirical studies on

---

[1] Karl Rahner, *Theological Investigations* 7, trans. David Bourke (New York: Herder and Herder, 1971): 15.

[2] William Johnston, S.J., *The Inner Eye of Love* (New York: Harper and Row, 1978), pp. 9-10. See also pp. 53f.

[3] See Karl Rahner and M. Viller, *Aszese und Mystik in der Väterzeit* (Freiburg i. Br.: Herder, 1939).

[4] Karl Rahner, "Die 'geistlichen Sinne' nach Origenes," and "Die Lehre von den 'geistlichen Sinnen' im Mittelalter," *Schriften zur Theologie* 12 (Zürich-Einsiedeln-Köln: Benziger, 1975): 111-72.

[5] Rahner, "Thomas Aquinas," *Everyday Faith,* trans. W. J. O'Hara (New York: Herder and Herder, 1968), pp. 185-90.

[6] See Rahner, "Mystische Erfahrung und mystische Theologie," *Schriften zur Theologie* 12:428 esp. See n. 7 below.

[7] Rahner "Teresa of Avila: Doctor of the Church," *Opportunities for Faith,* trans. E. Quinn (New York: Seabury, 1970), pp. 123-26.

[8] On Ignatius, see esp. Rahner, "The Logic of Concrete Individual Knowledge in Ignatius Loyola," *The Dynamic Element in the Church,* trans. W. J. O'Hara (New York: Herder and Herder, 1964), pp. 84-169; "The Ignatian Mysticism of Joy in the World," Theological Investigations 3:277-93; "Erfahrung des Geistes und existentielle Entscheidung," Schriften zur Theologie 12:41-53; "Einige Bemerkungen zu einer neuen Aufgabe der Fundamentaltheologie," *Schriften zur Theologie* 12:198-211; *Spiritual Exercises,* trans. K. Baker (New York: Herder and Herder, 1965). On penance, see Rahner, *Schriften zur Theologie* 11. *Frühe Bussgeschichte in Einzeluntersuchungen* (Zürich-Einsiedeln-Köln: Benziger, 1973).

mysticism of Carl Albrecht, a respected German doctor and psychologist,[9] have had a tremendous impact on Rahner's own theology.

For example, Rahner insists that Teresa of Avila does theology because "she teaches something about mysticism."[10] Both Teresa and John of the Cross, moreover, remain irreplaceable sources of theology because of the depth and clarity of their experiences of God which are paradigmatic of what we ought to discover in ourselves. These mystics also illustrate what contemporary theology should provide: initiation into the experience of our basic orientation to Mystery.[11] In fact, as this article will emphasize, practically all of Rahner's theology contains a mystagogical moment, a moment which attempts to evoke, awaken, purify, and deepen every person's core experience of being referred to loving, holy Mystery.

I. Rahner's Theology: A Mystical Theology

Although most commentators correctly emphasize the intellectual influence of Thomas Aquinas, Maréchal, Kant, Hegel, and Heidegger upon Rahner, most commentators have missed his real secret. His theology is intrinsically an authentic *mystical* theology which has resulted not only from his awesome mastery of the above, not only from his mastery of the mystical doctrine of the early Fathers of the Church, Thomas Aquinas, Bonaventure, Teresa of Avila, John of the Cross, Ignatius of Loyola, etc., but also from his own profound religious experiences based on the *Spiritual Exercises* of Ignatius of Loyola. He views these *Exercises,* moreover, as a "literature of piety which forestalls theological reflection, which is more fundamentally spontaneous than the latter, wiser and more experienced than the wisdom of the learned . . . a creative prototype . . . [and] a subject of tomorrow's theology."[12]

Insisting upon "the importance of living piety for academic theology,"[13] Rahner maintains that "his own theology proceeded from the experience of the Ignatian *Exercises* and was actually stamped in the light of the thought of such activity of the Spirit."[14] These *Exercises* imparted to Rahner one of the main pillars of his

---

[9] Rahner, "Mystische Erfahrung und mystische Theologie," *Schriften zur Theologie* 12:428-54. This article originally appeared as the Foreword to Carl Albrecht's *Das Mystische Wort. Erleben und Sprechen in Versekenheit,* dargest. und hrsg. von H. A. Fischer-Barnicol (Mainz: 1974).

[10] Rahner, *Opportunities for Faith,* p. 123.

[11] Ibid., pp. 125-26. See also *Theological Investigations* 7:14-15.

[12] Rahner, *The Dynamic Element in the Church,* pp. 85-87.

[13] Rahner, *Schriften zur Theologie* 12:358 [my translation].

[14] Ibid., p. 14 [my translation].

thought: whether or not we are explicitly and directly conscious of it, whether or not we open ourselves to it, our whole life is orientated to a loving, forgiving Mystery which is the basis of our existence. God is the loving, holy Mystery whose historical Self-communication has reached its high-point in Jesus Christ and become radically interior through the sending of the Holy Spirit. The *Exercises* have plunged Rahner into the Mystery of the ever-greater God, God-*above*-us, the Father, a God "beyond even the world of experience of the mystic"[15]; into the historical Revelation of Mystery, God-*with*-us, the Son; into the Intimacy of Mystery, God-*in*-us, the Holy Spirit.

Furthermore, this God communicates Himself in such a way that His specific Will for the individual can be discovered. Hence, our deepest, fundamental experience, what haunts the very roots of our being, is a God who remains Mystery, is the Word of Revelation to our spirits, and the Love which embraces us in utter intimacy.

What Rahner says about the Ignatian formula, "Finding God in all things," can also be said about almost all of his theology: "It is, in fact, the attempt of the mystic to translate his experience for others and make them share in his grace."[16] Taking his cue from Ignatius' conviction that the one making the *Exercises* will experience the immediacy of God's Self-communication,[17] Rahner's theological point of departure roots itself solidly in his own personal experience of God's Self-communication.[18] Unlike those commentators[19] who argue that Rahner's pious and spiritual writings are the overflow or application of his speculative theology, I contend that his philosophical and theological writings have been radically influenced by his own Ignatian religious experiences. His philosophy and theology, moreover, attempt to explicate what is intrinsic in these very experiences.

If philosophy for Rahner "is properly speaking a theology that has not yet arrived at the fulness of its own nature,"[20] and if philosophy must deal with "the depth of the human abyss . . . already . . . opened by God's grace and which stretches into the depths of God

---

[15] Rahner, *Theological Investigations* 3, trans. Karl-H. and Boniface Kruger (Baltimore: Helicon, 1967): 291.

[16] Rahner, *The Dynamic Element in the Church,* p. 155.

[17] St. Ignatius of Loyola, *The Spiritual Exercises,* trans. A. Mottola (Garden City: Doubleday, 1964). #15.

[18] See Rahner, *Foundations of Christian Faith* (New York: Seabury, 1978), trans. William Dych, S.J. Note how often Rahner appeals to transcendental experience throughout this volume.

[19] For example, Hans Urs von Balthasar's review of Rahner's *Geist in Welt, Zeitschrift für Katholische Theologie* 63 (1939): 378.

[20] Rahner, *Theological Investigations* 13, trans. David Bourke (New York: Seabury, 1975): 65.

himself,''[21] and if theology is living faith seeking reason, for "faith itself activates the critical and speculative faculties of the believer,''[22] then the roots of his philosophical and theological enterprise are permeated with a mystical eros. What Rahner says about Thomas Aquinas can also be said of his own theology: "Thomas' theology is his spiritual life and his spiritual life is his theology.''[23] The power, authenticity, and attractiveness of so much of Rahnerian theology issues from the theological transposition of his own Ignatian experiences. I definitely agree with Johannes B. Metz that Rahner's theology is "a type of existential biography . . . a mystical biography of religious experience, of the history of a life before the veiled face of God, in the doxology of the faith.''[24]

With this in mind, perhaps it becomes easier to understand why Rahner demands that theology in part must be a reduction into Mystery, maieutic, a mystagogy into the ultimate experience of the Spirit in the person's life.[25] He attempts to evoke, to awaken, to deepen, and to strengthen the basic experience of God's Self-communication which haunts the core of every person, at least as an offer.[26] Because of this mystagogical concentration, his theology begins and ends in a mystical moment: the *experience* of the lived, root unity of self-possessing knowledge and love penetrated by God's Self-communication.

Because Rahner understands the person as reference to Mystery, he can ask: "Is theology in this case anything more than an *anthropologia negativa,* i.e., the experience that man continually loses track of himself in the uncomprehended and intractable mystery?[27] He begins, therefore, with the human subject as experiencing divine mystery. Neither the human alone nor the divine alone suffices. The foundational reality in Rahnerian theology is the human person as reference to Mystery, the experience of which has foundational theological significance. Theology begins, therefore, with the theocentric depths of human experience, for theology is the work of the theologian as a human subject explicating his encounter with the ever-present God of love.

---

[21] Rahner, *Theological Investigations* 6, trans. Karl-H. and Boniface Kruger (Baltimore: Helicon, 1969): 78.

[22] Rahner, *Theological Investigations* 7:57.

[23] Rahner, *Everyday Faith,* p. 188.

[24] Johannes B. Metz, "Karl Rahner—ein theologisches Leben," *Stimmen der Zeit* (May 1974): 305-14.

[25] Rahner, *Schriften zur Theologie* 12:594.

[26] See Rahner "Reflections on Methodology in Theology," *Theological Investigations* 11, trans. David Bourke (New York: Seabury, 1974): 68-114.

[27] Rahner, *Theological Investigations* 9, trans. Graham Harrison (New York: Herder and Herder, 1972): 193-94.

It is not an exaggeration to say, moreover, that Rahner theologizes by critically reflecting upon the pressure points of his own spirit, a spirit filled with living Christian faith and an enormous empathy for the problems of the contemporary person. As he says: "In investigating these theoretical questions the starting point must be precisely *those* factors with which life confronts the concrete individual in his own personal and unique situation, and in the particular development of his own ideas."[28]

Although he theologizes from inside his own living faith, one should not overlook its radically *ecclesial* dimension. He insists that:

> Theology is only of interest when it constitutes a process of reflection . . . upon the faith of a Church which is actually using this faith as the basis of its activities . . . it is obviously part of any sound theological method to take as its starting-point the average and representative awareness of faith to be found in the Church as it exists in the concrete.[29]

Rahner's mastery of the Church's tradition has been reinforced by his experiences of the "authentic" in this tradition. Ignatius had a mystical memory by which he recalled previous mystical favors to taste them again and again; Rahner, too, has received through his studies and the *Spiritual Exercises* an *experiential* as well as an academic appreciation of the Church's past and present. His Ignatian religious experiences and his pastoral activities have sensitized him to the Church's and the contemporary person's needs. Aware of the authentic in the Church's past, sensitive to the catechism of the heart of the contemporary person, Rahner theologizes from within his own contemporary, ecclesial faith, but in a way which enables the contemporary person to see the truths of the faith in conjunction with his own experience and self-understanding. His, therefore, is a prophetic theology, a theology which "forth-tells." Mystically sensitive to both the past and the present, his theology speaks out of a mystically and critically assimilated past and present to address the contemporary person where he is in need. His theology explains the Church to the contemporary person and the contemporary person to the Church, because Rahner's living faith includes both, a typically Ignatian faith which loves both the Church and the world in God.

Convinced of the original, unreflected, yet lived justification of the faith,[30] Rahner's theological method explicates what we are prior to conceptualization. Because we live the faith before we reflect upon

---

[28] Rahner, *Theological Investigations* 7:57.

[29] Rahner, *Theological Investigations* 11:81.

[30] Rahner, *Foundations,* pp. 8-10.

it, and because this faith contains an element of "mysticism as the experience of grace,"[31] theological concepts explicate something *already* lived, experienced, and known because of God's universal Self-communication. And since "man always experiences more of himself at the non-thematic and non-reflexive levels in the ultimate and fundamental living of his life than he knows about himself by reflecting about himself . . . ,"[32] Rahner often emphasizes the unity-in-difference which exists between original Christian self-possession and reflection. Today's theology, therefore, should be a "living and courageous mystagogy"[33] into the core experience of grace, a theology which can heal the breach between a living piety and abstract theology. Theology must plunge into its deepest source, its slender root, its origin before it burgeons into the various branches of knowledge. It must explore the fine point of the person's spirit which has been lovingly drawn, illuminated, and embraced by Mystery. It must center upon the boundary between the human person and loving Mystery.

A colleague recently asked me how Rahner's theological method differed from that of most Catholic and Protestant theologians for whom faith plays a foundational role. Although I do not dispute that most theologians are men of faith, I do dispute that their theology results from an indirect, or transcendental reflection[34] on their own religious tradition in the light of *their own religious experiences* of Mystery and the "authentic" in that tradition. Most theologians do theology within an *academic* tradition which *presupposes* faith. Rahner's theology, on the other hand, begins from his own religious experience by which he critically evaluates the community's faith consciousness and by which he allows the community's faith experiences to be a critique of his own. His theology begins and ends in prayer, without the critical moment of reflection being swallowed up in some type of fuzzy mysticism. His own, yet deeply ecclesial, religious experiences are the vital element of his "first level reflection" as carried out in his excellent *Foundations of Christian Faith,*[35] and perhaps the point wherein his method is open to contemporary "narrative theology."[36]

---

[31] Rahner, "Mysticism," *Encyclopedia of Theology* (New York: Seabury, 1975), p. 1010.

[32] Rahner, *Theological Investigations* 13:123.

[33] Rahner, *Schriften zur Theologie* 12:100.

[34] See Rahner, "Transcendental Theology," *Encyclopedia of Theology,* pp. 1748-51.

[35] See n. 18 above.

[36] Klaus Fischer, *Der Mensch als Geheimnis* (Freiburg i. Br.: Herder, 1974), p. 405, "Ein Brief von P. Karl Rahner."

II. Ignatian Themes

Reflecting perhaps Ignatius' own interior tasting of God's immediate Self-communication and of the essentials of salvation history,[37]
Rahner's philosophy and theology center upon the human person as
reference both to Mystery and to history. Ignatius frequently directs
the exercitant throughout the *Exercises* to meditate or contemplate
the various mysteries of salvation history and to reflect upon himself
in their light. In a parallel fashion, Rahner employs a *mystical*
theological anthropology by splashing the truths of salvation history
against the mystical horizon of God's transcendental Self-
communication. Precisely because God creates in order to give
Himself, there is a correspondence between the person's nature and
this transcendental and historical Self-communication, a communication directed at the one perfect totality of man. Because of
the human person's historical nature, he must turn to salvation
history in view of its salvific character.

Rahner's method attempts to uncover the anthropocentric
anchoring to any truth of salvation history. There is, in this view, a
correlation between salvation history and the person's experience of
himself, a mystical correlation which transcends merely logical
deductions or explications. He explicates why the person must by his
very nature necessarily turn to the various mysteries of salvation
history. He explicates the "necessary" in this history and the
person-as-subject aspect of any saving truth. God's transcendental
and historical Self-communication answer the one ultimate question
which is lived by the graced, historical person. This means that the
various mysteries of salvation history are the multiple aspects of the
one answer given by Mystery making history to what the human
person means. The various mysteries and dogmas of the faith provide a variety of keys which unlock the various levels of the one
mystery of the human person. Because salvation history is radically
anthropocentric, i.e., aimed at the one perfect totality of the human
person, one can experience this history's mystical resonance with
something intrinsic to the human person.

By awakening the inner word from the person's transcendental
reference to Mystery through the outer word of saving history,
Rahner's method shows why the outer word serves this function,
explicates how the inner word is the horizon of meaning of the outer
word, and explicates their mutual relationship. Unless the inner
word is awakened and brought to itself through the outer word, it
cannot realize itself. Unless the outer word is seen and experienced
against the horizon of the inner word, it remains mere *information*,

---

[37] See esp. Ignatius, *Spiritual Exercises,* #2 and #15.

not *revelation*. Starting from graced human nature and using revelation to illuminate human experience, Rahner seeks to open the person to the experience of his own deepest mystery. Welding together the person's spirit/matter, individual/social, reference-to-Mystery/reference-to-history aspects, Rahner's mystical theological anthropology functions as a mystical depth psychology by explicating, thematizing, strengthening, and deepening the ultimate horizon of all meaning and experience. In short, Rahner has experienced that what concerns the entire person in his salvation, the existential significance of the facts of salvation history, cannot be made intelligible without a mystical transcendental theology. The truths of salvation history must be placed against the mystical, transcendental horizon of meaning.

This mystical theological anthropology also utilizes Ignatius' well-known methods of Election.[38] In the most important method for Rahner's purposes, the Ignatian exercitant finds God's individual will for him through the experience of congruence or incongruence between the particular object of choice and his primordial experience of grace as openness to Mystery.[39] Skilfully applying this categorical/supernaturally-elevated transcendental experience to theology, Rahner stresses that the contents of revelation must be grasped in conjunction with the fact of revelation, and vice versa. This points to a mystical hinge between the experience of revelation and its content. His mystical theological anthropology involves, therefore, the reciprocal movement from the experience of faith to the foundation of the faith, and vice versa.[40] As he says, "such a foundation of the faith has an 'inner' side and an 'outer' side; it is at the same time rational and pneumatic."[41] His theological method contains, therefore, both a rational and a mystical moment. These two moments are reciprocally related. But it is only the mystical moment which can close the gap between "the grounds for the credibility of Christian revelation and the concrete decision of faith."[42] Perhaps this explains why his theology must not only be studied, but also *prayed*. Perhaps this explains why the theologian himself must undergo a *conversion* in his own intellectual, moral, and religious life, if his theology is to advance.

---

[38] See esp. Ignatius, *Spiritual Exercises*, #175-89; Harvey D. Egan, S.J., *The Spiritual Exercises and the Ignatian Mystical Horizon* (St. Louis: The Institute of Jesuit Sources, 1976), esp. chapter 6.

[39] Rahner, *The Dynamic Element in the Church*, pp. 156ff.; Harvey Egan, *The Spiritual Exercises and the Ignatian Mystical Horizon*, pp. 108-09, 143-46.

[40] Rahner, *Schriften zur Theologie* 12:28-31.

[41] Rahner, *Schriften zur Theologie* 12:18 [my translation].

[42] Rahner, *Schriften zur Theologie* 12:208 [my translation].

Ignatius experienced on the banks of the river Cardoner a mystical "architechtonic" grasping of the truths of the faith. Rahner has also experienced to some degree that "there *is* an *experience* of grace, and this is the real, fundamental reality of Christianity itself."[43] The poets, saints, and those whose lives manifest the full meaning of existence as a whole have long fascinated him.[44] Because he has prayerfully tasted that Christianity is something total and single which can only be accepted or denied in its totality, what he says about Thomas Aquinas applies to his own thought: "[Thomas] always thinks on the basis of the whole and in relation to the whole."[45] Rahner's architechtonic appreciation instinctively leads him to theologize from the core of Christianity to explicate it as the "*one single* aperture which leads out of all the individual truths (and even errors) into *the* truth which is the unique incomprehensibility of God."[46] This no doubt clarifies his concern for "short formulas of the faith"[47] and his recent *Foundations of Christian Faith* which intends "to express the whole of Christianity and to give an honest account of it on a 'first level of reflection'."[48] Much of his theology is, therefore, architechtonic, a reduction into Mystery, not really unscientific, for "the unscientific nature of this different kind of discipline which we are striving for lies in the object, not in the subject and his method."[49]

Rahner's mystical theological anthropology cannot be reduced to a tract or to some regional element of his thought. The mystical remains not only at the heart of his theological method, but also of the theological content he explicates. For example, he frequently focuses upon the trinitarian structure of human existence, that the person is experientially referred to the ever-greater God who has definitively appeared in history and who graces his inmost center as Mystery, Revelation, and Love.[50] Then, too, we are experientially referred to the historical Jesus Christ because our entire being lives a "seeking Christology,"[51] for Christology is anthropology's absolute fulfillment. Jesus Christ is the historical person in whom we experience that the infinite question which we are has been definitively and irrevocably answered by loving Mystery. He is the paradigm of

---

[43] Rahner, *Theological Investigations* 9:41.

[44] Rahner, *Theological Investigations* 11:160.

[45] Rahner, *Everyday Faith*, p. 188.

[46] Rahner, *Theological Investigations* 7:61.

[47] Rahner, *Theological Investigations* 9:117-26; *Theological Investigations* 11:230-44.

[48] Rahner, *Foundations*, p. xii.

[49] Ibid., p. 10.

[50] Rahner, *Schriften zur Theologie* 12:301.

[51] Rahner, *Foundations*, pp. 206-12; *Schriften zur Theologie* 12:277-79.

mysticism's radical meaning: total self-surrender to loving Mystery so that one no longer belongs to self but to God. It is within *that* context that Rahner explicates the various mysteries of the one Mystery making history, a history towards which we must necessarily turn.[52]

The experience that the human person is of his essence he who must lose himself in loving Mystery, that his deepest essence is "the adoring acceptance of the sway of the mystery in dedicated love,"[53] actually grounds Rahner's mystical anthropology. The experience of the Church as those gathered in loving intersubjectivity to live and profess in a social-historical way the Christian good news, as "the awakening and interpretation of the most interior aspect in the human person, of the ultimate depth of his existence,"[54] also grounds Rahner's ecclesiology. Finally, the experience of true love of God, neighbor, and self remains intrinsically and mystically linked and provides one of the best short formulas of the faith.[55]

III. Towards the Meaning of the Word "Mystical"

Dissatisfied with the traditional mystical theology and disappointed by the contemporary lack of theological interest in mystical questions,[56] Rahner does offer, at first glance, a traditional view of mysticism. He states that the term "mysticism" can mean both "an experience, the interior meeting and union of a man with the divine infinity that sustains him and all other being"[57] and "the attempt to give a systematic exposition of this experience, or reflexion upon it (hence a scientific 'discipline')."[58] He insists, moreover, that "the mystic experiences the influence from the Absolute as that which is most inward in his own soul."[59] Mystical experience involves the "submerging of the soul in its source . . . and . . . is always experienced as a gift."[60] Rahner also accepts, at least provisionally,

---

[52] See esp. Rahner, "Remarks on the Importance of the History of Jesus for Catholic Dogmatics," *Theological Investigations* 13:201-12; "Mysteries of the life of Jesus," *Theological Investigations* 7:121-201.

[53] Rahner, *Theological Investigations* 4, trans. Kevin Smith (Baltimore: Helicon, 1966): 61.

[54] Rahner, *Schriften zur Theologie* 12:403.

[55] See esp. Rahner, "Experience of Self and Experience of God," *Theological Investigations* 13:122-32; "Reflections on the Unity of the Love of Neighbour and the Love of God," *Theological Investigations* 6:231-49.

[56] Rahner, "Mystische Erfahrung und mystische Theologie," *Schriften zur Theologie* 12: esp. 429.

[57] Rahner, "Mysticism," *Theological Dictionary*, trans. R. Strachan (New York: Herder and Herder, 1965), p. 301.

[58] Ibid., p. 301.

[59] Ibid., p. 302.

[60] Ibid., pp. 301-02.

"infused contemplation, in which God gratuitously makes himself known to the individual"[61] as the defined essence of mysticism.

But in addition to this traditional and obvious use of the term "mysticism," Rahner also creatively notes that:

> In every human being . . . there is something like an anonymous, unthematic, perhaps repressed, basic experience of being orientated to God, which is constitutive of man in his concrete make-up (of nature and grace), which can be repressed but not destroyed, which is "mystical" or (if you prefer a more cautious terminology) has its climax in what the older teachers called infused contemplation.[62]

Because of God's universal Self-communication, a Self-communication experienced at least as an offer, man is *mystical* man. The very heart of mysticism, experienced reference to Mystery, can be found in every person's primordial, albeit often repressed or anonymous, experience of God. To be sure, special depth, power, and purity of this experience characterize the mystic in the strict sense, but the lower levels of this experience belong to everyone.[63] Strictly speaking, every person is at least an anonymous mystic, and in this sense Rahner seems to agree with Origen who did not definitively separate even minimal experiences of God from mystical experiences.[64]

When Rahner says that "the devout Christian of the future will . . . be a 'mystic,' one who has 'experienced' something,"[65] he is referring to every person's primordial experience of God's Self-communication which can be deepened and intensified, to a greater or lesser degree. Since this core experience is found, at least implicitly, in all personal experience, all human experiences contain a thrust towards "an intensification which is directed towards something which one could in fact call mystical experience."[66] The existential deepening of radically personal acts, i.e., "the gradual ascent to Christian perfection,"[67] never occurs without a mystical moment.

The empirical aspects of mysticism provide Rahner with his theological point of departure. In fact, he derives "a vague empirical

---

[61] Rahner, "Contemplation," *Theological Dictionary*, p. 99; *Theological Investigations* 3:279.

[62] Rahner, *Opportunities for Faith,* p. 125.

[63] Rahner, *Theological Investigations* 3:280-81.

[64] Rahner, *Schriften zur Theologie* 12:128.

[65] Rahner, *Theological Investigations* 7:15.

[66] Rahner, *Theological Investigations* 3:23.

[67] Rahner, "Reflections on the Problem of the Gradual Ascent to Christian Perfection," *Theological Investigations* 3:3-23.

concept of Christian mysticism''[68] from the religious experiences of the saints. As he says:

> . . . all that they experienced of closeness to God, of higher impulses, of visions, inspirations, of the consciousness of being under the special and personal guidance of the Holy Spirit, of ecstasies etc., all of this is comprised in our understanding of the word mysticism without our having to stop here to ask what exactly it is that is of ultimate importance in all this, and in what this proper element consists.[69]

The extraordinary religious experiences of the saints, on the other hand, always happen in the normal realm of faith and grace. Rahner consistently emphasizes that even the deepest mystical experiences of the saints do not abandon the sphere of faith to become experiences which are no longer those of faith.[70] Theologically speaking, he refuses to see an intermediary stage between the beatific vision and the life of everyday Christian faith, for no higher experiences can be obtained in this life than faith experiences in the Holy Spirit.[71] In fact, for Rahner "the concept of 'mysticism' . . . is not the opposite of belief in the Holy Pneuma but rather identical with it."[72] But of utmost importance for an understanding of Rahner's mystical theology is his point that, theologically speaking, "mystical experience is not specifically different from the ordinary life of grace (as such)."[73]

The extraordinary experiences of the saints, therefore, are not specifically different from ordinary Christian experiences because they are mystical, but for another reason. Mystical experiences in the strict sense, the extraordinary experiences of the great saints, are extremely intense instances of a basically universal experience of God, and, hence, a deepening, purifying, and radicalizing of the "normal" life of faith.

Perhaps Rahner's most fascinating insight into the mystical experiences of the saints emphasizes that they are a particular manner or mode of the universal experience of God made possible by God's universal Self-communication. The specific way in which the great saints experience God belongs to *natural* psychology and to the *natural* abilities of the human person for concentration, meditation, submersion, self-emptying, and other comtemplative techniques often

---

[68] Rahner, *Theological Investigations* 3:279.

[69] Ibid., pp. 279-80.

[70] Rahner, *Schriften zur Theologie* 12:4, 432; *Theological Investigations* 3:279; "Mysticism," *Encyclopedia of Theology,* p. 1010.

[71] Rahner, *Schriften zur Theologie* 12:432.

[72] Rahner, *Theological Investigations* 7:15.

[73] Rahner, "Mysticism," *Encyclopedia of Theology,* pp. 1010-11.

associated with Eastern mysticisms.[74] *Psychologically* speaking, Rahner distinguishes mystical experiences in the strict sense from normal Christian experiences insofar as their natural, psychological foundation differs from that found in daily life. The "specific difference" between the extraordinary experiences of the saints (mysticism in the strict sense) and ordinary Christian experiences (mysticism in a broader sense) resides in the *natural* domain of the person, i.e., as an unusual psychological manifestation.[75]

This "unusual psychological manifestation," i.e., what specifies mystical experience strictly speaking, is a "natural, pure experience of transcendence when the mediation of categories either partly or completely ceases."[76] It has to do with a "purely non-conceptual experience of transcendence without imagery,"[77] a transcendence which is, to be sure, elevated by grace. Mysticism in the strict sense involves, therefore, the psychological manifestation of grace-elevated transcendence emerging into awareness and occupying, to a greater or lesser degree, the person's center of attention. In short, it is the fundamental experience of the human spirit's grace-elevated transcendence which enters explicitly into conscious focus without the usual mediation of concepts. The ever-present, implicit experience of grace-elevated transcendence becomes more explicit. The person becomes more explicitly aware of his "return" to self.[78] For Rahner, therefore, the key to mystical experiences in the strict sense is in the person's natural ability to "return" to himself.

Rahner does argue, on the one hand, for a "difference in kind"[79] between transcendence "as the necessary condition of any act of the mind, even the most ordinary, and transcendence explicitly experienced."[80] Indeed,

> the more intensive and 'mystical' the experience becomes, and the more the supernatural elevation of the transcendence exerts its influence . . . the clearer it must become that this emergence into awareness of transcendence and of the term to which it tends, discloses a transcendence qualitatively different from the merely concomitant and implicit form.[81]

On the other hand, Rahner expressly denies that the difference between the extraordinary experiences of the saints and the ordinary

[74] Fischer, *Der Mensch als Geheimnis*, p. 406, "Brief."

[75] Rahner, *Schriften zur Theologie* 12:434, 436; *The Dynamic Element*, p. 126 n. 24.

[76] Rahner, "Mysticism," *Encyclopedia of Theology*, p. 1011.

[77] Rahner, *The Dynamic Element*, p. 147.

[78] Rahner, "Mysticism," *Encyclopedia of Theology*, p. 1011.

[79] Rahner, *The Dynamic Element*, p. 145 n. 34.

[80] Ibid.

[81] Ibid., pp. 145-46 n. 34.

love and knowledge of Christians is itself supernatural. The difference consists in a type of "return" to self, an experience of transcendence without the usual mediation of categories, and belongs to "the natural order of psychology or parapsychology."[82] These unusual phenomena, with their natural substratum as a "return" to self, are "elevated by grace and put to a supernatural use, just as ordinary ones are."[83]

Mystical experiences in the strict sense, therefore, result from a particular mode of experiencing God in faith, hope, and love. The mode involves a natural, psychological "return" to self. These experiences, on the other hand, should not be devalued simply because they have a natural base, for as Rahner says:

> Insofar as it occurs in connection with the whole spiritual activity of man as the recipient of grace and is itself raised up by grace, this natural experience can, like every natural precondition of supernaturally 'elevated' acts (consciousness, freedom, reflection, and so on), be of great significance to man's salvation, be experienced as grace . . . and allow the supernatural act (of faith, love and so on) to remain even more deeply rooted in the person's inmost being.[84]

For example, feeding the hungry, giving drink to the thirsty, clothing the naked, etc., albeit natural acts in themselves, can be of extreme significance for salvation. So it is with contemplation, meditation, concentration, and self-emptying techniques which are natural in themselves, but can also be the means by which faith, hope, and love take even deeper hold of a person's core.[85]

To the extent, therefore, that a person can surrender his entire existence to loving Mystery and reach Christian maturity without the use of contemplative-meditation techniques, to that extent would Rahner say that mysticism is not a necessary aspect of every Christian life.[86] On the other hand, this "return" to oneself, even if not "technically" developed, even if only anonymously and implicitly employed, seems to be a necessary part of personal development, as contemporary psychology indicates. To that extent is mysticism a necessary dimension of all Christian living. In fact, an act of love of neighbor, contemplation, and martyrdom all contain to a greater or lesser degree of explicitness this "return" to oneself which enables the person to forget himself for the sake of the other. Rahner sees in

---

[82] Ibid.

[83] Ibid.

[84] Rahner, "Mysticism," *Encyclopedia of Theology*, p. 1011.

[85] Fischer, *Der Mensch als Geheimnis*, p. 406, "Brief"; Rahner, *Schriften zur Theologie* 12:432-33.

[86] Rahner, *Schriften zur Theologie*, 12:437.

Jesus' saving death, moreover, the historically visible and public victory of this "return" to self, of mysticism's goal: loving surrender to Mystery and its loving acceptance by this Mystery.[87]

Rahner also correctly insists upon the trinitarian, Christocentric, and world-affirming aspects of Christian mysticism.[88] He cautions against confusing an experience of oneness with the "world" with an authentic God experience, for one of the most important questions for a mystical theology is to clarify exactly what it is that the mystic experiences in radical nearness.[89] He dismisses pantheistic interpretations of the experience of God by emphasizing the unity-in-difference between God and the person in authentic, religious mystical union, points which need special emphasis today.[90]

It should be noted that Rahner frequently emphasizes the "natural" dimension of mystical phenomena.[91] In fact, he seems provisionally open to a "natural mysticism," i.e., a mysticism which "is simply the person's experience of his own pure spirituality,"[92] an experience of the divine infinity in the act of transcendence, but with a complete or partial absence of categorical mediation. On the other hand, he stresses that this natural "return" to self is *always* elevated by God's Self-communication. This means, for Rahner, that there are salvific mysticisms outside of Christianity, even if these non-Christian mysticisms interpret their experiences pantheistically.[93] To be sure, there are difficulties, for as Rahner asks:

> But the question then arises as to whether mysticism outside Christianity . . . is an "anonymously" Christian and therefore grace-inspired mysticism. Or, on the other hand, is Christian mysticism a "natural" mysticism just like non-Christian, although obviously under the influence of grace like all other free, moral actions of a human being, purified and free from baser elements like all that is naturally moral? Or are these two questions aimed after all at the same thing?[94]

What Rahner seems to be saying is that when the person's grace-elevated transcendence emerges explicitly into conscious awareness

---

[87] Ibid., p. 433-34.

[88] Rahner, "Mysticism," *Theological Dictionary*, p. 302.

[89] Rahner, *Schriften zur Theologie* 12:430.

[90] Ibid., pp. 430, 436.

[91] Ibid., pp. 432-36. "Mysticism," *Encyclopedia of Theology*, p. 1010; "Mysticism," *Theological Dictionary*, p. 302.

[92] Rahner, *Schriften zur Theologie* 12:435; Fischer, *Der Mensch als Geheimnis*, p. 407, "Brief"; Rahner "Mysticism," *Theological Dictionary*, p. 302; "Mysticism," *Encyclopedia of Theology*, p. 1010.

[93] Rahner, *Schriften zur Theologie* 12:436.

[94] Rahner, *Opportunities for Faith*, pp. 124-25.

154 Rev. Harvey Egan, S.J.

and is explicitly experienced and reflected upon as God's Self-communication, there is an example of specifically Christian mysticism. On the other hand, if this experience of God's Self-communication is interpreted in other ways which are in fact religious, there is an example of non-Christian mysticism. Finally, if this grace-elevated transcendence comes into explicit awareness by means of meditation techniques used solely for relaxation, concentration, etc., i.e., solely for *secular* purposes, there is an example of natural mysticism.[95]

Although Rahner frequently speaks of natural mysticism and the natural basis of mysticism, he still prefers to reserve the term "mysticism" for those extraordinary, psychological, grace-elevated and really supernatural experiences of the Holy Spirit.[96] On the other hand, he considers the restriction of the term "mysticism" for these extraordinary, supernatural phenomena to be a question of the strict use of *terminology*.[97]

IV. The Mysticism of Daily Life

Rahner can never be accused of minimizing the quality and depth of the "ordinary" Christian life of grace. Although most Christians do not experience in their lives mysticism in the strict sense, Rahner convincingly argues that the basic experience of God is not the privilege of a few, but is given in fact to all.[98] This experience not only appears in extraordinary forms in the lives of the mystics, but it also penetrates every aspect of daily life. One of the most appealing aspects of Rahner's thought is his mysticism of everyday life.

Inspired by Ignatius' "Finding God in all things," a "mysticism of joy in the world,"[99] and intellectually convinced that the human person is spirit-in-world, Rahner's is no theology or mysticism or pure interiority. The human person is basically mystic-in-the-world. Christian experiences, even the highest mystical experiences, therefore, "can only really take place in terms of that whole range of factors on the human plane which make up the manifold content of the Christian and Catholic faith."[100] Because the absolute Mystery communicates itself, and in so doing permeates and upholds all things, the human person must relate the multiplicity of his life's

---

[95] Fischer, *Der Mensch als Geheimnis,* p. 407, "Brief."

[96] Rahner, *Schriften zur Theologie* 12:435.

[97] Fischer, *Der Mensch als Geheimnis,* p. 409, "Brief."

[98] Rahner, *Theological Investigations* 11:153.

[99] Rahner, "The Ignatian Mysticism of Joy in the World," *Theological Investigations* 3:263-93.

[100] Rahner, *Theological Investigations* 7:57.

experiences and realities to this loving Mystery. Rahner's theology contains, therefore, not only a mystical moment which compresses all into Mystery; it also contains a mystical moment which unfolds Mystery's loving embrace of daily life. There is, therefore, a theology of everyday things, of work, of sleep, of eating, of drinking, of seeing, of sitting, and of standing.[101]

It is the *Easter* faith, a "faith that loves the earth,"[102] which establishes the indissoluble link between transcendence and history, mystical compression and mystical unfolding. It is precisely this Easter faith which guarantees that *every* dimension and aspect of earthly, human life will be integrated definitively by loving, transforming Mystery.[103]

There are, moreover, important "signals of transcendence," or experiences which underscore for Rahner the mystical depths of the human person which hold true for everyone, not only mystics in the strict sense. For example, the experiences of utter loneliness; forgiveness without expectation of being rewarded; radical fidelity to the depths of one's conscience; faithfulness, love, and hope, even when there are no apparent grounds for so doing; the bitter experience of the wide gulf between what we truly desire and what life actually gives us; a silent hope in the face of death—these and similar experiences are the experiences of the mysticism of daily life.[104]

In fact, whenever secular life is lived with unreserved honesty and courage; whenever the virtues of the world are practiced with courage; whenever there is a lived moderation without any thought of reward; whenever there is a silent life of service to others, there too, can be found the mysticism of daily life.[105] Because Rahner considers Christian anthropology to be the radicalization of profane anthropology, and grace as the radicalization of the human person's essence, perhaps *the* secular mystical experience for him is the courageous, total acceptance of life and oneself when everything tangible seems to be collapsing.[106] Anyone who is able to do this has implicitly accepted the holy Mystery which fills the emptiness of

[101] Rahner, *Belief Today,* trans. M. H. Heelan (New York: Sheed and Ward, 1967), pp. 13-43.

[102] Rahner, "A Faith that Loves the Earth," *Everyday Faith,* pp. 76-83.

[103] Rahner, "Über die Spiritualität des Osterglaubens," *Schriften zur Theologie* 12:343-55.

[104] Rahner, "Reflections on the Experience of Grace," *Theological Investigations* 3:86-90; *Schriften zur Theologie* 12:46, 591.

[105] Rahner, "Christian Living Formerly and Today," *Theological Investigations* 7:16-22.

[106] Rahner, *Schriften zur Theologie* 12:400; *Theological Investigations* 5, trans. Karl-H. Kruger (Baltimore: Helicon, 1966): 5-7.

both life and oneself. The one who does this, moreover, tacitly imitates Christ's self-surrender on the Cross to Mystery. As Rahner says:

> It must be realized that in earthly man this emptying of self will not be accomplished by practicing pure inwardness, but by the real activity which is called humility, service, love of our neighbor, the cross and death. One must descend into hell together with Christ; lose one's soul, not directly to the God who is above all names but in the service of one's brethren.[107]

It would be a serious misreading of Rahner, however, to see this being done only through explicitly religious deeds, for his concern centers on basic, ultimate human experiences which are not necessarily explicitly religious.

V. Concluding Remarks

Rahner's mystical theology is all the more remarkable when one considers the tradition out of which he comes. He had to overcome the radical divorce between spirituality and theology. The great saints and mystics, let alone the lived faith of the average Christian, were hardly considered important to theological reflection. Excessive extrinsicism plagued traditional theology and tended to view the human person as *spoliatus a nudo.* Too sharp a distinction between nature/grace forced a "thing-like" conception of grace which invaded the person from the outside, somehow elevated him, but did not affect his consciousness. Theology was not optimistic about salvation, seemed to view grace as in rather short supply, only sporadically given,[108] and viewed the mysticisms of the great world religions as demonic, pagan, or, at most, natural.

Theology tended to ignore the pressing questions which arose from the contemporary person's self-understanding and preferred the safe world of an excessively positivistic "Denzinger theology." Ignoring the common root and the salvific nature of the truths of the faith, they were examined in their plurality and "in themselves." The tract dealing with mystical theology remained increasingly isolated from the central tracts on the Trinity, Grace, Christ, Sacraments, Church, etc., and vice versa, in order to concentrate on a few select questions. The prophetic and charismatic gifts were hardly considered.

Although Rahner distinguishes between the mystical and the

---

[107] Rahner, *Visions and Prophecies,* trans. C. H. Henkey, S.J. (New York: Herder and Herder, 1964), p. 14 n. 12.

[108] Rahner, *Schriften zur Theologie* 12:431; Fischer, *Der Mensch als Geheimnis,* p. 408, "Brief."

prophetic,[109] he chides the history of mystical theology for its devaluation of the prophetic element in favor of "pure," infused contemplation.[110] He does indicate, moreover, that the prophetic may contain a mystical moment, for revelation takes place with "mysticism as the experience of grace."[111] He also stresses the mystical dimension of charismatic phenomena, which in his understanding appear to be the reverberations or echoes from the mystical experience at the person's core, overflowing into the various dimensions and levels of his psychic structure, as "the everyday face of mysticism."[112] Secondary mystical phenomena, such as levitations, visions, stigmatization, etc., often accompany mystical experience, but are not an essential aspect thereof.[113] On the other hand, Rahner maintains that the tradition had distinguished too sharply between infused contemplation and these secondary phenomena.[114]

His mystical theology transcends and reconciles the differences between the apophatic and kataphatic mystical traditions. Since "God is always greater than any image of himself and wishes to communicate himself as thus greater, in mystical experiences,"[115] Rahner defends the apophatic tradition's emphasis upon the clouds of forgetting and unknowing. On the other hand, the kataphatic mystical tradition is more in keeping with Christianity's historical, incarnational character.[116] Yet, "we can apprehend God in the sign (or in the form of a vision) only if we do not cling to the sign . . . as if it were the ultimate reality, God himself."[117] On the other hand, God will "one day reveal himself even to the pure mystic as the God of the transfigured earth because he is more than pure spirit."[118] Hence, unlike the radical apophatic tradition which stresses the forgetting of *all* created things, Rahner maintains that "the conceptual object which in normal acts is a condition of awareness of this transcendence can also become more transparent, can almost entirely disappear, remain itself unheeded, so that the dynamism

---

[109] Rahner, *Visions and Prophecies,* pp. 17-18; See also, *Hearers of the Word,* trans. M. Richards (New York: Herder and Herder, 1969), pp. 78-79.

[110] Rahner, *Visions and Prophecies,* pp. 20-21.

[111] See n. 31 above.

[112] Rahner, "Die enthusiastische und die gnadenhafte Erfahrung," *Schriften zur Theologie* 12:54-75, esp. p. 64.

[113] Rahner, "Mysticism," *Theological Dictionary,* p. 303.

[114] Rahner, *Theological Investigations* 3:279.

[115] Rahner, *Visions and Prophecies,* p. 58.

[116] Ibid., p. 14 n. 12.

[117] Ibid.

[118] Ibid.

itself alone becomes more and more the essential.''[119] Hence, the *transparency* of the incarnational dimension as a way of leading into Mystery proffers an excellent fusing of the apophatic and kataphatic elements of any genuinely Christian mysticism.

Due to Rahner's skilful union of God's universal Self-communication as the person's basic experience, with salvation history, his overall theology *is* mystical. Moreover, his mystagogical, theopoetical language; his appeal to the great saints and mystics as theological sources; his linking of charismatic, prophetic, mysticism of everyday life, and extraordinary mystical phenomena to a common root; his emphasis upon the unity of God, self, and neighbour experience; his mystical theological anthropology which begins with one's lived Christianity; the unfolding of the Christian mysteries from their root unity in God's Mystery as Self-communication making history; his emphasis upon the lived ultimate questions which cannot be asked as if we were somehow outside of them; his respect for theological critical reason which, however, begins and ends in prayer; his theology of mystical compression as well as mystical unfolding in daily life; the mystical anchoring of theology = christology = anthropology = ecclesiology = cosmology—all of this remains valid and must still be assimilated by the Church.

Rahner's theology is proof that theology is the man, that the theologian's daily life and spiritual life is the hermeneutical key to his theology. Rahner, like Thomas Aquinas is ''the mystic who adores the mystery which is beyond all possibility of expression.''[120] Not the ecstatic mystic, but the one who has experienced and prizes the ''silent contemplation'' so vividly described by St. John of the Cross. In short, Rahner is the theologian of Mystery whose theology contains a radically mystical moment, ''the last moment of speech before the silence, . . . the act of self-disposal just before the incomprehensibility of God disposes of one, . . . the reflection immediately preceding the act of letting oneself fall, after the last of one's own efforts and full of trust, into the infinite Whole which reflection can never grasp.''[121]

---

[119] Rahner, *The Dynamic Element,* p. 145.

[120] Rahner, *Everyday Faith,* p. 189.

[121] Rahner, *Christian at the Crossroads,* trans. V. Green (New York: Seabury, 1975), p. 53.

A Response to Fr. Egan

by Rev. Kenneth Baker, S.J.

At a time when many in the West are turning to Eastern mysticism, it is helpful to point out that Karl Rahner is preeminently a theologian of mystery, as Harvey Egan has done in his paper, "Mysticism and Karl Rahner's Theology." Unfortunately most of our contemporaries, both Christians and non-Christians, seem to be unaware of the great riches of mysticism in the Western tradition. Apparently they are unfamiliar with "The Cloud of Unknowing," John Tauler, Meister Eckhart, Ignatius of Loyola, Teresa of Avila, John of the Cross and a host of others. Christian mysticism offers such an imposing edifice that there is no reason why it should feel itself inferior to the Eastern brands or, indeed, take a back seat to any of them.

As Egan brings out clearly in his paper, Rahner is explicitly preoccupied with mystery in most of his theological writings. Of course, there is a certain tautology in stressing that a particular theologian is concerned with mystery since, if he is doing theology, by definition he must be concerned with mystery because God is *the* absolute mystery. But even though all theologians precisely as theologians are dealing with mystery, not all of them explicitly advert to this. One of the points that stands out in Rahner's theology is that he so often takes up explicitly the question of mystery and man's relation to mystery.

God is the absolute mystery because he is incomprehensible. In that sense there is and can be only one mystery. But God wills to communicate Himself to man. His will is mysterious, but he can make it known to us through revelation. Through the help of grace man can understand what God reveals to him, for to us has been revealed "the mystery of the reign of God" (Mk 4:11).

"Mysticism" or "mystical theology" presupposes a number of realities. It presupposes that there is such a thing as absolute mystery (God), and it also presupposes that man, or better, the mystic, can come close to that mystery in some way, can both know it and *experience* it. A mystery is something—either a reality or a truth—that is hidden. Without going into the problem of false mysticism, we affirm that the true mystic has come close to real mystery in some way, that he has had intense, extraordinary experiences of the incomprehensible God who is the ground of all being.

Fr. Egan has admirably succeeded in spelling out some of Rahner's principal insights and observations about the nature of mystery and mystical experience. In the paragraphs that follow I would like to add a few comments of my own.

The heart of Rahner's theological method is to be found in his conception of theological anthropology which, in turn, is closely related to (and in some sense derived from) his philosophical anthropology. Rahner's philosophy of man is spelled out in detail in his *Geist in Welt* and *Hörer des Wortes*. Whoever seriously desires to understand what Rahner is doing in theology has to study these two books carefully unless, of course, he is already familiar with Thomism and German transcendental philosophy, especially Kant, Fichte, Schelling and Hegel. For, it seems to me, it is not possible for an American trained in the pragmatic-English tradition to really understand Rahner at all without some foundation in the transcendental way of philosophizing which has been widespread in the German-speaking world since Kant. Rahner comes out of that tradition; he has adapted and taken over that tradition to such an extent that it shows up in everything he writes, including his beautiful *Encounters with Silence* (Newman Press, 1960).

For Rahner, man is "Geist in Welt," that is, "spirit in the world." "Spirit" means intelligence, freedom, openness to being, transcendence towards the fulness of all being; it means self-awareness, self-presence. Spirit for Rahner operates within an unlimited horizon of being. In the performance of any human act of knowing or loving, spirit manifests an anticipatory reaching out *(Vorgriff)* towards absolute being. Rahner arrives at this insight by analyzing particular human acts of knowing and willing (especially the *question*) and searching for the conditions of their possibility (transcendental reduction).

The procedure is sometimes called the "transcendental method." The method, for Rahner, reveals not only that man is spirit but also that there is identity and difference between spirit and being. Thus, knowing is being and being is knowing *(Sein ist Bei-sich-sein)*. In other words, being is self-presence.

To American ears this sounds strange. For to us it seems obvious that sticks and stones, which indeed exist, do not "know" anything, that they do not have self-presence or self-awareness. But for Rahner, being is ordered to self-presence; if it does not fully attain it in conscious knowledge (as is surely the case with sticks and stones) the reason is not to be found in the "being" present but in the material, limiting factors which prevent it from fully returning to itself.

The key to understanding Rahner is in the dialectic which goes on in man between absolute being present as the "horizon of being" unobjectively, unthematically as the condition of the possibility of knowing any particular being, and the concrete particular which is known objectively, thematically, categorically. The attentive reader of Rahner will soon note that the terms implicit-explicit, unthematic-thematic show up rather frequently. Thus, for Rahner, whenever a man knows some particular thing, such as that the grass is green, that is what he knows thematically; but in the same act he also knows absolute being unthematically, implicitly, unobjectively, that is, not as a particular object of knowledge.

Now since being is self-presence, according to Rahner, and since spiritual being can accomplish a full return in self-reflection, it follows that an entitative determination of spirit must be conscious—at least in some way. We know that divine grace is not just a juridical act in God; it is not something wholly extrinsic to man; rather, it produces an ontological change in the justified person. Rahner maintains, therefore, that there is such a thing in man as experience or consciousness of grace. However, in his writings on mysticism, some of which have been quoted by Egan, he stresses that there is a difference between the experience of grace on the one hand, and the experience of grace *as* grace on the other. Precisely what that difference is and how one can know for certain that one is experiencing grace *as* grace in a particular act is not spelled out and remains quite vague.

Another aspect of Rahnerian theology that should be mentioned here—one that is not explicitly treated by Egan—is the controversial "supernatural existential." We know from revelation that God has elevated man to the supernatural order. According to Rahner, God's decree elevating man to a supernatural end produces an intrinsic, ontological effect on man's existence. That effect is one of the structures of man's being; hence Rahner, using the terminology of Heidegger, calls it an "existential." Since it is above the realm of nature, and added to nature by a free decree of God, it must also be "supernatural." So what is the "supernatural existential?" It is "a permanent modification of the human spirit which transforms its natural dynamism into an ontological drive to the God of grace and glory."[1] According to Rahner, every human being is modified by the supernatural existential and according to what was stated above, it also affects, at least in some way, human consciousness so that there is an experience of this existential, even though it is not known explicitly as such.

The supernatural existential is not sanctifying grace; it is an internal modification of each person that enables him to respond to God's Word when it touches him in the preaching and witness of the Church. It is ordered to grace and glory, but it is not itself grace. However, it is supernatural and therefore it is unexacted, that is, it is not demanded by nature. It is a free gift of God's infinite love.

---

[1] Gerald A. McCool, *A Rahner Reader* (New York: Seabury, 1975), p. 185.

Rahner's ideas of spirit, being, grace and the supernatural existential are all very much involved in his theology of mysticism. In his view, if I understand him correctly, every person is in some sense a mystic because every person has the experience of grace. Of course, this does not help much in explaining what mystical experience is because the common understanding of the word is that it implies some extraordinary experience of God that is (essentially?) different from that of the ordinary man in the street. However, he does admit that mysticism in the strict sense should be reserved for extraordinary, supernatural experiences of God.[2]

What is a "mystical experience" according to Rahner? It is an "unusual psychological manifestation."[3] What specifies mystical experience strictly speaking is a "natural, pure experience of transcendence when the mediation of categories either partly or completely ceases."[4] Of course, it is an experience of transcendence elevated by grace. Because of his philosophy of man, Rahner allots more space to the natural operations of man's spirit than would the average neo-Thomistic philosopher.

A serious difficulty with Rahner's theory is that he explains mystical experience as something like a light shining into consciousness from the inside of man, but he does not explain, even within the limits of his own system, how the mind can, so to speak, set aside the categories of normal knowing and suddenly grasp its own transcendence, apparently as some kind of quasi-object of knowledge and love. His mystical theology is consistent with his own metaphysics of knowledge and his view of Uncreated Grace, but from a theoretical point of view it does not seem to shed more light on the phenomenon than the theory which explains mysticism as the result of a special gift of grace coming to the mind and will directly from the outside.

On the basis of his explanation, mystical experience seems to be for Rahner a purely interior affair—something that takes place in man's spirit, with the cooperation of the phantasm and perhaps the internal senses. Although he does not explicitly rule it out, in what I read of his mystical theology I saw no provision for the use of the external senses in mystical experience. Is there really no place for seeing, hearing, touching in such experiences? I would be interested in hearing what Fr. Rahner would have to say to this point. Cer-

---

[2] Karl Rahner, *Schriften zur Theologie* 12 (Zürich-Einsiedeln-Köln: Benziger, 1975): 435.

[3] Ibid., pp. 434, 436; *The Dynamic Element in the Church* (New York: Herder & Herder, 1964), p. 126 n. 24; Egan, p.

[4] Rahner, *Encyclopedia of Theology* (New York: Seabury, 1975), p. 1011; Egan, p.

tainly, there are many examples in the Bible in which patriarchs, prophets, Apostles and other holy people were encountered by God through visible symbols that affected their senses. Can these not also be legitimately characterized as "mystical experiences?"

Because of his theological anthropology, which has some of its roots in German idealism, phenomenology and Heideggerian existentialism, Rahner theorizes within the structures and categories of the transcendental method. This is both his strength and his weakness. It is his strength because it provides him with a logically coherent system for attacking every problem. It is especially suitable for a theological investigation of mystery and mysticism because for him all transcendence, which is what man is, is "transcendence into mystery."[5]

Its weakness is, it seems to me, that he concedes too much to modern rationalism, relativism and skepticism in his (wholly laudable) effort to express revealed truth in a way that is intelligible to the so-called "modern man." For example, liberal critics deny the possibility of miracles because, by definition, they violate the laws of nature and for them that is simply impossible. In his writings on mysticism Rahner does not explicitly agree with the rationalists, but he seems to agree with them implicitly in that, for him, all mystical experience takes place in man's spirit, that is, in the realm of self-consciousness and psychological acts. One gets the impression that he locates God's action in the mind in order to sidestep the objections of the rationalists to miracles and to avoid conflict with the demythologizers.

Such a position fits in logically with the transcendental method, but does it correspond with the experiences of the great saints and mystics? In his *Visions and Prophecies* Rahner makes many fascinating and illuminating observations on the visions and mystical experiences of particular saints.[6] But, surprisingly, he does not take the biblical data into account. For, there are many events in Scripture that qualify as mystical and that cannot easily be interpreted as *merely internal experiences* that bypass, so to speak, the external senses.

The following are certainly "intense" experiences of God that qualify as being mystical. They are also presented in Scripture as occuring outside of man's consciousness, that is, in the physical world that can be apprehended by the senses. Consider, for example, Moses and the burning bush (Ex 3:1-10); the transfiguration of Jesus during which Moses and Elijah appear to Him and are seen by the three Apostles (Mk 9:2-13 and par.); the disciples' experience of

[5] Ibid., p. 1002.

[6] Rahner, *Quaestiones Disputatae* 10 (Freiburg: Herder, 1963): 31-88.

Jesus after His resurrection (Mk 16; Mt 28; Lk 24; Jn 20 and 21); Paul's encounter with the resurrected Lord Jesus on the road to Damascus (Acts 9:1-9). Many more events from both the Old and New Testaments could be adduced, but the four listed are sufficient to make the point.

It seems to me that these Scriptural events qualify as valid "mystical" experiences. They also impinge on the external senses and so come from outside of man's naked consciousness. If this is correct, then it follows that at least some mystical experiences affect the external senses and so come to the mystic from the outside. And if that is so, then Rahner's theology of mysticism is at least incomplete.

Another point that could be raised here is Fr. Rahner's contention that all true mysticism is a species of the experience of grace in faith.[7] While granting the reality of "infused contemplation," he does not allow that mystical union can be anything more in this life than the experience of grace. The contemplation of grace is the Beatific Vision; that, of course, is reserved for those who die in grace and attain to the face to face vision of God. Rahner does not allow that there could be an intermediate state for the mystic. This position follows logically from his view of spirit, grace and transcendence. However, other explanations are possible, especially for those who do not accept the transcendentalists' view of God being present to man only as the "horizon of being"—and that unthematically, unobjectively. As Hans Urs von Balthasar said, if transcendental philosophy totally uses up the concept of objective knowing for the particular which is known categorically, then that is an error on its part; it does not at all mean that God cannot be known in some objective way.[8]

If transcendental philosophy, therefore, errs in claiming that God cannot be known in this life objectively, then there may be a mystical experience of God that is somewhere between faith and the Beatific Vision. True, as Scripture says, no one can see God and live. But certainly Elijah saw something of the glory of God and lived to tell about it (1 Kings 19:9-18). St. Paul was one of the greatest mystics in the history of the Church. "I know a man in Christ," he says, "who . . . was snatched up to the third heaven. I know that this man—whether in or outside his body I do not know, God knows— was snatched up to Paradise to hear words which cannot be uttered, words which no man can speak" (2 Cor 12:2-4). Did Paul merely experience his own unthematic transcendence towards God? Or did

---

[7] Rahner, *Schriften zur Theologie* 12: 432-33.

[8] *Cordula oder der Ernstfall* (Johannes Verlag, 1966), p. 68.

he receive a special favor from God that enabled him to catch a fleeting glimpse of the glory of the Lord?

Fr. Egan rightly stresses the influence of Rahner's own experience of the *Spiritual Exercises* on his theology of mysticism. A second influence is certainly his Kantian-transcendental method of theologizing, which has already been touched on. A third element, not mentioned by Egan, is the role of what is generally known as "German mysticism," that is, the mystical speculation in German-speaking countries that occurred between the 12th and 15th centuries. The names are familiar: Ludolf of Saxony, Meister Eckhart, John Tauler, Blessed Henry Suso, and the Fleming John Ruysbroeck.

Paul-Gundolf Gieraths describes the movement in this way: ". . . the German mystics spoke to the heart; following in the footsteps of St. Augustine, they primarily sought God in the soul itself, in the depths of the heart, in the 'bright spark of the soul' whose desire is only satisfied by breaking through to that 'darkest, deepest ground of the soul upon which God has stamped his divine image' (Tauler)."[9] That would be a fairly good description of Rahner's own mystical theology. Many of the words he uses to describe God are common to the German mystics, such as "divine darkness," "nameless region beyond all categories," "super-luminous darkness."[10] He has a certain preference for such words as "nameless," "incomprehensible," "obscure" and "darkness" when he talks about God. Perhaps some day a graduate student will do a thesis on the influence of German mysticism on Karl Rahner. I am sure that he would find abundant material.

Because of the internal cohesion of Rahner's whole system of theology—his "theological anthropology," immersion into one part of it very soon brings the student into contact with all of it. Our concern in these comments has been to make a few observations on his mystical theology in the light of Fr. Egan's paper on the same subject. Fr. Rahner has a dynamic, searching, penetrating, electrifying mind. When he zeroes in on a topic he makes it come alive and usually makes connections with other truths that have not been made before. Because of his view of spirit, his questioning never comes to an end. He believes that every answer merely gives rise to more questions, since spirit is transcendence into mystery. It has been said that all roads lead to Rome; for Rahner, all roads lead to mystery. I am grateful to my former professor for his profound articles on Christian mysticism. Let us hope that his many contributions will lead to a renewed interest in and a revival of Christian mysticism.

---

[9] *Sacramentum Mundi* 4:147.

[10] Rahner, *Theological Investigations* 4, trans. Kevin Smith (Baltimore: Helicon, 1966): 42.

A Response to Fr. Egan

by Dr. Keith J. Egan

The news that Fr. Egan would present a paper at this symposium in honor of Karl Rahner came as a delight to me. Fortunately Fr. Patrick Burns introduced me to Harvey Egan's work about a year ago when he asked if I would be interested in reading Fr. Egan's dissertation written under the supervision of Karl Rahner. Published by the Institute of Jesuit Resources in 1976 it appeared under the title *The Spiritual Exercises and the Ignatian Mystical Horizon.* Let not that ponderous title, the result no doubt of publishing a dissertation in a technical series, deter you from the profit to be gained by a careful reading of this book. It not only restores mystical perspective to an understanding of the *Spiritual Exercises* of St. Ignatius of Loyola; it raises and addresses with much help from the mystical horizon of Karl Rahner numerous points concerning religious experience which for too long a time have been relegated to a one dimensional understanding of the spiritual life. My anticipation of Fr. Egan's contribution at this symposium was heightened when I read the interview of Fr. Rahner which appeared in the March 10, 1979 issue of *America.* Few names are mentioned in that interview. One of them is that of Harvey Egan whom Rahner cites as working on a theme very important to Rahner.

My reading of Fr. Egan's paper and the presentation of the summary of his paper this morning have more than met my expectations and obviously the expectations of others. Harvey Egan's thorough knowledge of the voluminous writings of Karl Rahner and his grasp of the crucial questions concerned with the mystical character of Christian theology make Fr. Egan an apt guide for anyone who realizes that the loss of this character has deeply impoverished theology, a loss that despite advances continues to be keenly felt. Since we are a long way from a full recovery of the mystical character of Christian theology, I would stress this aspect of Karl Rahner's many major contributions to contemporary theology. It was entirely appropriate for Fr. Egan to engage himself with the many topics that emerge when one considers mysticism and Karl Rahner. One might note, in fact, that Harvey Egan's paper serves as a bibliographical introduction to the themes of mysticism and mystical theology as they appear so frequently in the writings of Karl Rahner. I for one intend to file the footnotes for his paper in a place for ready access. However, the plethora of information provided by Harvey Egan may make it difficult to discern the import for theology of Fr. Rahner's recovery of Christian theology's mystical character. Not without predecessors Rahner has acted as the chief midwife for the re-birth of a theology that has mystery at the very core of its identity.

Without a sense of mystery it was inevitable that theology would lose its wholeness, would fragment into narrow concerns. Even if it were possible, the restoration of tracts such as ascetical and mystical theology are not a priority. Rather the efforts to understand the journey to God ought to be kept closely in touch with the centrality of mystery. I believe that an address given by Karl Rahner on the occasion of the seven hundredth anniversary of the deaths of St. Bonaventure and St. Thomas Aquinas at the University of Chicago in 1974 is a landmark inquiry into the relationship between God and the human person. That address in two parts first presents an exposition of Aquinas' doctrine on the incomprehensibility of God. Part II probes the meaning of the incomprehensibility of God by way of the incomprehensibility of the human person. (*The Journal of Religion* 58, supplement [1978], s. 107-s. 125.) It is this stress on both God as mystery and the human person as mystery that enables one to develop an understanding of the journey to God as mystical. Before the mystery of God and that of the human person one must stand to explore the multi-levelled nature of the human journey to God. Never again should we try to view that journey from so tiny a bit of turf as a tract that is isolated from an orientation to mystery. If we foresake mystery we shall end up once again making rules the essence of holiness and being satisfied with pithy descriptions of the extraordinary phenomena of the few. Mysticism studied constantly in the light of mystery shall never be content to be so narrow. Karl Rahner has saved us from that narrowness, and Fr. Egan's paper is a good guide in discovering the full range of possibilities that Rahner's emphasis on mystery makes known.

Johannes Metz has warned us at this symposium of the danger of a notion of transcendence not grounded in history and human suffering. To do so he domesticated the hedgehog and the hare out of German lore. I would add that these two animals appear also in Medieval English literature. My acquaintance with them reminds me that they are both quadrupeds. To my mind the hedgehog and the hare may be more alike than different. Fr. Metz's warning is helpful and necessary. I would however not want to lose the emphasis of Rahner on mystery and the mystical character of theology. To conclude this comment may I say that Rahner's hedgehog might not be all that unlike Metz's hare?

As Fr. Egan has reminded us in his paper Karl Rahner has done so much in restoring a sense of the mystical in the Christian life that his achievement is difficult to over-estimate. For these achievements Harvey Egan's contribution is a major resource. I would add that I am grateful that Karl Rahner's work has retired the need for such tired old controversies as the Dominican/Jesuit debate over the normalcy of mystical experience in the Christian life without, however, a losing sight of the real issues that were and are behind such debates. The same comment can be made about the debates over the relationship of so-called acquired and infused contemplation. Fr. Egan has also demonstrated that Rahner has stressed what the great mystics have emphasized: mystical experience always occurs in the context of faith and grace. In so doing Rahner makes possible a theological understanding for example of St. John of the Cross, a doctor of faith. John of the Cross was a poet too. I would remind Fr. Egan that he might want to stress further Rahner's fascination with the relationship of poetic and Christian experience.

Fr. Harvey Egan has served us well this morning in pointing out all the riches that have resulted from the work of Karl Rahner, riches that make so attractive the meaning of the journey to God of the human person and of the human community. Harvey Egan's success will invite others, I hope, to take up a further exploration of Rahner's work and to think even of pursuing further unfinished questions in the writings of Karl Rahner. I suggest that the relationship between Christian mysticism and the mysticism of other religions is fertile ground for exploration. I especially urge further inquiry into the apophatic charcter of the Incarnation and the sacraments.

Theologians of the Middle Ages were frequently honored with titles that spoke volumes of the import of such persons as St. Thomas Aquinas, *Doctor Angelicus,* and St. Bonaventure, *Doctor Seraphicus.* Might not the work and dedication of Karl Rahner be succinctly remembered were we to accord him the title *Doctor Mysticus?*

An Identity Crisis In Christianity? Transcendental and Political Responses

by Rev. Prof. Johannes B. Metz

My topic concerning the identity crisis of Christianity provides me with the opportunity for sketching some representative positions in contemporary German and Middle-European systematic theology, namely transcendental theology, universal-historical theology, and political theology. In doing this, I am fully aware of the fact that the future of European theology is no longer what it used to be.

My reflections imply a criticism of Karl Rahner's transcendental theology. But this criticism is profoundly inspired by my admiration and gratitude to my mentor and close personal friend, Karl Rahner. From him one can learn even while criticizing him. Probably this kind of criticism is a better way of remaining faithful to his intentions. Theological loyalty has its own dialectics!

I. Identity Crisis: Symptoms and Non-Theological Theories

There are symptoms and theories of an historical crisis of identity in Christianity. Almost all the theories which seek to explain the structures and tendencies of the present age are implicitly theories about this crisis. For example, the neo-Marxist theory which affirms the Utopian content of Christianity but denies its strictly religious character; the theories of culture in Western middle-class societies on the basis of a logic of evolution which affirms the functions of religion in the development of culture but once again denies its indispensability; theories about the historical discontinuity of Christianity and the modern age; theories about the widespread but mostly unnoticed atrophy of the religious consciousness itself in our times; theories about the Christian Churches as "cognitive minorities," etc.

These non-theological and non-Christian theories about the historical crisis or even demise of Christianity are reflected in the minds of Christians and in the life of the Churches. Not only Christian intellectuals, but believers in general (and this is, of course, much more alarming) are beset by more and more doubts and anxieties. Is it not possible, at least in central Europe, to observe for the first time perhaps a widespread disappearance of inner and intense convictions about faith? Is there not, at all levels of society, an inability not only to be sorrowful, but also to be consoled? Is this inability not increasing? Is consolation not understood except as an impotent form of pacification? These symptoms and others that are related to them in the heart of Christian life today would seem to point to the real existence of a crisis of identity in Christianity of the kind that has already been established in theory.

How does theology understand the historical identity of Christianity in face of this situation?

II. Theological Theories About the Present Situation of Christianity: A Spectrum of Positions

I give to those theological theories about the present situation of Christianity that have been elaborated in argument and are therefore effective from the theological point of view the rather cursory description of *transcendental* and *idealistic* theories. This title therefore includes such different approaches as the universal-historical and the transcendental approaches. If I am lacking in consideration in my generalized description of these approaches, it is because I want to clarify in as few words as possible the intention underlying the post-idealistic narrative and practical-political approach of political theology.

Among the *universal-historical* approaches that are described (critically) in this paper as ''idealistic'' is not only Wolfhart Pannenberg's influential ontology of history and meaning which is strongly orientated towards Hegel and in which the idea of a meaning of history is not a category of practical reason, but (following idealistic traditions) a category of reflection. A universally historical and idealistic conception—in the sense of a stage in the history of human freedom that can be eschatologically and messianically integrated into Christianity—has also been provided by Jürgen Moltmann, in his impressive attempt to interpret the present situation of Christianity in the light of the revolutionary history of freedom. Theories of Christianity based on liberal tradition can also be regarded, for different reasons, as belonging to this approach. Despite all their individual differences, however, these theories have one thing in common: they all pay careful attention to history as the place where the crisis of identity has occurred in Christianity.

As opposed to this first group of theories, there is one consistently elaborated theological theory of the present situation of Christianity in the Catholic world (which has an influence far beyond Catholicism). This is the *transcendental theory* of *anonymous Christianity* as developed by Karl Rahner. In describing this theory as a transcendental and idealistic concept, I take as my point of departure a practical fundamental theology which understands itself as political theology. This post-idealistic theology is characterized by the cognitive primacy of praxis, that is, by the dialectics of theory and praxis. This praxis is basically political because there is no individual moral praxis which is politically innocent. For this post-idealistic theology the notion of God is basically a practical and political notion: God cannot be thought of at all unless this idea irritates and encroaches on the immediate interests of the subjects who are trying to think of it. Thinking about God is a review of interests and needs that are directly related to ourselves. Conversion, metanoia and exodus are not simply moral or educative categories—they are also and above all noetic categories. Stories of conversion and memories of exodus are therefore not simply dramatic embellishments of a previously conceived "pure" theology. On the contrary they form part of the basic structure of this theology. This practical-political structure of the idea of God is the reason why the concept of God is basically narrative and memorative (as well as the concept of truth). But let us return to Rahner!

The theory of anonymous Christianity sees the historical crisis of identity in the form of the dilemma that arises on the one hand from the increasingly obvious social particularity of the Church and on the other from the universal nature of the Church's mission and of God's saving will as represented in the Church. This theory seems to me to be dominated both by the central theological idea of God's free and universal will to save and by human respect for the hidden depths of man's existence, which is not open to absolute reflection and within which man is always to some extent anonymous even to himself. In his theory of anonymous Christianity, Rahner has only extrapolated his transcendental view of man as the being who has been withdrawn from himself into God or as the being who is "condemned to transcendence," who is "always already with God," even in every act of denial of God, and whose freedom consists (only) in accepting this being (in faith) or in suppressing it (in lack of faith). In his reflective articulation of this freedom, man has to take into account dissonances and even contradictions between what is explicitly said and what is done in fact, between acts of freedom and reflective self-assurance and so on. It would, of course, be impossible to examine here Rahner's profound and highly developed theory of transcendental faith, which is obviously based on an idealistic theory of knowledge and on the traditional doctrine of *fides implicita* and *bona fides*. All that I can do here is to point to the result of this approach when it is applied to a theological theory about the present situation of Christianity. Nowadays, the Church is no longer able to reach a great number of people and is bound to take seriously into account that it will not be able, in the future, to make many people and groups of people explicitly Christian. This means that, according to Rahner's theory, the salvation of these people can be seen by the Church as possible in an anonymous form of Christianity.

III. The Transcendental Theory of Anonymous Christianity: A Few Questions, Not Yet a Criticism

1. Does the doctrine of transcendental faith that is at the basis of this theory of anonymous Christianity not bear too strongly the marks of an elitist idealistic gnoseology? The great mass of people are saved by virtue of their *fides implicita* and their attitude of *bona fides*. The real relationships are known to the few who possess the "high gift of the wise." Rahner, whose entire theological disposition makes him turn away from an elitist attitude perhaps more than any other theologian, has himself raised this objection. His reference, however, to the marks of elitism in "sublime, aesthetic, logical, ethical and other forms of knowledge" which he believes apply to all men, but are only known to a few, is not convincing (at least for me). Full and explicit (!) knowledge of faith is after all a practical knowledge. In its distinctive character, it is incommensurable with purely scientific or idealistic forms of knowledge. It is possible to speak of an arcane knowledge in the case of a full knowledge of faith, but this arcanum cannot be the arcanum of a philosophical gnosis—an elitist idealism; it must be the arcanum of a practical knowledge. It cannot be the arcanum of a Socrates, but must be the arcanum of Jesus, in other words, the practical arcane knowledge of the imitation of Christ.

2. Do we not have, in this form of transcendental Christianity, a form of over-justification and over-identification of Christianity in the face of the growing historical threat to its identity? Is the historical identity of Christian faith not fixed, in this theory, to a basic anthropological structure, according to which man is "always already," whether he wants to be or not, "with God"? It would certainly be a fundamental misunderstanding of Rahner's transcendental theology if we were to assume that its aim was simply to introduce Christian faith subsequently into a previously existing anthropological structure. The transcendental process works in the opposite direction, according to Rahner's explicit description of it. The actual historical experience of man in Christian faith is generalized and becomes the "categorical" pre-condition for our understanding of man as an absolutely transcendent being. The question remains, however, as to whether it is possible to generalize by means of speculative thought a historical experience (such as that of Christian faith), which is always threatened because of its historical character and whose identity is always endangered for the same reason. It may

in fact only be possible to generalize this experience by means of a praxis for which no theological compensation can be found by transcendental reflection, but which must be remembered and narrated.

If we are to elaborate the idea of a narrative and practical Christianity further, we have first to extend our criticism, both that of Rahner's transcendental and idealistic theory and also (at least in outline) that of the universal-historical and idealistic conceptions. My criticism, then, is principally directed against the attempt to explain the historical identity of Christianity by means of speculative thought (idealism), without regard to the constitutive function of Christian praxis, the cognitive equivalent of which is narrative and memory.

IV. A Fairy-Story—to Read "Against the Grain"

To clarify what I mean by this criticism, I should like to recall one of the best known German fairy-stories, that of the hare and the hedgehog. One Sunday morning, the hedgehog is going for a walk in a ploughed field and a hare teases him about his bandy legs. He challenges the hare to a race in the furrows of the field. First, however, he goes home to breakfast because, as he tells the hare, he cannot run on an empty stomach. He then returns with his wife, who is exactly the same in appearance as her husband, and gets her to stand at the far end of the furrow. He himself stands at the other end beside the hare in another furrow. The hare falls for this trick. He runs and runs in his furrow, but the hedgehog is (in both positions) "always already" there. In the end, the hare falls dead from exhaustion on the field.

The "little ones" of this world, who are always slow and therefore deprived in life and for whose encouragement this fairy-story was presumably written, may let me perhaps tell this story "against the grain," in other words, against its own fully-justified intention and for a moment take the side of the hare, who runs and runs and in the end falls dead in the race, while the hedgehog wins by a cunning trick and does not even have to run. If we opt for the hare, we opt to enter the field of history, a field that can be measured in running the course of the race, in competition or in flight (one is reminded here of the images used in Pauline traditions for the historical and eschatological life of Christians). And this option for the hare also means that we must try to expose critically the idealistic guarantee of the threatened identity of Christianity. This guarantee leaves out of account the power of praxis to save the historical identity of Christianity and acts as a kind of theological hedgehog trick which aims to safeguard the identity and triumph of Christianity without the experience of the race (that is, without the experience of being threatened and possibly of being defeated).

V. The Exposure of the Hedgehog Trick, or a Criticism of the Transcendental and Idealistic Versions of the Guarantee of Identity

There are two versions of this hedgehog trick, both of which can be used to explain both the universally historical and the transcendental attempt to undermine history.

The *first version* of the hedgehog trick stands for the universal-historical and idealistic approaches. Like the two hedgehogs, those who suggest these approaches have the course of history in view. Because they view it from both ends, however, there is no need to enter it. The hare runs and the hedgehog stands in a deceptive duplication at the control-points of history as a whole. In this way, history is made into a movement of the so-called objective spirit which we have already seen through. And theology is made into a kind of information service for world history, but one that is consulted less and less by the public.

The ultimately promised saving meaning of history is not disclosed as it were while the course of that history is being run. It is not evoked, remembered and narrated (for all men) as a practical experience of meaning in the middle of our historical life. It is, so to speak, rigidified into a definition for reflection that cannot be affected by collective historical fears or threats of catastrophe and is therefore not in need of any hope provided with expectation. The present state of meaning has had all its wrinkles ironed out and is free of all contradictions. It is, as it were, "hopelessly" total. There is only a very weak eschatological and apocalyptical sense of danger and of the needs of the age . This eschatological consciousness has been successfully removed from the theologies of history and transferred to the realm of individual history.

The *second version* of the hedgehog trick stands for the transcendental and idealistic approach, the idea of transcendental Christianity. The hare runs and the two hedgehogs are "always already" there. In the North German fairy-story, the hedgehog husband and wife alternate with each other, calling: "I am here." By means of their transcendental omnipresence, they harass the hare to death. Is not—in this second version—the threatened historical identity of Christianity guaranteed for a too high price: the price of confusing identity with tautology? The two hedgehogs—the hedgehog's wife is exactly the same in appearance as her husband—stand for this tautology and the running hare stands for the possibility at least of historical identity. The running itself, during which it is also possible to fall flat on your face, belongs, together with its danger, to the guarantee of identity. Nothing can compensate for it transcendentally. In my opinion, everything else leads in the end to tautology—one hedgehog is exactly the same as the other, the beginning is like the end, paradise is like the end of time, creation is like the fulfillment and at the end the beginning repeats itself. History itself—with its forms of identity that are constantly threatened and in danger of being overcome—cannot intervene. The transcendental magic circle is complete and, like the two hedgehogs, it cannot be overcome *vae insuperabilibus.* One therefore suspects that the process of transcendentalization of the Christian subject may have been guided by a tendency to unburden and immunize. Would this process of transcendentalization not give Christianity a kind of omnipresence which would ultimately remove it from every radical threat in the sphere of history? Is the vanguard of the historical and apocalyptical attack made by Christianity and its identity not destroyed by this process of transcendentalization of the Christian subject and is the battle therefore not prematurely broken off?

VI. A New "But"

But: can there be another point of departure for Christian theology apart from the one that insists that the universal meaning of history and the historical identity of Christianity is already established? How could universally historical meaning continue to be called into question for theology? Has history not been saved a long time ago in the definitive eschatological action of God in Jesus Christ? Is it not essential for theology to argue as both the approaches that are criticized here do, that is, transcendentally or universal-historically? Is Christian theology in this sense not necessarily idealistic? And should it therefore, for its own sake, not accept the criticism that it does not take history seriously with all its contradictions, antagonisms, struggles and sufferings, and that it makes an ''as if'' problem of it? Does not every other attempt lead to a contradictory idea of a conditioned salvation or to a confusion of salvation and Utopia?

But how can these idealistic ''solutions'' themselves avoid the danger of regarding the history of salvation as a totality without reference to the subject, in other words, of looking over the heads of the people who are bowed down under their own histories of suffering? Does this one, universal history of salvation that is founded in Christ not take place in the concrete mystical-political histories of salvation?

But how does this take place? And how is it possible to speak about it if, in the case of salvation history, the very notion of history constituted by concrete subjects is overlooked? Finally, should the salvation of the whole of history that has been promised at the end of time be reduced to a harmless, teleological history of meaning in which it is no longer possible to consider seriously, let alone provide a conscious theological assessment of, the catastrophic element that is present in that history?

VII. A Plea for a Narrative and Practical Christianity

It is because of the existence of these questions that I make a plea for a narrative and practical structure of Christianity, its historical identity and its idea of eschatological salvation.

In this context, it is important to point to one very decisive factor. As distinct from pure discourse or argument, narrative makes it possible to discuss the whole of history and the universal meaning of history in such a way that the idea of this universal meaning is not transferred to a logical compulsion of totality or a kind of transcendental necessity. As a result of this the mystical-political histories of individuals would be of secondary importance in comparison with the saving meaning of history as a whole and could only be incorporated subsequently into the framework of a definitive history dissociated from the subjects. In the narrative conception of Christian salvation, however, history and histories—the one history of salvation and the many particular histories of salvation—merge together without diminishing each other. The individual histories do not take place without regard to the previously narrated history of salvation and the history of salvation is able to assimilate the individual histories. The narrated (and remembered) universality and definitiveness of the meaning of history mean that the historical praxis of opposition to meaninglessness and to the absence of salvation is not superfluous, as though it were transcendentally or universal-historically guaranteed, but indispensable.

The universality of the offer of salvation in Christianity does not have the character of a transcendental or universally historical concept of universality. It has rather the character of an "invitation." The inviting logos of Christianity does not in any sense compel. It has a narrative structure with a practical and liberating intention. If this is expressed in Christological terms, it means that the salvation that is founded "for all men" in Christ does not become universal via an idea, but via the intelligible power of a praxis, the praxis of following Christ. This intelligibility of Christianity cannot be transmitted theologically in a purely speculative way. It can only be transmitted in narrative—as a narrative and practical Christianity.

It is also clear from this that the so-called historical crisis of identity of Christianity is not a crisis of the contents of faith, but rather a crisis of the Christian subjects and institutions which deny themselves the practical meaning of those contents, the imitation of Christ.

The imitation of Christ is a question of decisive importance for the version of the identity crisis that is served up every day in many varieties of the criticism of religion and ideology and which has become popular, within Christianity, in the catchphrase: "Yes to Jesus, no to the Church." What we have here is a deep suspicion, rooted in the pre-rational Christian consciousness, that the living identity of the Christian body with Jesus has become lost in later Christianity, that Christianity cast off its conformity to Christ a long time ago and that many of Jesus' intentions were long ago successfully taken over by other historical movements. This suspicion cannot be reduced simply by interpreting more subtly the historical attitude of Christianity, in other words, by a more scholarly form of hermeneutics and a more critical reconstruction of the history of Christianity. It can only be diminished by providing evidence of the spirit and power of Christianity in consistent imitation of Christ, in other words, by practical conformity to Christ. Our memories of the failure of Christianity and the deeply rooted disappointments felt by individuals and whole groups and classes of people cannot be theoretically explained away. For even successful historical research cannot exempt us from these collective memories of suffering, i.e., we would not be regarded as in any sense justified in the presence of those memories. It is clear, then, that this version of our Christian identity crisis also compels us to accept the praxis of following Christ and points at the same time to the urgent need for a narrative and practical Christianity.

VIII. Conclusions

This narrative and practical Christianity of the following of Christ is a *political* Christianity, for the following of Christ always has a dual mystical and political structure. This mystical and political Christianity implies a criticism of that dominant form of Christianity which is making a last attempt to achieve universality by transforming the messianic religion of the following of Christ into a middle-class religion which functions as a legitimating ideology for the priorities, aspirations and security of middle-class society.

The *theology* of this narrative and practical Christianity makes necessary new *loci* and new subjects of theology. Alongside academic theology, which reflects the division of labour of middle-class societies, a new type of theology is called for which could perhaps be described as a mystical-political biography, i.e., a theology which is fully aware of the historical and social situation of its subjects.

On the occasion of *Karl Rahner's* seventy-fifth birthday, I have tried to show that his theology can be understood as a biography in which the narrative elements form the substructure of the transcendental reflection. In this sense Rahner truly belongs to the classics: we can often find support for objections to his theories in the broader context of his own thinking.

A Response to Fr. Metz

by Rev. Matthew L. Lamb

On the basis of both Prof. Metz's lecture and his recent book, *Faith in History and Society,* I understand his political theology as related dialectically to Prof. Karl Rahner's transcendental theology. The relation is dialectical inasmuch as Metz negates and affirms Rahner's theology. He negatively criticizes the transcendental-idealist conceptuality Rahner employs in formulating his theological positions, but Metz affirms the intellectual and spiritual perform-ance out of which Rahner theologizes. Indeed, the negative criticisms are meant to emphasize that intellectual and spiritual per-formance by giving it a more concretely historical and narrative articulation. These negations and affirmations might be termed, to borrow the procedures of Paul Ricoeur, a hermeneutics of suspicion and a hermeneutics of recovery. Acknowledging the limits of brev-ity, I shall first outline the negative suspicions, and then sketch how they promote a positive recovery.

I. A Political Hermeneutics of Suspicion Regarding Transcendental Theology

Disagreements are usually a function of the proximity of the divergent positions. More volumes than even Rahner himself has written would be needed to expound the intellectual and spiritual indebtedness of Metz to his mentor and close personal friend, Karl Rahner. The proximity upon which their intellectual disagreements began and continue is their shared conviction that Catholic fun-damental theology must effectively promote a critical questioning of contemporary cultures and societies from the perspective of the Christian faith and Catholic traditions, as well as a critical question-ing of traditional religious beliefs and institutionalized practices within Christianity and Catholicism from the perspective of the con-tradictions in contemporary cultures and societies. This shared con-viction led Metz, from 1966 to the present, to develop a new political theology which included (among many other elements I cannot men-tion now) a hermeneutics of suspicion regarding Rahner's transcendental theology. At the risk of oversimplification, the follow-ing are some of the main criticisms of this political hermeneutics:

1. A suspicion that Rahner's transcendental theology is too dependent upon a metaphysical conceptuality derivative from the traditions of German Idealsim run-ning from Kant's *Critique of Pure Reason* through the right-wing Hegelians to Heidegger and Maréchal.

2. A suspicion that such a metaphysical conceptuality, unable to thematize the concrete origins of ideas and concepts, too easily spills over into a somewhat romanticist idealization of originating, pre-thematic experience as unifying and unproblematic, thereby downplaying the concretely contradictory and problematic character of human experience in history and society.

3. A suspicion that this metaphysical fascination with ideas and an unproblematic originating experience does not provide strong enough foundations to criticize the fascination of instrumental rationality with technique and its cultural offspring, middle-class consumerism, since both fascinations neglect the concreteness of historical and social human subjects.

4. A suspicion that a fundamental theology formulated with such a metaphysical conceptuality would promote an idealized universality of humanity constituted in a pre-apprehension of God, paralleling an idealized universality of anonymous Christianity which, like the hedgehog, would project the illusion of having won the race without having actually run. Concepts do not move.

5. A suspicion, finally, exists that the theological foundations of Christian faith should not introduce us into the concept of Christianity so much as into an understanding of *both* the genuinely pre-religious conflicts and questions (the identity-crisis of becoming human subjects) to which the memory of Christian narratives respond, *and* the intellectual, moral, and religious imperatives of being doers of the Word as well as hearers of the Word (the identity-crisis of becoming Christian subjects).

If I understand Metz correctly, this hermeneutics of suspicion regarding the metaphysical conceptuality of Rahner aims, not at simply negating his transcendental theology, but at actually *realizing* its intention of turning to the subject (anthropocentrism) concretely in our personal, social and ecclesial practice. The hermeneutics of suspicion ground a hermeneutics of recovery.

II. A Political Hermeneutics of Recovery Regarding Transcendental Theology

Metz calls our attention to how the intellectual and spiritual performance of Rahner's theologizing breaks through the metaphysical conceptuality of transcendental idealism.[1] The hermeneutics of

---

[1] This is clearly brought out in Metz's *Glaube in Geschichte und Gesellschaft* (Mainz: Gruenewald, 1977), pp. 195-203.

suspicion is concerned with distancing us from the conteptuality in order that we really experience the historical tensions of contemporary questioning intelligence thirsting for what no concept or idea could ever satiate. We are reminded of Marx's criticism of Hegel. The political hermeneutics of suspicion seem more directed at us, the readers in front of the text, than at the performance of Rahner behind the text. Metz warns us that it would be a false and distorted reading of Rahner's work to view it as a calm conceptual unfolding from *Spirit in the World* to the latest volume of the *Theological Investigations*. Rahner must not be left to some dry, academic history of ideas course. At the end of his lecture Metz indicated the classic quality of Rahner's theology: "we can often find support for objections to his theories in the broader context of his own thinking." That broader context, I suggest, is the intellectual and spiritual performance of Rahner's theologizing. It is on this basis that a narrative and practical hermeneutics of recovery would read Rahner's transcendental theology, not as disclosive of an "always already" achieved Christian identity, but as imperatives impelling us towards personal and social transformations of a world "not yet" truly human and "not yet" truly Christ-like. Without the hedgehog the hare would not have run.

Among the many elements in Metz's political hermeneutics of recovery, I would like to single out three. First, in the essay Metz referred to at the end of his lecture he showed how Rahner introduced the concrete human subject into his reflections on doctrinal conceptuality.[2] Rahner has taught us to read Church doctrine as the expression of a praxis-grounded existential biography of the Christian community. What Rahner began for dogmatics, political theology would extend to the whole of theology. The latter must be grounded, not on concepts and ideas, but on the dynamics of historical and social human subjects striving to live out the call to conversion, metanoia, or exodus as intellectual, moral, social and religious imperatives. Here the recovery of political theology is very close to the transcendental method of Prof. Bernard Lonergan.

Second, as I already mentioned, political theology recovers the transcendental thrust by understanding it, not as disclosive of human beings "always already" before God, but as imperatives to transform ourselves and every human being into more attentive, intelligent, reasonable, responsible, and loving subjects—subjects, as Metz writes, who respond to the demands of their historical times and social experiences, seeking ever anew to realize truly human and Christ-like identities in their world; humans who realize that

---

[2] This essay is published in the reference given above, pp. 195-99.

their presence to God calls them to be truly responsible human subjects.[3] The social sins of racism, sexism, ecological destruction,
political and economic oppression cannot be adequately counter-
acted within the churches and society at large by pious or indignant
moralisms, nor by cleverly conceived techniques. They require profound conversions of personal, social, cultural, economic and
political conduct or praxis. To argue, for example, that multina-
tional corporations should continue collaborating with and supporting the apartheid government in South Africa because this provides
some jobs for some black South Africans can be a technique of eva-
sion, a rationalization whereby we evade *our* responsibility because
we thereby deny the majority of South Africans the ability to exercise for themselves *their* responsibility as truly human subjects. It
overlooks the fact that South Africa is constitutionally the only state
in the world legally based upon white supremacy.

Finally, a political hermeneutics recovers the concrete history of
suffering through which Rahner theologized. Metz has reminded us
that in honoring Karl Rahner we are confronted more with the
challenge of an abiding question than with the comfort of a com-
placent answer. Metz's own critical questioning of Rahner's
transcendental theology should call our attention to the concrete
historical context of Rahner's writings. Rahner loved the Church
enough to challenge official policies when those contradicted the
demands of fidelity to the ongoing *traditio* or handing on of the faith.
Nor was it in the cheap grace of a romantic idealism that Rahner
gained insight into how anthropocentrism is profoundly theocentric.
That insight concretely emerged within the darkness and despair of
a human and historical identity-crisis, the apocalyptic dimensions of
which can only be glimpsed in the many histories of suffering spread
across two World Wars. Only a mind and heart steeped in the
mystery of the Crucified would have the audacity to think of
humanity as "Spirit in the World" and "Hearer of the Word"
through the din and carnage of Germany in the late 1930's and
1940's. If the narrative folly of the Cross confounds the so-called
wisdom of this world (by some estimates almost half of all natural
scientists in the world are engaged in military-related research), we
dare not imagine that the identity-crisis of humanity etched in the
holocaust of those years is now behind us. While millions of human
beings today go without sufficient food and shelter, the ovens of a
million Auschwitzes are neatly produced and packaged with all the
cool logic of the nuclear arms race. Just as, in the words of
Lonergan, "there are real theological problems, real issues that, if

---

[3] Cf. Ibid., pp. 57-76.

burked, threaten the very existence of Christianity,'' so there are real political problems, real issues that, if burked, threaten the very existence of humanity.[4] Metz's political theology, by showing how the identity-crisis of Christianity is intimately related to the identity-crisis of humanity, recovers critically the central insight of Rahner into the God-centeredness of human-centeredness in the dying and risen Christ. We shall honor Rahner worthily, Metz reminds us, not by simply repeating or rearranging the conceptuality he used, but by following the underlying intentionality of his life dedicated to Christ and Catholic theology.

---

[4] Cf. Bernard Lonergan, *Method in Theology* (New York: Herder & Herder, 1972), p. 140.

A Response to Fr. Metz

by Rev. David Tracy

It is an honor to add my congratulations to the incomparable Karl Rahner and to provide a brief response to the brilliant paper of my colleague at *Concilium* and my friend, John Baptist Metz.

As all of Metz's work makes clear—as his most recent book *Faith in Society and History* decisively clarifies, Metz's own theological creativity and his own program of a political theology have not lessened his respect and his debt, at once creative and critical, to Fr. Rahner.

Indeed his paper may be read as a critical tribute to Rahner. (Above all) it is a *tribute* to Rahner, whose own rigorous transcendental theology may also be read, as Metz observes, as a theological biography narrating in classical form a twentieth century Catholic Christian's reinterpretation of both the great Catholic tradition while yet speaking to and in the contemporary situation. Yet Metz's paper is also clearly a *critical* tribute formulated from the perspective of Metz's own practical fundamental theology. Where Rahner will emphasize the cognitive identity crisis of the contents of faith of Christianity in modernity and thereby develop a transcendental program for theology, Metz will insist upon the political-ethical crisis of subjects and institutions of Christian identity today and thereby develop a political theology dependent upon the *intelligible* logos of *praxis*. Where Rahner will develop his daring method of retrieval of the contemporary meaning of the doctrines into his own systematic array of concepts, Metz will appeal not to transcendental argument and concept but to narrative and memory and will insist, in that very appeal, upon their fully practical and cognitive status. Where Rahner will concentrate principally upon the individual subject, Metz will shift that concentration, not from the subject, which remains central, but to the political, social subject. Where Rahner will concentrate his theological energies upon a method of retrieval of the contemporary meaning of the classical doctrines, Metz will retrieve above all the "memories of the suffering of the oppressed" throughout the centuries and the powerful negations of the present status-quo as those negations are embedded in the apocalyptic texts of the New Testament. Where Rahner will re-express the mystagogical experience of the Christian, Metz will develop a political theology which is at the same time a mystical-political theology.

The differences in their approaches—differences which cannot be minimized without sacrificing the seriousness of both positions—are differences yet grounded in a joint emphasis upon the *subject* as *subject* and upon the identifiably religious, Christian, indeed mystagogical resources of the tradition. In the brief time allotted, it is impossible, of course, to pay either a proper tribute or to provide an adequate critique of either position, or to do more than suggest what I believe to be the profound unity-in-difference (to recall a favorite concept of both Metz and Rahner) of these two major theologians. I have indicated some of the issues above that such a critical comparison would need to address. In the remaining time, allow me to follow through on Metz's own emphasis upon narrative and indicate very briefly how Rahner's emphasis upon the "always-already" reality of redemption and Metz's emphasis upon the negations of the present and the "not-yet" are both grounded in the narratives which function as normative for us all, the passion-narratives of the New Testament. I do not engage in this exercise in order to suggest any easy reconcilliation between the two positions—indeed I do not believe that one is available. Nor do I plea for a lazy pluralism encompassing "a little of this and a little of that." Rather I make these suggestions to show how the real differences between Rahner and Metz are differences finally grounded in the unity-in-difference of the narratives of the New Testament itself.

My question, therefore, is: If we are to concentrate upon narrative, as Metz urges us to do, then what do our classical narratives—the gospels—disclose of the reality of the always-already and of the not-yet of Christian *praxis* and thought? What finally do these narratives narrate?

These narratives of the passion, let us note, end in the transformation of the event of resurrection disclosing the significance of passion and the whole ministry of deed and word, and disclose as well, in John, Rahner's "always-already" reality of incarnation, of universal grace in history and nature. And still the reader cannot avoid noticing that the narratives do not really end. Even in Luke-Acts the story moves on into an open future to "all" whose reality has been disclosed proleptically in Jesus. A tension pervades these narratives between a fulfillment of the eschatological Kingdom of God in the ministry, passion, and resurrection of Jesus Christ and an as yet unfulfilled hope for the end-time and for all, the living and the dead, in that Kingdom. Above all the negative symbols, apocalyptic and cross, disclose the "not yet" character of the narrative: the story which ends in the incredible paradoxical triumph of cross-resurrection and begins by that ending its passionate demands that the reader, like the hare, really enter history, its conflicts, its contradictions, its suffering, as we all, in our individual histories and in history itself, head to the whole and the not-yet-foreseen end.

It is true that the very concentration of these gospel narratives upon the single person and proclamation of Jesus in the narratives and upon the proclamation of Jesus Christ by the whole confessing narrative concentrates the attention of any individual reader, as such a narrative of a single life must, upon her/his own individuality as authentic or inauthentic. And yet the constant presence of the apocalyptic negations, the ''not-yet,'' throughout the gospel narratives remind the sensitive reader not to transform the radical importance of individual decision into the myopic concern of individualism—even for salvation. The ''not yet'' of this eschatological Kingdom proclaimed by Jesus, the ''not yet'' of the future transformation proclaimed in the narrator's confession of Jesus Christ and in the narrative's own non-end reminds the Christian that no Christian can turn this call to radical personal decision, to real and authentic individuality, into a compulsive concern with myself and my salvation, into the false security of an already present salvation. The *no* of that not yet, like the yes of the command to love the neighbor, is a no to all that: an enabling *praxis* to real, active concern with the other, indeed with all the living and the dead, especially the ''privileged'' ones of the Christian gospel and the ancient prophets—the underprivileged, the poor, the outcasts, the repressed, the tax-collectors and sinners, the oppressed. Only when that *all* comes will the total hope and radical promise of these narratives be fulfilled. Only then will the story end.

In the time-in-between (for the Christian our time) this narrative and its plot of this Jesus who taught, ministered, was crucified, and raised by God, this Jesus Christ the Lord whom this community experiences and proclaims will be the narrative by means of which Christians try to focus and live out the individual stories of their lives. A life of Christian discipleship means the opposite of any easy security in the authentic reality of the *already;* rather it is an empowering, always-already present vision and *praxis* as witness to a life like that disclosed in this story (the life of this Jesus now proclaimed as the crucified and risen one; now confessed, with Paul, as he *in whom* we live). The prophets and apocalyptic-minded among us, like Metz, are likely to resonate to one temporary end of the story of the crucified one: the frightening and shaking ''not-yet'' cry of Jesus in Matthew and Mark, ''My God, my God why have you forsaken me'' (Matt 27:46; Mk 15:34)? The more ''ordinary'' Christian—a type which the gospel also honors and for whom it demands that attention must be paid—is more likely to overhear the trusting words of Luke's crucified Jesus, ''Father, into your hands I commend my spirit'' (Lk 23:46), and its disclosure of the reality of fundamental trust. The mystics and all those who honor authentic religious manifestations of cosmos from chaos, all those who, like

Rahner, sense the ground of all in ultimate mystery and radical grace are likely to turn to the words in the narrative of John's exalted as crucified one: "It is accomplished" (Jn 19:30).

Yet whatever classical route of spirituality or theology individual Christians take, none of us can forget that the Christian narrative must finally be remembered in its entirety: as a whole of real negation and real exaltation, of real suffering and active love, as a proclamation and manisfestation of the Crucified and Risen One who lived, lives, and will live; as a narrative which has not ended and will not end until all the living and the dead are touched—how, like the hare and the hedgehog alike, *we know not;* as a narrative which discloses the tense and paradoxical presence of both the utter reality of the "always-already" graced state which *is* ours and, at the same time, the reality of the "not-yet" negating all present securities; as a narrative which disallows *any* assumption that the reality of the "not-yet" is not as real as the "always, already" presence of God in creation, covenant, and the radical, universal grace of Jesus Christ at the heart of the lived tension of Christian identity and Christian theology. Perhaps in the spiritual existence of that recognized tension of both incarnation and apocalyptic, of both the always-already and the not-yet, the Christian theologian may yet recognize the profound unity-in-difference of the New Testament narratives. Perhaps also a recognition of that unity which I have tried here too hurriedly to express will free us all to honor the affinities that all of us sense towards the real unity-in-difference of the always-already reality disclosed by the theology of Karl Rahner in its manifestation of our grounding in radical grace and ultimate mystery, and the classical *praxis* of the negations present in the *imitatio Christi* disclosed in the political-mystical theology of John Baptist Metz.

Current Problems in Christology in Latin American Theology

by Rev. Jon Sobrino, S.J.

Translated by Dr. Fernando Segovia

For this study in which I wish to honor the theological work of Karl Rahner, I have chosen a theme which has been radically present in his work from the very beginning: the theme of God. As Rahner himself has declared, Christianity basically proposes only one thing: ". . . that the great Mystery remains eternally a mystery."[1] And if some have claimed, often by way of criticism, that Rahner's theological work is anthropological in character, it is no less true that his anthropology is also deeply theo-logical: "Whether he is consciously aware of it or not, whether he is open to this truth or suppresses it, man's whole spiritual and intellectual existence is orientated towards a holy mystery which is the basis of his being. . . . It is our most fundamental, most natural condition, but for that very reason it is also the most hidden and least regarded reality. . . . We call this God."[2]

Rahner has always insisted that this radically theo-logical point of departure is the only one that can do justice to any type of reflection on the ultimate nature of Christian faith. Consequently, he has cautioned against beginning the theological task with too hasty a christological and *a fortiori* ecclesiological reduction.[3] Yet, at the same time, he has claimed that the experience of God as absolute mystery is always an historical experience, i.e., it can be experienced only through an experience of that which is categorically historical. Thus, the experience of the mystery of God, of the whence and whither of transcendence, can take place only within specific historical experiences.[4]

In this study, I wish to describe the experience of God from the perspective of a specific historical reality which I shall call "the church of the poor." That is, I wish to describe how the mystery of God is experienced as mystery in this relatively concrete and historically specific channel, a channel which can be clearly differentiated from other such channels. In so doing, I believe that the

---

[1] Karl Rahner, "Questions of Fundamental Theology and Theological Method," *Theological Investigations* 5, trans. Karl-H. Kruger (Baltimore: Helicon, 1966): 6.

[2] Rahner, "The Need for a Short Formula of Christian Faith," *Theological Investigations* 9, trans. Graham Harrison (New York: Herder and Herder, 1972): 122.

[3] Rahner, *Foundations of Christian Faith. An Introduction to the Idea of Christianity*, trans. William V. Dych (New York: Seabury, 1978), p. 13.

[4] Ibid., pp. 51-52.

church of Latin America and Latin American theology can contribute directly to the task of theological reflection on the mystery of
God. It is precisely this type of reflection that many superficial critiques and evaluations would argue is missing from Latin American
theology, given the latter's supposed preference for the historical
efficacy of liberation rather than for the mysterious or numinous element of the faith.[5]

Before proceeding to elaborate the theme in question, I wish to
make certain preliminary observations that will be of help in
understanding the meaning and direction of this study:

1. When I speak of "the experience of God" or of "the church of
the poor," I do not pretend to shed light directly on these concepts
or on this mutual congruence. Nor is it my intention to demonstrate
thereby the reasonableness of faith or, in the words of Rahner, "to
give people confidence . . . that they can believe with intellectual
honesty."[6] Rather, my goal is simply to show that such an experience of God does exist—and this in itself may prove to be a
valuable pastoral aid.

2. I take it for granted that the transcendental experience of God
is made concrete in specific historical channels. Thus, although
theoretically one could give a generic description of the universal
experience of the mystery of God, such an experience, given its concrete character, will always be conditioned by and made possible
only within specific historical channels. More specifically, I wish to
affirm that it makes quite a bit of difference whether one believes in
God within an ecclesial configuration or outside of one, or even
within one particular historical configuration of the church, such as
the church of the poor, or another such configuration. Moreover,
the difference arises not only because of the different doctrines of
God that are formulated in the various ecclesial channels, but also
because of the concrete historical nature of the channels themselves.

---

[5] It is true that liberation theology has not given as much attention to the theme of
God as to other themes. It is also true that when it has done so, it has tended to concentrate on reflections concerning the knowledge of God and the practice of justice.
See, e.g., J.P. Miranda, *Marx and the Bible. A Critique of the Philosophy of Oppression,*
trans. John Eagleson (Maryknoll, N.Y.: Orbis, 1974). Nevertheless, from its very
beginnings liberation theology has preserved the dimension of the mystery of God as
mystery, even if it has done so in the context of an examination of the spirituality of
liberation rather than in the context of a systematic study of God. See, e.g., G.
Gutiérrez, *A Theology of Liberation. History, Politics and Salvation,* ed. and trans. Sr.
Caridad Inda and John Eagleson (Maryknoll, N.Y.: Orbis, 1973), pp. 189-208; L.
Boff, *La experiencia de Dios* (Bogotá, 1975).

[6] Rahner, *Foundations,* p. 12. For the different pastoral perspective, in a profound
sense, of European and Latin American theology, see J. Sobrino, "El conocimiento
teológico en la teología europea y latinoamericana," *Estudios Centro Americanos*
322/323 (1975), pp. 427-34.

3. I also take it for granted that one can experience God within the church of the poor and that one can do so as mystery, i.e., as an experience that goes beyond the concrete channel itself. I also believe that in this concrete channel of the church of the poor one can recover certain fundamental Christian doctrines of the experience of God that, from an historical point of view, have not been as palpably present in other ecclesial channels.

4. When I speak of "the experience of God" in "the church of the poor," I wish to emphasize the fact that the individual believer cannot exclude, even in his own transcendental experience of God, his dependence on other human beings, on their own specific historical situation, and on the experiences of God that these others have. It is not the same to believe in God as an individual as it is to believe in God as a member of a community. Indeed, one could even argue whether the former option is a possibility at all, given the social nature—itself transcendental—of man. Be that as it may, however, what I do wish to emphasize in this study is the latter option: the importance of the ecclesial reality as a social and communitarian reality for the experience of God.

5. I take it for granted as well that the faith of the individual believer is colored not only by the ecclesial reality as a communitarian reality, but also by the concrete characteristics of that very same reality. More specifically, I take it for granted that a real and historical configuration of the church as the church "of the poor" will influence directly the life of the individual believer. Further, such a configuration will affect not only the most obvious levels of that individual's life, e.g., those of liturgy and ethical praxis, but also the theo-logical level of the experience of God.

6. In what follows, I proceed to describe the experience of God in the church of the poor, first of all, from a descriptive and expository point of view rather than from a directly polemical or apologetic one. I am, therefore, quite aware that the present study represents a description of ecclesial life within a specific time and situation, viz., that of various churches in Latin America today. Strictly speaking, this description does not pretend to be universal in character. Yet, at the same time, if the description should yield more accurately, from an historical point of view, that which is essential to the experience of God according to revelation, then the description becomes to a certain extent normative as well as indirectly polemical or apologetic. Further, one would also have to affirm that one could find today within the church of the poor a "better"—though by no means unique—channel for the experience of God.

If on the one hand it is correct to say that both the transcendental nature of the experience of God and the eschatological reservation prevent one from singling out a unique and exclusive locus for the experience of God, it is also true that they do not demand that all possible historical loci for such an experience be considered to have the same validity. Further, if one takes all of revelation into account, such a minimalist position demands and justifies a search for the "most adequate" locus for the experience of God. That which comes at the end does not relativize all that precedes; rather, it demands a proper subordination or hierarchy.

7. I should also like to emphasize that whatever is said here concerning the experience of God in the church of the poor does not presuppose or give way to triumphalism or mechanicalism. I speak of the church of the poor as a structural channel for the experience of God. As such, I do not claim that all individuals within that church share in effect the same profound experience of God, nor is it my claim that Christian faith within that church is beyond all dangers, as if completely protected by life insurance and no longer borne in fragile vessels made of clay. What I do wish to affirm is the structural importance of the church of the poor for the experience of God of the individual believer. Nevertheless, I have deliberately chosen to reflect on that structure because I believe that therein one does find an experience of God of such substance that it is not only important, but also, in its character as channel, normative.

8. Finally, I wish to affirm that whatever is to be considered normative in the church of the poor is ultimately, but not exclusively, to be attributed to a very specific understanding of Jesus Christ and of christology. The fundamental goal of this christology is to reevaluate the historical Jesus, specifically his status as son of God, i.e., as the one who is historically related to the Father and dependent on his own historical situation.[7] Briefly stated, the fundamental goal is to reevaluate Jesus' *own* faith: to let Jesus become not only the primary content of our own faith, but also a structural model for that faith, i.e., to let him emerge as "an extraordinary believer,"[8] the one who first lived the fullness of faith (Heb 12:2).

The second goal of this christology presupposes that the radical historicity of Jesus demands that his own subjective experience of the Father be mediated through his concrete, historical life, through the actions and goals of that life. Therefore, it seeks to single out the more important and, from an historical point of view, the more firmly established aspects of Jesus' experience of the Father. Among these one would have to include his fundamental and foundational

---

[7] This was the fundamental goal of my previous work, *Christology at the Crossroads,* trans. John Drury (Maryknoll, N.Y.: Orbis, 1978), esp. pp. 41-235.

[8] L. Boff, *Jesus Christ Liberator,* trans. Patrick Hughes (Maryknoll, N.Y.: Orbis, 1978), p. 113.

relationship to the Kingdom of God as the mediator of that Kingdom; his ministry toward the poor as the primary recipients of his message; his historical solidarity with the socially oppressed of his time; his total immersion in the historical conflicts occasioned by his mission; the persecution and death which he accepted as part of his own destiny and as logical and historical consequences of his own mission.

The third goal of this christology is to accept the fact that it is possible and necessary for the experience of God to relive these fundamental historical structures of Jesus' life. The possibility of reliving these structures is already quite evident in Latin America, even if new mediations are always necessary. The need to relive them follows ultimately from one's own acceptance of Jesus' call to follow him. Furthermore, the intrinsic reasonableness of this call, given its character as call, cannot be analyzed or debated. Indeed, if the call is not accepted as an essential part of one's own experience of God, then any further reference to Jesus as the historical revelation of the Son of God would have to be seriously questioned.

The church of the poor claims no monopoly on the experience of God or on the understanding of Jesus, but it does believe that it can relive more adequately Jesus' original experience of God within its own channel.

I. The Importance of the Ecclesial Channel of "the Poor" for the Experience of God

When I speak of "the church of the poor" in this section, I refer to its primary historical constitution or to what one could call its first ecclesial substance. In what follows, I select from that historically primary ecclesial reality only three elements that can shed further light on the importance that a determined ecclesial reality has for the experience of God. These are: the communitarian nature of the experience of faith; the variety and complementarity of historical experiences within that communality; the importance of the active presence of the poor in the church.

A. Historical Communality of Ecclesial Faith

From its very inception, the church has been conceived as embodying a double dimension of immanence and transcendence, of historical channel and experience of faith. This double dimension appears in programmatic fashion in its very first self-definitions: the church as "the people of God," "the body of Christ," "the temple of the Spirit." That which one calls faith in God has been found to entail from the very beginning a double relationship. The first relationship is with its own direct object, viz., God, while the second is with the historical locus in which that object appears as an object of faith in correlation with that locus, that is to say, with whatever it is that is meant both historically and materially by such terms as "people," "body," and "temple."

If the importance of the locus in which the experience of God takes place is taken seriously, then, for example, whatever it is that is meant by the term "people" will have important consequences not only at the level of administrative organization, liturgy, and ecclesial praxis, but also at a more profound theo-logical level. Further, these consequences flow not only—as is obvious—from the teachings *concerning* God that the members of this "people" receive from the revelation, the tradition, and the magisterium of the church, but also from the very fact that being a "people" will influence directly the act of faith in God.

If that is the case, then the individual who has an experience of God should not be seen merely as an individual subject, but rather as an individual subject *in* the church, *in* the people of God. Likewise, the experience of God of that individual will be dependent on and influenced by not only the object of his faith, but also the historically concrete ecclesial reality in which it takes place.[9] Given the rather familiar ring of this terminology, this distinction may appear prima facie to be rather trivial, but it is extremely important. On the one hand, it is clear—as every form of existentialism and personalism has emphasized—that only the individual person as such and not a corporate structure can have an experience of God. Yet, at the same time, if the faith of that individual is to be ecclesially Christian, then it must of necessity be shared with others and open to the faith of these others in the Pauline sense of "bearing and being borne." One could even debate, given the transcendental character of the communality of the individual subject, whether at the philosophic level an experience of God can take place that is not

---

[9] Rahner (*Foundations,* p. 343) also presents this truth generically: "By the very nature of man and by the very nature of God, and by the very nature of the relationship between man and God when God is understood correctly, the social dimension cannot be excluded from the essence of religion. It belongs to it because man in all of his dimensions is related to the one God who saves the whole person. Otherwise religion would become merely a private affair of man and would cease to be religion." Furthermore, he comes even closer to the intention of my own reflections when he states (Ibid., p. 389): "No one develops and unfolds from out of the purely formal and antecedent structure of his essence. Rather, he receives the concreteness of his life from a community of persons, from intercommunication, from an objective spirit, from a history, from a people and from a family, and he develops it only within this community, and this includes what is most personal and most proper to himself. This is also true for salvation and for the Christian religion, and for the Christianity of the individual."

essentially related to or dependent on the experience of God that others have. Be that as it may, I believe that at the ecclesial level the faith of the individual subject cannot properly be called faith unless it is both a witnessed faith—a faith that is shared with and actively oriented toward others—and a faith that needs witness—a faith that is influenced by and dependent on the faith of others. A properly ecclesial faith is, therefore, a faith that is experienced before "a great cloud of witnesses" (Heb. 12:1) and needs "the mutual encouragement of each other's faith" (Rom. 1:12).

Consequently, I wish to emphasize, although at a very generic and formal level, that the experience of God of the individual subject must of necessity be open to the faith of others and that an important part of that experience of God is the individual's own awareness of the fact that he is dependent on and to a certain extent influenced by others in the experience of the mystery of God. It is in this profound sense that I wish to affirm the fact that faith is ecclesial by nature, where the adjective "ecclesial" is not to be understood from a doctrinal point of view—that is, as a presentation of teachings and doctrines concerning God—but rather as making explicit the essential communality of the individual subject, even at the level of the experience of God. In this way, one may speak radically of the church as "the people" of God.

B. Variety and Complementarity of the Historical Experience of Faith

It should be clear from the preceding presentation that a simple multiplication of the individual subjects of a faith does not of itself establish the ecclesial nature of that faith. That is not the proper way to understand how this reality of being a "people" influences or determines the faith of the individual. Rather, it should be clear by now that the ecclesial character of the experience of faith refers to the different and complementary configurations signified by the term "people." From the very beginning, the church accepted an historical configuration of that term. In so doing, it also accepted the different historical situations of its members as well as the different historical mediations of the experience of God.

Paul's declaration to the effect that "there is neither Jew nor Greek, free man nor slave, male nor female" (Gal. 3:28) should not be seen as contradicting this fundamental point. If it is possible, on the one hand, that a particular theological reading of this study could conclude that therein the importance of the concrete historical situation for the experience of faith is relativized, a different theological reading of the same study—and specifically one that would pay close attention to the polemical undertones of that text—could very easily reach the opposite conclusion: even being a Greek, or a slave, or a woman can be a possible mediation of faith. From its very beginnings, it must be said that the church never sought to abolish historical differences—indeed these cannot be abolished!—but rather to accept and incorporate them into its own self-definition as a "people."

Thus the church accepted a diversity of cultures and of social configurations regardless of their minority or majority status. It accepted the diversity of abilities and of "charisma," of talents and contributions from different individuals and groups of individuals, necessary for the constitution of a social body. It accepted the diversity of functions essential to any social organization. It accepted the historical deprivation and misery of many—indeed, of the majority—of its members as well as the spontaneous and related desire for redemption and liberation. Finally, it accepted the heartfelt urgency on the part of other members to dedicate themselves to that task of liberation.

It does not really matter to what extent the church consciously accepted such a diversity into its own historical configuration or what theological reflections flowered from such an acceptance; what does matter is the fact that the acceptance took place. The fact that one finds in the church many members in different historical situations presupposes ipso facto that they have different historical experiences and that these experiences cannot be relativized by any subsequent theologizing, but rather must be shown to be mediations of faith. This means that the church accepts automatically diversity and complementarity in the experience of God, an experience which, insofar as it is transcendental in nature, can be formally described as being universal to all human beings, but, insofar as it is concrete, depends on concrete historical configurations.

Furthermore, this diversity of experiences should give way to complementarity both for historical reasons, viz., the social nature of a human being, and theological reasons, viz., the mutual encouragement of faith. The historical situations and experiences of *others* as well as the way in which God is experienced within them will be extremely important for *one's* own experience of faith. For example, that experience of God which takes place in the midst of historical deprivation and is lived in situations of real and permanent misery will be quite different from that experience which urges others into the service of God. However, the deprivation of the former will turn the urgency to serve of the latter into a determined mediation of the experience of God. Similarly, the altruistic service of the latter will influence and modify the experience of God of the former, that is, of all who live in total misery. Yet another example. The experience of God which takes place among church officials in positions of power, be they of an intellectual, administrative or pastoral nature, will be quite different from the experience of the dispossessed. However, the faith of the latter can influence the service and the faith of the former, and this service in turn can influence the faith of the historically dispossessed.

This diversity of historical situations among the different members of the church prevents the experience of the individual subject, even at the level of the experience of God, from ever becoming a purely individual experience. If one takes seriously the unlimited breadth of the mystery of God, then this very fact of diversity will not only be simply accepted, but will be positively received and valued, because this multiplicity of experience constitutes in effect the only way to correspond asymptotically to the mystery of God. And it is because of this mystery that of necessity belongs to God that the proper experience of God can take place only when there is an openness to the different historical experiences of others. It is in this sense that I refer to the importance of the diversity and complementarity of the different experiences and situations within the church and to their importance for the experience of God of the individual.

C. The Importance of the Poor in the Church for the Experience of God

The only reason that I have taken time out to recall something which is already well known is to prepare the way for a fundamental assertion: a specific church will offer a specific historical channel for the experience of God by vigorously adopting the historical and primary fact of the poor and by allowing that historically primary fact to become the very center of its own ecclesial self-definition and mission. Such an emphasis on the importance of an historical fact, insofar as it is historical and free of any theoretical reflection, for the totality of the church is nothing new, whether in principle or in fact. Indeed, the church has been historically organized, for example, on the basis of such facts as hierarchy or celibacy. As a result, these facts of hierarchical power or celibate life have become historically primary facts on the basis of which both the totality of the church and the hierarchical ordering of its values have been understood historically. For example, if one accepted the hierarchy of the church as its primary ecclesial fact, then one would propose the use of authority and the demand for obedience as historical mediations for the experience of God. Similarly, if one accepted the celibate way of life as the primary fact, then one would propose freedom for service and the aloneness of man before the mystery of God as proper historical mediations.

What I wish to affirm above all is the importance of the adoption of what one could vaguely call "the world of the poor" as the primary and central fact within the church, so that the church itself may be called, "the church of the poor." In what follows, I should like to begin a description of this church by giving examples of what may not yet be properly called "the church of the poor," even though one may find in these descriptions scattered elements of the proper definition.

First of all, the church of the poor goes beyond what the second Vatican Council understands and proposes by the term, "the people of God," even though the Council may have in effect prepared the way for the emergence of the church of the poor by abandoning a very effective hierarchical conception of the church, viz., a church that was conceived and organized from the very top of a pyramidal structure of ecclesial power. The new description of the church as "the people of God" helped to restore a fundamental historical and corporate reality to the church, but that was the extent of the change. The Council, despite its profound consideration of charisma, did not go beyond a theological democratization of the church. It failed to find in that new description of the church a center with sufficient historical strength to reorganize all Christian and ecclesial realities.[10]

Secondly, the church of the poor goes beyond the image of a church that shows concern for the poor, even though such a concern is desirable in itself and represents a fundamental dimension of the church of the poor. Strictly speaking, however, such an interest in the poor remains an ethical, not an ecclesial, concern for the poor. A church *for* the poor is not necessarily a church *of* or *from* the poor. In such a church, the poor would not yet constitute an historical prin-

---

[10] I do not mean to belittle in any way the contribution of Vatican II to an understanding of the church as the people of God. One may even find in the Vatican II documents references to the poor as the privileged within the church and to the persecution that characterizes the status of the church as a pilgrim (e.g., *Lumen Gentium,* 8). However, the Council did not attempt to restructure the church around these truths. In an excellent and by now classic study of the church as the people of God, Y. Congar ("The Church: The People of God," *The Church and Mankind,* ed. E. Schillebeeckx, Concilium, no. 1 [Glen Rock, N.J.: Paulist, 1964], pp. 11-37), shows the uses and the limitations of this concept in the II Vatican Council. Thus, for example, God is said to have saved his people from Egypt, but the oppressed whose cries reached God are not mentioned (Ibid., pp. 20-21). Likewise, the inequality that exists within the people of God is said to be organic and functional, so that in effect certain benefits accrue to the entire people of God. However, social inequality is not mentioned, so that the partiality of God with respect to his people does not appear (Ibid., pp. 21-22).

ciple for the configuration of the church, even though they may very well be the principle recipients of the mission of that church.

Thirdly, the church of the poor goes beyond the collectivity of all the poor and the oppressed, whether in the church or outside of it, even if they are fully aware of their oppression and self-interests and thus constitute a very specific class within the church. In principle, the church of the poor does not emerge from a negation of other ecclesial elements in a social conflict, even though such a conflict may in effect exist.

The church of the poor thus goes beyond these three preceding descriptions—the church as the universalistic, theologically democratic people of God; a church with an ethical concern for the poor; a regional or class church—even though elements from these descriptions may be found in the historical process of the church of the poor and important channels for the experience of God may exist within them, e.g., the experience of democracy and solidarity, the experience of conflict, and, to be sure, the ethical experience of service.

At this point, I should like to turn to a positive description of the church of the poor.[11] First of all, the church of the poor is a church the social and historical basis of which is to be found among the poor. As such, it is a church which has as its basis the majority of human beings, who both individually and collectively constitute the real poor not only because of their natural condition of poverty, but also because of their historical condition of impoverishment by the riches of others. It is these poor, therefore, that are said to constitute the very basis of the church. Such a description shows how different the Latin American understanding of the phenomenon of "base communities" is from that of the developed nations, since the latter takes the essential characteristics of these communities to be the small number of their members and, by comparison with the institutional church, a seemingly greater degree of freedom and initiative for the spirit of God.

Secondly, the poverty that characterizes the poor of this church can be concretely distinguished from that spiritual poverty which constitutes a basic openness to the spirit of God as well as from that

---

[11] On the church of the poor, see F. Soto, ed., *Cruz y Resurrección. Presencia de una Iglesia nueva* (Mexico, 1978); G. Gutiérrez, *Teología desde el reverso de la historia* (Lima: Lib. Studium, 1977); *Iglesia de los pobres y Organizaciones populares* (San Salvador: UCA Editores, 1979); *Estudios Centro Americanos* 348/349 (1977); issues, devoted to the state of the church in Latin America; G. Gutiérrez, "The Poor in the Church" and R. Muñoz, "The Function of the Poor in the Church," *The Poor and the Church*, ed. N. Greinacher and A. Müller, Concilium, no. 104 (New York: Seabury, 1977), pp. 11-16, 80-87. On declarations of Latin American episcopates that reflect this type of theology, see *Los obispos Latinamericanos entre Medellín y Puebla* (San Salvador: UCA Editores, 1978).

metaphysical poverty which is correlative to and inherent in the limited condition of every human being. The final document of the Third Conference of Latin American Bishops and Puebla gives a vivid description of the poor from the point of view of this first social level:[12]

>—the faces of young children, struck down by poverty before they are born, their chance for self-development blocked by irreparable mental and physical deficiencies; and of the vagrant children in our cities who are so often exploited, products of poverty and the moral disorganization of the family;

>—the faces of young people, who are disoriented because they cannot find their place in society, and who are frustrated, particularly in marginal rural and urban areas, by the lack of opportunity to obtain training and work;

>—the faces of the indigenous peoples, and frequently of the Afro-Americans as well; living marginalized lives in inhuman situations, they can be considered the poorest of the poor;

>—the faces of the peasants; as a social group, they live in exile almost everywhere on our continent, deprived of land, caught in a situation of internal and external dependence, and subjected to systems of commercialization that exploit them;

>—the faces of laborers, who frequently are ill-paid and who have difficulty in organizing themselves and defending their rights;

>—the faces of the underemployed and the unemployed, who are dismissed because of the harsh exigencies of economic crises, and often because of development-models that subject workers and their families to cold economic calculations;

>—the faces of marginalized and overcrowded urban dwellers, whose lack of material goods is matched by the ostentatious display of wealth by other segments of society;

>—the faces of old people, who are growing more numerous every day, and who are frequently marginalized in a progress-oriented society that totally disregards people not engaged in production.[13]

---

[12] For a theological analysis of what is meant by "the poor" in Latin America, see G. Gutiérrez, *A Theology of Liberation*, pp. 287-302; I. Ellacuría, "Las bienaventuranzas come Carta Fundacional de la Iglesia de los pobres," *Iglesia de los pobres y Organizaciones Populares*, pp. 105-18.

[13] John Eagleson and Philip Scharper, eds., *Puebla and Beyond: Documentation and Comentary,* trans. John Drury (Maryknoll, N.Y.: Orbis, 1979), ch. 3, The Final Document, "Evangelization in Latin America's Present and Future," Pt. 1: Pastoral Overview of the Reality that is Latin America, 32-38.

Thirdly, the poor described above deserve preferential attention on the part of the church in their own concrete historical situation and regardless of ". . . the moral or personal situation in which they find themselves."[14]

Fourthly, the poor within this church become the hermeneutical principle for a primary concrete expression of important Christian concepts and realities.[15] Thus, for example, the notion of objective sin may be interpreted from this perspective as anything which brings death upon human beings and the children of God; the concept of Good News as that which is addressed to the poor as its privileged recipients[16] and thus forms a transcendental relationship with them; the first objective of the ethical praxis of the church as the liberation of the poor through the establishment of justice and the decision to achieve this objective in active solidarity with them; the concept of a theology of history as one which is presented from the point of view of the poor, "from the underside of history."[17]

The church of the poor, however, goes beyond an acceptance of the poor as the social basis of the church or as the primary recipients of its mission. A true church of the poor must look at poverty from the perspective of the Beatitudes. The latter propose in effect a salvific kenosis which in order to be salvific must be a kenosis. "Become poor as long as there is poverty in the world; identify yourselves with the poor."[18] The spiritual basis of the church of the poor must include a voluntary acceptance of poverty, the adoption of an attitude of effective solidarity with the real poor, and an acceptance of the persecution that results from the just nature of this solidarity. The church of the poor represents, therefore, an attempt to find the ecclesial and Christian *spirit* of poverty, that is to say, to spiritualize poverty and misery and not simply to endure them as cruel facts of human existence. It must be emphasized, however, that this proposed spiritualization cannot be achieved by a mere desire to become poor. In order to be truly a sacrament of salvation, where

---

[14] Ibid., Pt. IV: À Missionary Church Serving Evangelization in Latin America, 1142.

[15] The document cited above (see n. 14) has attempted to do this in the following paragraphs: 1141-44, 1148-52.

[16] According to J. Jeremias *(New Testament Theology: The Proclamation of Jesus,* trans. John Bowden [New York: Charles Scribner's Sons, 1971], p. 116), the Good News was directed "to the poor alone."

[17] G. Gutiérrez, *Teología desde el reverso de la historia,* pp. 42ff. The reference has been translated into English by the translator of this article.

[18] I. Ellacuría, Las bienaventuranzas como Carta Fundacional de la Iglesia," p. 177. The reference has been translated into English by the translator of this article.

salvation is understood as a real kenosis,[19] the church must accept real poverty, must become poor itself in an act of solidarity with the poor, and must actively defend the causes of the poor. Poverty, powerlessness and persecution constitute in effect the real and material condition for a church which is in keeping with the will of God to arise and for the possibility of an experience of God within such an ecclesial channel to take place. If one takes seriously the promise of the Kingdom of God to the poor and the persecuted, then one must affirm that there is something inherent in poverty and persecution that directs human beings to the Kingdom of God. As a result, the church of the poor can provide an historical channel for an authentic experience of God, and it is the nature of this experience that I wish to pursue in the following section.

II. The Experience of God in the Church of the Poor

The mystery of God has been historically conveyed in many different ways by many different historical experiences, even though these experiences may be considered to be formally similar insofar as they are channels for that mystery. The sapiential, apocalyptic, prophetic and existential tradition of both the Old and New Testaments testify to this diversity. The absolute nature of the mystery of God does not prevent specific historical experiences from pointing to or conveying that mystery. Rahner himself, for example, has recently emphasized the importance of three types of experiences for what he calls a searching christology: an appeal to absolute love for the neighbor; an appeal to readiness for death; an appeal to hope in the future.[20]

From the perspective of the church of the poor, the unconditional rejection of scandalous poverty and the unconditional acceptance of salvific and liberating impoverishment may be said to constitute the fundamental appeals. While it is true that any of the above-mentioned experiences can be a channel for the mystery of God if and when such an experience is taken to its ultimate expression, it is also true, given the historical situation of all human beings, that the choice of one or the other of these experiences in coming to know the mystery of God is extremely important. Rahner himself has emphatically declared that ". . . it is equally obvious that the present-day situation of man, in which he has to achieve the total fullness of his own selfhood . . . also in a very essential sense imposes

---

[19] I. Ellacuría, "La Iglesia de los pobres, sacramento histórico de la liberación," *Estudios Centro Americanos* 348/349 (1977), pp. 707-22.

[20] Rahner, *Foundations,* pp. 295-98. See also Rahner, *Ich glaube an Jesus Christus* (Einsiedeln: Benziger, 1968).

its own distinctive stamp upon this experience. . . .''[21] What does remain theoretically open to question—although I myself am of the opinion that the point is beyond discussion—is whether the present situation of the Latin American believer, a situation which in its concrete historicity is quite different from that of the European believer, is in effect essentially determined by the massive, oppressive, scandalous and challenging fact of the absolute poverty of the masses.

This present situation of the Latin American believer and the primary experience which is obtained therein give rise to different expressions of the experience of God. To be sure, such expressions may also be found in other ecclesial channels which cannot be historically described as the church of the poor, but it is only within the church of the poor that these expressions allow their own contents to become much ''more evident.'' At first glance, this process of allowing the contents to become ''more evident'' would appear to be a rather small contribution to the task of theoretical reflection on and logical analysis of the experience of God, particularly since the contents, once conceptualized, can be subsumed under other ecclesial realities. However, I would argue that the process itself is extremely important, because the evidence for the concept becomes thereby more operatively transparent as it becomes ''more'' evident. What is more evident can be easily subsumed under what is evident and, as a result, can be presumed to be known, but one can also argue that in becoming ''more'' evident, the contents themselves become absolutely evident.

I should like to emphasize this latter point because what follows is not new, or at least not radically new, in terms of its purely conceptual formality. To speak of life, love, conversion or hope would appear to be nothing other than a routine repetition of what is frequently discussed in the field of theology. Yet, it may be that in making concrete the formality of the concepts, the concepts themselves acquire new ''evidence,'' since the reality that lies behind the concepts does not exist as universal ''genera,'' of which the ''species'' are but an application, but rather as concrete and specific realizations.

A. The Experience of the God Whose Kingdom is Near

Rahner has declared that ''there is really only one question, whether this God wanted to be merely the eternally distant one, or whether beyond that he wanted to be the innermost center of our

---

[21] Rahner, ''The Experience of God Today,'' *Theological Investigations* 11, trans. David Bourke (New York: Seabury, 1974), p. 150.

existence in free grace and in self-communication.''[22] Christianity assumes this question by claiming that God has shattered his symmetry of distance and nearness and in his free grace has drawn near.

The church of the poor makes concrete this fundamental experience of God as nearness in grace by affirming, in biblical language, that the Kingdom is near and the Good News is being preached to the poor. Thus, the introduction of the poor as the hermeneutical principle in the primary experience of God makes concrete all generic truths concerning the God of the Kingdom. Several important points concerning the experience of the mystery of God follow from this position.

First of all, the transcendental relationship that exists between the God of the Good News and all men is seen as being mediated by the more concrete correlation that exists between the Good News and the poor. The latter are accepted as constituting the primary recipients of the Good News and, therefore, as having an inherent capacity to understand it ''better'' than anyone else. The obediential capacity of man to become a hearer of the word is thereby made concrete as the obediential capacity of the poor and the impoverished to hear that word as the Good News and thus as a word of grace. It also follows logically that it is only to the extent that man adopts the perspective of and shows solidarity with the poor that he will have the capacity to hear the Good News exactly as it was preached in history.

This historical disposition of the poor presupposes their historical capacity to hear the Good News in its formal character as ''grace,'' that is, as something which is totally unexpected and freely given, and as ''content,'' i.e., as life itself. In this regard, the response of Jesus to the disciples of the Baptist is well known: ''the blind receive their sight and the lame walk, lepers are cleansed and the deaf hear, and the dead are raised up, and the poor have the good news preached to them'' (Mt 11:5; Lk 7:22). This text clearly identifies the poor and, at the same time, shows what happens to them when the Kingdom of God draws near. What happens is that the poor receive life once again, since from the point of view of both the ancient world and linguistics, these types of persons—the blind, the lame, lepers, etc.—are always described in terms of death: ''According to the thinking of the time, the situation of such men was no longer worth calling life; in effect, they were dead . . . now those who were as good as dead are raised to life.''[23]

Thus, the preaching of the Good News in the church of the poor becomes in effect the recovery of the original truth concerning God

---

[22] Rahner, *Foundations*, p. 12.
[23] J. Jeremias, *New Testament Theology,* p. 104.

the Creator among those who would appear to have the least claim to be his children. God is a God of life and, therefore, life itself becomes a primary mediation of the experience of God. All the complexities of life—its abundance, its threat, its demand, its misery—reflect the complexities of the experiences of God. The words of the famous dictum, "gloria Dei, vivens homo," should not be looked upon as mere words. Life is the primary mediation of God. Only within the church of the poor is that insight recovered in the very midst of that life which is for the most part threatened, stymied and destroyed. The life that emerges out of such a historical situation is well acquainted with the mystery of God.

Secondly, although the affirmation that the God of the Kingdom "is near" breaks through that fundamental symmetry of distance and nearness, it does not abolish the dialectic of the presence and the hiddenness of God—a dialectic which has been summarized in the well-known expression, "already, but not yet." Indeed, the need to preserve that dialectic represents one of the fundamental experiences of the mystery of God as mystery, since the "not yet" of God is perceived as always surpassing his "already." That dialectic may be expressed in several ways. Philosophically, it may be conceived as the presence of the ground of being in all beings and as the inadequacy of concrete beings vis-á-vis absolute being. Existentially, it may be conceived by seeing God as that which is most intimate to a human being and, because it is most intimate, as overflowing the human being. Biblically, it may be perceived as the tension which exists between creation and eschatology, between absolute origin and absolute future.

That experience of the dialectic which takes place in the church of the poor does not discredit the ones mentioned above, but it does concretize them from the perspective of the poor. This experience becomes ultimately an experience of a history which includes both grace and sin, both manifestation as well as hiddenness on the part of God. The church of the poor knows that the Kingdom of God has not yet come, because sin, the very nature of which is to cause death, is still very much present. The church of the poor knows that as long as there exist innumerable victims of the oppression of men against their fellow men and that as long as countless other men are regarded as human refuse, undone by the appetites of the powerful, the Kingdom of God cannot be said to have come. On the other hand, if the Good News is preached to the masses, if this ultimate dignity as children of God and this status as the privileged before God is effectively proclaimed, if they manage miraculously to achieve human solidarity, if they actively regain this dignity and begin to defend their so-called "rights"—a situation which amounts, in effect, to a reliving of the original creation—then it may be said that the Kingdom has come. Again, it is true that the experience of the manifestation and the hiddenness of God, of the "already, but not yet," may be expressed in many ways. However, the description of that experience within the church of the poor is privileged, because it captures from within and in its most historical essence what it means to let God be God.

Thirdly, it is a typical feature of the church of the poor, and one which is historically demonstrable as well, to experience the coming of God in his Kingdom not only as destiny (joyful because of its character as grace and yet somber because it occurs in the midst of sin) but also as a task which is demanded by God and which corresponds to God's own mode of approaching. It is an experience that seeks to correspond to that God whose Kingdom approaches. Obviously, that correspondence is as complex as the mystery of God itself. In recent years, many have pointed to hope as the primary mode of corresponding to that God who is coming. To be sure, hope, as I shall point out later on, is an important element of the experience of God that takes place in the church of the poor. But an even more primary mode than hope and a mode that will provide the necessary conditions for that hope to be Christian is the practice of love. If hope hopes that the otherness of God will one day become fullness, the practice of love attempts to correspond to that eternal content of the mystery of God. Ultimately, the practice of love is an attempt to capture the mystery of God from a Johannine perspective: "If God so loved us, we also ought to love one another" (1 Jn 4:11). That is to say, it is an attempt to grasp at the same time the character of the mystery of God as a free gift and of its content as a task to be carried out.

In the church of the poor, this basic affirmation concerning the practice of love as the primary element in the experience of the mystery of God is mediated by its own historical situation. First of all, within that situation the practice of love cannot be considered simply as one of the many possible mediations of God or even as the one that is selected as the most privileged; rather, love becomes that mediation which lies at the very center of the experience of God and gives meaning to all other mediations. Such a conception of the practice of love recapitulates both the Pauline teaching of Galatians 5:14 and Romans 13:8-9—"For the whole law is fulfilled in one word, 'You shall love your neighbor as yourself' "—and the Johannine message of 1 John 4:16 and 18—"God is love."

Secondly, the practice of love is seen in that church as an urgent task. The poor cannot wait. It is, therefore, not a question of calmly and collectedly accepting the proposition that love is the ground of being itself and concluding that the practice of such love befits its character as ground; on the contrary, it is a question of realizing that love demands of its very nature its urgent actualization. Love consists, to put it in biblical terms, in becoming a neighbor to someone in need before that individual becomes a neighbor to oneself.

Finally, the neighbor is seen in this church in his concrete historical reality. It is true that, given the social nature of a human being at every level of life, interpersonal relationships will develop so that in effect some human beings will become one's neighbor at every level of life. However, it is also true that there exists the overwhelming historical fact of the impoverished masses who demand that we become their neighbors. Indeed, one could find in this situation the basis for a solution to the problem of justice. At this time, however, all I wish to affirm—and that is sufficient in itself—is that the practice of love in the church of the poor includes of its very nature that attitude of Jesus which is reflected in the "misereor super turbas" of Mark 6:34, that is to say, the act of becoming a neighbor not only to individuals whom the "I" encounters as a "you," but also to collective entities such as the great majority of the human race and of the Latin American continent. Any practice of love that would exclude from its very center this urgent task of becoming a neighbor to these masses cannot be called a mediation of the experience of God. In the end, such a conception of love would constitute a docetic view of creation: a view that would not accept creation as it actually is, but rather would restrict itself to those areas of human experience where one could choose ahead of time to become a neighbor to someone else.

I would emphasize at this point that the above discussion does not represent by any means a new theoretical truth concerning God or the experience of God. There have been many who have claimed that God is a God of life and of love; many who have claimed that life and love constitute mediations of God and that sin is the reason for his hiddenness; and many who have claimed that a practice of love which gives life to those without it is a privileged mediation of the experience of God. I would simply want to add that the church of the poor provides a structural channel in which these generic affirmations may become fully operative and effective truths. The reason for this claim lies in the historical and material constitution of the church of the poor. Within that church, the affirmation that life is a mediation of the mystery of God becomes obvious in the midst of institutionalized death; similarly, the affirmation that the praxis of love is a privileged mediation of the experience of God also becomes obvious amid those who have surrendered in similar fashion to apathy, indifference and injustice. After all, those narratives of the

Old and New Testaments that speak of the self-revelation of God and of his offer to become our God and to make us, all men, his own people, begin with the following words: "I have seen the affliction of my people . . . and have heard their cry . . ." (Ex 3:7; 6:5). To this exalted truth of the loving nature of the mystery of God, the church of the poor would simply add that such love is historically preceded by the cries of the poor that reach God. Given this position, the church of the poor will always proclaim that which is eternally true concerning the mystery of God, viz., his loving nature, but it will do so only from the perspective of those who find themselves the most deprived similarly of any love.

B. The Experience of the Greater God

The nature of God as mystery includes of necessity being beyond all control, being the totally other, being "the greater being." This aspect of God may be experienced in various ways. In this section, I wish to discuss only two important elements of this experience of God as the greater being, both of which are common in the church of the poor: conversion and the permanent process of conversion.

Conversion may be defined as a turning toward the "true" God. Such a definition has two very important components: 1. the aspect of "turning," of changing the direction of one's life; and 2. the idea that such a "turning" is directed toward the "true" God. As a turning toward God, conversion implies, to be sure, the notion of change, but it is a change which should be more precisely understood as a rupture. There is no question that a change without rupture can be indicative of an experience of the greater God; however, such a change would not alter fundamentally the basic nature and experience of man. A rupture, on the other hand, is a change that allows man to come face to face with the greater God as the one who is totally other.

Given this definition of conversion, the church of the poor attempts to find that concrete historical situation which—in unison with the workings of grace—can provide the channel for such a radical change and, indeed, demand it. For the church of the poor, that concrete situation is to be found historically whenever the radical nature of "the other" becomes most obvious, questioning directly one's own identity and demanding that one become "an-other." Such a concrete historical situation, it claims, is to be found among the poor.[24] Thus, for this church, the poor historically

---

[24] See E. Dussel, "Domination—Liberation: A New Approach," *The Mystical and Political Dimension of the Christian Faith,* ed. Claude Geffré and Gustavo Gutiérrez, Concilium, no. 96 (New York: Herder and Herder, 1974), pp. 34-56.

constitute otherness, i.e., they constitute that which becomes "the other" to the individual and to the church as such; the poor embody the unconditional "No!" of God to the world, i.e., they embody that which one must become and which cannot be ignored by any theodicy; the poor provide a positive direction for the initial stages of the process of conversion, i.e., they provide the task of their liberation as the unconditional "Yes!" of God to the world, a liberation which cannot be relativized by any eschatological reservation. It is clear, therefore, that the church of the poor locates and identifies an historical situation where conversion can take place, i.e., a situation where "the other" exists and demands that one become "an-other."

Perhaps the most important point—although from the point of view of pure theoretical reflection it would appear to be rather trivial—is the fact that the experience of conversion takes place very frequently in the church of the poor. Just as Rahner has correctly pointed out that it is very difficult for a modern human being, that is, for a human being within the perspective of the developed nations, to experience guilt and, therefore, conversion,[25] it must also be pointed out that conversion does take place in the church of the poor and that it can be conceptualized precisely because it does take place. Further, it seems, as far as the phenomenon can be analyzed empirically, that conversion takes place because the very real presence of objective sin in this church makes it extremely difficult to repress subjective guilt. It is "easier" to be aware of one's own status as a sinner in the midst of sinful poverty, even though one may not be able to define in exact terms the relationship between one's subjective guilt and objective sin. Objective sin makes it easier to differentiate between what is and what ought to be, to grasp the qualitative as well as the quantitative dimension of this difference, and to realize how urgent it is to change from what is to what ought to be.

As a human experience, therefore, conversion involves a "turning," an experience of change and rupture. As a theological experience, however, it also implies a turning toward the "true" God. Once again, what I propose here is nothing fundamentally new; the only difference lies in the perspective from which it is presented, viz., the poor as the locus for conversion. From that perspective, to turn toward the "true" God takes on a very specific meaning: it means to turn toward a God who lives and gives life. In Latin America—at least in the way it is generally experienced—conversion does not mean a turning toward God in the face of agnosticism and

---

[25] Rahner, *Foundations,* p. 91.

atheism, but rather a turning toward the true God in the presence of other gods who cause death. The faces of the poor become a positive mediation of the true, but hidden, God insofar as they are also a mediation of those false gods who choose death as the channel for their revelation.

Thus, conversion as a theological experience is not a turning toward God in the face of atheism, but rather in the face of idolatry. The experience of the church of the poor is not one where men call upon many gods, some of which are true and some false, or where they fail to call upon any god at all. It does not involve the question of epistemological disagreement when calling upon the gods or when failing to call upon them. Rather, it has to do with an experience of two very real alternatives: a situation where men encounter death, where they are dehumanized and impoverished, in the name of a specific god, be it a religious god or a secular god such as ''democracy,'' ''private property,'' and ''national security''; or a situation where, in the name of a different god, life is given to them or, at least, actively sought for them. The idolater, therefore, is not someone who errs epistemologically in the process of defining his transcendental experience of God, but someone who brings death upon other men in the name of some god. Similarly, the true believer is not someone who has correctly defined his transcendental experience of God, but someone who gives life to others in the name of this God.[26]

Consequently, the experience of conversion is an experience of God as the greater being primarily because he differs radically from all men. When this experience takes place among the poor, it includes the realization that one must turn toward life, because the real alternative is to cause death. Rahner himself has declared: ''God is always greater . . . than culture, than science, than the Church, the Pope, and all forms of institution. . . .''[27] The church of the poor provides an objective basis for such a claim. God is not only greater because what is uncreated is greater than any creature and because what is unlimited is greater than what is limited, but also because all that is created and limited can ultimately be measured by only one criterion, viz., whether it brings about life or death. God is greater because He guarantees life and because no creature can call upon the name of God in order to disregard life, or to discourage it, or, even worse, to destroy it. Herein lies the fundamental experience of conversion, of turning toward a true God.

---

[26] I have examined this choice between the God of life and the gods of death in greater detail in a forthcoming work, *La aparición del Dios de vida en Jesús de Nazaret.*

[27] Rahner, in *The Jesuits. The Year Book of the Society of Jesus,* 1974-75 (Rome: Curia Generalizia, S.J., 1975), p. 32.

Conversion is, first of all, a turning toward the God of life; however, this is but the beginning of the process of conversion. If conversion is to be Christian, it must also include a constant search for the concrete will of God. Rahner has written as follows: "Is it necessary to discover the will of God because it is not possible fully to know what is willed, here and now, by God, simply by way of a Christian use of reason (principles of reason and faith plus analysis of the situation), because a man must take into account on principle and not merely as a hypothetical case not normally met with in practice, that God may make known to him some definite will of his over and above what is shown by the Christian use of reason within the framework of Christian principles applied to the particular situation?"[28]

Given the possibility that God may reveal his will to man, the conclusion is inevitable: man must always be open to the process of coming to know the concrete will of God in varied ways. In addition, however, particular attention must be given to that historical channel which makes it possible for the diverse will of God to be revealed in the course of history. This channel includes, first of all, life itself—its transitory character; its different stages; its surprises and disappointments; its changes and failures, etc. However, I would argue—and I do not mean to deny thereby the importance of the channel of human changeability—that the church of the poor provides a historical channel that demands that life become a theological process in search for the will of God. This channel is made possible by a dialectic which is inherent in and essential to the church of the poor. In this church, one finds two fundamental affirmations that are true only when considered dialectically. The first one includes an incessant condemnation of oppressive poverty and a determined resolve to eradicate it; the second involves the adoption of a real kenosis, that is, a life of voluntary poverty and an attitude of solidarity with the poor.[29] It would be relatively easy from both a theoretical and a practical point of view to designate only one of these poles as the mediation of the experience of God. A much more difficult task is to claim that both poles represent the correct mediation of that experience. However, it is precisely because of this structural and, therefore, permanent difficulty that the experience of God has to be characterized as a process and the task of man described as a search for the will of God, as an attempt to discern that will. Fur-

---

[28] Rahner, *The Dynamic Element in the Church*, trans. W. J. O'Hara, Questiones disputatae, no. 12 (New York: Herder and Herder, 1964), p. 91.

[29] Liberation theology was well aware of this dialectic from the very beginning, e.g., G. Gutiérrez, *A Theology of Liberation*, pp. 299-302; I. Ellacuría, "Las bienaventuranzas come Carta Fundacional," pp. 117-18.

ther, to undergo this process and undertake this task is, in effect, to relive Jesus' own process in his search for a "messianism" that could adequately describe his own mission.

That lack of knowledge which is inherent in man's knowledge of God, that a priori inability to manipulate God which is inherent in the process of letting God be God, and that possession of God which is true possession only when understood as a way of God further characterize this process. As a result, the church of the poor may be said to undergo the experience of a search for the will of God and thus the experience of the greater God. However, this experience should not be seen as the result of a decision made by the church of the poor on the basis of knowledge acquired through theoretical reflection, but rather as a process which is demanded by its own structure, i.e., as an attempt to sustain the search for a synthesis which can never be adequately attained. And it is this experience that constitutes the historical mediation of letting God be God.

C. The Experience of the Lesser God

The privileged perspective of the previous reflection should be obvious: this is also an historical characteristic of the church of the poor. At this point, I believe it would be helpful to treat this perspective thematically, i.e., as an element in the experience of God. First of all, the proposition that God's nature has to be absolute in character has been a long accepted teaching in both the philosophical and the Christian traditions. If this claim were to be denied, then God could in no way be considered the absolute origin or the absolute future or the absolute Lord of history.

However, this true proposition may give rise to a rather serious error in the understanding or description of the experience of God. God can be said to be present in all things as their ultimate ground and horizon, but he cannot be said to be present equally in all things. This is a second traditional Christian doctrine: God is present in man, in the neighbor. If God is present in all things, he may be found in all things; however, this proposition in and of itself does not solve the problem of a concrete access to God or that of a hierarchical arrangement within such an access so that he may indeed be found in all things. Consequently, out of this situation emerges the expression, "the lesser God," an expression which is metaphorically correct, but no less metaphorical than that of "the greater God." What this expression means is that one cannot approach God in the same way from all experiences, but rather that such an approach must take place from adequate experiences and, more specifically, from those experiences which prima facie would seem to have absolutely nothing to do with God.

Rahner has correctly stated that the claim, "whoever searches for God has already found him," represents authentic Christian teaching. However, this teaching must be made concrete through another authentic Christian teaching: "The question is not whether someone is seeking God or not, but whether he is seeking him where God himself said he is."[30] That locus consists of the world of the poor as I have described it above. The search for this concrete locus may be historically difficult—a real difficulty, for example, in the context of the developed nations. However, the difficult nature of this task does not prevent one from emphasizing formally the privileged position of the poor in the experience of God or from claiming that the very attempt to determine who the poor actually are—regardless of the success of such an enterprise—is important for the experience of God.

From the point of view of philosophical reflection, it is clear that God cannot be reached directly from the absolute character of the totality of existence and history. However, the position that he must be reached only from the perspective of the poor is possible only within Christian faith. Consequently, the church of the poor, in recalling what it takes to be the fundamental truths of revelation, "justifies" an access to God that is privileged in nature.

First of all, the revelation of the mystery of God has been accomplished in terms of a "lessening," a kenosis. Indeed, the incarnation of Christ presupposes a double "lessening." The first one consists of the fact that he became man—a teaching which has been held and revered by all of Christian tradition. The second, proclaimed and emphasized by the church of the poor, consists of the fact that he became weak and showed solidarity with the poor. Although from a logical point of view, this second "lessening" could be regarded as being accidental to the life of Jesus—that is, as if his incarnation could have just as easily taken place in another context and showed a different kind of solidarity—from a historical point of view this is impossible. "I have been sent to preach the Good News to the poor." It is always possible to interpret this text as one more text of the life of Jesus and not to draw any logical conclusions from it. Likewise, it is also possible to interpret "the poor" to mean "all men." However, if these words have not totally lost their meaning and if the entire life of Jesus is taken into consideration so that his own partiality can be observed from the point of view of his tragic end, then it is clear that in Jesus' life one may find a partiality and a solidarity that are historically constitutive. Such a partiality, which takes place at the second level of kenosis of the Christ and not at the

---

[30] J. P. Miranda, *Marx and the Bible*, p. 57

first, forms part of the "surprise" that the incarnation itself brings and that corresponds, as Rahner himself tells us,[31] to a certain lack of knowledge on the part of man concerning himself prior to the incarnation. If Christ has something really historical to say concerning what it means to be a man and concerning the kinds of relationships with other men that are necessary in order to become such a man, then it is clear that "man" himself becomes a mediation for the experience of God if seen from a very specific perspective: "man" as someone who is poor or who shows solidarity with the poor.

Secondly, if the proper appellation for Christ is not only that of "man," but also that of "son," then it follows that he himself has an experience of the Father, an experience of God, and that that experience becomes a prototype for our own experience of God. He is the faithful witness that has lived the faith first and in fullness (Heb 12:2). In his concrete way to the Father, Christ himself becomes the way for us to the Father. I cannot analyze in detail at this point the way of Jesus, but I do wish to affirm that both his objective way as well as what can be discerned of his subjective experience have been shaped by the perspective of the poor and by his partiality for them. Neither the controversies nor the exposé of oppressive religious traditions nor the prophetic denunciation of the rich, the priests, the intellectuals and the politicians nor the threats and persecutions in the course of his life nor above all his own end can be understood simply as consequences of his defense of "man"; rather, they should be seen as direct results of his defense of "the poor." It is this partial perspective of his mission—a partiality which may also be observed in his subjective experience, given his messianic temptations, his prayers, his knowledge or lack of knowledge with respect to the coming of the Kingdom—that Jesus fundamentally requires of anyone who wishes to follow him. Further, it is this following which in turn constitutes the only way for us to become sons in the son and thus to have the experience of the Father. Finally, this following, which may also be described as a taking up of the cross, is also historically privileged, given the reasons why the way to God is a way to the cross.

Thirdly and finally, the church of the poor finds its constitutive partiality in the famous passage of Matthew 25. The passage may be read in two ways: as a simple demand for ethical action in the church or as having more pronounced consequences for an understanding of the formal nature of the experience of God. In the first reading, the act of reaching out to the neighbor in an attitude of love and

---

[31] Rahner, "On the Theology of the Incarnation," *Theological Investigations* 4, trans. Kevin Smith (Baltimore: Helicon Press, 1966), pp. 107-11.

service already constitutes, to be sure, a historical gesture in which the transcendental necessity of love for the experience of God is made concrete.

In the second reading, however, this act of reaching out to the neighbor, as presented in Matthew 25, also functions as a mediation of the experience of God. The unity of love of neighbor and love of God constitutes a profound truth; however, this truth will remain a simple tautology or be construed as pure idealism unless the generic aspect of the three terms in question—love, neighbor and God—is shattered and made concrete. I believe that the description of Matthew 25 carries out in effect this historical function of shattering and making concrete. The poor as poor and not simply as men serve to shatter the previous interest of natural man—and "natural" should not be understood here in its technical meaning of opposition to a "supernatural" elevation—and to provide the basis for a response to questions such as, what is love, who is the neighbor, and, more fundamentally, who is God. This natural egocentric interest of man—and "egocentric" should not be understood here in a moral sense, but rather in a structural sense—is shattered when love takes place previously where there is no reason or hope for a fulfilling gratification. And when this happens, the natural understanding of God may also be shattered in a fulfilling extrapolation of the self-understanding of man.[32] The claim that God may be found in the poor of Matthew 25 should hardly be called self-evident, and the acceptance of that claim should be even less self-evident. However, if the claim is true, then the contrary affirmation is also true: the experience of God demands in and of itself a certain amount of scandal, but a scandal that can be perceived only from the perspective of the poor.

This constitutive partiality of the experience of God does not invalidate the universality of other experiences where God can be found, and it does single out that experience without which the others could be considered generic experiences of a mystery, but not necessarily Christian experiences of God. There is an ultimate theological reason for this assertion: "Become poor as long as there is poverty in the world; identify yourselves with the poor."[33] As a result, one must seriously ask whether all Christian teachings should not be mediated by this partiality, whether the locus for raising a question and awaiting a response concerning truth, love or freedom

---

[32] This is an experience which J. Moltmann, following D. Bonhoeffer, has described in his recent work, *The Crucified Christ; The Cross of Christ as the Foundation and Criticism of Christian Theology* (New York: Harper & Row, 1974), and which takes place daily in the church of the poor in the presence of the crucified majorities.

[33] I. Ellacuría, "La Iglesia de los pobres," p. 717.

should not be the privileged world of the poor, and whether ultimately the above mentioned correlation, "gloria Dei, homo vivens," should not be understood in terms of yet another correlation, "gloria Dei, pauper vivens."

If this partiality—this "preferential option for the poor," as the Puebla document calls it—is rejected or dismissed as being exaggerated, opportunist and manipulative, then the question must be raised as to whether there exists any other locus for the experience of God which can be considered more Christian and more historically possible than that of the church of the poor. It is impossible, on the one hand, to reject this partiality in favor of a position that emphasizes the universality of the experience of God: the total character of any experience must always be expressed through a more concrete element of that experience. Similarly, it is impossible to reject it in favor of a position that emphasizes the fundamental equality of all concrete experiences of God: both from the point of view of history and of Christian tradition, this would be a misunderstanding of the fact that poverty is an historical product of the dialectic of oppressive wealth. Although one may claim to be at the margin of these two poles of history, in effect such a position can never be actually realized. History presents a very real choice: to understand the absolute mystery of God from the perspective of power or from that of poverty. To reject one partiality is to accept the other. If one does not think and live from below, one will think and live from above. If one does not experience God as a God who empties himself for men, one will experience him as a God of power without dialectic, i.e., as power without service, where service is understood historically in terms of the cross and of scandal.

D. The Experience of the Crucified God

As scandalous as such a proclamation may seem, one must affirm vigorously and without compromise that the experience of God implies in and of itself the notion of scandal. Many of the teachings of the faith point directly to it. The fact that God became flesh, that the son humbled himself even unto death on the cross, that the wisdom of God was manifested in the cross, that the anguished cry of Jesus on the cross was met with silence, and that grace now overflows where sin used to abound: from the point of view of both philosophical and religious reason, these truths are not self-evident, but scandalous. Indeed, even within Christian faith itself, it is a rather difficult task to take these truths seriously or to preserve them as a substantial element of the experience of God.

In the church of the poor, this scandal appears first and foremost through the scandal of history itself and points directly to what has traditionally been called the problem of theodicy. The difference is that neither the problem nor the solution are formulated in traditional terms. Thus, for example, the primary scandal in this church is not the need to reconcile the misery of the world with the nature of God, but rather the very existence of this misery in the world.[34] Likewise, the solution is not sought in an understanding of God that would allow for a conceptual reconciliation of the misery of the world with the nature of God. The church of the poor accepts, consciously or unconsciously, the fact of the scandal of history and—this is the fundamental point—uses it as a basis for its own structure. It does not seek to organize itself on the basis of what men call power, wisdom or beauty, but rather on the basis of the poor, the persecuted and all those crucified by history. It does not blame God for this situation. That attitude, as surprising as this may be, simply does not exist. On the contrary, the church of the poor looks upon God as its own ally on the basis of a certain intuition into the nature of God and its relatedness to the historical scandal as well as on the basis of a concomitant realization that salvation and liberation have to be secured through this scandal of history and not outside of it.

Moltmann has spoken of a "crucified God," and we are all aware of the difficulties of that terminology and of the necessary qualifications that have to be made. Nevertheless, the fact remains—and this is specially evident in the church of the poor—that unless one introduces the notion of scandal into one's conception of God, the nature of his salvific redemption will have been thoroughly misunderstood. This does not mean that the expression itself is frequently used in the church of the poor; what it does mean is that the reality conveyed by the expression is commonly found in that church. Indeed, one may even speak in that context of a "crucified people" as the primary scandal and as no longer a partial, but rather a specifically privileged locus for the experience of God.

At the same time, it is a fact that from the abyss of this scandal hope rises triumphant, confessing God as the absolute future or, in more typical Latin American language, as the liberator, the one who can be trusted. There is hope in the church of the poor. Further, it is not a naive kind of hope, since the church itself is born out of a situation where one would expect only despair or resignation. The church of the poor knows that the just man does not fare well, that the poor who struggle for their dignity are oppressed, and that those who show solidarity with them are persecuted. Indeed, it almost seems as if the oppressor has in effect the final say in and concerning history.

---

[34] J. Sobrino, "El conocimiento teológico," pp. 440ff.

In such a situation only one kind of hope can exist: that peculiarly Christian mode of hope that Paul calls hope "against all hope." At the same time, it is precisely in such a situation that one finds a possible structural channel wherein the scandalous aspect of God may be truly grasped. The characteristic darkness of faith—that element of *sacrificium intellectus* which is always a part of faith—is mediated therein by the black darkness of hope. If in spite of and through such a situation hope arises and endures, then it is clear that a very profound experience of the totality of history and of existence itself takes place in the church of the poor. This experience goes beyond a simple hope for a favorable outcome or a naive trust in optimistic mechanisms and solutions; it is much more profound than that. It is above all an acceptance of the enduring presence of truth, love and justice in the world. It is, furthermore, an affirmation to the effect that God can be found in the world, specifically, in the abysmal misery that exists in that world. Thus, the most important task of the church of the poor is not to attempt to formulate or employ these theological positions explicitly, but to continue to hope. If such hope does endure, then one may conclude that there exists within this church a mediation of the experience of God, a knowledge that God's silence is not his final say concerning history, and a conviction that the executioner does not ultimately triumph over his victims.

The ability to continue to hope in this way constitutes in effect the Christian utopia. To believe, despite everything, in the resurrection of Jesus and of all history becomes its generic formulation. This is the privilege, both tragic and joyful, of the church of the poor: to opt for hope where there should be none. Such hope goes against hope itself, but it is not groundless. If on the one hand the power of sin again and again clouds our understanding of God as the Creator, as the guarantor of life, and points us toward the crucified God, on the other the generosity of service, the raising of the consciousness of the poor with respect to their own dignity as sons of God, and their struggles and concrete gains serve to ground and strengthen anew this very vulnerable attitude of hope. It is within such a dialectic that hope endures as a process toward the mystery of God. He who hopes does not possess, but is on the way to possession. He who hopes against hope, who keeps that absolute mystery alive, is on the way to God, a God whom he will have to regard both as a crucified God and as the absolute future without any possibility of ever synthesizing the two affirmations. In undertaking and continuing in this difficult way of hope, one believes that the road does have an end.

To keep hope alive refers not only to the subjective experience of continuing to hope, but also to the adoption of and perseverance in the Christian praxis of love and justice in a world that is marked by conflict and in which persecution and martyrdom abound. This hope against hope, this mediation of the experience of God, is not grounded on its own power or on the act of waiting itself or on a belief in a promising future. Rather, it arises out of the historical practice of love, despite the seemingly impotent character of this love. For this hope the darkness of the future is grounded in the darkness of the present, that is, the persecution that characterizes the lot of the just man. But the light of the future is also grounded in the light of the present, that is, the ultimate human experience that he who loves has in effect fulfilled the law and that no one has greater love than he who dies for his brother. In the end, the church of the poor will be able to describe this experience only by way of negation, as is the case in all sound theological work. It has no adequate knowledge of the future, of the meaning of fullness or of the mystery of God. However, it is quite aware of the fact that unless it adopts this attitude of hope—that is, a hope which is active and fruitful, but also against all hope—it will have failed to correspond adequately to this mystery.

III. Conclusion. Historical Experience and Faith in God

The acceptance of the claim that specific historical experiences can serve as authentic mediations of the experience of God is already an act of faith and indeed the most fundamental act of faith, since it accepts thereby a correspondence between the historical and the theological structures of reality. This faith always presupposes "more"—and this quality of "more" may be interpreted in different ways, e.g., as "beyond" or "in the future" or "in the past" or "more profound"—than what the historical experience itself conveys. As a result, faith always implies a leap that cannot be adequately analyzed from the purely historical level of the experience.

Thus, faith in the mystery of God does not arise automatically from specific historical experiences, not even from those I have described above. This claim is historically correct: many who have not approached history or its meaning from the perspective of the mystery of God have had experiences fundamentally similar in nature to the ones described above. It is also theologically correct: faith in God has always been regarded as a grace and a gift, categories which theology employs to affirm the discontinuity that exists in principle between faith and historical experience.

At the same time, it is also true that there can be no faith without a historical experience. There are two basic reasons for this claim: the fact that faith does exist, that one does come to believe; and the fact that the quality of faith does differ, since faith—when it is understood primarily as a concrete reality in the believer and not only as a true, generic formulation—will vary according to different historical experiences. Therefore, while it is true that history does not automatically give rise to faith, it is also true that faith cannot exist without the historical experience.

Consequently, in analyzing what I have called the "experiences" of God in the church of the poor, I have attempted above all to describe in detail how the church of the poor, in its concrete historical reality, provides different types of experiences that can be accepted as historical mediations of the experience of the mystery of God. I have tried to do no more than this, but also no less. The fundamental point of this enterprise has been to make all subjective experiences dependent on objective historical reality. In so doing, I have tried to avoid a noble, but rather dangerous position: that of a purely conceptual view of the nature of faith. It is true that in the act of desiring to have faith, an individual is already adopting a subjective attitude which somehow corresponds to that element of faith which we call availability. However, that desire by itself, i.e., independent of all objective conditions of history, may remain nothing but a pure and empty desire, or, even worse, it may try to interpret, even by basing itself on a reading of the Scriptures, the content of faith, the mystery of God, from the perspective of its own subjectivity, i.e., ignoring all objective criteria. By way of contrast, the church of the poor offers a historically objective channel for the experience of God, a channel through which all generic attitudes and contents of the faith, which as generic realities are certainly to be found in the Scriptures, can be made concrete.

In the church of the poor, one may also find that element of *sacrificium* essential to faith. It is clear that faith implies a *sacrificium intellectus:* although the Church has always proclaimed the mystery of God as comprehensible, it has also declared it to be incomprehensible. It is impossible to relate to that mystery unless one is willing to abandon reason by an act of reason. In order to have an adequate knowledge of God, one must be willing to give up knowledge, even though one may know the reason for the lack of knowledge. The church of the poor interprets this *sacrificium* of the intellect in terms of a greater and more complete sacrifice, the *sacrificium vitae.* It is in the context of real life, of history, that man must give up an understanding of the ultimate mystery of life as well as the claim to have the final and absolute say concerning history. Further, it is also in that context that man must be willing to give of his own life and even give up his own life in order to be able to correspond to the mystery of life. The mystery of God will remain hidden without this fundamental sacrifice in and of life. The *sacrificium intellectus* will become a part of that *sacrificium vitae;* the reverse, however, is not necessarily true.

At the same time, one may also find in the church of the poor a locus for understanding God, a locus where faith can become an *obsequium rationabile.* The experiences I have mentioned above—the emphasis on and the urgent call for love and justice, the creative nature of history, the hope that endures—make this God in whose name they take place a "comprehensible" God. In these experiences the individual comes to an awareness of himself by unleashing a positive type of history, that is, by immersing himself in the flow of life and of the creation of life. When it is viewed in this way, faith does not alienate; on the contrary, it reflects and embodies what is most positive in history and it unleashes true history.

Finally, in the church of the poor one finds a locus where faith can be experienced as an *obsequium,* that is, in terms of gift and gratitude. The endurance of hope where there should be only despair, of love and justice where a prudent withdrawal would be much more realistic, of the conviction that love grounds all reality: these are all signs that what is impossible has become possible, that we have been given something which is greater and stronger than our own selves, something which imposes itself upon us and before which all we can do is utter a final word of thanksgiving.

Like any other ecclesial channel, the church of the poor has limitations and, as such, is subject to a certain characteristic element of danger with regard to its faith in God. This danger is grounded not only on the natural limitations and sinfulness of its members, but also on its own specific structure. It may appear, first of all, as a possible weariness in continuing to hope against hope and in striving to preserve the tension between the struggle against scandalous poverty and the commitment to an active life of poverty. It may also appear as an increasing desire to look to the historical process itself for some hope of a solution, thus limiting the role and reality of the mystery of God.

Nevertheless, despite these dangers, the church of the poor provides an objective—and indeed the best—locus for a life of faith. It does not in and of itself weaken the mystery of God, as many of its detractors have claimed; rather, it strengthens and widens it. It seeks to recover the tradition of the church and to enrich it. In attempting to make faith in God more concrete in its own specific way, it provides a verification of that faith: it recovers much more adequately the evangelical roots of belief in Jesus and it unleashes new history according to the Spirit of God. This verification constitutes in effect the ultimate warranty for its own faith as well as for the claims that its historical experiences can serve as mediations of the experience of God and that it is the nature of God itself that unleashes these specific experiences.

A Response to Fr. Sobrino

by Dr. Fernando Segovia

To an exegete of the New Testament and/or a historian of the early church, a study such as the present one on the experience of God in the church of the poor by Fr. Jon Sobrino is a most interesting piece of work. The central thesis of the work, as I see it, is the claim that the church of the poor has a privileged hermeneutical position in contrast to other historically conditioned, ecclesial or non-ecclesial, experiences of God, because its own experience of God corresponds very closely to—one could almost say "duplicates"—that of Jesus, the Son of God, i.e., an experience of partiality for and solidarity with the poor.

In the last few years, several exegetical studies have appeared that deal precisely with the issue of the poor and of poverty as the ideal way of life for the followers of Jesus in the early Church. I am referring, above all, to two works by the German exegete, Eduard Schweizer: the first, a commentary on the Gospel of Matthew [*Das Evangelium nach Matthäus,* Das Neue Testament Deutsch, no. 2 (Göttingen: Vandenhoeck & Ruprecht, 1973)]; the second, a subsequent study on the character of the Matthean community [*Matthäus und seine Gemeinde,* Stuttgarter Bibelstudien, no. 71 (Stuttgart: KBW Verlag, 1974)]; and one—which is really a summary of positions taken in earlier articles—by another German exegete, Gerd Theissen [*Soziologie der Jesusbewegung. Ein Beitrag zur Entstehungsgeschichte des Urchristentums* (Munich: Chr. Kaiser Verlag, 1977)].

First of all, it is Schweizer's opinion that the Matthean community represented a group of Christian believers who renounced home, family, and worldly goods, and became instead wandering charismatic prophets. Similarly, Theissen would see some of the earliest followers of Jesus, those who were largely responsible for the transmission of the *logia* of Jesus, as embracing a similar type of life, i.e., a wandering life of prophetic preaching and healing. Furthermore, both men would see the respective subjects of their studies, i.e., the Matthean community and the earliest transmitters of Jesus' *logia,* as claiming that their lifestyle corresponded to and duplicated that of the Lord Jesus.

Against this exegetical background, it is most interesting, I repeat, to read Fr. Sobrino's work. In effect, what the present study represents is an ardent call on the part of a contemporary systematic theologian to the church at large to become a church of the poor, to take up an active life of poverty, a life not altogether unlike that of the wandering charismatic prophets traced by Schweizer and Theissen in the early church. Furthermore, such a call is sounded primarily on the very similar claim that only such a life, only such an experience of God, authentically recovers and duplicates that of the historical Jesus himself, fulfills Jesus' own unquestionable and unanalyzable call to his followers, and represents a deeper and more effective grasp of the absolute mystery of God.

In what follows, I should like to respond to Fr. Sobrino's call and grounds for that call primarily as an exegete and a historian, although, to be sure, the paper could be approached and evaluated from a number of different angles, e.g., systematics, sociology, economics, political science. The response will consist of certain *caveats* on the following three points: 1. the historical Jesus' experience of God; 2. the privileged hermeneutical position of the church of the poor; 3. the goal or rewards of the church of the poor.

1. *The historical Jesus' experience of God.* To a contemporary exegete of the New Testament, Fr. Sobrino's strong and confident position on the possibility of reconstructing the historical Jesus is most unexpected. To someone who, for seven decades now, has stood in the shadow of Albert Schweitzer's *Von Reimarus zu Wrede* (1906); who is accustomed to speaking of the Markan Jesus, the Matthean Jesus, the Lukan Jesus, the Johannine Jesus, the Jesus of the Q tradition, but seldom discusses the Jesus of Nazareth; who rarely encounters in the scholarly journals of his field an article dealing with the historical Jesus; and, finally, who is used to arranging his texts according to elaborate form, redaction and literary methodologies; to such a person, any mention of the historical Jesus is treated only with extreme reluctance and with great trepidation.

For someone raised in this methodological background, Fr. Sobrino's work is, I repeat, most unexpected. The position taken with regard to the historical Jesus in this work is very clear and very strong. It is foreshadowed in the eighth presupposition found within the introduction and then succinctly summarized in the third section of Part II, entitled, "The Experience of the Lesser God." I reproduce those words:

> . . . then it follows that he himself has an experience of the Father, an experience of God, and that that experience becomes a prototype for our own experience of God . . . In his concrete way to the Father, Christ himself becomes the way for us to the Father. I cannot analyze in detail at this point the way of Jesus, but I do wish to affirm that both his objective way as well as what can be discerned of his subjective experience have been shaped by the perspective of the poor and by his partiality for them.

Thus, Jesus' own experience of the Father is dominated by his partiality for and solidarity with the poor and stands as a beckoning call—a call whose reasonableness cannot be analyzed—to all believers. Fr. Sobrino also provides the reader with examples of those objective events in Jesus' life (e.g., the controversies; the accusations against oppressive religious traditions; the denunciations of the rich, the priests, the intellectuals and the politicians; the threats and the persecutions) and subjective attitudes (e.g., his messianic temptations; his prayer) that confirm the existence of such a partiality.

As an exegete of the New Testament, I should like to offer at this point a *caveat*. Any reconstruction of the historical Jesus or of a particular Christian tradition cannot abandon or do without a rigorous application of the existing exegetical methodologies; otherwise, such an enquiry runs the danger of mixing different layers of tradition or of not including important elements or texts from that tradition. Let me give two examples that point out these methodological difficulties.

It seems to me, first of all, that any attempt to reconstruct the historical Jesus—and especially one that would make the end result of such a reconstruction an unanalyzable call—must come to terms with Jesus' imminent expectation of the arrival of the Kingdom of God as reported by several writers of the New Testament. Thus, for example, one finds the Jesus of the Synoptic traditions making the following prophecies: in Mk. 8:34-9:1 par one finds Jesus telling the disciples about the conditions of discipleship and promising in v. 9:1, "Truly, I say to you, there are some standing here who will not taste death before they see the Kingdom of God come with power"; again, in Mk. 13:30-32 par, as part of the apocalyptic discourse, Jesus tells the disciples, "Truly, I say to you, this generation will not pass away before all these things take place"; finally, in Mk. 14:62 (Mt. 26:64), within the trial scene, Jesus responds to the question of the High Priest as follows: "I am; and you will see the Son of man sitting at the right hand of Power, and coming with the clouds of heaven."

Likewise, in what is regarded by many as the earliest written document of the New Testament, I Thessalonians, one finds Paul, in the Exhortation section of the letter (4:1-5:22), relaying to the community instructions from the Lord Jesus. One of these instructions has to do with the fear among the Thessalonians that those who have died will not meet Jesus when he returns; Paul assuages those fears as follows (vv. 4:13-18): "For this we declare to you by the word of the Lord, that we who are alive, who are left until the coming of the Lord, shall not precede those who have fallen asleep."

Thus, any reconstruction of the mission and message of the historical Jesus that leaves these texts out of consideration must justify methodologically such a serious exclusion. If, on the other hand, the texts are accepted, then their relationship to other elements of the reconstructed message must be shown, e.g., partiality for the poor (cf. A. Schweitzer's radical interim ethics). Finally, if the texts are accepted and if the call of Jesus is not to be analyzed in terms of its reasonableness, then the failure of these prophecies to come true presents a very serious challenge to the believer.

A second example. In the first section of Part II of the paper, entitled, "The Experience of the God Whose Kingdom is Near," Fr. Sobrino employs Jesus' response to the disciples of John from Mt. 11:2-6/Lk. 7:18-23 (Mt: "Go and tell John what you hear and see: the blind receive their sight and the lame walk, lepers are cleansed and the deaf hear, and the dead are raised up, and the poor have the good news preached to them") as a direct example of the partiality of the Good News for the poor. In this passage, Jesus' miracle working powers clearly indicate that he is "the one who is to come."

Yet, in another part of the same synoptic tradition, within the parable of the sower and its explanation (Mk. 4:1-20 par), one finds Jesus making a distinction between the disciples and the crowds, i.e., those who, according to the Gospels, come to Jesus because of his miracle working powers and his exorcisms and who have been characterized by Fr. Sobrino as the oppressed. That distinction runs as follows: "Then, the disciples came to him and said, 'Why do you speak to them in parables?' And he answered them, 'To you it has been given to know the secrets of the kingdom of heaven, but to them it has not been given. For to him who has will more be given, and he will have abundance; but from him who has not, even what he has will be taken away. This is why I speak to them in parables, because seeing they do not see, and hearing they do not hear, nor do they understand' " (Mt. 13:10-13). On the basis of this text, one could conclude that the crowds, the oppressed, are not receiving the fullness of the message.

Again, this attitude, this distinction, if excluded, must be justified methodologically; and, if included, must be reconciled with other parts of the reconstructed message, e.g., the partiality for the poor. I offer these examples as *caveats,* not as refutations.

2. *The privileged hermeneutical position of the poor.* To a contemporary exegete of the New Testament, i.e., someone who is accustomed to drawing comparisons among the different, and sometimes conflicting, christologies of the New Testament and to tracing the different, and sometimes conflicting, interpretations of Christian discipleship based on these christologies, any affirmation of the diversity of opinion, such as the one espoused by Fr. Sobrino, is most heartening.

Again, I reproduce his words (taken from the second section of Part II of the paper, entitled, "Variety and Complementarity of the Historical Experience of Faith"):

> From the very beginning, the church accepted an historical configuration of that term. In so doing, it also accepted the different historical situations of its members as well as the different historical mediations of the experience of God. . . . Thus the church accepted a diversity of cultures and of social configurations regardless of their minority or majority status. It accepted the diversity of abilities and of 'charisma,' of talents and contributions from different individuals and groups of individuals, necessary for the constitution of a social body.

However, at the same time that a diversity in experiences of God is being recognized, a hierarchy is being affirmed on the basis of a present reconstruction and reliving of the experience of God of the historical Jesus. The following texts are indicative: the first is taken from the sixth presupposition in the introduction; the second, from the third section of Part II of the paper, entitled, "The Experience of the Lesser God":

> In what follows, I proceed to describe the experience of God in the church of the poor, first of all, from a descriptive and expository point of view. . . . Yet, at the same time, if the description should yield more accurately, from an historical point of view, that which is essential to the experience of God according to revelation, then the description becomes to a certain extent normative as well as indirectly polemical or apologetic. Further, one would also have to affirm that one could find today within the church of the poor a "better"— though by no means unique—channel for the experience of God.

> This constitutive partiality of the experience of God does not invalidate the universality of other experiences where God can be found, and it does single out that experience without which the others could be considered generic experiences of a mystery, but not necessarily Christian experiences of God.

As an exegete and historian, I should like to offer at this point a second *caveat*. The exegete is used to seeing in the earliest Christian traditions and christologies an ever present danger to absolutism, toward the development of a certain Christian elitism. Thus, from the point of view of the exegete, any talk of a deeper or more effective contact with or grasp of *the* Christian tradition is received, once again, with great trepidation. The exegete would rather see a position enter into serious dialogue with the range of christologies and forms of discipleship in the canon out of which we work as members of a church—all of which would lay claim to contact with the historical Jesus.

3. *The goal or rewards of the church of the poor.* I should like to end my response with a question which is an implicit *caveat.* When the exegete examines the texts and the reconstructions of the groups or communities outlined by both Schweizer and Theissen, he or she sees that the radical ethic espoused in these writings—an ethic which is accompanied in both cases by charismatic activities—looks forward to an imminent return of the Lord and to the retribution of good and evil: those who have suffered here will very soon find rest in the next world, in the Kingdom; those who have persecuted here will soon be punished in that place where there is the weeping and the gnashing of teeth (see, e.g., Mt. 25:10b-12, 8:11-12; Lk. 13:22-30). My question is as follows: in the apparent absence of apocalyptic fervor, what is the ultimate goal of the church of the poor? What goal can it have or can it present that will allow it to preserve its privileged status? This is not immediately clear to me from the argumentation of the present study.

I conclude these remarks by emphasizing the fact that the *caveats* should be taken in the spirit of a closer dialogue between systematic theology and biblical studies and by extending my thanks to Fr. Sobrino for a very challenging and well-reasoned line of argumentation.

A Response to Fr. Sobrino

by Rev. Joseph Komonchak

Jon Sobrino has written an interesting paper on an important topic. It attempts to move Karl Rahner's thought in a direction which I think Rahner would admit to be valid and necessary but which he has not himself attempted to follow. In some of the more densely packed paragraphs of his *Foundations of Christian Faith,* Rahner has defended the necessarily ecclesial character of Christianity.[1] This defense is based on earlier positions on the inescapable concreteness of the experience of grace which is the heart of Christian existence.[2] As concrete, this experience is mediated by an individual's time and place, language and culture, past and present, by the freedom of others and the chances for the exercise of his own freedom. This inescapable historicality and sociality of existence provides the basic anthropological ground for Rahner's "indirect" vindication of the ecclesial character of Christianity.

Where Sobrino advances beyond Rahner is in the effort to describe in their fully concrete reality the only transcendentally oriented subjects that exist—*incarnate* subjects. For that incarnation or embodiment of unlimited subjectivity, which is, of course, central to Rahner's thought, always has quite concrete economic, social, political, cultural locations. To say, as Rahner does, that the transcendental experience is mediated by the categorical is to say, as Sobrino presumes, that the experience of transcendence is economically, socially, politically, culturally mediated.[3] The excitement provoked by the "political turn" in general and by Sobrino's essay in particular is that they force us theologians to descend from our abstract heavens to deal concretely with human subjects in all their particularity and concreteness; or at least—if that suggests too severe a criticism of alternate approaches—to cause us to reconsider those categorical mediations within which we tend to take it for granted that the questions about the meaning and value of human existence and, through them, about the meaning and value of Christianity, must be asked. Most of us, I suspect, tend to agree with Bultmann against Barth that the key to interpretation is the "pre-understanding" we bring to Christian texts and Christian proclama-

---

[1] Karl Rahner, *Foundations of Christian Faith: An Introduction to the Idea of Christianity,* trans. Wiiliam Dych (New York: Seabury Press, 1978), pp. 322-23, 342-43, 345-48; see also pp. 389-90.

[2] Ibid., pp. 14-43, 94-97, 106-7, 138-42.

[3] The point is simply an extension of Levi-Strauss' statement, "Whoever says 'Man' says 'Language,' and whoever says 'Language' says 'Society' " (Quoted without further reference in Arthur Brittan, *The Privatised World* [London: Routledge and Kegan Paul, 1977], p. 15).

tion. Less often do we attend to the taken-for-granted character of our own pre-understanding, and we tend to overlook the degree to which our categorical pre-understandings channel the power, focus the light, and constrict the range of the experience of transcendence offered us in grace and in Gospel.

By the taken-for-granted of the pre-understanding which we bring to the Gospel, I mean what is known in answering such questions as: which questions are we asking of the Gospel? in what categories? on what assumptions? for what purposes? with what self-consciousness? It is, of course, impossible to approach the Gospel without presuppositions; all we can do is to try to be self-critical about them, to reduce their taken-for-granted character, perhaps first of all by self-reflection: if now the Gospel says to us what it once did not say, why now does it say that? What prevented our hearing it earlier? What enables us to hear it now? What might we not be hearing now? Perhaps by this means a way might open which could lead, first, to a more critical control of our own interpretative efforts and methods and, secondly, to a common ground on which differences in interpretation can be civilly and effectively addressed.

A second point on which Sobrino advances Rahner's thought is an immediate corollary of the first. For the ecclesial character of Christianity which Rahner urges in a very formal way is here again *concretely* addressed and described. Sobrino is not speaking of the Church in general, nor of the Church as theologically defined, but of *a* Church concretely existing in the world. He begins with the assumption that Christian subjectivity is *shared* subjectivity, *ecclesial* subjectivity, but the shared, ecclesial character of this subjectivity has the same concreteness and particularity as individual existence. This is not to deny the universality of Christian ecclesial subjectivity, any more than our common humanity need be threatened by our wondrous individuality. But it is to suggest the need for theologians to speak *concretely* about the Church as self-realized in history, as realized *here* rather than *there,* among and in *this* people, rather than *that,* in *this* situation rather than *that, now* rather than *then.* The differences implied here do not affect only matters external and peripheral, but the realization in a concrete body of human beings of those distinctive meanings and values, centered on the figure of Jesus Christ, which constitute the Christian Church. This is not to suggest something new—the history of theology or the history of Christian art offers enough evidence that the self-realization of the Church has differed down through the ages—but what is suggested here too seldom finds its way into ecclesiologies. A concrete and practically effective Christianity will have to be much more self-conscious and self-critical about the way in which it becomes and is the Church, here and there, now and later, everywhere and always.

Sobrino's point was dramatically illustrated in a conversation I had with him this morning. He was apologizing for the late arrival of his paper, but, he said, things have been rather bad in El Salvador— a fourth priest had recently been found murdered. Well, if that is the context in which you are the Church, the Gospel sounds different than it does at a typical theological symposium. The Gospel is heard in different tones; the threat out of which hope arises is felt differently; the Cross stands in different judgment and offers different comfort; the business of being a Christian and of gathering as the Church *means* differently, and Sobrino's statements about the Church of the poor and oppressed—as, for example, that "there is something inherent in poverty and persecution which directs human beings to the Kingdom of God"—can only be properly understood and evaluated if that context is known and appreciated.

It may be easier for us to agree with these two basic advances which Sobrino has made than with his application or at least its conclusion with regard to the Church of the poor. Rather than address this point directly, I want to suggest two steps that may prove helpful for an engagement with his thought to be a genuine conversation, challenging both him and those who may disagree with him.

First, I think that we need a series of empirical studies, historical, sociological, theological, of the concrete mediations of faith in and by social milieux and in and by the diverse realizations of the Church. Our phenomenologies of faith have generally been too formal and too individualistic. And it will only be by serious descriptive and analytic study that we will be able, on the one hand, to put flesh on the bones of our transcendental anthropologies and, on the other, to prepare the way for a genuinely self-critical and concretely effective contemporary ecclesial mediation of Christ's grace, truth and power.

The second suggestion concerns Sobrino's argument for a privileged position of the Church of the poor vis-à-vis the Gospel. His biblical and christological arguments need to be addressed seriously and with the appropriate disciplines; but beyond that there is need for a fuller working-out of the fundamental anthropology on which the issue between him and those who disagree with him on this point turns and which, I think, is more often assumed than articulated and defended. The question Sobrino raises cannot be settled adequately either biblically or christologically; in fact, I believe that the resolution of the biblical and christological issues depends on a critical anthropology which treats the person as a concretely incarnate subject, whose incarnation is not only bodily but also economic, social, political and cultural. But Catholic theology, I fear, is only beginning to address that very difficult and basic task.

The Preunderstanding of the Theologian

by Dr. Thomas Ommen

I. The Problem

The purpose of this paper is to explore the role of faith in theology. Must the Christian theologian be a Christian believer? Is a personal acceptance of the Christian message and a self-understanding defined in Christian terms a prerequisite for doing theology? These questions, in various forms, have been asked many times in the history of Christianity and have usually been answered affirmatively. Anselm's concept of theology as *"fides quaerens intellectum"* is clearly the dominant model in both Protestant and Catholic traditions. Articles on theological method in the basic theological lexicons and important classical and contemporary statements on theological method reveal the predominant influence of what I shall call in an abbreviated way the Anselmian model. My intention in this essay is to challenge this traditional understanding and to suggest an alternative to the Anselmian model of theology. I shall argue that Christian faith is not a requirement for doing Christian theology.

Such an argument does not deny the obvious fact that most Christian theologians are Christians. As a matter of fact, most Christian theologians are believers. They were usually drawn to the study of theology because of their faith convictions, and these same convictions have an important role to play in determining the theological approach adopted and the selection of theological questions which are understood to be important. Whether a Christian faith stance is in principle necessary to theology, however, is a distinct question. As a matter of fact most Christian theologians are Christians, but is this a necessary part of theology? Is it true that the person without Christian faith cannot do the work of theology?

Such an assumption is increasingly under attack today. A number of contemporary theologians have pointed to the need for a reassessment of the classical understanding of the role of faith in theology. Some examples of this critique might be briefly pointed out. In several works, Schubert Ogden has maintained that the intellectual legitimacy of theology is most undermined by two widely held assumptions: 1) that theology has to appeal to special criteria of truth accessible only to the believer; 2) that the theologian as such has to be a believer already committed to the truth of the claims that theology seeks to establish. Theologians often point to these principles as the guarantee of the uniqueness of theology, and yet, in so doing, Ogden is convinced, they endanger the credibility of the theological enterprise.[1] Ogden's alternative to both assumptions is that theology must appeal to universal criteria, which extend beyond the boundaries of the faith community, and that faith is not necessary in the enterprise of theology.[2] As Ogden succinctly remarks: "even though faith without theology is not really faith at all, theology without faith is still theology and quite possibly good theology at that."[3] In *Blessed Rage for Order* David Tracy adopts a similar position: "The present work holds that the Christian theologian *qua* theologian need not be an explicit believer."[4] And, at another point:

> The Christian theologian, by professional and, thereby, ethical commitment, has resolved to study that tradition's past and present claims to meaning and truth. Ordinarily, he will choose to do so because he has committed himself to a Christian self-understanding. Yet, in principle, such commitment need not be the case. In principle, the fundamental loyalty of the theologian *qua* theologian is to that morality of scientific knowledge which he shares with his colleagues, the philosophers, historians, and social scientists. No more than they, can he allow his own—or his tradition's—beliefs to serve as warrants for his arguments.[5]

"Revisionist" theology, as Tracy understands it, if it is to meet the challenge of the post-Enlightenment period, must revise the classical understanding of the role of faith in theology. A third example of a critique of the Anselmian model is Wolfhart Pannenberg's defense of the scientific character of theology in *Theology and the Philosophy of Science*[6] which rests in large part on a careful separation of theological criteria from faith presuppositions. Indeed, one of the fullest treatments of faith in theology is in the recent German discussion of *Wissenschaftstheorie* in which Pannenberg's work is located.[7] Faith cannot properly function in the justification of theological claims, Pannenberg maintains. Only this model of theology, in which faith has no "probative" value, frees it, in Pannenberg's opinion, from a subjective method in which religious claims could not be given an

---

[1] Schubert Ogden, "What is Theology?" *The Journal of Religion* 52 (1972):4.

[2] Ibid.

[3] Ibid., p. 38.

[4] David Tracy, *Blessed Rage for Order* (New York: Seabury Press, 1975), p. 36, n. 16.

[5] Ibid., p. 7.

[6] Wolfhart Pannenburg, *Theology and the Philosophy of Science* (Philadelphia: Westminster Press, 1976).

[7] See, e.g., Gerhard Sauter, *Wissenschaftstheoretische Kritik der Theologie. Die Theologie und die neure wissenscaftstheoretische Diskussion* (Munich: Chr. Kaiser Verlag, 1973); H. Peukert, *Wissenschaftstheorie-Handlungstheorie-Fundamentale Theologie* (Düsseldorf: Patmos Verlang, 1976); Wolfhart Pannenberg *et al*, *Grundlagen der Theologie* (Berlin: Kohlhammer Verlag, 1974).

intersubjective grounding.[8] Other examples could be added to those of Ogden, Tracy and Pannenberg. All suggest a growing dissatisfaction with the Anselmian model.

Why has this dissatisfaction emerged? One reason, but I think a secondary one, is the presence of unbelief within the theological community. While most Christian theologians are believers, many are not. As Gordon Kaufman observes: "Whereas in earlier generations those who called themselves theologians all in some sense 'believed in God' or presupposed the reality of the God about whom they wrote, in our time even this minimal level of agreement cannot be assumed."[9] Once asked in an interview what united the faculty and students at Harvard Divinity School, Harvey Cox remarked that it was not really a shared foundation of Christian belief but the fact that they all "took religious questions seriously."[10] This seems to me to capture the mood of much contemporary theology. Not so much an assumed framework of shared Christian belief, but an interest in Christian tradition and the intention to take that tradition "seriously" shapes much of the theological enterprise. At times this non-believing approach represents a loss of a previously held belief. To discuss theological method today, one must take account of what Van Harvey has called the "alienated theologian."[11] But even the believing theologian is often a mixture of belief and unbelief. Some elements of Christian faith are personally accepted, but others may not be. The dilemma of trying to fix the line where one crosses from belief to unbelief and thus from the possibility to the impossibility of doing theology is recognized even by those who defend the importance of faith in theology and will have to be examined more closely.

Another type of "unbelieving" theology must also be recognized, especially in view of the many religious studies programs in secular and non-denominational settings. Such programs are producing increasing numbers of theologians who adopt theology as a career in the same way that one might choose to become a biologist or a chemist. Academic interest rather than a faith commitment is at the origin of and shapes the form of such theological work. Can the theological reflection of such individuals be recognized as theology? Or perhaps more to the point, can it be recognized not to be theology?

---

[8] Pannenberg, *Theology and the Philosophy of Science,* pp. 60-61.

[9] Gordon D. Kaufman, *An Essay on Theological Method* (Missoula: Scholars Press, 1975), p. ix.

[10] I heard Cox make this remark in an interview on public television some years ago. I have since misplaced the reference.

[11] Van A. Harvey, "The Alienated Theologian," in *The Future of Philosophical Theology,* ed. Robert A. Evans (Philadelphia: Westminster Press, 1971), pp. 113-43.

I should add at this juncture that I am not suggesting that these forms of non-believing theology can be simply put in a category of · religious or historical studies in which one carefully avoids the truth question. I understand Christian theology to be the reflective investigation of the meaning and truth of the Christian witness of faith.[12] Whatever decision is made on the *subjective* importance of faith in the work of theology, the *objective* importance seems to me self-evident. The theological community has a responsibility to critically interpret and assess the Christian witness of faith in its past and present forms and to mediate this tradition in contemporary terms. Such a correlation involves practical as well as theoretical dimensions, as the political theologians have emphasized. It also involves the reflective examination both of the meaning and truth of Christian claims. To "bracket" the truth question or to leave it out of theological argument is not to do theology. I stress this because one way of envisioning an unbelieving form of Christian theology might be to see it as an exploration of forms of Christian religious experience in which no theological consideration is given to the truth of Christian beliefs concerning God, Christ, and other religious matters. Analogously, religious studies are sometimes perceived as a description of human religious experience in which the truth question is "bracketed."[13] The force of the question of the role of faith in theology is felt only when one recognizes that the task of Christian theology includes the issue of the truth or falsity of Christian claims.

The presence of unbelief in the theological community is one reason for the reassessment of the role of faith in theology. A more important reason, I believe, is the desire to make theology a form of public discourse. There is a felt need today to ground theological reflection on criteria which reach beyond the circle of faith. Such an imperative has always been implied in the claim of the Christian witness itself to provide a decisive illumination of the meaning of human existence. Although the symbols of Christianity reflect a particular and special tradition and experience, they point beyond this limited setting. To theologically examine the claim of Christianity itself is thus to look for the connections between the experience of Christian faith and common human experience in its widest sense, including the experience of the unbeliever. The character of the Christian message alone would spur the search for a public form of theological discourse.

---

[12] I am indebted for this formulation both to Ogden and Tracy, although they do not use these precise words.

[13] This is, for example, the method employed by Peter Berger in *The Sacred Canopy: A Sociological Theory of Religion* (Garden City: Doubleday, 1966).

Today, however, other questions have arisen which touch more directly on the role of faith in theology and its impact on the public character of theology. One such factor is the post-Enlightenment understanding of the marks of a genuine science. The validity of scientific method is tied to the possibility of reasoned discourse and exchange. This implies a suspicion of all claims which are based, in the last analysis, on an assumed authority or on a personal religious conviction and are not accessible to the rational assessment of another individual who does not recognize that authority or share that conviction. One of the features of argumentation, theological or otherwise, which is intended to secure intersubjective agreement is the appeal to evidence which can be recognized by more than a limited or special audience. As Gordon Kaufman has put it, theology should be "a generally significant cultural enterprise with universal and public standards, not a parochial or idiosyncratic activity of interest only to special groups."[14] To maintain that the theologian must be a believer committed in advance to the assertions he or she is trying to justify undermines, in my opinion, this public character of theology. Such a conception of the theological enterprise produces what David Tracy has called a "clash" between the loyalty of belief and the ethical demands of critical reason. A tension arises between loyalty to tradition, the faith stance of a community, or the authority of Scripture and that critical rationality which treats all claims of faith as hypotheses.[15] To overcome such a tension is to seek a rational control over theological statements analogous to that in other disciplines. Such control becomes especially important in an age of interdisciplinary discourse in theology. Can theological method be justified in a wider setting of the humanities, or is it an anomaly? To answer this question is to determine the place of theology in the university.

The presence of unbelief in the theological community and the concern to make theology a form of public discourse lie behind the current critique of the Anselmian model of theology. They point as well to a necessary distinction which should be made in any examination of the role of faith in theology. Two dimensions of the problem stand out. First, there is the question of the role of faith in what I shall call the preunderstanding of the theologian. Is faith essential to the act of theological understanding? Does it supply a necessary pretheoretical context for the theory of theology? If this were true, then the unbeliever would lack the experience required to understand the subject-matter of theology just as someone who is deaf might be con-

---

[14] Kaufman, *An Essay on Theological Method*, p. x.
[15] Tracy, *Blessed Rage for Order*, pp. 4-14.

stitutionally unable to understand music theory. Another form of the problem of the role of faith in theology is the question of its use in the justification of theological claims. Does faith necessarily enter the structure of theological argumentation? Does the theologian depend on faith presuppositions in reasoning, and is faith necessary in order to see the validity of such theological reasoning? One could maintain that faith has a role in theology in the first of these senses but not in the second. Pannenberg, for example, admits that faith may have a *heuristic* but not a *probative* importance in theology.[16] It might motivate the theologian and shape the questions the theologian asks. The mind is not a blank slate waiting to be filled in. Thus the personal faith of the theologian might provide a basis for making certain conjectures and determine the investigation of certain topics. But such personal faith cannot properly determine the probative force of theological argument. Whatever the faith status of the theologian, and Pannenberg seems to leave open the possibility of an unbeliever doing theology, this should have no bearing on the justification of theological claims. The evidence for the latter should be public in character and not available only to a believing theologian or to a believing reader of a theological work.[17]

My original hope in writing this paper was to explore both dimensions of the role of faith in theology—the heuristic and the probative. This proved to be too massive a project within the limits of this paper. My focus, therefore, will be on the first problem, the heuristic role of faith. Must it be a part of the preunderstanding of the theologian? In this analysis, I have found two strands of philosophy to be of great value in clarifying the issues: hermeneutical theory and language analysis. Both of these philosophical discussions will be employed in the analysis of the role of faith in theological preunderstanding which follows.

II. The Preunderstanding of the Theologian

A. The Concept of Preunderstanding

That aspect of the problem of the role of faith in theology to be considered is the preunderstanding of the theologian. The concept of "preunderstanding" is a product of the hermeneutical discussion of the last two centuries.[18] Hermeneutical theory has emphasized the

---

[16] Pannenberg, *Theology and the Philosophy of Science,* pp. 320-21.

[17] Ibid. See also pp. 344, 285-86.

[18] For an overview of the hermeneutical discussion see Gerhard Ebeling, "Hermeneutik," in *Die Religion in Geschichte und Gegenwart* 3, 3rd ed.; Emerich Coreth, *Grundfragen der Hermeneutik* (Freiburg: Herder, 1969); Richard Palmer, *Hermeneutics* (Evanston: Northwestern University Press, 1969); and Ommen, *The Hermeneutic of Dogma* (Missoula: Scholars Press, 1975), pp. 61-104.

impact of the interpreter's horizon of experience on every act of interpretation. This is clear in text-interpretation, the primary focus of hermeneutics, but it applies to other acts of understanding as well. No form of understanding, theological or otherwise, is completely presuppositionless. We always understand in terms of a preexisting fabric of prereflective and reflective experience. What is understood is shaped by those questions which are asked in the act of interpretation.

A formatively important articulation of the concept of preunderstanding is in the work of Martin Heidegger.[19] Any phenomenon is understood, Heidegger stresses, to the extent that it can be connected in some way to the experience of the interpreter. An interpreting subject understands in terms of his or her concrete experience of being-in-the-world. This is reflected in the "as" structure of understanding. Phenomena are perceived "as" something—"as" chairs or trees—i.e., by being located within the existing experience, categories, and preconceptions of the interpreter. All understanding depends upon a prepossession *(Vorhabe)*, a preconception *(Vorgriff)*, or a foresight *(Vorsicht)* of meaning. "Any interpretation which is to contribute understanding must already have understood what is to be interpreted."[20] This hermeneutical circle has special importance in the humanities which take human experience as their field of interpretation.

This is not to say that an interpreter simply reproduces what he or she already knows. Particular anticipations of meaning are properly tested in the act of interpretation to determine their appropriateness to the subject matter that the interpreter is trying to understand. A correction of preconceptions can occur in such instances. Appropriate anticipations of meaning are worked out in encounter with the phenomena to be understood so that they reveal rather than conceal the subject-matter.[21] *Some* preconception or anticipation of meaning is necessary, however, to make understanding itself a possibility. To attack this forestructure of meaning as a "vicious circle" to be avoided at all costs in the name of scientific objectivity is simply to misconceive the nature of understanding.[22] No simple separation of the subject and object in understanding is possible. Meaning emerges "for" someone in a specific context and thus in relationship to a knower's projections and intentions.

[19] Martin Heidegger, *Being and Time* (New York: Harper & Row, 1962), pp. 188ff.

[20] Ibid., p. 194.

[21] Ibid., p. 195.

[22] Ibid., p. 194.

This accentuation of the importance of the horizon of experience of the interpreter in every act of understanding offers a useful entrée into the specific problem of this paper. One might ask: What preunderstanding is required in the work of theology? The subject-matter of theology is the Christian witness of faith, and the task of theology is the reflective examination of the meaning and truth of that witness. Are there some specific structures of experience which the theological interpreter must possess, and is believing acceptance of the Christian message among these? What experience might be missing in the non-Christian which would prevent him or her from doing theology?

My intention is to raise these questions in an examination of three basic approaches to theological preunderstanding which are representative of contemporary theology and which emphasize the importance of faith in theology. I shall also critically assess these approaches and develop an alternative position. Understandably, any selection which is intended to give an overview of modern theology must leave many important theological options unexplored. The limits of this paper prevent a more comprehensive treatment. Hopefully, the examples I have chosen will illuminate broad areas of theological work. There is, I am convinced, on this particular issue of the role of faith in theology, a remarkable consistency in Catholicism and Protestantism in the affirmation of one form or other of an Anselmian position.

B. The Supernatural Basis of Theological Preunderstanding

One defense of the notion that theology is dependent upon the faith of the theologian, particularly characteristic of Catholic theologians, relies on the distinctive supernatural character of the reality which theology investigates. Theology in this model is properly talk about God. But the reality of the divine is not available for study as are the realities explored by the other human and natural sciences.[23] While the other sciences build upon the data of experience, theology builds upon the data of revelation. The mystery of God can be rationally approached only to the extent that God reveals himself. As Edward Schillebeeckx has put it: ''The capacity of this science to grasp reality can only be based on the supernatural cognitive aspect of the act of faith, because it is in this only that con-

---

[23] On this point see, for example, Marie Dominique Chenu, *Is Theology a Science?* (New York: Hawthorn Books, 1959), pp. 11-12 and Rene Latourelle, *Theology: Science of Salvation* (Staten Island: Alba House, 1969), pp. 31-32.

tact is made with the reality of revelation."[24] Theology, in this sense, however much it may be in its unfolding a work of reason, is in its inception a gift of God. It depends on an exterior revelation, the Word of God, which comes to expression, in particular, in Christian tradition. Theology also requires the "inner word" of the grace of faith which motivates the theologian's assent to revelation.[25] Together the "inner" and "outer" word comprise the gift of faith upon which the theologian reflects. Unless there has been, by the light of faith, a recognition that certain historical realities are an actual revelation of God, the theologian has no real ability to construct a theological argument. Faith raises the mind to an otherwise inaccessible object.

This notion of the distinctive supernatural reality which theology investigates highlights the difference between theology and religious studies. The unbelieving theologian might very appropriately explore the forms of Christian experience. Religious experience is as accessible for examination as any other aspect of human experience. An understanding of what a particular individual or community *thought about* God requires no faith presuppositions. But theology must move beyond assertions about the nature of religious experience to assertions about the nature of God. The latter claims cannot be made from an uncommitted stance, but must reflect a personal acceptance of God's revelation. The transition from talk about the reality of religious experience to talk about the unseen reality of God is dependent upon an act of faith.

This notion of the distinctive supernatural character of the object which theology studies appears in the distinction often drawn between biblical exegesis and church history, on the one hand, and biblical and historical theology, on the other. The history of the people of Israel or of the early Christian community, for example, can be examined by the unbeliever. An unbeliever might as readily as the believer locate the *Sitz im Leben* of a particular scriptural text or recognize the impact of Gnostic thought on the writings of St. Paul. But the felt need and ability to see in such history the hand of God is the product of faith. Only the believer can see in the events of the history of Israel or early Christianity the deeper spiritual significance. Congar points out, in a similar way, that only a Catholic believer would be likely to see particular texts as "evi-

---

[24] Edward Schillebeeckx, *Revelation and Theology*, 3 vols. (New York: Sheed and Ward, 1967), 1:99-100.

[25] On the "inner" and "outer" word see Edward Schillebeeckx, *Revelation and Theolgy* 1:95-99; Rene Latourelle, *Theology: Science of Salvation*, p. 3; and John Connelly, "The Task of Theology," in *Proceedings for the Catholic Theological Society of America* (1974): 20-29.

dence" for a doctrine of papal infallibility.[26] Faith thus supplies the ability to see "through" certain historical events to the revelation which they contain. As the line is crossed from history to historical theology and as history is seen as revelation, an act of faith becomes an essential interpretative requirement in theological work.

An important qualification is often added to this traditional view of theological preunderstanding. This is the awareness that theology is not itself an act of piety or devotion but a work of reason. The affective insights or religious feelings of the believing theologian must be translated into rational terms. Religious devotion cannot replace the scientific work of theology. The personal experience of faith is of no theological value unless it is rationally justified and articulated in an intelligible manner. This distinction of the personal faith of the theologian and the value of theological reasoning is reflected in Congar's observation that a life of charity is not formally required for the work of theology.[27] The depth of a personal commitment to Christianity cannot be the criterion for good theological work. Similarly, although Schillebeeckx defends the need for faith in theology, he goes on to say that ". . . it may not even be claimed that theology is impossible without a personally experienced religious life."[28] While it is possible to talk about God only from a committed stance, from within an experience of encounter with the divine, the depth of this experience cannot be specified too exactly. There is a reluctance to recognize a possibility of talking about God from a standpoint completely outside an experience of faith, but the precise faith commitment required must be defined rather marginally. No theologian is an example of complete belief. The existential situation of most theologians today is a mixture of belief and unbelief.[29] Consequently, the precise line which separates the believing theologian from the unbeliever, who is incapable of doing authentic theology, is very difficult to draw. René Latourelle observes, in fact, that it may be impossible from the outside to distinguish the work of the "formal heretic" who lacks the light of faith from the work of the authentic theologian.[30] One wonders, having read this, exactly what faith supplies if it may have no discernible effect on the form of theological reflection.

---

[26] Yves Congar, *The History of Theology* (Garden City: Doubleday, 1968), pp. 236-37.

[27] Ibid., p. 269.

[28] Schillebeeckx, *Revelation and Theology* 1:101-2.

[29] Connelly, e.g., makes this observation in "The Task of Theology," p. 33.

[30] Latourelle, *Theology: Science of Salvation,* pp. 32-33, n. 2.

Critique

In this first "supernaturalist" approach to theological preunderstanding we have examined, faith is required to bring the theologian in contact with a supernatural reality "above" the world of ordinary experience or an act of God "behind" the events of biblical history. An access to an unseen dimension is opened in faith which is closed to the unbeliever. This model is unsatisfactory, it seems to me, above all because it downplays the obvious historicality of the object which theology studies. Christian theology is the reflective examination of the meaning and truth of the Christian witness of faith, but the "witness" here referred to is within history and experience. It is a mistake to think that there is a "supernatural" part of it which only a believer can see. Let me illustrate this point with two examples.

One often finds the assertion, as I noted earlier, that faith opens the biblical interpreter or biblical theologian to a deeper spiritual meaning which the unbelieving interpreter cannot recognize. At one time Raymond Brown followed the lead of a number of other Catholic exegetes in locating this deeper meaning of the Bible in a "fuller sense," the *sensus plenior,* which appears only to the eyes of faith.[31] After years of biblical study, however, Brown was forced to conclude that the distinction of the literal and fuller sense had no practical importance in his exegetical work. In theory, he could affirm the distinction of the fuller from the literal or historical meaning of the Bible, but his interpretation worked through the normal channels of historical understanding.[32] There was only a literal or historical meaning which the believing interpreter might be inclined to interpret "as" revelation, but there was no special spiritual meaning accessible only to the believer.

Similarly, doubts have been raised about the common form-content distinction employed in Catholic systematic theology in the interpretation of dogma. This model distinguishes the revealed "essence" or "content" of dogmatic statements from their historical "forms." In its movement through history, a dogmatic statement is necessarily recast in different concepts and modes of expression, just as it was initially expressed in the language and thought forms of a particular period. Within this historical development, however,

---

[31] Raymond Brown, *The Sensus Plenior of Sacred Scripture* (Baltimore: St. Mary's, 1955). For a discussion and critique of the notion of the *sensus plenior* see R. Lapointe, *Les trois dimensions de l'herméneutique* (Paris: Gabalda, 1967), pp. 32-42.

[32] Brown expresses his doubts about the *sensus plenior* in 'The Problems of the Sensus Plenior," *Ephemerides Theologicae Louvanienses* 43 (1967): 460-69. See also his article on "biblical interpretation" in the *Jerome Biblical Commentary,* p. 616.

according to the form-content schema, a core of revealed truth remains the same. At the center of historical development and flux is a stable, unchanging "content" of faith which is identical through the history of the Church although its expression may vary. What is defined in dogma, the inner content, is a deeper or fuller sense which goes beyond the scope of investigation of critical history, but which is nonetheless "there" in the dogmatic text.[33]

The problem with the form-content schema posed by hermeneutical and historical awareness is this: how is such an inner kernel of meaning to be located? Can the linguistic "form" of a definition be in fact distinguished from an inner content which the believer recognizes? Edward Schillebeeckx, a theologian who has employed the form-content distinction in the past, has since questioned its usefulness. The meaning of dogma always emerges in a concrete act of understanding from a vantage point within history. The distinction between the dogmatic essence, perceivable by the believer, and its historical mode of expression is therefore "virtually meaningless and unmanageable precisely because this 'essence' is never given to us as a pure essence, but is always concealed in a historical mode of expression."[34] Schillebeeckx's statement echoes Brown's observation on the *sensus plenior.* No "pure" or spiritual content of faith is ever supplied which is itself not originally historical in meaning and accessible only in a historical act of understanding. A growing recognition of historicality has brought an unwillingness, indeed an inability, to separate "historical" from "spiritual" meaning in scripture or dogma and a new attentiveness to the hermeneutical problem.[35] The attempt of theologians to locate the spiritual content of dogmatic teaching founders, as does the *sensus plenior,* on the historicality of the Christian witness of faith and ultimately the historicality of revelation.

What these examples illustrate, I would maintain, is that the theological investigation of the Christian witness of faith, whether conducted by the believer or unbeliever, appeals to the same historical facts and to the same fabric of human meanings. There are no distinctively supernatural facts or realities which only the believer can recognize. Bultmann is quite right in stressing that the unbelieving and believing interpreters of scripture employ the same method.

---

[33] For some examples of an appeal to a form-content distinction see Schillebeeckx, *Revelation and Theology* 1: 256 and Michael Schmaus, *Preaching as the Sacrament of the Encounter with God* (Staten Island: Alba House, 1966), pp. 130-34.

[34] Edward Schillebeeckx, "Toward a Catholic Use of Hermeneutics," in *God the Future of Man* (New York: Sheed and Ward, 19868), p. 12.

[35] For a full discussion of this issue see my *Hermeneutic of Dogma* (Missoula: Scholars Press, 1975).

The Bible has to be interpreted as any other book would be interpreted.

This is not to say that theology is confined to assertions about human experience. Obviously, the meaning and truth of Christian claims concerning God are necessary to theology. But God is not "there" as an object, even of a supernatural kind, in theological reflection, but only *indirectly* as an inference from experience. The crucial question in theology based on a wider model of pre-understanding than the Anselmian would be whether that inference could be rationally supported in terms of criteria which the unbeliever could recognize. Certainly, the believer may have a conviction of God's direct presence, but this cannot properly be the basis of theological argumentation. I must stress that I am not talking about the origin of Christian faith in Christian believers, but about the nature of theology. Whatever "direct" experience the believing theologian claims has no bearing on the validity of theological argumentation. The theses of faith become the hypotheses of the theologian. "Direct religious experience acquires intersubjective validity only by becoming relevant to men's understanding of the world and of themselves."[36] The crucial question in a reflective justification of the theological notion of God, for example, is whether the hypothesis of God fits and illuminates human experience. As Gordon Kaufman puts it, the notion of "God," like that of "world," is logically different from notions which we have of objects of experience. The former are "imaginative constructs" created by the mind for certain intra-mental functions. Theology must break out of the notion that God is an "object" of study, even of a supernatural kind.

> "World" and "God" are not objects directly describable but are constructs or images by means of which men and women: a) conceive or picture the multiplicity and plurality of experience and life as having some unity, order and wholeness (the concept or image of world), and b) grasp this ordered context of life not as ultimately threatening or even as merely neutral with respect to what is humanly valuable and meaningful, but as informed by purpose, meaning and loving care (the concept of God).[37]

A theological justification of the meaning and truth of the concept of God would be an attempt to rationally verify that the imaginative construct "God" fits the totality of experience. Or, to use Pannenberg's formulation: "the science of God is possible only indirectly, in relation to reality as a whole."[38]

---

[36] Pannenberg, *Theology and the Philosophy of Science,* p. 301.

[37] Kaufman, *An Essay on Theological Method,* p. 26.

[38] Pannenberg, *Theology and the Philosophy of Science,* p. 314.

This same need for a rational justification of theology's starting point applies to the concept of revelation. To claim that theology is grounded in God's revelation does not provide a clear and unambiguous beginning for theological reflection. The concept of "revelation" like that of God cannot simply be presupposed as something given and clear. Gordon Kaufman puts this awareness in these terms:

> I am not holding that it is false to claim that theology in some sense—indeed, in a theologically very important sense—may have its foundations in 'God's revelation.' I am holding that it is a mistake to suppose that that claim tells us how to begin our theological work, i.e., that it tells us where we as theologians, as human thinkers, can or should turn to do theology. Theology is and always has been a human work: it is founded upon and interprets human historical events and experiences; it utilizes humanly created and shaped terms and concepts; it is carried out by human processes of meditation, reflection, ratiocination, speaking, writing and reading. We as theologians can perform only these human activities; we cannot in any way do God's speaking, acting, inspiring or providential guiding. Our theological work has to be understood, therefore, entirely in terms of what *we* can do on the basis of what is available to us. If in the course of that work we conclude that God also has been involved in it and with it, making himself known in and through human experience and revealing himself through particular historical sequences—and that therefore the ultimate foundation of theological work is God's self-revelatory activity—that will be a highly significant conclusion. But it is important to note that this claim about God's guidance and revelation will be a conclusion, not an opening premise; it rests upon prior foundations in experience, reflection and reasoning, and these must be uncovered and made clear if we are to come to a genuine understanding of what we are doing when we are theologizing.[39]

The claim to revelation, while it may be important in theology as a "conclusion," requires justification. It cannot be a premise for theological investigation. One is therefore pushed out of the circle of faith in supporting the claim that a revelation has occurred, with an appeal to wider criteria that would include the unbeliever. This cannot be provided, it seems to me, if a believer's insight into revelation is taken as the foundational basis for theology.

---

[39] Kaufmann, *An Essay on Theological Method,* pp. 3-4.

C. The Existential Setting of Theological Preunderstanding

Many Catholic theologians tend to stress the supernatural object or subject-matter of theology and thus the importance of faith. The next two approaches to theological preunderstanding to be considered point more to the *subjective* pole of theology. Because they have this common focus, I shall present both before adding my critical reflections. The existential defense of the role of faith in theology, more characteristic of Protestantism, emphasizes the gap between theoretical reasoning on matters of religion, to which the unbeliever is confined, and existential or personal understanding, which is available only to the believer. Because of the need for the latter, at some crucial point faith becomes important in the work of theology. A personal involvement and existential participation in Christian symbols is, in this approach, essential to Christian theology. This is especially the case when one includes in theology the need to assess not only the meaning but the truth of Christian claims.

Langdon Gilkey and Rudolf Bultmann provide explicit models of the existential approach to theological preunderstanding. Gilkey, for example, has pointed to the value of a neutral, philosophical grounding of the meaning of Christian symbols but finds a believing method essential when the theological focus shifts to the truth of such symbols. The "prolegomenon" or introduction to theology which Gilkey constructs in *Naming the Whirlwind*[40] is intended to show the meaningfulness of religious symbols in general and Christian symbols in particular. Such an introduction is not dependent on the insights of faith. It appeals rather to the religious dimension in common human experience which can be generally recognized and raised to light by phenomenological analysis.

While a method not dependent on belief is essential to the theological justification of the meaning of religious symbols in terms of ordinary experience, however, it cannot ground the *validity* or *truth* of such symbols. The transition from the prolegomenon to theology proper is made possible by the theologian's reception in faith of the truth of a particular set of religious symbols.[41] But such a reception of particular symbols or a particular manifestation of the sacred does not occur on the plane of theoretical reason. It occurs more on the prereflective level, in the context of a particular community, as the theologian experiences certain symbols as answers to the fundamen-

---

[40] Langdon Gilkey, Naming the Whirlwind (Indianapolis: Bobbs and Merrill, 1969).

[41] Ibid., p. 460.

tal questions of life. Gilkey emphasizes the importance in theology of special moments of experience in which one perceives, in a deep personal way, a divine revelation, in Christian or in some other form. It is in such recognizable hierophanies that the "gospel" is heard which releases us from the "law" of an otherwise alienated and inauthentic state of existence. Or, to put it somewhat differently, in such moments of experience a religious answer is heard to the universal questions of human life. There is here a clear analogy to the Catholic stress on the supernatural dimension of theology, but one phrased more in terms of the relationship of law and gospel and question and answer than of nature and supernature.

An approach to theological preunderstanding similar to Gilkey's is in the work of Rudolf Bultmann. Bultmann's model of theological preunderstanding is developed in light of the Heideggerean analysis of the forestructure of understanding.[42] As a biblical exegete, Bultmann was especially concerned with the problem of scriptural interpretation. The preunderstanding *(Vorverständnis)* of the interpreter is a necessary component in the interpretation of scripture. Interpretation is grounded in the interest of the interpreter—in the question brought to the text. For those texts such as Scripture, which reflect fundamental human concerns, the appropriate question is that of the *meaning of existence itself*. The interpreter must feel the "claim" of the text on this personal level in asking the question of the meaning of his or her life. "The most 'subjective' interpretation is in this case the most 'objective,' that is, only those who are stirred by the question of their own existence can hear the claim which the text makes."[43] For a scientific interpretation, this question is appropriately put in the reflective and thematic terms of philosophy. Bultmann felt the best available philosophical articulation of the question of the meaning of existence was in the work of Martin Heidegger.

An involved or personal reading of scripture stops short, however, of a demand for explicit Christian faith. Bultmann's desire to locate a preunderstanding in theology which is in some sense "universal" stands out. There is no "believing" hermeneutic for the Bible. In this sense, his work is an anticipation of the revisionist theology of the present day. The Bible must be interpreted as any other book

[42] For Bultmann's discussion of preunderstanding and hermeneutics in general see "Is Exegesis Without Presuppositions Possible? in *Existence and Faith,* ed. Schubert Ogden (Cleveland: World Publishing, 1960), pp. 289-96 and "The Problem of Hermeneutics," in *Essays Philosophical and Theological* (London: SCM Press, 1955), pp. 234-69.

[43] Bultmann, The Problem of Hermeneutics," p. 256; cf. "Is Exegesis Without Presuppositions Possible?" p. 294.

would be interpreted. But this means that there must be some foundation in common human experience for an understanding of talk about God. The biblical witness obviously articulates the meaning of existence not on a purely human or historical level, but by referring man beyond the world to God. In Bultmann's understanding, the question of God arises within common human experience and can at least be raised by philosophy. There is a clear parallel here to the position of Gilkey we already examined. Language about God is in principle understandable by anyone simply because existence includes religious dimensions and points beyond itself for an answer to the human dilemma.

Anyone can ask the question of God, as long as the question is personally important, and understand the meaning of scripture as language about God. But there is a gap for Bultmann between the awareness of the question of God, which anyone can possess, and the understanding of the Christian witness as an authentic *answer* to that question—as gospel. In the Catholic theology we examined earlier, faith brings the theologian into contact with the supernatural content of revelation. In Bultmann, faith brings the theologian in an inward way to recognize in the gospel of Jesus Christ the forgiveness of sins and the release from a striving for a self-guaranteed security. The paradox of the Cross appears only to the eyes of faith as an act of God. Such an insight is normally attained not in the study of scripture but in hearing the oral word of proclamation. In faith, the theologian is prompted to recognize the Word of God in the human meanings of the Bible, the act of God behind the closed continuum of history which the Bible describes.[44] As in the Catholic positions considered earlier, a mysterious reality, accessible only to the eyes of faith, is that revelation which the Christian kerygma communicates. The validity of the revelation is recognized, not on the level of theoretical reason, but in the inwardness of personal experience.

To put Bultmann's position in terms drawn from analytic philosophy which we found earlier in Gilkey, while anyone, including the unbeliever, can understand the *meaning* of the Christian message, the *truth* of that message can only be understood and assessed from the standpoint of faith. Thus if theology is the reflective examination of the meaning and truth of the Christian witness of faith, Bultmann would confine the latter theological task to the believer. Such an undertaking, even by the believer, is obviously curtailed by the limits of theoretical reason. Faith is needed to get at the truth. Only the believer can understand the truth-claim of the Christian witness because this is mediated not on a reflective, but on

---

[44] See Bultmann's discussion of the concept "act of God" in *Kerygma and Myth*, ed. H. W. Bartsch (New York: Harper & Row, 1961), pp. 196ff.

a personal or existential level. The unbeliever is constitutionally unable to assess the truth-claim of the Christian kerygma.

D. The Linguistic Setting of Theological Preunderstanding

We turn now to a third approach to theological preunderstanding, one which stresses the connection between language or linguisticality and the role of faith in theology. Such a position is evident in the development of Heidegger's and Bultmann's work in the hermeneutical theory of Hans-Georg Gadamer. Bultmann, as we have seen, balances the importance of a "universal" preunderstanding, accessible to the unbeliever, and the unique ability of the believer to recognize and assess the truth of the Christian kerygma. Gadamer stresses a more exclusive role for faith because of the connections he makes between preunderstanding, or "prejudgments" as he prefers to call them, and human language. Experience for Gadamer, and thus preunderstanding, are shaped by the language an individual has learned. We experience the world "as" this or that because of the language we have been taught. Thus the problem of theological preunderstanding becomes the problem of linguistic conditioning. There is a clear parallel to Gadamer's stress on the importance of language, with significant implications for theology, in Anglo-American linguistic analysis. I shall refer to both of these discussions in clarifying this linguistic approach to theological preunderstanding. Let us first consider Gadamer.

In their models of preunderstanding, Heidegger and Bultmann stress the experience which is reflected in being-in-the-world and thus accessible in principle to anyone. Gadamer stresses, on the contrary, that such prejudgments come from the tradition in which the interpreter is rooted and to which he or she belongs. The mind of the interpreter includes a fabric of meanings which have been provided by tradition. This body of traditional presuppositions is part of the horizon of interpretation and is the medium for the encounter with history.[45]

The problem of theological preunderstanding is thus set by Gadamer in the context of what he would call "effective-history" *(Wirkungsgeschichte)*. Theological work properly reflects a life-involvement on the part of the theologian in the experience and

---

[45] See, e.g., Hans-Georg Gadamer, *Wahrheit und Methode: Grundzüge einer philosophiscen Hermeneutik* (Tübingen: J. C. B. Mohr, 1965), p. 261. [Eng. tr. *Truth and Method* (New York: Seabury Press, 1975), p. 245]. For Gadamer's discussion of "effective-history" *(Wirkungsgeschichte)*, which is crucial to his notion of tradition, see *Wahrheit und Methode*, pp. 284ff. [*Truth and Method*, pp. 267ff.]

language of the Christian community. A continuity of experience links the horizon of past Christian communities and the texts they produced to the interpreter in the present. As the theologian is molded by the Christian community and its uses of language, he or she is introduced into a chain of experience which extends back to the scriptural beginnings of the tradition. This bond of experience and language functions much more on the prereflective than on the reflective level. If we are to make any sense at all out of the Christian witness in the texts of St. Paul or Thomas Aquinas, this linguistic continuity is presupposed.

Gadamer's view that the decisive theological preunderstanding is that shaped by involvement in a particular community leads him to criticize Bultmann's notion of a "universal" preunderstanding in biblical interpretation. To understand the scripture as the "divine proclamation of salvation" is to carry the interpreter necessarily beyond a simple "scientific or scholarly interpretation of its meanings."[46] It is not at all clear to Gadamer what it means to say that the Bible is to be interpreted in the same way as one would interpret any other book, and that the preunderstanding required is given with human life itself. The questions Gadamer directs to Bultmann make his objections quite clear:

> Does there exist in every man a previous connection with the truth of divine revelation because man as such is concerned with the question of God? Or must we say that it is first from God, i.e. from faith, that human life experiences itself as being affected by the question of God? But then the sense of the presupposition that is contained in the concept of foreunderstanding becomes questionable. For then the presupposition would be valid not universally but soley from the viewpoint of true faith.[47]

As Gadamer sees it, the appropriate preunderstanding in theology is shaped by the interpreter's education and involvement in the Christian community. "The existential foreunderstanding, which is Bultmann's starting-point can only be a Christian one."[48]

This rather clear position becomes somewhat clouded, however, when Gadamer asks himself whether the question of God might still be taken seriously in the absence of any particular religious commitment or training. While this seems for Gadamer to be possible, it is difficult to attain. The Marxist, for example, is likely to recognize not the question of God in history, but the working of class interest.

---

[46] Gadamer, *Wahrheit und Methode,* p. 314. [*Truth and Method,* pp. 295-96].

[47] Ibid., p. 314 p. 296ı.

[48] Ibid.

The presupposition of the question of God as a serious one "is obviously valid only for someone who already sees in it the alternative of belief or unbelief in the true God. Thus the hermeneutical significance of fore-understanding in theology seems itself theological."[49] To understand Christian texts is to allow oneself to be claimed by belief as a real possibility. The interpreter must allow himself "to be addressed—whether one believes or whether he doubts."[50] Interestingly, with this last statement, Gadamer seems to qualify his earlier demand for a distinctively Christian preunderstanding. Presumably, one could understand texts referring to God as long as the question of God is taken seriously as a real possibility for one's own life, even if "doubt" rather than "belief" is the end-result of interpretation. But Gadamer is unwilling to see such a question being taken seriously outside of a context of explicit faith.

There is a striking parallel to Gadamer's linguistic approach to preunderstanding in the Wittgensteinian tradition of philosophy prevalent in England and America. Although the terminology changes in the transition from the Continental to the Anglo-Saxon milieu, the problem of preunderstanding remains an issue with important implications for theology. Moreover, there is a current dispute in analytic philosophy which touches directly on the concern of this paper. On one side of the dispute, stressing the determining importance of faith, is a group of philosophers such as D. Z. Phillips and Paul Holmer who represent what has sometimes been called "Wittgensteinian fideism."[51] On the other side of the dispute are other interpreters of Wittgenstein who are critical of the fideist approach and whose work resembles the concerns of revisionist theology. Patrick Sherry's recent book, *Religion, Truth and Language Games*[52] would fall into this category. It is to the first of these options, Wittgensteinian fideism, especially as it is represented in the writings of Phillips and Holmer, that I would like to briefly turn at this point. Both Phillips and Holmer have explicitly dealt with the issue of theological preunderstanding and thus are appropriate

---

[49] Ibid., p. 315 [p. 296].

[50] Ibid.

[51] For a discussion of the key figures in and principles of Wittgensteinian fideism see Kai Nielsen, "Wittgensteinian Fideism," *Philosophy* 42(1967): 191-209. A theologian whose work reflects this approach is Anders Nygren, *Meaning and Method. Prolegomena to Scientific Philosophy of Religion and Scientific Theology* (London: Erworth Press, 1972).

[52] Patrick Sherry, *Religion, Truth, and Language Games* (New York: Barnes and Noble, 1977). See also James Richmond, *Theology and Metaphysics* (London: SCM Press, 1970) and Basil Mitchell, *The Justification of Religious Belief* (New York: Macmillan, 1973).

examples of this particular fideist option from the standpoint of this paper.

At the foundation of this particular approach to preunderstanding is a view of the nature of language which Wittgenstein furthered in his later writings. For the Wittgensteinian—as for Gadamer—the meaning of language is imbedded in particular social and historical contexts. To understand language one must understand the specific context in which it is used, the "language-game" of which it is a part. It is a mistake, therefore, to understand language in an abstract way, divorced from its concrete historical and social setting, just as it is a mistake to reduce the many uses of language to a single use, say that of science, as the logical positivists were inclined to do. Different rules govern different regions of language, and these rules are determined by the communities in which a particular use of language originates. Therefore it is a mistake to confuse the language-games and different rules of religion and science. Generally, the rules are not explicit and are not precisely stated, so one does not learn the rules by memorizing definitions. One becomes part of a language-game, as Jerry Gill has noted, ". . . by participating successfully in the give and take of ordinary discourse."[53] A language-game is appropriated more on the tacit or prereflective than on the reflective level. Understandings of reality are shaped as language is learned, even though we are normally not reflectively aware that this linguistic conditioning and thus this patterning of experience has taken place.

Wittgensteinian fideism, in particular, stresses the autonomy of the Christian language-game and the internal character of its criteria of meaning and truth. Because the rules of the Christian language-game are limited to a particular setting, there is a resistance to a search for public criteria of theological discourse. The limits of this paper prevent me from going more deeply into this question, which relates more to the probative than to the heuristic role of faith in theology. It is, however, one of the most important areas of discussion today. To what extent can Christian claims be rationally justified in a public forum, appealing to more than Christian uses of language? This is an issue which has prompted a variety of theological and philosophical statements in the analytic tradition and one to which I plan to return at another time.

But the topic with which we are concerned, the role of faith in theological preunderstanding, comes very quickly into the Wittgensteinian discussion as well. Learning the uses of religious language

---

[53] Jerry Gill, *The Possibility of Religious Knowledge* (Grand Rapids: Eerdmans, 1971), p. 104.

means participating personally in the give and take of ordinary discourse. Learning how to use Christian language starts on the practical level of involvement in a Christian form of life. The foundation of a theological system, D. Z. Phillips tells us, is the "non-formalized" theology "which is the religious way of life carried on by the person who is constructing the theological system. In so far as this is true, theology is personal, since it is based on one's own experience of God. Where the connection between theology and experience is missing, there is danger of theology becoming an academic game."[54] The idea of God is learned in a community and given shape by the language game in which the theologian participates on a practical or "non-formalized" level. The stories or "pictures" one learns, especially in childhood, reflect the "primitive theology" upon which all more reflective theology is based. This grammar of religious discourse on the ordinary level ultimately defines for the theologian what can sensibly be said and what cannot.[55]

The meanings of Christianity are properly conveyed, according to Holmer, by learning "how" to be religious, not by studying "about" Christianity. There is a mistaken notion, Holmer believes, that theological reflection on ordinary Christian language can clarify and justify it in a secular age. Unless meaning is already there on the ordinary level, reflection is useless. Theology's task is descriptive, not constructive or generative.[56] It simply observes and carefully describes the uses of language already at work within the Christian community. The technical language of theology is a function of ordinary language, and the latter is properly learned in a "passionate assimilation" of the Christian witness by the believing theologian. A knot in theological understanding is more than likely not a problem of method or conceptuality, but a problem in the character of the theologian. Knowledge "about" a religious form of life isn't enough. Religion is a "how," a way of living more than a what.[57] To understand the Christian witness and way of life fully, one must participate in it in a personal way, sharing that particular pattern of belief and practice.

Even the atheism which matters, Phillips stresses, isn't a theoretical denial of the existence of God, but a recognition by the

[54] D. Z. Phillips, *Faith and Philosophical Inquiry* (London: Routledge & Kegan Paul, 1970), pp. 8-9.

[55] Ibid., p. 5. Cf. pp. 117-19 and *The Concept of Prayer* (New York: Schocken Books, 1966), pp. 50-51.

[56] Paul Holmer, "Language and Theology: Some Critical Notes," *Harvard Theological Review* 58 (1965): 258.

[57] Holmer, "Wittgenstein and Theology," in *New Essays in Religious Language,* ed. Dallas High (New York: 1966), pp. 25ff.

unbeliever that the activity of religion means nothing to him. Such an individual is at a loss to know what to do with prayer, creeds, etc. Whether one is speaking of belief or unbelief, the relationship to God that is authentic is on the level of existential involvement and day to day patterns of behaviour. There is no "theoretical" knowledge of God, Phillips emphasizes, and thus it is impossible to rationally justify or disprove the existence of God.

> To ask whether God exists is not to ask a theoretical question. If it is to mean anything at all, it is to wonder about praising and praying; it is to wonder whether there is anything in all that. This is why philosophy cannot answer the question 'Does God exist?' with either an affirmative or a negative reply.[58]

One is moved to a recognition of the truth of religious claims concerning God not on the theoretical level, but only in a setting in which religious activities such as prayer come to mean everything to an individual. While it is perfectly appropriate to treat some matters as hypotheses which may or may not be true, the existence of God cannot be a "fact" in this sense. It makes no sense for the believer to say, even as a theological exercise, that God might not exist. A religious claim concerning God is "absolute." One puts one's trust in such a claim and is willing to sacrifice for it.[59] There is an enormous gulf between the person who believes in God and one who does not.

Thus the Wittgensteinian fideists drew a conclusion which is analogous to that we noticed earlier in Bultmann. Knowledge of the truth of religious claims concerning God occurs in an inward experience, produced by living involvement in a community and its uses of language, which cannot be translated onto the level of theoretical reason. Because there is no theoretical knowledge of God, there is no way for the unbeliever to carry on this dimension of the work of theology. Or to put it more accurately, even the believer can neither rationally justify nor criticize religious claims concerning God in a public forum which would include the unbeliever. The "enormous gulf" between belief in God and unbelief makes such a conversation between the two difficult if not impossible.

Summary

In our examination of existential and linguistic approaches to theological preunderstanding, we found a variety of ways of stressing the necessity of faith in theology. Both the existentialist model

---

[58] Phillips, *Religion Without Explanation* (Oxford: Basil Blackwell, 1976), pp. 176ff.
[59] Phillips, *Faith and Philosophical Inquiry,* p. 90.

and that of Wittgensteinian fideism stress the limits of theoretical reason. God cannot properly be approached and understood in hypothetical terms. A believing and loving relationship is at the foundation of an authentic understanding of the divine and thus of a theology which includes such understanding as an essential part of its undertaking. Explicit Christian belief is pointed to as the foundational basis of a judgment of the truth of Christian claims. While a non-believing method may suffice in showing the meaning of religious symbols, faith is required when the theologian turns to the issue of Christian truth.

In Gadamer and the analytic philosophers the central importance of faith in theology is defined in linguistic terms. Participation in ordinary discourse, within the Christian community, communicates Christian ''effective-history'' or the Christian ''language-game.'' The reflective work of theology is properly grounded in what Phillips calls this non-formalized theology which is learned in day to day Christian life. Both Gadamer and the Wittgensteinian fideists are critical of ''universalizing'' tendencies in theology. Because of the determinative importance of a personal involvement in a concrete historical tradition, Gadamer rejects Bultmann's model of a universal preunderstanding. Similarly, the Wittgensteinians point to the autonomy of the Christian language-game and the inappropriateness of seeking public criteria of theological discourse.

While the main thrust of these existential and linguistic approaches is in support of a fideistic theological preunderstanding, there are counter-tendencies as well. Bultmann, in particular, wants to ground theology in a wider context of experience not limited to the circle of Christian faith. For him, a reflective understanding of the fundamental questions of human life is the appropriate preunderstanding. Similarly, Gilkey's ''prolegomenon'' to theology is a phenomenological examination of religious dimensions in common human experience in order to show the meaning of religious symbols. Even in Gadamer, as we noted, some ambiguity surrounds the possibility of an unbeliever ''seriously'' asking the question of God and thus understanding the Christian witness.

Critique

My intention in this final section of the paper is to critically assess these existential and linguistic approaches to theological preunderstanding and to suggest an alternative to the Anselmian model of theology.

My first criticism echoes a main theme in what David Tracy has called ''revisionist theology.'' I have touched on this criticism before, and it is behind the concern to make theology a form of public discourse. If the Christian message and Christian theology are intended to provide an illumination of human existence in general, then theological preunderstanding must be located in common human experience and not in the particular experience accessible only to a member of the Christian community. Some preunderstanding of the subject-matter of Christian tradition is required in theology, much as preunderstanding forms a part of every act of understanding. To say that such preunderstanding *must* assume the form of explicit Christian faith, however, is to undermine not only the possibility of theology as public discourse but the truth-claim of Christianity itself. David Tracy made this point forcefully a few years ago at the annual convention of the Catholic Theological Society of America in response to John Connelly's defense of the necessity of faith in theology. Tracy remarked:

> . . . our common human indeed secular experience will more than suffice for the properly subjective or experiential element needed to interpret the Christian tradition. This seems to me to follow unless we are to maintain . . . that religious meaning (either as a religious dimension to our common human experience or as explicitly religious experience) is somehow radically separated from our common human experience. If it is thus radically separated, then clearly it cannot provide the adequate pre-understanding of the subject-matter needed to interpret religious texts. If, however, it is not thus separated but on the contrary present in our common human experience, then the latter seems clearly to suffice as the preunderstanding needed.[60]

The meaning and truth of religious claims are linked to their potential to illuminate human existence. This is not to deny an experience of mystery, but if mystery is humanly significant, then it is more than an esoteric experience available only to the few who happen to have been raised in or to have found their way into a Christian or some other religious tradition. If "redemption in Christ" means something important, then presumably it also has a connection to the basic fabric of human experience. If that connection to experience is a part of Christian claims, then it is not at all clear why only the explicit Christian can attain a reflective understanding of Christian beliefs. The criteria which theology properly employs extend beyond the Christian community. But if they do, then they should be recognizable and usable by more than the Christian.

There is an interesting development in Wittgensteinian thought which accentuates the point I am making. D. Z. Phillips' early

---

[60] Tracy, "Response" to John Connelly, *Proceedings of the Catholic Theological Society of America*, 1974, pp. 70-71.

writings stressed the autonomy of the Christian language-game and the internal character of its criteria of meaning and truth. In some of his later essays, however, Phillips has expressed misgivings about his description of religious beliefs as a distinctive language game. If such a language game were in fact an isolated and distinct concern, then it would be difficult to see why it would be so "cherished" by believers and not confined to a limited role in life.[61] Moreover, there is the risk of implying that purely internal criteria might be used to justify what in a wider setting would appear as nonsense.[62] In his later writings, Phillips has stressed instead that religious language, including that of Christianity, is not cut off from other language games. Basic life experiences such as birth, death, suffering, shared by more than a Christian audience, shape religious discourse. Religious language always flows over into other contexts. It is intended to say something about the world as a whole, and not just about the particular institution in which it originates.[63] A similar stress on the interpenetration of the Christian and other language games has been made by other Wittgensteinian philosophers, especially the critics of Wittgensteinian fideism.[64]

This notion of the resemblance of the religious and other language games has been carried even farther by Gordon Kaufman. Kaufman maintains that the language of Christian tradition is not restricted to the Christian community but is imbedded in the history of Western culture. It is thus not necessary to be raised in a Christian community to gain familiarity with religious concepts: ". . . all Westerners, simply by virtue of their cultural inheritance, have the necessary rudiments of vocabulary and conceptuality and imagery to begin engaging in theological investigation."[65] It is not enough simply to say that a wider experiential setting has shaped Christian language and practice. The converse must also be said. Christian language, including the notion of God, has had an impact on Western culture. The Western non-Christian thus has a form of involvement in what Gadamer would call "effective-history," and the Wittgensteinian, the Christian "language-game." For Kaufman, this suffices as a starting point for Christian theology.

---

[61] Phillips, *Faith and Philosophical Inquiry,* pp. 78f., 94ff.

[62] Ibid., p. 78.

[63] Ibid., p. 126.

[64] See, e.g., Jerry Gill, "Tacit Knowing and Religious Belief," *International Journal for Philosophy of Religion* 6 (1975): 84; Dallas High, *Language, Persons and Belief* (New York: Oxford University Press, 1967), p. 72 n. 5; W. D. Hudson, *A Philosophical Approach to Religion* (New York: Barnes & Noble, 1974), pp. 22-25.

[65] Kaufman, *An Essay on Theological Method,* pp. 8-9, cf. p. 17, n. 7.

To point in this way to the general human significance of Christian claims is to open the possibility, it seems to me, for a wider basis of theological preunderstanding than the Anselmian model permits. A person may stop short of becoming a Christian and still have the ability to understand and reflectively interpret Christian claims. What is important, in the last analysis, is that the questions religious faith is intended to answer be real ones and accessible to more than the explicit believer. If the theologian is capable of recognizing the human questions to which religious language responds, then theology is possible. Being able to ask the appropriate religious questions, not affirming in a personal way a particular answer, is the condition for Christian theology.[66] The individual who can ask the appropriate questions, even if he or she stops short of Christian faith, can examine the Christian witness to see how and to what extent these basic questions are reflected in and responded to by Christian symbols.[67] What is important in theological preunderstanding is not a particular assertion, even of the reality of God in Christ, "but only the question to which this assertion and the whole system of assertions it constitutes are the answer."[68]

This line of argument presupposes a distinction between understanding or reflecting upon and assenting to the meaning and truth of religious claims.[69] It is precisely this distinction which is dissolved in the existentialist identification of authentic understanding with existential involvement. If only the believer can understand the statements made and the concepts involved in a profession of belief, then it is difficult to see what happens in a loss of faith. Consider the case of a Christian theologian who has lost his or her faith. Does such an individual who loses faith lose the possibility of theological understanding as well? This makes little sense—to me at least. Is it not more accurate to say that such an individual has lost faith but not theological understanding? But then there is a difference between theological understanding and believing. Schubert Ogden makes an analogous point in a number of essays when he suggests that some form of understanding must precede and be distinct from the act of faith. "If it were true that one must first

---

[66] Ogden, "Theology and Religious Studies," *Journal of the American Academy of Religion* 46 (1978): 14.

[67] Ibid.

[68] Ogden, "Response" to John Connelly, *Proceedings of the Catholic Theological Society of America,* 1974: 64.

[69] For the discussion in analytical philosophy see, e.g., Alisdair MacIntyre, "Is Understanding Religion Compatible with Believing?" in *Rationality,* ed. Bryan Wilson (New York: Harper & Row, 1970), pp. 62-77; Christopher Cherry, "Understanding Religious Belief," *Religious Studies* 10 (1974): 457-67; and Humphrey Palmer, "Understanding First," *Theology* 71 (1968): 107-14.

believe the Christian witness before he can understand it theologically, there could be no difference between disbelieving the witness and not understanding it—wherewith the original hypothesis could only be false, there being no basis for asserting that belief is prior to theological understanding."[70]

As Karl-Otto Apel has observed, there is little consideration by Wittgenstein on the phenomenon of a loss of faith or the problem of the role of linguistic communication in an elimination of incomprehension.[71] One understands only when he or she is taking part in a particular language game, participating in a particular form of life. But neither Wittgenstein nor—it seems to me—most of his followers, give much attention to the problem of attaining this familiarity if one is not already in such a state of participation. This, incidentally, is where the hermeneutical discussion could contribute much to the analytic tradition.

The necessary distinction between understanding and believing is further reflected in the ambiguity noted earlier of trying to specify the degree of faith required to make theological understanding possible. If every theologian is a mixture of belief and unbelief, but never a complete believer, where does one draw the line between the possibility and the impossibility of doing theology?[72] How would anyone know when he or she is in a position to undertake theology? Earlier we noted the distinction made by a number of Catholic theologians between piety, charity, or depth of religious experience and the quality of theological reasoning. If one accepts this distinction, it is difficult to understand how there can be any valid discernible grounds for answering that question. These and other ambiguities surrounding the relationship of understanding and believing seriously undermine, it seems to me, the Anselmian model of theological preunderstanding.

Another aspect of the distinction of theological understanding and believing needs to be noted. Many of the human sciences, such as anthropology and history, depend on the ability of an interpreter to understand language games and forms of life of which he or she is not a part.[73] An anthropologist who is an "outsider" can form an

---

[70] Ogden, "Response" to Connelly, p. 64.

[71] Karl-Otto Apel, *Die Transformation der Philosophie* 1 (Frankfurt: Suhrkamp Verlag, 1973): 367-69. cf. Apel, *Analytic Philosophy of Language and the Geisteswisselnschaften* (Dordrecht, Holland: D. Reidel, 1967), pp. 53ff.

[72] Ogden, "What is Theology?" pp. 36-37.

[73] See Apel, cited in n. 71 of this paper. See also the lively debate over the method of anthropology between Alisdair MacIntyre, "The Idea of a Social Science," in *Rationality,* ed. Bryan Wilson, pp. 112-30 and Peter Winch, "On Understanding a Primitive Society," in *Rationality,* ed. Bryan Wilson, pp. 78-111.

understanding of Vietnamese culture or a modern historian of the institution of chivalry without directly taking part in those traditions. Especially in the anthropological example, it is not enough to appeal, as Gadamer might do in the case of chivalry, to a participation in a common process of effective-history. A question arises even with reference to chivalry. Is the twentieth century historian any closer in principle to that institution and its practices and beliefs than the contemporary Western non-Christian is to the practices and beliefs of Christianity? And yet historical and anthropological understanding occurs. The horizons are merged.

The analogy of history and anthropology point as well, I recognize, to some limits in a non-fideist model of theological preunderstanding. The person who lives in the time of chivalry or who is born into and brought up in Vietnamese culture has obvious advantages over the outsider. A direct familiarity with the practices and beliefs of the community, for example, stands out. The outsider never fully duplicates the spirit or depth of experience of another age or culture. The Christian "insider" has a direct familiarity with rituals and their meanings and with concepts like "sin," "grace" or "God." The believer may more easily develop and sustain an interest in the theological enterprise. But I do not see anything in principle which would prevent the outsider from *acquiring* the necessary familiarity to do theology. Such an outsider would stop short of an involvement on the level of what Newman might call "real assent." But he or she could attain an understanding of the use of religious concepts or of the meaning of doctrines and practices. As Patrick Sherry observes:

> Those who lack a religious interest may indeed not know how to use religious concepts and therefore fail to fully understand the relevant activities, doctrines, etc. Moreover, it is probably true that the most direct path to learning about the real point of religion is to participate in prayer, meditation and other spiritual practices, in an attempt to achieve some degree of spiritual transformation and holy living; this participation acquaints one with the background in life which makes religious concepts meaningful. But there is nothing to prevent the outsider coming to understand the religious way of life, particularly by studying the beliefs on which it is based, even though he will lack the experiences and relationships which characterize direct participation.[74]

I might add to Sherry's remarks the observation that an outsider may also have theological advantages. He or she may bring an expe-

---

[74] Sherry, *Religion, Truth and Language Games,* p. 132.

rience to theology which direct participation may not provide—a sensitivity for other points of view and horizons of experience, an absence of dogmatism and short-sightedness. Such a critical form of preunderstanding can be incorporated creatively into the theological enterprise. A certain cultural, historical or experiential distance from a way of life has a way of making its limitations quite clear.

The possibility pointed to here of a critique of a religious way of life brings us to a final crucial point in this consideration of theological preunderstanding. Are there criteria of truth, which are available to what I have called the outsider to Christianity, that could be employed in theological reflection? In the introductory section of this paper, I noted the distinction between the heuristic and the probative roles of faith in theology and my intention, given the limits of space and time, to focus on the former. Some attention, however, must be given to the problem of justifying or verifying theological claims. The problem has risen in the positions examined earlier. Gilkey and Bultmann recognize a limited role for non-believing preunderstanding in theology in the interpretation of the *meaning* of Christian claims, but draw the line when the attention of theology shifts to the question of *truth*. The truth insight comes, they believe, in an inner experience of grace which cannot be converted into the theoretical terms of a theological argument. If one does not "bracket" the truth question in theology, and I don't believe it can or should be, then this separation of meaning and truth must be challenged.

My first observation is that Bultmann's and Gilkey's position depends on certain assumptions about the relationship of law and gospel or nature and grace which are clearly in the Neo-Orthodox tradition of theology. This is especially true of Bultmann. He holds that while common human experience raises the question of God, the only access to the reality of God is through faith in Christ. The "fallen" character of human existence, as Bultmann understands it, points to this necessity. The criteria of meaning in theology must reflect common human experience, but the ultimate object of theology is found only in a believing relationship to the Christian kerygma. Moreover, this insight cannot be validated as true in any sense on the level of reflection. Unlike Bultmann, Gilkey does not want to restrict the working of grace to those individuals who have heard the Christian gospel. But like Bultmann, and this brings Gilkey's thought more in contact with transcendental Thomism, Gilkey wants to preserve the importance of an experience of revelation through explicit religious symbols in Christian or non-Christian form. Without this personal transformation by recognizable religious symbols, life's basic questions would remain unanswered.

The alternative to this position—clear in the revisionist theology of Ogden and Tracy—is to locate a universal working of grace that is not tied to such specific historical forms. As Ogden has noted, the modern theologian in the liberal tradition does not need to look for some "new" event of God's grace other than that present in human life as such.[75] This is what distinguishes Ogden's approach from traditional Protestant and Catholic positions, where a clear distinction of law and gospel or nature and supernature is maintained. The alternative to the traditional position is to see the final depth of existence as graced "in existence as such, and not in a second altogether gratuitous act of God's grace."[76] Christianity and other religions disclose or re-present an original possibility granted with existence itself. The revisionist exploration of "basic" or "existential" faith is an example of this conviction. At this moment, I am inclined to agree with Ogden and Tracy that this alternative view of nature and grace can only be maintained in terms of neo-classical or process metaphysics.

In addition to seeking a wider "natural" setting of an understanding of God, a second basic requirement for a public forum of theological validation of Christian claims is the ability to reflectively determine the truth of Christian assertions without appealing to a unique insight of Christian faith. I emphasize *Christian* faith in this statement, because both Ogden and Tracy, for example, appeal in the last analysis to faith, but it is a basic or existential faith available to anyone and not restricted to the Christian community.[77] Gilkey, Bultmann and the Wittgensteinians challenge the possibility of a reflective determination of religious truth. They link the verification of Christian claims, in the last analysis, to an insight which only the Christian can have. There are a number of alternative conceptions of theological criteria of truth today: the neo-classical metaphysics of Ogden and Tracy, Pannenberg's universal history, pragmatic or political criteria, various models of unrestricted communities of discourse which Apel and others have pointed out. The full analysis and exploration of the value of these models of theological validation is an undertaking which will have to wait. The key to all these strategies of theological verification and the basis for a public forum of theological reflection are criteria of religious truth not dependent upon the particular foundation of Christian faith. To recognize such criteria of theological truth is to recognize the possibility for the non-believer to understand, assess and construct theological arguments about the meaning and truth of the Christian witness of faith.

---

[75] Ogden, "Present Prospects for Empirical Theology," in *The Future of Empirical Theology,* ed. Bernard Meland (Chicago: The University of Chicago Press, 1967), p. 75.

[76] Ogden, "The Reformation We Want," *The Anglican Theological Review* 54 (1972): 265, 270-71.

[77] See, e.g., Ogden, "The Task of Philosophical Theology," in *The Future of Philosophical Theology,* ed. Robert Evans, pp. 55-84, for a thorough analysis of "basic existential faith."

A Response to Dr. Ommen

by Rev. Peter Schineller, S.J.

The paper of Dr. Ommen, as he indicates, is part of a larger project on the exploration of the role of Christian faith in theology. In his paper he deals with the heuristic role of faith, but does not move into the probative role of faith. My own comments do not pretend to do full justice to the argument of his project or even this significant part of his project. Rather, I wish to isolate the central issue of his paper in a way that will lead to a clear discussion. I see this issue as follows: is Christian faith a requirement for doing Christian theology?

My basic response, in contrast to Dr. Ommen, is to answer *yes,* Christian faith *is* required for doing Christian theology. But at the same time, I wish to comment on the usefulness of the question, and show that it is a complex, and often misleading question. It can become an all too theoretical or formal question, and I am not sure of its practical consequences. In other words, I do not see clearly how the way that I answer it will affect the way I do theology, read theology, or teach theology. This questioning of the question arises from many and varied discussions I have had over the past several years precisely in debating this issue of the need for Christian faith for doing Christian theology.

Why do I respond that Christian faith is necessary for doing Christian theology? My answer comes from how I define "doing Christian theology." In my view, we can and must distinguish between (a) the task of commenting on theology, and (b) doing theology. The first task may consist of reflecting upon, reporting on, describing the position of another theologian or a part of the Christian tradition. This I take to be part of the task of a religious studies approach to Christian theology. In contrast to this I would speak of (b) doing theology as the task of making claims about the nature of Christian faith and standing behind these claims and arguing for them in one's own name. In other words, one is not merely understanding or examining another's position, but is affirming one's own. I admit, by the way, that this task of "doing Christian theology" is a rare occurrence. Most theologians speak or write about method in theology or comment on the theology of other theologians or persons of faith. Few attempt constructive Christian theology in this clearly defined sense.

To clarify further the issue at stake, I suggest that we become more specific, and instead of talking about Christian theology in general, talk about Christology in particular. Christian tradition has affirmed that Jesus is the Christ, Lord and Savior. I fail to see how a theologian can affirm and argue for this as the truth, and not stand behind it as a Christian believer. I grant it is true that one could report the affirmation of others (such as Rahner, Barth, etc.) concerning Jesus as the Christ, and not affirm the claim as one's own; but in this case, in my framework, one would be doing religious studies rather than Christian theology.

To further clarify this distinction between doing religious studies and doing Christian theology, let us suppose that we find a text or essay that makes high Christological claims, but we do not know the name of the author of the text, and it is written in the third person. On the one hand, since the text does present valid Christian theology, one could say that *if* the author agrees with the content, then he or she by definition is a Christian believer. If, on the other hand, the author does not agree with the claims, but is describing another Christian's position, then, from the viewpoint of that author, he or she has done religious studies rather than Christian theology. In either case, if the text makes Christological claims, then someone's faith stands behind the text, either the immediate author of the text, or the person the immediate author is commenting on.

Turning more specifically to the paper of Dr. Ommen, I note that he presents two reasons why he seeks to justify the possibility of doing Christian theology without Christian faith. The first is the desire to make theology a form of public discourse. While I agree with this goal, I do not think that it necessarily involves the possibility of doing Christian theology without faith. Take for example the theology of the person we honor here, Karl Rahner. His theology, even if it begins from faith, and proceeds in the Anselmian mode of "fides quaerens intellectum," has become public discourse. So too, the writings of Augustine, Teilhard, Barth, arising from faith positions, have become public classics.

A second reason for justifying the possibility of doing Christian theology without Christian faith comes from the presence of unbelief in the theological community. The theologian, more and more, is a mixture of belief and unbelief. While this statement of Dr. Ommen may well be true, it does not lead to his conclusions. For while there may be unbelief in the theologian, when one does Christian theology, one writes or speaks from one's Christian faith or belief. And if one speaks or writes from one's unbelief, then one is not doing Christian theology. Furthermore, if the theologian were to completely lose his or her faith in Jesus as the Christ, as Lord and Savior, then surely that theologian's theology would change. One could still understand the theology of another Christian, but ultimately the nonbeliever would say it is wrong, it is not my position, since I no longer believe that Jesus is the Christ.

At stake in the discussion, therefore, are two different ways of describing what it means to do Christian theology. The reason why Dr. Ommen says that the nonbeliever can do Christian theology is because he is willing to leave out the personal commitment or faith of the theologian. The theologian need not stand behind the truth claims he or she affirms. In my way of thinking, such a person, by definition, is doing religious studies, and not Christian theology.

In my opening remarks, I mentioned that I would like to question the question. Two factors lead me to this. First, I now teach in a professional school for ministry, rather than a college or university. This context, in which theology is closely related to ministry and praxis, has shaped the way in which I conceive of the nature and goals of Christian theology, and pushes me to a closer relationship between Christian faith (and hope and love) and doing Christian theology. Secondly, I would ask how a theology of liberation would respond to the question at issue. It seems to me that here again, with a continual interaction of theory and praxis, they might well question the reality or usefulness of the question. In fact, a theologian of liberation would probably affirm that not only is faith required for doing Christian theology, but also a commitment to charity and justice.

In conclusion, I hope that I have demonstrated the complexity of the question, the need to clarify terminology, and even some of my own dissatisfaction with the question. I also hope that I have shown the possibility of a different answer, namely that Christian faith *is* required for doing Christian theology.

A Response to Dr. Ommen

by Rev. Roland J. Teske, S.J.

Dr. Ommen's thesis is that Christian faith is not a requirement for doing Christian theology. The sense of the thesis is that one need not be a believing Christian in order to do Christian theology, though one does require the Christian witness of faith as the object of one's reflective investigation. The Christian theologian then is Christian in the context of this paper only in the sense in which I am a Manichaean theologian when I study the Manichaean witness of faith.

Dr. Ommen's thesis is a conceptual, not an empirical, thesis. That is, he does not appeal to the existence of non-believing Christian theologians to establish their possibility, though he does inform us that there are many such. He wishes to establish the more interesting thesis that the concept of doing Christian theology need not presuppose the possession of Christian faith on the part of the theologian.

The paper defines theology as "the reflective investigation of the meaning and truth of the Christian witness of faith." From the paper I am not entirely sure whether that definition is intended to include everything that may legitimately be called theology or whether it means that at least what falls within the scope of that definition may be legitimately called theology, even if there are other legitimate forms of theology that do not fall under that definition. While I have no problem in admitting that what a non-believing theologian does may be legitimately called theology, I do not agree that everything that has been legitimately called theology can be done by the non-believing theologian. Even David Tracy, who is cited by Dr. Ommen in support of his thesis, has said, "A defining existential characteristic of systematic theology is its insistence that the theologian as theologian is a faithful member of a particular religious tradition."[1]

In Dr. Ommen's view of theology, the object that theology studies, namely, "the Christian witness of faith," falls "within history and experience." To illustrate "the obvious historicality" of theology's object, he uses as examples scriptural texts and dogmatic statements. He insists that theology "must break out of the notion that God is an 'object' of study, even of a supernatural kind." I gather that for Dr. Ommen the object that theology studies is principally texts that express the Christian faith.

---

[1] David Tracy, "The Public Character of Systematic Theology," *Theology Digest* 4 (1978): 400.

I can see no reason why a non-believer cannot study such Christian texts and grasp their meaning as well as, if not better than, some believers. I agree with Dr. Ommen that the distinction between understanding and believing is necessary. It would make believing a completely irrational act if one had first to believe before he had any understanding of what was to be believed. I can see no reason why one's understanding of the Christian witness of faith might not be highly developed without one's assenting to its truth.

On the other hand, I find difficulty with the idea that a non-believing theologian can also reflectively determine the truth of the Christian witness of faith. While Dr. Ommen speaks of determining the truth of Christian assertions independently of faith, from the perspective of my tradition there are some truths that God has revealed that cannot be known to be true except by accepting in faith what God has revealed. Besides such mysteries there are also some truths that God has revealed that can be known by human reason without faith. For example, it seems to me that the non-believing theologian might very well determine that an assertion, such as, there is a God, is true. He would be operating as a philosopher, but his determination of such a truth ought surely to add interest to his work in theology.

Moreover, the non-believing theologian might also come to see that the Christian faith provides an understanding of human existence such that it would be reasonable to assent to the truth of the Christian faith. However, for the non-believing theologian to determine the truth of such assertions as, the Son of God became man, would from the perspective of the Catholic tradition involve a rationalism that reduces faith to reason. I find no problem conceptually with a non-believing theologian deciding that the Christian witness of faith is not true or that there is not sufficient evidence to settle the question.

Dr. Ommen says that faith is not able to provide premises for theological argumentation. This claim leads me to believe that his definition of theology is meant to exclude from the scope of theology what he terms theology in the Anselmian model or what has been called dogmatic or systematic theology. When Dr. Ommen speaks about faith, he refers to it as "affective insights or religious feelings," "religious devotion," or "a conviction of God's presence." Now, if one thinks of faith exclusively in terms of pious religious feelings, one would be correct, I suspect, in claiming that faith cannot provide premises for theological argumentation. However, when theologians operating within the Anselmian model speak of faith seeking understanding, they include as essential to faith intellectual assent to truths revealed by God. When the Catholic tradition insists upon the intellectual character of faith, it means that as an intellectual act faith grasps reality, that faith is an act of the intellect whose object is being or what is, and that in faith reality is known—specifically, the reality of the mystery of our salvation worked by God in Christ. With such a view of faith the believing theologian has revealed truths that can serve as premises for theological reflection. On the other hand, for the non-believing theologian there are no known revealed truths to be understood. There might be propositions whose interrelation and coherence can be grasped, but without faith as intellectual assent those propositions are not known to be true. Perhaps Dr. Ommen is making the same point when he says that the theses of faith become the hypotheses of the theologian. That is, for the non-believing theologian theology will attempt to understand not what is known to be true, but what is not known to be true and might be either true or false.

Furthermore, if faith is viewed as an intellectual assent to the truths that God has revealed, the believing theologian does know distinctively supernatural facts and realities, though Dr. Ommen says that there are no such facts or realities that only the believer can recognize. For a fact is a truth, and a supernatural fact is a truth that cannot be known by human reason without God's revelation accepted in faith. And if faith is an intellectual assent to what God has revealed, the believer does know supernatural truths or facts and does know realities that the non-believer does not know. For the believing theologian operating in the Anselmian model, the object of theology is not historical texts, but the realities known in the intellectual assent of faith to the word of God. Whereas the object of theology for the non-believing theologian is obviously historical, the object of dogmatic or systematic theology for the believer is the truths God has revealed in Christ and the realities grasped in those truths, at least some of which are not historical.

What I find lacking in Dr. Ommen's paper is any indication that theology might not be all of one piece, that there might be areas of theological reflection that do presuppose faith as well as other areas where faith might not be a prerequisite. I would suggest that his oversight of the element of intellectual assent in faith causes him to view faith as being unable to provide any supernatural truths for the believing theologian and to reject the idea that theology deals with God.

In closing I would like once again to cite David Tracy who says, while speaking of the public character of systematic theology, "Indeed what Christian theologian will not agree that Luther speaks for the entire Christian tradition when he states: 'Faith and God—these two belong together'?"[2]

---

[2] Ibid.

MAKING HEAVEN AND EARTH
Catholic Theology's Search for a Unified View of Nature and History

by Rev. Leo O'Donovan, S.J.

Catholic thought over the last decade has become increasingly political, turning from the comprehensive ontology and dogmatics of its recent past to a more flexible and responsive concern for social change. Where there had been a synthetic perspective on an ordered cosmos in which integral humanism would be a realizable goal, we now find sobering analyses of oppressed societies and urgent calls for a new world order. The cosmological optimism which characterized Teilhard de Chardin's thought can scarcely compete today with the sociopolitical pessimism of political and liberation theologians whose hope for the world seems largely confined to its future. In view of the Catholic community's emerging sense of its relation to a world recently shocked into awareness of economic inequity and the limits of growth, this new pessimism, which is really an awakening to historical experience, seems unavoidable. It is time that *Heilsgeschichte* gave way, if not to Robert Heilbronner, then at least to a harder realism about human life in its social concreteness.

And yet there are signs that our desire for a socially transformative theology may in certain respects be shortsighted or premature. The renewed desire to find the living unity between doctrine and ethics, between faith and justice, is scarcely an ambition we can now abandon. But I want to suggest in this essay that while so many of us have been turning whole-heartedly to this question as the central one for our future, significant voices in the scientific community have been proposing alternate views of the human situation, views which can seriously affect planning for human society in the future. Jacques Monod, the French Nobel Laureate, was among the first of these in our decade, when he summoned modern society to choose once and for all between mythologized religiosity or scientific objectivity and then to commit itself to an ethic of knowledge.[1] More recently, Edward O. Wilson has captured public attention with his programmatic study, *Sociobiology*,[2] and its anthropological sequel, *On Human Nature*,[3] which proposes that human behavior is wholly

---

[1] *Chance and Necessity: An Essay on the Natural Philosophy of Modern Biology* (New York: Knopf, 1971). Cf. L. J. O'Donovan, "Science or Prophecy? A Discussion with Jacques Monod," *American Ecclesiastical Review* 167 (1973): 543-52.

[2] Cambridge, Mass.: Belknap Press of Harvard University Press, 1975.

[3] Cambridge, Mass.: Harvard University Press, 1978.

rooted in human heredity and that the basic values for our species, as for every other, are survival and reproduction. Voices from other disciplines also place humanity entirely within nature. In the realm of social science, B. F. Skinner has capped his long career in behaviorist psychology by proposing a view of humanity which confidently appraises our situation "beyond freedom and dignity": Instead of seeking change in the human heart, we must develop a technology of behavior that will first change our environment and thus ourselves.[4] Analyzing human social activity within a larger natural system, the Club of Rome's report on *The Limits to Growth* insisted that the balance between human demands and the world's natural resources is seriously endangered.[5] Our confidence about the constant expansion of technological systems has eroded in view of the needs of ecological and social balance. No wonder that the World Council of Church's proposed colloquium of "Faith, Science and the Future" asks how faith and science may together contribute to the struggle for a technologically and ecologically sustainable society.[6]

In a wide variety of ways, then, our decade has witnessed the beginnings of a significant reassessment of the relations between the natural and the political or historical orders. I want to argue that no significant theology of history or political theology can realistically prescind from conversation with these voices, no fully public theology can be developed apart from the naturalist foundations with which they are concerned. To understand historical change adequately we must continue to relate it to the development of nature studied by natural and social sciences. More specifically, I want to suggest that dialogue with evolutionary thought is more significant for theology than we have commonly thought in recent years. To understand the history we are called to live in response to God's new covenant, I believe, we must be equally aware of the earth we have been given as the environment for our hopes. We are, in fact, ineluctably a part of that earth; the God who calls us to

---

[4] *Beyond Freedom and Dignity* (New York: Knopf, 1971).

[5] Cf. Donella H. Meadows et al., *The Limits to Growth* (New York: Universe Books, 1972). Mihajlo Mesarovic and Eduard Pestel, *Mankind at the Turning Point* (New York: Dutton, 1974). Jan Tinbergen, Coordinator, *Reshaping the International Order* (New York, 1976; Bergenfield, New Jersey: New American Library, 1977). Ervin Laszlo et al., *Goals for Mankind* (New York, 1976; Bergenfield, New Jersey: New American Library, 1978). D. Gabor et al., *Beyond the Age of Waste* (Elmsford, N.Y.: Pergamon Press, 1978).

[6] *Faith, Science and the Future.* Preparatory Readings for a World Conference Organized by the World Council of Churches at the Massachusettes Institute of Technology, Cambridge, Mass., USA, July 12-24, 1979. Ed. Paul Albrecht, Geneva, 1978.

liberation has called us at the same time to make with him a heaven *and* an earth that may one day be renewed forever.

I. Recent Contributions

In the next two sections of this essay, I shall review the state of the question between theologians and evolutionists. A long journey in the history of thought has been travelled since T. H. Huxley, at the height of the romantic period in evolutionary theory, wrote: "One of its greatest merits, in my eyes, is the fact that it occupies a position of complete and irreconcilable antagonism to that vigorous and consistent enemy of mankind—the Catholic Church."[7] This supposedly irreconcilable antagonism between the theory of evolution and Catholic faith in a redeeming creator gave way gradually to the conviction that inasmuch as each view is relevant to a different aspect of our experience in the world, both can be held intelligently by the same person. During the Second Vatican Council, in fact, when interest in the thought of Teilhard was at its height, the concept of evolution was received and used in conciliar documents in a variety of ways, particularly in *Gaudium et Spes,* the Pastoral Constitution on the Church in the Modern World. There the Council spoke typically, for example, of humanity's passing "from a rather static concept of reality to a more dynamic, evolutionary one."[8]

Vatican II's references to the evolutionary perspective in contemporary thought represent a notable change in climate from Pius XII's cautious recognition in 1941 and 1950 that a moderately evolutionary conception of human origins might be doctrinally acceptable. But it was not clear how much the change was one of principle. Some fundamental characteristics of a Christian anthropology were outlined in the Pastoral Constitution, but the sketch of a Christian cosmology present in the preparatory texts of Mecheln and Ariccia dropped from the final document almost entirely. The Council spoke of evolution, as do most contemporary theologians, in an extremely general and undefined way. Its lack of clarity on the term mirrored a similarly varied usage in the history of ideas. There may be general acceptance of the evolutionary conception of human origins, but there is much less consensus on whether an evolutionary

---

[7] Quoted in Phillip G. Fothergill, *Evolution and Christians* (London: Longmans, 1961), p. 13.

[8] Cf. Wolfgang Klein, *Teilhard de Chardin und das Zweite Vatikanische Konzil.* Ein Vergleich der Pastoral-Konstitution über die Kirche in der Welt von heute mit Aspekten der Weltschau Pierre Teilhards de Chardin (Munich, Paderborn, Wien: F. Schöningh, 1975); and L. J. O'Donovan, "Was Vatican II Evolutionary? A Note on Conciliar Language," *Theological Studies* 36 (1975): 493-502.

model is possible for understanding the universe and humanity's place in it. As Karl Rahner has remarked, "the 'peace' established between sacred theology and the present-day scientific theory of man's evolutionary origins . . . is only the basis and pacific condition of a genuine encounter between the various branches of study concerned with man."[9]

Teilhard remains the central figure in this encounter, and it may well be that the decline of popular enthusiasm for his writings now provides a more apt atmosphere in which to analyze them more critically and productively.[10] His basic law of complexity-consciousness is that the growing complexity of natural organization provides the basis for the full emergence of reflective thought; his converse principle of differentiating unity holds that the convergence of independent centers of consciousness personalizes rather than merely individualizes them; together these continue to provide a provocative translation in historical, dynamic terms of the classical, static relation between the unity and plurality of being.[11] Around him we find a wide spectrum of theologians whom he has inspired, from Dutch theologians like Piet Schoonenberg,[12] to liberation theologian Juan Luis Segundo.[13] Teilhard has especially attracted the comment of thinkers trained in both Christian tradition and the life sciences. Some, like Olivier Rabut, are generally favorable to him, although critical of particular aspects of his thought. Rabut, for example, takes the evolving universe as a starting point and seeks to develop from it the conception of a Source of meaning which could

---

[9] *Hominisation: The Evolutionary Origin of Man as a Theological Problem* (New York: Herder and Herder, 1965), p. 45. See also Rahner's "Theology as Engaged in an Interdisciplinary Dialogue with the Sciences," and "On the Relationship Between Theology and the Contemporary Sciences," in *Theological Investigations* 13 (New York: Seabury, 1975): 80-93 and 94-102. The World Council of Churches' *Faith, Science and the Future* notes: "It is sometimes said that the old conflict between science and religion is dead. That is too cheerful a statement. It would be better to say that the tensions and conflicts have changed. Science is less likely than in the past to seem to *refute* religion, although it still refutes many formulations of religious beliefs. It is more likely to challenge religion—to ask people of faith why they believe in God, what they mean by talking of God and of God's action in the world" (p. 16).

[10] Cf. Donald P. Gray. "The Phenomenon of Teilhard," *Theological Studies* 36 (1975): 19-51; Hans Küng, *Existiert Gott?* Antworf auf die Gottesfrage der Neuzeit (Munich: R. Piper, 1978), pp. 201-6, 704-6.

[11] Sharing Teilhard's prophetic social commitment, Bernard Delfgaauw has developed an ontology and metaphysic of these central themes. In his three volume work *Geschichte als Fortschritt* (Cologne: Bachem, 1962, 1965, 1966) he argues for an understanding of the evolutionary process as the condition of possibility for the progress of freedom. Later I shall myself argue the need to qualify such a thesis by the recognition of freedom's enduring dialectical dependence on nature.

[12] *God's World in the Making* (Pittsburgh: Duquesne University Press, 1964).

[13] *Evolution and Guilt* (Maryknoll, N.Y.: Orbis Books, 1974).

be identified with the God of Christian revelation and faith.[14] Others, like Werner Bröker, have developed their views in seeming independence of Teilhard but with significant structural similarity. Bröker wants to hold that "evolution as a dynamic variation in time is not only a phenomenon of life (of the individual, of races and species), but just as much a phenomenon of the cosmos and of history."[15] Concerned chiefly with discovering an encompassing meaning for a world in process of becoming, he interprets evolution as creation's capacity through its own activity to develop the necessary conditions for encountering God in salvation history. It is precisely the discontinuity of history, however, which leads other scientist-theologians to reject the Teilhardian synopsis of cosmic, organic and cultural evolution. Raymond Nogar, for example, had argued earlier in his career that the traditional argument for the existence of God from the observance of order in the world receives a progressive and dynamic re-interpretation from the synthetic theory of evolution, which understands nature as maintaining its overall stability through a process of adaptation in which constancy and variation are natural correlatives. But the more Nogar meditated on the discrepancy between arguments for God from the wisdom of order and the dramatic meaning injected into history by the cross of Christ, the more he concluded to the necessity of radically revising his earlier views.[16]

It is striking that each of the examples I have cited takes "meaning" more or less explicitly as the middle term of its argument. Each argument, furthermore, suggests the need for scientific cosmology and anthropology to be critical and to examine the presuppositions of their basic objectifications. Each author also recognizes that the integration of the evolutionary viewpoint into a more empirical and historical Christian consciousness is still at a programmatic stage; more adequate formulation of theological topics such as original sin merely foreshadows a larger task. Having moved beyond the apologetic perspective of Lecomte du Noüy and his effort to justify God's ways with us through an inspection of evolutionary evidence, the contemporary issue is not to identify but to relate the perspec-

---

[14] See his *God in an Evolving Universe*, trans. William Springer (New York: Herder and Herder, 1966) and also *Dialogue avec Teilhard de Chardin* (Paris: Éditions de Cerf, 1958).

[15] *Der Sinn von Evolution. Ein naturwissenschaftlichtheologischer Diskussionsbeitrag* (Düsseldorf, 1967), p. 40, my trans. See also Brökers "Aspects of Evolution," in *The Evolving World and Theology: Concilium* 26 (New York-Glen Rock, N.J., 1967): 7-24, which is a selection from his book.

[16] Compare his *The Wisdom of Evolution* (Garden City, N.Y.: Doubleday, Mentor-Omega, 1966), first published in 1963 (Garden City, N.Y.: Doubleday), and *The Lord of the Absurd* (New York: Herder and Herder, 1966).

tives of evolution and faith.[17] To do so we need a method of interpretation that will do justice to both, an approach to meaning that
will neither restrict it unduly nor generalize it unhelpfully. Whether
one considers the biblical revelation to have fostered primarily the
development of natural science or the exploitation of nature, "the
present crisis calls for a new description of the human ontological
position and the ethical values of his scientific and technological
attempts to change the surface of the earth."[18]

Serious opposition, rather along Nogar's later lines, has been
voiced precisely to that project, from a fairly traditional perspective.
Hans Urs von Balthasar has offered a wide-ranging critique of the
evolutionary world view as applied to Christian faith. Von Balthasar
grants that an encounter between Christianity and the idea of evolution must indeed take place, in fact that a remarkably successful
example of such encounter is already found in the nineteenth century with Vladimir Soloviev. Nevertheless, he argues, eschatological
faith must always recall that the resolution of time which God
intends is not effected by the world's development: it can only be
vertically achieved through union with the Incarnate Word who is
present until the end of time in the Church which is his body and
bride. Von Balthasar emphatically rejects the possibility that Christians can dismiss the idea of evolution as "secularized theology."
But he is less successful, I think, in coming to terms with the actual
status of the question: how the process of evolution may express
God's purposes and whether humanity in any sense can be its goal.
One may distinguish philosophical from theological questions at this
point, "philosophy of evolution" from "eschatology." But this runs
the danger of avoiding the roots of the issue in the one world meant
for God's fulfillment; it emphasizes transcendent fulfillment, in
other words, to the neglect of the immanent.[19]

Likewise, Hans-Eduard Hengstenberg represents a scholastic philosophy and theology which has sought to renew scholastic principles
through dialogue with twentieth century philosophy, especially Max
Scheler's. Hengstenberg has repeatedly addressed himself to the
relation between Christian thought and the theory of evolution.[20]

---

[17] Cf. Harold H. Oliver, "The Complementarity of Theology and Cosmology,"
Zygon 13 (1978): 19-33.

[18] *Faith, Science and the Future*, p. 41.

[19] Von Balthasar's theology of history and its relation to evolutionary thought are
discussed in my "Evolution under the sign of the Cross," *Theological Studies* 32
(1971): 602-26, and God's Glory in Time," *Communio* 2 (1975): 250-69.

[20] See especially his *Evolution and Schöpfung* (Munich: A Pustet, 1963) and *Mensch
und Materie* (Stuttgart: W. Kohlhammer, 1965). These depend on his earlier anthropological and metaphysical studies such as *Das Band zwischen Gott und Schöpfung*
(Paderborn: Verlag Bonifacius-Drukerei, 1940), *Autonomismus und Transzendenz-
philosophie* (Heidelberg: F. H. Kerle, 1950), and *Philosophische Anthropologie*, 2d ed.
(Stuttgart: W. Kohlhammer, 1960).

Despite useful analyses on the ideological potential of evolutionism, however, he appropriates the idea of evolution too philosophically and uses an unsatisfactory conception of scientific method. As in Bröker and von Balthasar, Hengstenberg attributes a form of interior freedom to material reality before the advent of human consciousness, but he does so with an ontology that appears more anthropo-morphic than anthropo-logical. To this extent the evolutionary process could have meaning quite apart from humanity, while the theory of evolution would appear to have little real relevance for explaining human origins. Hengstenberg's own theory of creation, finally, which purports to be distinct from theology and yet remains curiously dependent on it, is overly static and a-historical; it is unsuited to sustain the real conversation he himself has often urged between adherents of a methodologically exact theory of evolution and a renewed but traditional Christian understanding of creation.

Two final and major representatives of contemporary Catholic thought represent a much more positive integration of the idea of evolution into their reflection on Christian experience. Both Karl Rahner and Bernard Lonergan use a form of transcendental method in theology, and each of them has proposed a mediation of the horizons of evolutionary theory and Christian faith. Rahner has elaborated a conception of transcendent divine causality according to which human spirit is the goal of world process but achieves its true fulfillment only in the man of Nazareth who lived out radical solidarity with men and women of every condition and through whom humanity is promised final union with God.[21] Rahner has concentrated on the dimension of transcendental causality and its correlate of active self-transcendence in the process of evolution. I think it can be shown, furthermore, that in *Geist im Welt* he had already developed an understanding of innerworldly causality which bears striking resemblances to his later considerations on active self-transcendence, the former viewpoint employing with respect to knowledge a deductive, a priori causal analysis from above, while the latter emphasizes development from below, the temporal unfolding of the material conditions from which knowing spirit is meant to arise.

Lonergan's point of departure is likewise a cognitional one, but in a way that is meant to have methodological consequences for understanding all objective reality and, as it appears in his later

---

[21] L. J. O'Donovan, "Der Dialog mit dem Darwinismus. Zur theologischen Verwendung des evolutiven Weltbilds bei Karl Rahner," in *Wagnis Theologie: Erfahrungen mit der Theologie Karl Rahners,* ed. Herbert Vorgrimler (Freiburg: Herder, 1979), pp. 215-29.

thought, for permanently renewing conversion to the Christian horizon. His theory of emergent probability effects a transposition into verifiable psychological terms of scholastic theses on equivocal causality, latent virtualities, and the education of form from matter. His distinction and explanation of the classical, statistical, genetic and dialectical methods required for an adequate understanding of our concrete world introduces a high degree of clarity and precision into a discussion which all too often simply equates the concepts of evolution, development, process, or even history.[22] For the most part his reflection on evolution seems to have restricted itself to the categorical order. But this emphasis should not be considered without acknowledging his basic assertion of self-transcendence as the law of being. I will later suggest that his approach is complementary to Rahner's.

II. The Future of a Dialogue

Criticism of evolutionary theology by political and liberation theologies is a progressivist critique countered by more conservative theologians whose concern is not that evolutionary thought will excessively confine theology but that it will subvert faith's basic concern for transcendence. In my own view, however, the most fruitful critique of an evolutionary model comes neither from the left nor from the right but from the center. It may be simply framed in the question: How will our new understanding of reality as evolutionary affect our understanding of God's redemption of his creation? New, or at least more comprehensive, categories in ontology will be required, I am convinced, if we are to hold the meanings of both evolution and faith in some reasonable relation to one another.

Even among authors who agree that evolutionary theory poses important questions for theology, however, there is a tendency to subsume such questions under older ones already familiar to classical theology. In that case, however, the life sciences only provide striking illustrations for issues that can be recognized quite apart from them. Philosophers of science can add with some justice that evolutionary theory to a significant extent merely intensifies the process view of the world inaugurated by mechanics between Galileo and Newton. Dominique Dubarle has written, for example, that "the opposition of evolutionist ideas to the fixist ideas of the ancient cosmology is only, in certain respects, a second face to the clash between the ancient conceptions of the movement of bodies and the essential principles of scientific mechanics." The acceptance of mod-

---

[22] Cf. L.J. O'Donovan, "Emergent Probability and the Method of an Evolutionary World View," *The Personalist* 54 (1973): 250-73.

ern mechanics already began to make it possible and natural to represent the universe as one in evolution. "In this respect, the life sciences only effect a re-enforcement of the evidence already inscribed in the unfolding of the sciences of inanimate nature."[23]

To this objection one may reply that the theory of evolution has not more but also not less relevance for Christian faith than other basic scientific approaches through which post-modern society conceives and projects its world. Like depth psychology and cybernetics, it contributes to forming the concrete experience and understanding of the world in which we come to believe or not to believe in a redeeming creator. The claims of faith may make their appeal to our hearts and existence more centrally and directly, but the person to whom the Christian message is proclaimed today is one who knows we live in an evolving world. What meaning this whole process may have is indeed a question structurally similar to questions about the meaning of life with which humanity has always been posed. If the latter, more general question concerns believer and unbeliever alike more immediately than the former, more special one, that should not surprise us. There is a natural, existential priority and depth to the question of life which allows it to be both particular and highly inclusive, at once deeply personal and yet always directed toward a fuller grasp of meaning. At this level, every answer becomes the source of further questions. The evolutionary perspective, however, is not merely one aspect among others for the life sciences; it *constitutes* them as sciences. It emphasizes process, as modern mechanics did, but it does so in a radically new way: with respect to life itself, which cannot help but be of more interest to us than the sheerly material. Evolutionary thought thus involves a novelty which should not be minimized by the suggestion that Christianity was always evolutionary in instinct. The notions of "common descent with change" and "discontinuous continuity" should be emphasized in theological reflection just as much as those of dynamism and process.

In addition, the argument that evolution is merely the way creation is accomplished is more deceptive than it seems. This has been a common position, from the time of the American romantic liberal theologian John Fiske, who used to insist that "evolution is God's way of doing things,"[24] to the French neuro-physiologist Paul

[23] Both quotes from "Evolution et évolutionnisme," *Lumière et Vie* 6 (1957): 499-514, at p. 501, my trans. Cf. Dubarle's "La science et la vision unifiée de l'univers. Les conceptions d'Einstein et l'apport de Teilhard de Chardin," in René Maheu et al., *Science et synthèse* (Paris: Gallimard, 1967), pp. 48-66, esp. at p. 61.

[24] Quoted in Richard H. Overman, *Evolution and the Christian Doctrine of Creation* (Philadelphia: Westminster Press, 1967), p. 102. See also John Dillenberger, *Protestant Thought and Natural Science. A Historical Study* (London: Collins, 1961), pp. 230-32.

Chauchard, who writes that "it is necessary simply to recognize that the evolution of matter and of life is just the manner in which the creative act accomplishes itself. . . . Creative evolution is an *evolving creation.*"[25] But there are significant ambiguities in such statements. In the first place, a philosophical or theological concept (creation) is specified immediately by one from natural science (evolution). Secondly, such formulations usually mean to include the historical dimension of creation but often fail to ground this inclusion; and yet the unity of organic and historical process is precisely one of the central problems the theory of evolution raises for an integrated understanding of our world. Finally, authors who propose the thesis that evolution is simply the manner in which God creates generally disregard the question of the relation between the orders of creation and redemption. It was with more precision, then, that Père Sertillanges one day said to Bergson, "Creative evolution is not an evolution that creates, *but an evolution where there is creation*"—to which Bergson gave his agreement.[26] In a world which modern science has discovered to be evolutionary, another and more fundamental type of thought concludes to the constant origin of this evolutionary world from an eminently good creator. Only as a programmatic integration of the two approaches, scientific and theological, therefore, is it appropriate to say that God creates by means of evolution. The statement should serve to encourage rather than to conclude contact between the two modes of thought.

The discussion between evolutionists and theologians is thus in many ways an exemplary one for interdisciplinary study. The exchange consisted far too long in attacking and defending respective positions, rather along the lines of the famous debate between Bishop Wilberforce and T. H. Huxley. But with a certain peace established between the two parties, as we have seen, a mutually beneficial dialogue appears to be possible. Interest on the part of Catholic theology was strong throughout Vatican II and Paul VI's theology of development. The imminent danger of now neglecting the dialogue, however, is a major concern of this essay.

Writing of the encounter between Christian faith and secular ideologies, Karl Lehman has urged that the very possibility of the discussion must first be kept alive. For this to be possible, he suggests, one must "avoid from the start hasty evaluations, or else be critical with respect to them: for example, the condemnation of ideologies as 'the power of the devil,' 'substitute religions,' 'idols';

---

[25] *La création évolutive* (Paris: Éditions Spes, 1957), p. 125.

[26] As reported by Rabut, *God in an Evolving Universe,* p. 49; cf. Küng, *Existiert Gott?,* pp. 204f.

describing each other by means of standardized slogans; polemical and overly simple reductions to other historical phenomena (such as autonomism, sociologism, communism, etc.).'' Lehmann calls for an open and exploratory faith. ''By faith's commitment we are more obliged to a deepened exploration of the truth in an adversary's position than one would be by the commitment which a party ideology can perhaps demand for the understanding of other parties.''[27] An open dialogue must be fostered. It will be all the more necessary to the extent that evolutionary theorists tend towards the kind of comprehensive world-view which we remarked in our opening paragraphs. For if every philosophy inevitably bears within itself the germs of a theology, then practice has also shown that students of evolution inevitably expand their strictly scientific thinking into a more generalized theory—as when G. G. Simpson writes on *This View of Life,* C. H. Waddington on *The Ethical Animal,* Julian Huxley on *Religion Without Revelation,* or Theodosius Dobzhansky on *The Biological Basis of Human Freedom.* In view of every science's propensity to open towards a more inclusive grasp of reality, then, Lehmann's remarks provide timely advice for the theologians.

Here we may also note a benefit scientists may expect from the discussion. Theologians are encouraged by evolutionary theory to consider humanity's place in the universe more correctly: to pay closer attention to the vagaries of natural and historical process; to value the process itself as well as its possible outcome (its ''how'' or content as well as its ''why'' or goal); to conceive in a new way the immense extent and variety of our common density in a universe which is billions of years old. But then theorists of evolution may also expect from theology a sober critique of the extrapolations biology makes towards a more generalized anthropology. They have a right to expect an understanding of the human condition which serves as a *negative* criterion only to the extent that it *positively* includes a deeper and more comprehensive truth. Theorists of evolution have a right to expect that theological interest in the fundamental characteristics of humanity's place before God (''foundations'') may also shed light on scientific presuppositions about the emergence of the human species (''origins''). If the central question in current study of the mechanism of evolution is the generation of new species, then criteria for identifying such new species must be clarified. Criteria for identifying the human species can neither be taken for granted, nor can they be left entirely to a science which concerns itself with only a part of human experience. Once such

---

[27] ''Die Herausforderung der Kirche durch die Ideologien,'' in *Handbuch der Pastoraltheologie* 2 (Freiburg, 1966): 148-80, quotes at p. 170 and 168-69, my trans.

criteria have been elaborated, furthermore, we cannot assume that they will always be correctly understood and applied. If theologians, in other words, seem currently to be more concerned with foundational questions than with questions of origins, the latter should still not be excluded.[28] This is particularly true in regard to a theological evaluation of evolution. The foundations of the human situation are only adequately grasped when they serve somehow to illuminate humanity's full history in the universe. As we continue to learn the implications of our temporality , we would do well not to forget theology's ancient sense of the mutual relations between protology and eschatology.

It seems, therefore, that the first meeting ground for theologians and theorists of evolution is established when evolutionists reflect on the presuppositions of their science and on its ideological consequences. Material exchange between the two disciplines should lead to mutual re-examination of basic categories of meaning, as I shall show later. The most immediate practical discussion, however, probably develops from the recognition that partial views of reality are always tempted to make absolute claims and must regularly be prevented from doing so. Theologians can only expect to be listened to seriously, however, if they have some awareness of how evolutionists themselves pose their questions. A theological reflection on evolution should specify the conception of evolution used and who represents it. All too easily theologians speak of Darwin and evolution without realizing that their actual discussion partners are neo-Darwinists and their critics.

Methodologically, I would also note that just as the dialogue between theologians and evolutionists tends to cut across denominational lines, so too it fits only with difficulty into the more common divisions of theological subject matter. One might characterize the discussion as pertaining, in von Balthasar's words, "to a general Christian understanding of history, which establishes itself as a third discipline at the point where the two perspectives [of biblical revelation and world history] meet and a 'supernatural' light falls on the 'natural.' "[29] In terms of Lonergan's distinction of functional specialties in theology, it appears that four of these—history, dialectics, foundations, and systematics—would in various ways be concerned with a theological appropriation of evolution. At any rate the discussion can scarcely be confined to fundamental or foundational

---

[28] For an emphasis on foundations almost to the exclusion of the question of origins, see Karl-Heinz Weger, *Theologie der Erbsünde*. Quaestiones disputatae 44 (Freiburg: Herder, 1970).

[29] *A Theological Anthropology* (New York: Sheed and Ward, 1967), p. 169, trans. slightly amended.

theology. It is an inter-disciplinary question which also has repercussions for issues pertaining to doctrinal or systematic theology.

III. Nature and History: The Limits of an Evolutionary Model

Having renewed some major contributions to the dialogue, I turn now to consider some of the categories which may be used analogously by both theological and evolutionary thought. It will be helpful to ask first how one may speak about the unity of organic and historical (psychosocial) evolution. The question is the evolutionary variant of the general question about the relation between nature and history or freedom. It should serve to indicate both the limits and the serviceability of an evolutionary model in theology.

We have already met the basic objections to an evolutionary approach. It is said to overemphasize the more or less inexorable character of an impersonal process, neglecting the historical freedom which should be the focal phenomenon for any adequate philosophy or theology today. Nogar and others consider it a "biological fallacy" to use evolution as a means of understanding history. Political and liberation theologians criticize the adequacy of an evolutionary model for inspiring a program of self-critical social commitment. Harvey Cox anticipated their view well when he wrote that like apocalypticism, "evolutionism . . . fails to provide the perspective on the future needed for politics today. True, one can derive a certain comfort from the conviction that reality is moving towards a predetermined telos. But when this attitude informs our planning, it can inhibit imagination and discourage radical new initiatives. Any teleological philosophy obscures the fact that history is radically open, has no predetermined end and will go on where man takes it and nowhere else."[30] Still others reject the evolutionary model as detracting necessarily from the transcendently free self-involvement of God. Indeed, life scientists themselves are by no means in agreement as to how thoroughly evolution can be said to "explain" the phenomenon of man. Nor is it a foregone conclusion for them that the universe can be considered a unity.

In fact, however, authors interested in an evolutionary model commonly wish to argue an analogy, at once a continuity and a discontinuity between natural and human history. They intend to pursue a middle course between a reductionism in which higher forms are accounted for only by lower ones and a false spiritualism

---

[30] "Evolutionary Progress and Christian Promise," in *The Evolving World and Theology: Concilium* 26: 35-47, at p. 44. As we shall see, however, it is imperative to distinguish between teleology and predetermination.

in which higher forms are accounted for without lower ones. Normally they do not represent Lamarckianism, which proposes development through the inheritance of acquired characteristics. Neither do they support social Darwinism, which flatly asserts that nature provides the adequate pattern for human behavior. "Darwinian naturalism" may continue to prevail as a dominant scientific ideology, and in that respect critique of ideology has a proper and important role. But this does not dispense us, as Ernest Becker has forcefully argued, from fidelity to the tradition of scientific naturalism.[31] A fundamental condition for understanding human life is that it must be explained in relation to the animal kingdom—without being reduced to that.

We must avoid isolating ourselves in history, in other words, just as much as we must avoid isolating God in eternity. Paul Chauchard has written that the essential task of current theology is "to put God back at the heart of his work. . . . [It] is entirely correct to insist on God's personal character as love present to the heart of man, but it is necessary all the same not to forget the creator God, that grand materialist through whom the material universe exists and, by organizing itself, becomes capable of spirit."[32] Chauchard urges a cosmological extension or complement to the immanentism which has played so large a role in French thought since the late nineteenth century (in Bergson, Blondel, and the modernists, for example) and which was also widespread in recent secular theology. As we seek to interpret God's workings in history we must also look for his purposes in a universe that is more than just a stage for history's play.

This concern for the unity of freedom and nature, of history and cosmos, has made itself felt in various ways in recent Catholic thought. Werner Bröker, for example, attributes in effect a fundamentally dialogic character to the material creation even prior to the origin of humanity. Von Balthasar and Hengstenberg both admit inchoate forms of consciousness and freedom at this stage. Rahner speaks in another way of the one history of humanity's one world. In this connection Olivier Rabut has remarked that "the term 'consciousness' (or 'pre-consciousness') attributed to inert matter seems acceptable to us, if excessive conclusions are not drawn from it." It would mean that "consciousness (that is psychism) in superior living creatures is *prepared* at the beginning of the series by appropriate arrangements. As long as it is left at that, one does not expose oneself to any serious objection, though the appropriateness of the choice of words might be contested. Teilhard enunciates a

---

[31] See his *Angel in Armor* (New York: G. Braziller, 1969).

[32] *La création évolutive*, p. 127, my trans.

principle with good reason which one might call the phyletic principle—nothing appears that was not prepared from all time.''[33]

But what exactly is meant by the word "prepared," which Rabut himself emphasizes? Does it simply state the presence of those prior conditions and causes necessary for successive stages of evolutionary solutions to increasingly complex problems? But then the term introduces an element of finality which is not explicitly accounted for. A similar objection can be raised to Nogar's distinction between prehistory and history, by means of which he hopes to avoid the "biological fallacy." What precisely is the criterion for referring the prehuman phase of natural development to the human? What makes prehistory in any strict sense of the word "historical?" It would see that "prehuman" and "prehistory" are phenomenal descriptions which natural science may use with good reason but whose full justification depends on philosophical criteria.[34] This is not to question the legitimacy of objective frames of reference as used by science. But it suggests that these objectifications themselves raise further questions about their critical grounding.

Various analogies have been proposed in an attempt to solve this problem. In Bröker's approach through the idea of salvation history, an analogy is drawn between God's formulation of humanity as his mode of self-expression outside of himself and evolutionary creation's formulation of humanity as its answer beyond itself to God. The two formulations, one emphasizing descent, the other ascent, are then united in the world's one history of salvation. Von Balthasar argues that the emergence of humanity is written into nature from the beginning. He draws an analogy between nature and humanity, the history of nature and the history of humanity on the one hand and, on the other, Old Testament history and the appearance of Christ. In each case a radically new event is prepared through the dynamism of the goal in question. For both Rahner and Lonergan human self-transcendence is proposed as the primary analogue for conceiving the emergence of truly higher forms in the evolutionary process; this self-transcendence, furthermore, stands in a relation of possibility to true fulfillment through God's gracious act of self-giving.

---

[33] *God in an Evolving Universe,* quotes at p. 51.

[34] Schoonenberg remarks: "When we start from the phenomena established by science, we witness only a gradual transition from animal to man. Hence the use of the term 'prehuman' can be meaningful. But this does not oblige us to give up the question: Is this or that form a man or not? . . . Can we admit that there are degrees in the self-consciousness which affirms one's own being and that of God, and are there gradations in the freedom which determines its attitude toward God? It is certain that there are degrees in their active self-realization, but we cannot conceive that there could be degrees in the self-realization of *being*-a-person" (*God's World in the Making,* p. 54).

The tendency of all these analogies can be summarized in a still simpler one proposed by Gisbert Greshake: the relation of evolution to history is analogous to the relation between history and its fulfillment.[35] A similar suggestion sets the past development of the world, including the history of Israel, up until Christ in analogy to its present development, including Christianity, up until the Eschaton.[36] In each case, one should note, the event towards which the respective processes tend is nevertheless radically new and free, not simply to be derived from the potentialities of the previous process considered in and for itself. If history is to be seen as transcending nature, then the fulfillment of history through God's gracious judgment must be conceived as still more mysteriously transcendent. But what, if anything, holds such an analogy together? Recent reflection on analogical thought suggests that its most basic form is the analogy of reference or transcendence rather than the analogy of proportionality. In view of that, let us try to discover a unifying point of control in human experience which can both generate and criticize the analogies we have mentioned. That central point of reference, I propose, is an experience and idea of finality which is usually the most unsatisfactory aspect of theological reflection on evolution. In our discussion of finality in the next sections we shall see that dialogue between evolutionary thought and theology also helps to clarify some of our basic conceptions with regard to transcendence, self-transcendence, causality, freedom, fulfillment, and the unity of the world.

IV. Finality and Transcendence

All too commonly, theologians simply assert that the incarnation is the goal of world development, a goal present from the beginning through a "power of attraction."[37] With somewhat more precision, Michael Schmaus says of the material universe that "humanity was

---

[35] *Die Auferstehung der Toten in der gegenwärtigen theologischen Diskussion* (Essen: Ludgerus-Verl., 1969), pp. 373ff.

[36] This is George Lindbeck's formulation, cited by Henri de Lubac, *Athéisme et sens de l'homme* (Paris: Éditions du Cerf, 1968), pp. 139-40. In a similar way Karl Rahner distinguishes between the period of natural existence when humanity was embedded in nature and still threatened by it, and the period of truly hominized existence, when humanity is co-responsible and co-creative of its environment; cf. his *Foundations of Christian Faith,* trans. William Dych (New York: Seabury, 1978) pp. 168ff.

[37] Cf. Jean Mouroux, *Le Mystère du Temps* (Paris: Aubier, 1962), who in this respect is close to von Balthasar, although his interest in the question of evolution is considerably less. More generally, cf. Franz Mussner, "Schöpfung in Christus," *Mysterium Salutis* 2 (Einsiedeln: Benziger, 1967): 455-61; and Karl Hermann Schelke, "Die Schöpfung in Christus," in *Die Zeit Jesu,* ed. Gunther Bornkamm and Karl Rahner (Freiburg: Herder, 1970) pp. 208-17.

from the very beginning the goal. It is questionable whether natural science can strictly prove such a finality in the direction of humanity. For the philosophically and above all for the theologically thinking person this finality is certain."[38] But then the manner in which that finality is conceived is obviously crucial. It will neither interest the evolutionist nor have lasting value for the theologian if finality is asserted without being shown to have a specific structure.

The question is all the more important since evolutionists and theologians repeatedly misunderstand each other on this point. On the one hand, "scientific integrity" leads certain philosophers or theologians to deny that it is possible to speak of finality in evolution in any justifiable scientific sense prior to a thematized knowledge of God. On the other hand, so astute a philosopher and commentator as Madeleine Barthélemy-Madaule writes that "when Teilhard appeals to orthogenesis, it is because the paleontologist in him invokes a concept which seems indispensable to him. . . . If he had not been a Christian, he would have been obliged, as a scientist, to appeal to an orthogenesis."[39] As if in direct reply, Theodosius Dobzhansky says in *Mankind Evolving:*

> Teilhard de Chardin saw that the evolution of matter, the evolution of life, and the evolution of man are integral parts of a single process of cosmic development, of a single and coherent history of the whole universe. Furthermore, he saw in this history a clear direction or trend. Regrettably, he described this trend as "orthogenesis," but if I understand him aright, he did not mean to imply that evolution is an uncreative unfolding of preformed events. . . . unfortunately he lacked familiarity with modern biology.[40]

Straddling these various positions, one can speak of evolution as a development which does not take place in a straight line but which comes to have humanity at its term. This assertion as it stands, however, will scarcely satisfy those self-contained theories of evolution which either refuse to ask whether the human species is the highest form achieved in the evolutionary process or else consider the question itself invalid. Finally, the highly general idea of evolution used by many theologians often leads scientists to object that the descriptive concept employed by science has been replaced by a teleological concept, one that ascribes to the material universe a cer-

---

[38] "Materie und Leben in theologischer Sicht," in *Matrie und Leben. Naturwissenschaft und Theologie* 7 (Freiburg, 1966): 255-68, at p. 265.

[39] *Bergson et Teilhard de Chardin* (Paris: Éditions du Seuil, 1963), p. 159. Mme. Barthélemy-Madaule does add, however, that Teilhard intended to correct, renew and integrate the idea of orthogenesis (pp. 159f.).

[40] *Mankind Evolving* (New Haven: Yale University Press, 1962), p. 347.

tain "primordial capacity" for "higher development." The scientist is seldom satisfied to hear that philosophers and theologians are concerned to integrate the knowledge of humanity and its world provided by the life sciences, that their goal is a holistic view with practical perspectives on our actual future in this world. We see, once again, that the need is to mediate possible scientific and theological meanings of evolution rather than to place them merely side by side.

Here, in order to appreciate the relation between the descriptive formal causality which can be considered the province of natural science and the final causality which can only be grounded by further reflection of a philosophical-theological kind, fundamental distinctions must be drawn. We may begin by recalling Lonergan's conception of finality as "the dynamic aspect of the real."[41] Finality is understood in this view not according to deductivist or determinist models but as "an effectively probable realization of possibilities."[42] Finality in this sense is to be conceived not merely as a dynamism but in a certain sense as a directed dynamism: "For it knows proportionate being as constituted by explanatory genera and species of central and conjugate potencies, forms, and acts. It knows that potency stands in some dynamic direction to form, that form stands in some dynamic direction to act, that coincidental manifolds of act stand in some connection with potency to higher forms."[43] To this extent, precisely from the perspective of immanent formal intelligibility, I would not accept the scepticism of Rabut and others with regard to the notion of finality. I do agree, however, that a complete conception cannot be derived from this perspective alone. For, as Lonergan adds about his own notion of finality (and only later develops while discussing the existence and nature of God): "Just what the dynamic direction may prove to be, is a further question. But at least in some sense, dynamic direction is to be affirmed."[44] In order to sustain this notion of a dynamism which has a directed character in at least certain verifiable respects, in order to reach a complete understanding of finality, in other words, I would agree that an understanding of final causality in the strict sense is required.

For if the dynamic aspect of the real "is no less the sadness of failure than the joy of success, . . . to be discerned no less in false starts and in breakdowns than in stability and progress,"[45] never-

---

[41] *Insight* (New York: Philosophical Library, 1957), p. 446.

[42] Ibid., p. 448.

[43] Ibid., p. 447.

[44] Ibid.

[45] Ibid., p. 448.

theless this dynamism has witnessed the emergence of a species which values success and failure quite differently and which sets itself goals accordingly. If the proper conception of final causality is only possible when the human agent is explicitly brought into consideration, this is because the good can only act properly as a cause for mind or spirit desiring it and then efficiently seeking to realize it. Lonergan is correct, I believe, in ascribing a non-deductivist, nondeterminate, but partially directed dynamism to the real. And this dynamism does manifest a formal parallelism to the dynamism of mind, to our experience of a heuristic structure of inquiry and reflection. But neither the former dynamism, the process of the real in general, nor the latter, the mind's, can be qualified as fully successful until the mind's dynamism in fact refers the general dynamism of the real to worthwhile goals. Only humanity, as any evolutionist will admit, can ambition such comprehensive goals. One may reasonably argue, then, in agreement with Michael Polanyi, and along lines found also in Rabut and Lonergan, that all living beings manifest a "logic of achievement."[46] For "living beings," as Polanyi says, "can be known only in terms of success or failure. They comprise ascending levels of successful existing and behaving."[47] But Polanyi also goes on to show that "we can know a successful system only by understanding it as a whole."[48] Living beings thus pose questions not only about success but about wholeness.

Now, with respect both to the limited notion of finality we have been discussing and also to the need for conceiving the system of organic life in terms of its success or failure, I want to adduce important confirmation from a recognized master of scientific methods. In a recent monograph Jean Piaget has presented a persuasive argument that refines and develops the view that all organic reality has a problem-solving character.[49] Seeking to explain how organisms actually reach success or failure, Piaget asks what role behavior has in the mechanisms of evolution. He proposes his hypotheses in

---

[46] *Personal Knowledge. Towards a Post-critical Philosophy* (New York: Harper Torchbooks, 1964; first published 1958), esp. chaps. 11-13. Teilhard had written in *The Phenomenon of Man,* trans. Bernard Wall (New York: Harper, 1959): ". . . In interpreting the progressive leaps of life in an active and finalist way we are not in error. For if our 'artificial' constructions are nothing but the legitimate sequel to our phylogenesis, *invention* also—this revolutionary act from which the creations of our thought emerge one after the other—can legitimately be regarded as an extension in reflective form of the obscure mechanism whereby each new form has always germinated on the trunk of life" (pp. 222f., emphasis his).

[47] Ibid., p. 381.

[48] Ibid.

[49] *Behavior and Evolution,* trans. Donald Nicholson Smith (New York: Pantheon Books, 1978).

strictly organic and physical terms, but his materialism seems clearly
to be an "open" one; it entails a "logic of the organs" from which
instincts can be derived, a "logic of actions" linked especially with
sensorimotor activity, and ultimately a "logic of concepts" characteristic of properly intelligent forms of life. Behavior is the central
conception. By it Piaget means all action directed by organisms on
their environment in order to change either the conditions of the
environment or the organisms' situation in relation to it. The critical
question is whether or not behavior can be said to have a formative
role in evolutionary processes, whether an active and causally
significant function may be ascribed to the organisms themselves
which are involved in evolution.

Piaget's proposal aims not merely to take a middle course between
Lamarckianism and neo-Darwinism but to transcend them both.
For Lamarckianism, behavioral changes are the source of all evolutionary variations inasmuch as they are determined by the environment. For orthodox neo-Darwinism, evolutionary innovation is a
result of chance variations whose adaptive advantage emerges in the
course of natural selection. Lamarck himself, however, seems to
have wrestled with a dualism between organizational factors in the
organism and determination by outside circumstances. Piaget thinks
a synthetic resolution of this dualism is possible if behavior is treated
as an extension of organization. He takes his first clue from J. M.
Baldwin, whose idea of "organic selection" held that an organism
effects variations in its congenital capacities by accommodating
them to new environmental conditions. The major correction to
Baldwin's approach must be to see such effects not as a gradual fixa-
tion but as a replacement, in technical terms the replacement of the
phenotype by a genotype.[50]

Ethologists generally acknowledge that the organism does make
differentiated adaptations ("adequations," for Piaget) which come
to "match" environmental circumstances. Out of fidelity to neo-
Darwinist principles, however, they view such matching not as
active construction on the part of the organism but as strictly fortuitous. Piaget, on the contrary, wants to emphasize the role of the
organism's internal environment and of changes that may occur
there under the influence of new phenotypes. This is how he moves
beyond both Lamarckianism and neo-Darwinism. "For the internal
environment clearly also plays a part in selection: changes in it are
on this reading at once more or less direct *effects* of the external

---

[50] A genotype is the genetic constitution of an individual or a group; a phenotype
is the discernible interaction of genotype and environment that constitutes the
visible characters of an organism.

world, brought about through the mediation of the phenotype (Lamarckian factor), and *causes* of the selection of mutations occurring at the same time more or less randomly (the Darwinian factor)."[51] Furthermore, whereas natural selection can apply only to survival and to the differential rate of reproduction of the species, "intraselection" can also become a factor in adequation.

Cybernetics also contributes towards Piaget's theory, since it has helped evolutionists to recognize that biological causality always implies the operation of feedback systems. Thus C. H. Waddington has proposed the notion of "genetic assimilation," conceiving interaction with the environment as a circular process in which the phenotype is a response to the organism's surroundings, but a response which remains subject to genetic control and must be taken over by the genotype in order to be preserved. Piaget considers this notion of selection under genetic control ambiguous. Is the new genotype simply the result of a predictable union of already given elements? That would account neither for the creative aspect of evolution nor for the constitution of new forms of behavior that can generate new organs such as legs or wings. Piaget argues that the new genotype must rather be the outcome of a progressive reorganization by the organism: in the interaction between the genome and the regulatory systems of epigenesis,[52] a series of trial forms is produced as the organism adjusts to disturbances in its surroundings; among these, those that meet the disturbances effectively can be retained as "successful innovations."

Drawing then on Paul Weiss's theory of the hierarchy of dynamic, self-structuring and self-restoring systems, Piaget proceeds to suggest that behavior in its early manifestations may be considered innate in the sense that it is a synthesis of preformations and constructions. But what of its more developed forms and especially such remarkable achievements as instincts and intelligence? He suggests a solution invoking interactions between the various levels of the organism's organization. It is known as the process of phenocopy, in which "new varieties of behavior are generated by phenotypical accommodations before the advent of hereditary forms."[53] The process may be described as follows. When a disequilibrium in the epigenetic system is brought about by environmental influences, it

---

[51] Ibid., p. 40. On biological causality, cf. Piaget's *Biology and Knowledge. An Essay on the Relations between Organic Regulations and Cognitive Processes* (Chicago: University of Chicago Press, 1971), pp. 126ff.

[52] Genome: the total chromosomic apparatus, including its hereditary features. Epigenesis: development through gradual diversification and differentiation of an initially undifferentiated organic form.

[53] Piaget, *Behavior and Evolution*, p. 67.

causes the genome to try different genic variations or solutions as ways of meeting the disequilibrium. Wherever such genic variation is able to overcome conflict with the organism's own internal environment, an internally generated reconstruction will have occurred and will *replace* earlier traits of the phenotype. Phenocopy thus acts as a mediation between environmental influences and behavioral genic factors. A new organic form occurs not simply because of an environmental influence mechanically received and repeated but rather because of an interactive process in which the influenced organism itself actively influences the direction of the process.

The origin of instincts poses a further difficult problem for such an approach. Can Piaget also explain the formation of species-specific activity by means of his hypothesis of a genetic mechanism that can apply a certain *savoir-faire* to the environment? His response is a thesis on the genesis of hereditary behavior which includes three complementary hypotheses. First, there are "elementary" varieties of behavior which indicate phenotypical accommodation. Secondly, where elementary behavior is hereditary, it has been produced by phenocopy. Thirdly, complex specific behavior which occurs at levels of performance that cannot be acquired by phenocopy alone must be understood as the product of a series of combinatorial, compensatory, and constructive mechanisms which may be postulated as existing beyond the anticipatory and generalizing mechanisms already found at the elementary levels. By distinguishing seven main processes that constitute these mechanisms, Piaget is able to establish a deductive explanatory model for the origin of instincts. Here too he is able to find a logic immanent to physical reorganization and to transcend the neo-Darwinist conception of a range of fortuitous variations which are externally selected.

In conclusion, Piaget views the organism as an open system. The dual goal of its behavior is to expand its environment and to increase its own living capacities. Transcendence, he notes repeatedly, is the essence of behavior. Such behavior has an intrinsically adaptive character which is manifested from three points of view: from its teleonomy or goal-directedness, aiming to produce results in the outside world; from its specialized adequations, the development of a *savoir-faire* which is appropriately described in terms isomorphic with cognitive systems; and from the fact that selections brought about by the internal environment act as mediators between the internal environment and the orientation of new variations. In these three essentials, behavior differs from the ordinary variations of which neo-Darwinists speak. It constitutes a mechanism which is unique in terms of its mediated and yet continuous relationship with the environment. Piaget concludes that it should be regarded as the principal factor in evolution. And so he distinguishes finally between two complementary forms of evolution, variational and organizing. Variational evolution is one that brings variations into already organized systems. But organizing evolution is the one in which developments are subordinated from the outset to two teleonomies, one external, with respect to the origin of new hereditary behavioral forms, and one internal, with respect to the organs serving as instruments of such behavior. For this organizing evolution it is behavior that is the motor.

My report on Piaget's theory has had two purposes. Negatively, I want to emphasize how misleading it can be for theologians to accept uncritically the theoretical constructions of neo-Darwinian evolutionary theory and their generalized consequences. Positively, I suggest that Piaget has developed a convincing material view of finality which also remains open to more than a purely materialist position. As we have seen, he considers behavior's most basic characteristic to be the widening of its environment: "It is of the essence of behavior that it is forever attempting to transcend itself and that it thus supplies evolution with its principal motor."[54] Behavior is described in terms isomorphic with the basic procedures of human intelligence not because intelligence is presumed to be present at the earliest stages of evolutionary development, but rather because one must conceive mechanisms with enough heuristic value to account for the remarkable formation of the variations that arise in the evolutionary process. Piaget distinguishes sharply between theories that explain evolution by an appeal to final causality and his own view, which instead posits a teleology in terms of causal mechanism. He also distinguishes sharply between instinct and intelligence. "The generality of these [seven elementary] processes certainly proves that intelligence is rooted in the life of the organism . . . , but this is no reason to conflate intelligence and instinct."[55] It is strong warrant, however, for recognizing the basic analogy between natural and personal processes.

V. Self-Transcendence and Fulfillment

No doubt Piaget's hypotheses represent a minority report today. But they cannot simply be rejected as a recurrence of the vitalism which Monod and others deride. His method is not to suppose a non-physical, vital principle in organisms but to detail the processes of their material organization and activity. And if he emphasizes the

[54] Ibid., p. 139. Cf. Piaget, *Biology and Knowledge*, pp. 348ff.
[55] Piaget, *Behavior and Evolution*, p. 94. Cf. *Biology and Knowledge*, pp. 361ff.

transcendence of the organism, he also refuses to make any immediate appeal to a directive intelligence ''behind'' such transcendence.

With the emergence of intelligence in the human species,
however, a new capacity emerges in evolutionary process, the reflective transcendence of the truly *self*-constructing animal.[56] Human
behavior seeks always to expand its environment not only objectively but subjectively; a capacity for self-transcendence is manifest
in the progressive union of objective and reflective activity. As
Polanyi puts it, ''man's supreme position among all known
creatures is safely established; but at the same time the study of
man's rise extends thereby far beyond biology into our acceptance of
what we believe to be man's nature and destiny.''[57] It is within the
issue of human freedom, therefore, as the crucial challenge to be met
rather than a direction simply to be followed, that we find
manifested just what the ''dynamic direction of the real'' (as
Lonergan calls it) may prove to be. It is only in human persons' free
realization of themselves and the community of their fellow human
beings that the finality of the evolutionary process can be seen to be
''directed'' in the full (intentional) sense of the word and thus subsumed under a truly final causality. This interpretation, bearing as
it does on the essence of human freedom, necessarily transcends the
bounds which the life sciences set for their modes of thought. It bears
on a fundamental option, in fact, from which subsequent and
enriching reflection lives, but which reflection can never supplant or
even fully formulate.

If it cannot be expected of evolutionary theorists as such that they
affirm final causality in the process of evolution, neither can it be
taken for granted that a more comprehensive reflection on evolution
will discern the possibility of its ultimate success, of its direction
towards a finally successful goal. Here I would recall the view of
most contemporary philosophers of history that philosophy alone is

---

[56] ''The uniqueness of intelligence lies in free compositions of a variety and
specificity always subject to revision in function of a constant constructive activity.
For it is the individual himself who is subjected to his problems, who chooses or in-
vents them, whereas the elementary processes we call anticipations, generalizations,
combinations, etc., cannot be categorized as intelligence because they are not intentionally organized and used by an individual subject with a specific, new solution in
view'' (Piaget, *Behavior and Evolution*, pp. 93ff.).

[57] Polanyi, *Personal Knowledge*, p. 386. For Polanyi it is the rise of human consciousness which is the ''orderly innovating principle'' which directed the process of
evolution and which made anthropogenesis possible. ''But I must admit once more
that I would not feel so certain of this, had I not before me the rise of human personhood, which manifestly demands the assumption of finalistic principles of evolution'' (Ibid., p. 402).

unable to affirm a total sense for history. A faith, however, may commit itself rationally and freely to a full sense of history and evolutionary process as God's own goal. A theologian of history like von Balthasar will emphasize the vertical character of time's resolution, with the development of the world serving rather amorphously as God's vessel for this resolution. But I am more persuaded by Rahner's thesis that the true fulfillment of humanity and its world is possible only through God's grace bringing about a transcendent fulfillment which is at the same time the immanent fulfillment of the one redeemed creation.[58] The active self-transcendence discernible in the evolutionary process is ultimately possible only by reason of the creative presence of the ground of this process itself. This ground can be understood as present to the process precisely by empowering it to develop new and higher forms of reality; when the process reaches the human species, we have the full paradigm for active self-transcendence, the created possibility for final fulfillment through communion with God's own reality. It is then that ground and goal may be conceived as one.

Lonergan found the prototype of emergent probability in human intelligence, but his analyses with respect to the evolutionary perspective were restricted to categorical considerations of the process and to a careful distinction and elaboration of the various methods required for comprehending it adequately. During the period of *Insight,* his conception of the human person's transcendence towards the God of Christian revelation was an aspect of his thought which even his most distinguished commentator thought insufficiently developed.[59] More recently, however, he has made the concept of self-transcendence clearly central to his thought, emphasizing its place in all created activity up to and including the self-transcendence of freedom and religious conversion. It is precisely this dimension on which Rahner's thought has centered. It is the openness of all created process to divine presence that he emphasizes as the perspective necessary for integrating various categorical analyses and causal inquiries.

To be sure, the conception of self-transcendence will profit from a more detailed consideration of its social character. A sociology of knowledge will be relevant for such development, as will a sociology of choice and decision making. To understand evolution fully, as we have seen, the decisive aspect of self-transcendence is the self-transcendence of free human acts which alone are capable of ratify-

---

[58] See esp. Rahner's "Immanent and Transcendent Consummation of the World," *Theological Investigations* 10 (New York: Herder and Herder, 1973): 273-89.

[59] David Tracy, *The Achievement of Bernard Lonergan* (New York: Herder and Herder, 1970), p. 249, n. 29, and p. 253, n. 34.

ing the final and fulfilling direction of evolution made possible by a creator who is at once transcendent and immanent to the process. A more comprehensive approach to the experienced self-transcendence of humanity, the only final clue we have for discovering a direction in evolution,[60] seems all the more evidently appropriate and necessary when one recalls that we arose on this earth, biologically, as a human species and are intended, according to God's promise, to be joined in communion with him as one body, forming one new people. Once again, however, the effort to develop a more social conception of human self-transcendence should proceed not apart from but in dialogue with evolutionary science. We cannot afford to overlook analogies with the activity of organic life and its systemic character. Finally, the extension of the conception of self-transcendence would do well to take into consideration the purpose-free, aesthetic element in human experience. This would provide another critical base for a reflective understanding of recent evolutionary theory's own renewed emphasis not only on teleonomic activity but on another, apparently universal, immanent tendency of life: its constant development of aesthetic structures and forms. There might be an important point of contact here with the Augustinian argument concerning the *pulchritudo universi*.[61] And this aspect of evolution also underlines the need for the kind of restricted anthropocentrism which this essay proposes.

In summary, we have been looking for the aspect of human experience which could ground the various analogies that suggest a unified conception of the evolutionary world in its natural, historical and eschatological dimensions. This we found in the full finality which human beings experience in their free self-transcendence as persons in community. Charged with responsibility for the proximate success of the evolutionary process which it is now called upon to direct in part, the human community can also become aware that a final fulfillment for that process is possible, a fulfillment, however, of which we can only be confident through loving faith and hope. Just as the evolutionary process has been marked by predation and extinction, furthermore, we must also recognize the basic risk of misusing our opportunity and turning it to destructive rather than constructive ends. The problem of evil is located centrally rather

---

[60] As Charles Birch writes in *Nature and God* (London: SCM Press, 1965): "The most directly accessible clue we have to the nature of the universe is neither the electron, nor amoeba, but man. What is man? That is the relevant question to ask. It is man's self-awareness that leads him to ask this question" (p. 60).

[61] From the viewpoint of evangelical theology, Gerhard Gilch in *Das Spiel Gottes mit der Welt* (Stuttgart: Steinkopf, 1968) esp. chap. 1, has made an effort to connect theology of play with evolutionary theory.

than peripherally in a view of reality that sees history as the decisive realm for a freedom based in nature, a not yet settled challenge to the possible fulfillment of organic development.

Greshake has taken a similar approach to free self-transcendence as the privileged experience for conceiving the unity of evolution and history against the horizon of their eschatological fulfillment. He argues that freedom neither annuls nor separates itself from the material process of evolution which precedes it. Rather "it preserves what preceded it by establishing meaning and goal for the dynamic openness of that process. The transcendence of humanity is therefore essentially a 'transition' which dialectically comprehends both elements in unity: what is given and what is free. And since for this reason history is also essentially grounded in the dialectical interaction of already given necessity and freedom, the transition from evolution to history does not bring . . . evolution to an end." Greshake emphasizes discontinuity, however, as well as continuity. "Only from the standpoint of history does evolution manifest itself as history's presupposition and condition; only from the standpoint of history does the structural unity of evolution and history manifest itself." Finally, he summarizes their relation to the promised future of history: "Seen from the standpoint of evolution (an imaginary standpoint of course), history is underivable and unverifiable, although, once the turn to history has taken place, it proves itself to be that toward which evolution tended and in which it finds unity, meaning and goal. So also the unverifiable fulfillment of history must be conceived as a new, underivable dimension in which evolution and history are perfectly preserved."[62]

The "imaginary standpoint" Greshake mentions, however, is one imposed upon the human community to the extent that it is co-responsible for the possible success of evolution and history in their human issue and even in their divinely promised fulfillment. The dialectical unity of a dynamic nature and a truly human history is an ontological expression for our hope of a new creation. It is additional reason for rejecting all oversimplified conceptions of the time in which we are called upon to make decisions with eternal implications. Full human time certainly cannot be conceived cyclically, but neither the linear model nor spiral variations on it are satisfactory either.[63] One may properly differentiate various types of time from a theological point of view, with Mouroux and von Balthasar. But

---

[62] Die Auferstehung der Toten, p. 377, for all three quotes, my trans.

[63] Cf. Walter J. Ong, S.J., "Evolution, Myth and Poetic Vision," *New Theology* No. 5, ed. by Martin E. Marty and Dean G. Peerman (New York: Macmillan, 1968), pp. 222-52.

these types do not cohere with each other in terms of any mathematically representable form. Rather, they open into the mystery of freedom which grounds the historical dialogue between a humanity responsible for preparing a new heaven and a new earth and the God who is the source and goal of both. To any vertical conception we should prefer the biblical *kairos,* the "now" of self-transcending time, which criticizes and surpasses all other models. Only a free self-transcendence in response to the address of a loving creator can constitute that "today" in which the promises of yesterday can be brought to full realization in a common tomorrow (cf. Heb 3:7-14; 2 Cor 6:1-2).

VI. One Universe Or One Creation?

If we believe in a redeeming creator as the final goal of a human history which comprehends and includes the evolutionary process (not merely intentionally but actively), if we hope for communion with God as the only fulfillment of evolutionary history which deserves that name in its proper sense, then a biological fallacy is ruled out from the start. Humanity cannot finally be described in terms of nature alone; on the contrary, nature can only be fully understood with reference to humanity. This judgment only becomes possible against the horizon of a fulfillment promised by God; it is nonetheless significant for a true understanding of the world. It projects a unity of nature and history which does not foster a gnostic approach to the life of faith in the world, precisely because it highlights the central character of faith's responsibility. The extent of human accountability is deepened and broadened by the recognition of our evolutionary origin and situation; our capacities both for good and for evil are projected on a wider screen. At the same time, our commitment to a scientific naturalism receives a further, confirmatory seal. This does not rule out further advances in biological science but rather expects them. Our unity with the material universe from which through God's free initiative we have sprung is transformed into responsibility. Nature must be understood to have a real independence of humanity, and yet there is a work of salvation to be done in her. "Jesus of Nazareth is not the end of the process God started with his creation: he is the anticipation of a new earth and a new relationship between humanity and nature."[64]

Contemporary believers have a natural desire not to compartmentalize their belief in God on the one hand and their experience of the natural universe on the other. They seek to discover a unity between

---

[64] *Faith, Science and the Future,* p. 43.

the God to whom they ultimately entrust their own history and that
of their fellow human beings and the God who creates the evolving
universe investigated by science. When Christians realize that they
"come at the same time from the natural universe and from a divine
action superior to every capacity of cosmic nature, . . . God is
revealed to their reflection as the supreme origin of that which is
specifically human in them, as the origin of human liberty itself, that
liberty whose primordial manifestation is the liberty to create proper
to human beings as makers."[65] The conception of the unity of
cosmic, organic and historical evolution may not yet be fully
grounded for natural science. The unity of the universe may at present be rather postulated than proven. Still this should pose no fundamental objection to the greatest single systematic advantage of the
evolutionary idea: that its projection makes possible philosophically
an immanent conception of the unity of the universe and confirms
theologically a similarly immanent conception of the unity of creation. For the theologian also approaches the unity of creation as one
which is assured by faith but which nevertheless remains a promise,
only eschatologically to be achieved. As the New Testament says in
one of its latest summary formulations: "We have his promise, and
look forward to new heavens and a new earth, the home of justice"
(2 Pt 3:13).[66]

It is thus a false dilemma to ask whether the universe is a natural
unity on its own terms or only a divinely willed unity on God's
terms. Instead we should say that an ultimate unification of the
universe is intended by God *insofar* as he means his redeemed creation to become fully one in its final, eschatological transformation.
"Unity," as we have seen, is an ontological expression designating
the complete dynamic perfection of a realized "new creation." Seen
from a purely cognitional point of view, such unity cannot yet be
adequately verified. To this extent, it is also true that the critical
function of intelligent faith is able to orientate itself in the process of
the universe more than to project a specific content for its situation.
The specific content is provided by particular sciences of humanity
and its world—the actual material origin of the planet, our
similarities and dissimilarities to our forebears in the animal
kingdom, the conditional patterns of our psychological processes,
etc. These must regularly be integrated into a reasonable context for

---

[65] Dominique Dubarle, "Technique et création," in *Mensch und Technik. Naturwissenschaft und Theologie* 9 (Freiburg, 1967): 67-76, at p. 75, my trans.

[66] Cf. Is 65:17, 66:22; Apoc 21:1. In this connection we badly need to develop a
theology of the Spirit as guarantee of the world's fulfilled unity. Cf. 2 Cor 1:22, 2
Cor 5:2, 5; Eph 1:13; 1 Cor 2:9-10; Jn 17; and, among conciliar texts, especially
Gaudium et Spes, art. 38.

responsible action. Humanity's unity with itself and its evolutionary universe is supported by a wide range of evidence, but it is basically heuristic, a unity to be discovered. And if we recall the central notion of the person's free self-transcendence within the human community, then it should be clear that heuristic unity is not an abstract projection of the ideally possible unity of the created universe. It is a concrete challenge to humanity, individually and collectively, to make of its variegated experience something whole and finally valid and to face the risk that it may fail to do so. The question is not so much one of conceiving a heuristic unity of the universe but of operating within what Michael Polanyi has called a "heuristic field." The apparently fragmented universe of our experience serves as the heuristic field for our discovery of true unity—with our fellow human beings, with our world, with ourselves, and ultimately with God. The lines of force in a heuristic field do not stand merely for the expectation in principle that the universe can be one, nor for a finally reconciling divine intervention which renders it one. Rather they stand "for *an access to opportunity, and for the obligation and the resolve to make good this opportunity, in spite of its inherent uncertainties.*"[67]

At this point a commitment to scientific naturalism must transcend itself to become a rational and responsible commitment to the understanding and policy of men and women who can lead us in realizing such opportunities. "This corresponds," as Polanyi says, "to the extrapolation of biology into ultra-biology, where the appraisal of living beings merges into an acknowledgement of the ideals transmitted by our intellectual heritage. This is the point at which the theory of evolution finally bursts through the bounds of natural science and becomes entirely an affirmation of humanity's ultimate aims."[68] An immanent reflection on the finality of nature leads to a consideration of the purpose of history. But the dialectic I have proposed between them implies a continuing interaction, not merely the relation of linear advance suggested by an irreversible, progressivist dialectic. Today we are learning all too painfully the consequences that flow from abusing our natural environment. If we are truly called to cooperate with the One who is maker of heaven and earth, a reverence at the task is due to all its dimensions. And yet we are right to direct our commitment by our community's personal hopes. "For the emergent noosphere is wholly determined as that which we believe to be true and right; it is the external pole of our commitments, the service of which is our freedom. It defines a

---

[67] Polanyi, *Personal Knowledge*, p. 403, emphasis his.
[68] Ibid., p. 404.

free society as a fellowship fostering truth and respecting the right. It comprises everything in which we may be totally mistaken."[69]

Christian faith in every age must discern the prophetic horizon of true fulfillment from which it is called to be the new people of God inhabiting a new creation. In an evolutionary age marked also by great political and economic unrest, faith must newly commit itself to the living hope "that the human race might become the Family of God, in which the fullness of the Law would be love."[70] This summons to ultimate liberation must have the character of personal cooperation with the ultimate source and ground of the world process who makes its fulfillment possible. There is no final sense, then, in contrasting the *Deus spes* with the *Deus creator*. "God can only be the absolute future of humanity, because he is the beginning and the ground of all reality. Only because God is Alpha can he also be Omega."[71] Only because he is the explanatory ground of every finality in our evolutionary universe can he also be its ultimate and final fulfillment. That fulfillment does not bring creation's dynamism simply to an end. It is an abiding and final actualization, the lasting and dynamic realization of the Christian vision of a new heaven and a new earth where men and women "may have life, and have it in all its fullness" (Jn 10:10).

---

[69] Ibid.

[70] *Gaudium et Spes*, art. 32; cf. *Lumen Gentium*, art. 9.

[71] Walter Kasper, *Glaube und Geschichte* (Mainz: M. Grünewald, 1970), pp. 139f., my trans.

A Response to Fr. O'Donovan

by Dr. William O'Brien

My response to Fr. O'Donovan's paper will fall evenly into two parts. In the first part I aim to identify the particular concern which animates his recent work and which constitutes the seriousness of this particular paper. In the second part I will pose several questions raised for me by Fr. O'Donovan's central thesis.

Part I

In the first place it is to be emphasized that Fr. O'Donovan's remark that "there are signs that our desire for a socially transformative theology may in certain respects be shortsighted or premature" is not the comment of a theological or political conservative, let alone reactionary. It is rather the *warning* of a radical thinker, one who has for at least the last fifteen years been attempting to see through rather than around ever changing if ever painful presents to the most fundamental issues which combine to constitute the contemporary horizon. It is not his intention to deflect attention from deteriorating economic, political, and social conditions or from the warfare, famine, conquest and death that mark our times as apocalyptic. It is doubtful that anyone could. Not even the NCAA finals can deaden the nerves of more and more people who are awakening to the gravity and the complexity of the present moment.

What matters enormously to Fr. O'Donovan and what should concern everyone here is *how* those who are awake relate to what is happening in our times. For the way a person understands his life and what is going on in it is intimately related to the breadth of his moral vision and the range of his moral competence, just as, negatively, an inability to relate to the events of life describes an absence of moral vision and moral impotence. But the ways of understanding what is happening in our lifetime are many. While no one could reasonably expect a theology to incorporate every imaginable perspective, Fr. O'Donovan is convinced that a theology which ignores one of the dominant perspectives, namely, the scientific, will have little hope of shedding light on the future as it emerges dynamically, let alone of helping "to make heaven and earth."

In other words, Fr. O'Donovan sees no reason to doubt that the future awaiting us will be any less the product of scientific advance (as well as, of course, economic, political and social forces) than it has been in the recent past. And the world that comes to be will bear witness to the breadth of vision of those whose decisions help to shape it. Nor is it accidental that science has contributed so significantly to the shape of the modern world. Fr. O'Donovan's interest in science is not to be ascribed to his absorption in a myth or to his uncritical acceptance of a scientific world-view. The reason he is interested in science, the reason any thinking person ought to be interested in science, is that science is interested in persons as *natural* beings first and foremost. That they are social, political, and historical beings cannot blur the fact that they are also "of earth," are related to nature. And if it is likely that the most far-reaching decisions shaping the future of people on this planet will be all but determined by how *that* relation is conceived, Fr. O'Donovan's warning to those who might be tempted to devote their energies exclusively to thinking through a theologically responsible strategy for political and social change is a timely warning. Unless theologians are prepared to underwrite a future uninformed by the values they profess, it behooves them to take an intelligent part in the conversation with scientists whose compassion for the miserable of the earth is no less than their own. As Fr. O'Donovan put it suc-cinctly, "while so many of us have been turning wholeheartedly to this question (of a socially transformative theology embodying a liv-ing unity between faith and justice) as the central one for our future, significant voices in the scientific community have been proposing alternative views of the human situation, views which can seriously affect planning for human society in the future."

I hope with these initial remarks I have sufficiently underscored the importance of Fr. O'Donovan's concern to fix attention on issues which will be no less fundamental after than before the revolu-tion.

Part II

The thesis Fr. O'Donovan wishes to defend is that an adequate understanding of historical change is impossible apart from a con-sideration of the development of nature that is studied in various natural and social sciences. Although he nowhere offers an explicit critique of current political theologies, he leaves the impression that they rest upon a mistaken philosophical position which sharply distinguishes the natural from the personal, nature from history. Hence his interest in searching for a *unified* view of nature and history. The model he proposes is the evolutionary model.

I will not repeat here Fr. O'Donovan's admirable summary of the varied Roman Catholic responses to various conceptions of evolu-tion. He wishes to enter into the discussion at a critical point: the contested claim that there is an analogy, at once a continuity and a discontinuity, between natural and human history. He is particu-larly interested in Gisbert Greshake's proposal that the relation of evolution to history is analogous to the relation between history and its fulfillment. He realizes the speculative character of the claim and asks bluntly, "What, if anything, holds such an analogy together?" The analogy will be sound, he thinks, if there is an experience and an idea of finality which can be critically affirmed. While theology has tended to be weak at this point in the past, O'Donovan finds in Lonergan's conception of finality as "the dynamic aspect of the real," or "a directed dynamism," a promising path. Certainly one of its virtues is its frank recognition of failure, false starts, and breakdowns as part of evolutionary process. Furthermore, the researches of Jean Piaget lend empirical support. If behavior may be understood as an extension of organization, then behavior can be said to have a formative role in the evolutionary process, the neo-Darwinian thesis is effectively undermined, and there is a strong warrant for positing a basic analogy between natural and personal processes.

Of course, O'Donovan is not so sanguine as to expect evolutionary theorists to affirm final causality. On the other hand, he sees no real obstacles to a "faith's committing itself rationally and freely to a full sense of history and evolutionary process as God's own goal." Furthermore, the active self-transcendence discernible in the evolutionary process may be taken as an indication of a divine ground for the process itself. Finally, our future participation in the direction of that process may be understood as the summons to ultimate liberation.

When I set Fr. O'Donovan's paper aside last week and began to mull over its contents, I found myself wishing that there would be in his vision—for in the end I believe he is more positing a vision than advancing an argument—a bit more of the precariousness of the process itself, and, in particular, an understanding of evil that includes a sense of our radical involvement in it rather than one that sees it as "an issue," "a not yet settled challenge to the possible fulfillment of organic development." And again I fould myself wishing that he, like Loren Eiseley pondering the immense journey of man, would have been left with the skull of the Strandlooper resting in his hand raising the dreadful but genuine question of whether the process is oriented toward man after all. Related to these wishes, I have two questions, which I would prefer to state in reverse order. For the second question is much more serious than the first. Fr. O'Donovan, just how open-ended is the evolutionary process for the believer? And how is one to understand the passion, death and resurrection of Jesus Christ in relation to evolutionary process?

In conclusion, I would like to express my gratitude to Fr. O'Donovan for calling me back to concerns which I have let lie for many years with his fine paper, and to Fr. Kelly for inviting me to participate in this symposium honoring one of the most distinguished theologians of our time. It has been a privilege to be here.

A Response to Fr. O'Donovan

by Dr. Dean R. Fowler

Fr. O'Donovan encourages a dialog between science and theology. In fact he argues that any significant theology must be conversant with the naturalist foundations of science, in particular, evolutionary theory. (p. 270) As a basis for discussion of this thought-provoking paper, I raise three questions concerning the nature and implications of the encounter between science and theology. 1) What posture should theology assume toward science in light of *theoretical pluralism?* 2) What are the implications of science regarding the structure of the creation; in particular, the structure of human existence? 3) What are the implications of science regarding the nature of God? Answers to the second and third questions necessarily depend on the answer given to the first question.

I. The Posture of Theology vis-à-vis Scientific Pluralism

Fr. O'Donovan recognizes the significance of a pluralism of explanations in alternative scientific theories. In the face of this ambiguous situation where alternative scientific explanations exist for the same empirical phenomena, what *criteria* should be used by theologians to assess the viability of the theoretical foundations of a particular scientific theory? Because of theoretical pluralism the criteria cannot be simply empirical or scientific. Fr. O'Donovan suggests that the criteria must finally be theological. For example, he argues that theology must supply "a sober critique of the extrapolations biology makes towards a more generalized anthropology." (p. 279) At the same time, he is sensitive to the importance of scientific criteria for meaning as witnessed in his discussion of Piaget. If we are to maintain a real dialog between science and theology, is it not also the responsibility of science to critique the foundations of theology? This in turn raises the question of the "truth" of theological claims. Is theology one discipline along side of others in an interdisciplinary dialog?

I would suggest that the theologian's criteria for determining the viability of the foundational principles of any discipline must be broadly interdisciplinary, not merely theological. The test of a specific discipline rests in the broad applicability of its claims when they are generalized to other disciplines. Science cannot rest on scientific criteria alone, nor can theology rest on theological criteria alone.

II. Science and the World

Fr. O'Donovan focuses his attention on the implications of the evolutionary vision of reality concerning nature and human existence within the context of redemption. He argues that our understanding of reality as evolutionary requires "new, or at least more comprehensive, categories in ontology." (p. 276) In this context he explores the meaning of finality, transcendence, freedom and fulfillment. However it is not clear whether the new categories of ontology modify the *form* or the very *content* of our understanding of the human situation in relation to redemption. Several theologians have argued that the form of theological issues varies according to the mentality of an age, but that the content—the essential structure of existence—remains the same throughout the ages. If the implications of science alter the *content* of our understanding and not merely the form, does this mean that advances in science serve as a vehicle to a keener insight into the structures of reality? But if the content of our understanding changes with the advances of science where new categories of ontology are used to understand existence is it meaningful to speak of the "essence" of Christianity? For example, can the essence of Christianity as it relates to the question of redemption be formulated in either static or dynamic evolutionary concepts of reality without altering the nature of the essence?

III. Science and God

While it is not Fr. O'Donovan's purpose in this paper to develop a doctrine of God, he does speak of God as the one "who calls us to liberation" (pp. 270-71) and as "the ground and goal" of the evolutionary process (p. 293) and as "at once transcendent and immanent to the process." (p. 294) Does a new ontology of the creation also imply a new ontology for understanding God's nature and God's relationship with the world? If it does, *how* does the dialog with science stimulate the quest for understanding God's nature?

Several Protestant theologians, who have been engaged in dialog with the sciences, have developed doctrines of God using the dynamic categories of process and becoming. Wolfhart Pannenberg's theology of hope speaks of God as the not yet, which will be. John Cobb's process theology speaks of God consequent upon the advance of the world. However, the final justification for these dynamic doctrines of God are rooted biblically, not scientifically. Does the shift from static to dynamic evolutionary concepts of reality also require a shift to an ontologically dynamic understanding of God?

Given the tentative and provisional character of scientific theory, it would be irresponsible for theologians to simply take over the vision of reality promoted by a particular scientific position in the formulation of a doctrine of God. Legitimate theology, I believe, is not mere adaptation of the faith to new insights in science. Rather, the encounter with new scientific ideas calls attention to aspects of the faith that were previously overlooked or de-emphasized. Theology emerges from the selective and adaptive remembrance of the past as creatively transformed through interdisciplinary encounters in the present.

Christianity and the New Man: The Moral Dimension—Specificity of Christian Ethics

by Rev. Bruno Schüller, S.J.

What exactly is the specificity of Christian ethics? For a decade or longer this question has engaged moral theology; and not only moral theology. At least in the German speaking countries there are exegetes, dogmaticians, and philosophers who obviously regard the question as too important to be left to the moral theologians alone. Eminent scholars like Heinz Schürmann (New Testament), Hans Urs von Balthasar and Josef Ratzinger (dogmatics)[1] as well as Robert Spaemann (philosophy)[2] took the floor and pronounced on the issue. Even the German Bishop's Conference, two years ago, dedicated an entire day of study to the clarification of the question. To my mind, however, confusion rather than clarification is the outcome of all these debates, characterized by a proliferation of seemingly irreconcilable views. How is an outcome like that to be explained? Permit me to explain it in words of Cardinal Newman: "Half the controversies in the world are verbal ones; and could they be brought to a plain issue, they would be brought to a prompt termination. . . . This is the great object to be aimed at in the present age, though confessedly a very arduous one. We need not dispute, we need not prove—we need but define. At all events, let us, if we can, do this first of all; and then see who are left for us to dispute with, what is left for us to prove."[3]

Applying Newman's advice to the controversy at issue, I consider it a necessity not to start with the question whether there is something like a specifically Christian ethics and wherein it consists, but first to clarify the possible meanings of the term "ethics" and the qualifying adjective "Christian." Otherwise we cannot be sure that we ourselves know what sort of a question we are asking and what we are entitled to take for a sound answer. Let me attempt to do a bit of this semantic enquiry by introducing two distinctions into the present discussion, the first referring to the term "ethics," the sec-

---

[1] Joseph Ratzinger, ed., *Prinzipien christlicher Moral* (Einsiedeln: Johannes-Verlag, 1975), containing three essays: 1. Heinz Schürmann, "Die Frage nach der Verbindlichkeit der neutestamentlichen Wertungen und Weisungen"; 2. Ratzinger, "Kirchliches Lehramt—Glaube—Moral"; 3. Hans Urs von Balthasar, "Neue Sätze zur christlichen Ethik."

[2] Robert Spaemann, "Woven handelt die Moraltheologie?, *Communio* (1977).

[3] *Newman's University Sermons* (London: SPCK, 1970), p. 200.

I wish to express my appreciation to Rev. Anthony Litwinsky for his kind assistance in preparing the English version of this paper.

ond to the adjective "Christian." There is a basic difference between paraenesis and normative ethics. Thus it is imperative to tell these two things apart. Again, there is a basic difference between the truth-value of an assertion and its psychogenesis, between epistemology and psychology; this too is a difference not to be overlooked, but carefully to be taken into account.

First, the distinction between paraenesis and normative ethics.[4] Let me begin with a short definition. Normative ethics is concerned with finding out whether and why a contemplated course of action is morally good or bad, right or wrong. In other words, normative ethics tries to justify moral prescriptions and to determine their exact content. It owes its existence to the vital question: "What ought we to do?" (in biblical language: "Lord, what would you have me do?") There are other biblical expressions which very aptly describe the activity of normative ethics: *dokimazein ta diaferonta, probare potiora,* "discern the things that really matter" (from the moral point of view) (Phil 1:9), and *dokimazein, probare,* "discover the will of God and know what is good, what it is that God wants, what is the perfect thing to do" (Rom 12:2). Thus, one question belonging to the realm of normative ethics might be whether it is morally justifiable to take the life of a terminally ill patient when he requests it.

In contrast to this, what do I mean by paraenesis? Briefly: moral admonition and moral rebuke. Old Testament scholars have coined the terms "admonition-speech" and "rebuke-speech," (in German, *Mahnrede* und *Scheltrede*) since very often the prophets had to practice this sort of speech. Greek rhetoric uses the equivalent expressions *logos protreptikos* and *logos elenchtikos.* Now, paraenesis in the form of admonition tries to move its hearers to do that which *they already know* they ought to do. As can be learned from the Pauline epistles, it expresses itself by asking, encouraging, arousing, entreating, imploring, adjuring, confirming and so forth. Paraenesis in the form of rebuke remonstrates with its hearers that they are acting in a way *they know* they ought not to act. It expresses itself in accusing, unmasking, exposing, convicting and finding guilt. It appeals to conscience, calling for repentance and amendment.

All this is easy to understand. There is only one thing that has to be mentioned and kept in mind. Paraenetic discourse *as such* neither can nor means to impart moral *knowledge.* To admonish or to rebuke is essentially different from making statements on the licitness or illicitness of a certain course of action. Thus it makes little sense to ask whether a piece of paraenetic discourse is true or false. Requesting, exhorting, encouraging, all belong to what tradition calls *verba efficacia,* i.e., performative speech acts. We should judge

---

[4] Compare this distinction with Bruno Schüller, *Die Begründung sittlicher Urteile* (Düsseldorf: Patmos, 1973).

paraenesis by whether it is warranted or not, whether it succeeds or fails, whether it moves the hearer or leaves him unmoved.

This fact provides us with a useful technique for identifying paraenetic discourse. When one reformulates a paraenetic utterance, contrary to its very nature, as a statement on the moral character of an action, he usually gets nothing but a tautology or an analytically true assertion. For example, the fifth commandment, translated literally, reads as follows: "Thou shalt not commit murder!" Now, "to commit murder" means to kill wrongfully, to kill even though one is not allowed to do so. Therefore, if taken for an assertion on right and wrong, the fifth commandment amounts to the following: Killing, whenever not allowed, is not allowed. An assertion not particularly informative, to be sure; a statement analytically true. Small wonder that the decalogue is an outstanding specimen of paraenetic discourse. Let us look briefly at the fourth commandment. We often use the words "father" and "mother" in a prescriptive sense. In this case "father" and "mother" mean those persons to whom a son or a daughter owes special love and attention. Given the prescriptive meaning of the words in question, the statement, "It is thy duty to honor thy father and thy mother," proves to be a mere tautology. Yet as an admonition it is obviously blameless. For that is one way to give expression to an admonition. Listen to St. Paul: "Render therefore to all their due, tribute to whom tribute is due; revenue to whom revenue is due; fear to whom fear is due; honor to whom honor is due" (Rom 13:7). These verses impart no information. All the same, when listening to them, we cannot deny that we need to be told what they tell us. We need exhortation, all of us, not only information. The technique just applied to the decalogue lets us recognize that the catalogues of virtues and vices in the New Testament (as well as the so-called "house-tables," sets of exhortations addressed to the various members of the family,) also belong to the category of paraenetic discourse.

With the distinction between normative ethics and paraenesis in mind, let us now turn to a *locus classicus* of Christian ethics, the sequence of Gospel and Law, of the divine indicative and the divine imperative. It gives the impression that Christian ethics is based on a ground exclusively its own. The relationship of Gospel and Law is particularly clear in Ephesians 5:1 f.: "Be imitators of God as his dear children. Follow the way of love, even as Christ loved you. He gave himself for us. . . ." The moral imperative, "follow the way of love," has as its standard the love of God and of Christ for us. It invites us, therefore, to *imitate* the love of God and of Christ. *Imitatio Dei, imitatio Christi.* But at the same time, the love of God and of Christ is given as the ground, the reason *why* Christians ought to follow the way of love. As exegetes like Rudolf Bultmann and Heinrich Schlier point out,[5] we must read the quoted verse in this way as well: "imitate God's ways *because* you are his beloved children," "follow the way of love *because* Christ has loved you." In short, the love of God and of Christ is both the *ground* and the *standard* for the love which is expected of Christians. The same relationship is expressed in what may be called the Christian formulation of the commandment of love of neighbour in John 13:34: "I give you a new commandment: love one another. Such as my love has been for you, so must your love be for each other."

As you well know, there are numerous passages in the Pauline corpus where we find this sort of connection of the moral demand to the Gospel as the Word of God working for the salvation of mankind. To cite just a few texts: ". . . as those whom God has reconciled, be reconciled with God!" (2 Cor 5:19); ". . . as those who have died to sin, sin no more!" (Rom 6:2) Often the Gospel is worded in a way that it appears as the standard for the Law only insofar as the Gospel, expressed by an "Is-Sentence," is simply repeated by an "Ought-Sentence," the latter intimating the Law: "We *are* the ones who already live in the Spirit; *therefore* we *ought* to follow the ways of the Spirit" (Gal 5:25). Obligation is based on being—*agere sequitur esse;* the obligation of a Christian follows from his being a Christian.

The Old Testament says of the Law that it is grounded in the deeds of Yahweh for the salvation of Israel. The New Testament relationship of Gospel and Law can readily be recognized in the Old Testament relationship of Covenant and Torah. Before Yahweh issues his moral requirements in the Ten Commandments, he reminds Israel that he is the one who saved them from the slavery of Egypt. No doubt, the connection of the moral demand to God's saving activity is characteristic of biblical ethics as a whole. But since the New Testament Gospel, incarnate in the person of Jesus Christ, is distinct from the Old Testament Gospel, it may be supposed to give also to the moral demand its own distinct character.

All this has been said quite often and strikes us as rather obvious. But if Judeo-Christian ethics has its own ground and standard, then shouldn't it be unique in itself, standing out in sharp relief against all the rest of what is commonly known as ethics? It would appear so. But then what does "ethics" mean in this context? What in the relationship of Gospel and Law has the force to immediately convince us?

[5] Rudolf Bultmann, *Das Evangelium des Johannes* (Göttingen: Vandenhoeck and Ruprecht, 1964), p. 403; Heinrich Schlier, *Der Brief an die Epheser,* 4th ed., (Düsseldorf: Patmos-Verl, 1963), pp. 230 and 255.

Let us take a closer look. Deuteronomy 15: 12-15 gives the regulations for freeing slaves. If the slave is a Hebrew, he should be set free
after six years of service and he should be provided with the
necessities of life. Following this regulation comes the reason for it:
"Remember that you too were once slaves in the land of Egypt, and
the Lord, your God, ransomed you. That is why I am giving you
this commandment today" (v.15). The relationship of Gospel and
Law in this passage can be reduced to the following summary statement: Just as you who were once a slave have been set free, so must
you set your own slaves free. When hearing an utterance like this, do
we not feel ourselves reminded of something quite familiar to us?
What is it that links the Gospel as ground and the Law as its consequence? It is one of the oldest ethical maxims, the Golden Rule.

In its basic form the Golden Rule can be stated thusly: Do unto
others as you would have them do unto you. Now, if we are permitted to assume that each wants *good* to be done to him, then the
Golden Rule can be restated in two more forms, referring either to
what has already taken place or to what is expected to take place: 1)
others have done good to you, so do good to them; 2) do good to
others, and they will do good to you. If we go one step further and
include God or Christ with "the others," then we most clearly
perceive the Golden Rule to connect Gospel and Law, Covenant
and Torah: God has done good to you, now you do good to others.

Is there anything that follows from this insight? The connection of
Law to Gospel can hardly have anything to do with normative
ethics. The Golden Rule, as stated in Matthew 7:12 and in Luke
6:31 defines what is morally good. But moral good is only a *necessary*
condition, not the *sufficient* condition for determining what is morally
right. And what is more, when used to connect Law to Gospel, the
Golden Rule is not analysed and grounded, but rather called to
mind in order to serve the purpose of admonition. The appeal, "Do
good unto others, just as God has done good unto you!" means the
same as "Do what the Golden Rule demands!" This again is
equivalent to, "Do what is morally good!" To address others in this
fashion is clearly to be engaged not in normative ethics, but in
paraenesis.

We find this conclusion corroborated when we have a closer look
at the context of the cited passages. The regulation of Deuteronomy
15, that you may not keep one of your own people in slavery for
longer than six years, can scarcely be proved to be a morally right
regulation by recalling that Yahweh freed Israel from the slavery of
Egypt. The rightness of this regulation is taken for granted. The
memory of being liberated is meant to stimulate the listener to
observe this regulation: "set your slave free when it is your duty to

set him free." As Gerhard von Rad says about this passage: ". . . it raises the question of obedience at the most personal level of conscience in the hearer."[6]

As we have seen, the paraenetic character of the Decalogue can readily be inferred from the fact that its commandments, if stated as assertions on right and wrong, have the logical form of moral truisms. The Gospel of God's saving activity must be reformulated in two different ways accordingly as it refers to the first or the second table of the Commandments: 1) Yahweh has set you free from slavery to strange gods, therefore you shall not have any other god besides Yahweh; 2) Yahweh has done right to you, therefore you shall do right to others.

In Ephesians 5:3 ff., the moral imperative "follow the way of love" is specified by a catalogue of vices and virtues. Follow the way of love: therefore no lewd conduct, promiscuity, lust; no obscene, silly, or suggestive talk; no idolatry. Instead, let there be thankfulness, goodness, justice. This way of defining love by contrasting it to a series of vices allows us to presume that it is already taken as a matter of course that all moral rules are summed up in the one rule of love. In this case the word "love" is already being used as a moral value-term, just like "goodness" and "justice." In point of fact, the word "love" occurs in some Pauline catalogues of virtues. Thus the appeal, "Follow the way of love" can be translated, "Do what you already know you ought to do."

One does well to make oneself explicitly aware of what the New Testament means by the love of God and of Christ. It is the love of one who reconciles men to himself, who sets them free from sin, who makes them just and who charges them to serve the cause of justice. It is a love which relates to man as a moral being; by consequence a love which already in itself is characterized as moral. So morality is the subject-matter not only of the Law, but even of the Gospel. Already the language of the Gospel is the language of morals.

Granted, the Gospel is a divine *indicative,* it expresses itself in "Is-Statements": God loves you; Yahweh has set you free; Christ forgives your sins; you have died to sin and are now charged to serve the cause of justice. However, all this is obviously an *ethical* indicative. It talks about the *facts* of God's dealing with mankind and about man's present situation, yet at the same time all these facts are appraised from a moral standpoint. It is an ethical indicative just like the sentence, "Peter is just." This sentence, if made explicit, means that Peter treats equals equally, which is what justice

---

[6] Gerhard von Rad, "Das fünfte Buch Mose," *Das Alte Testament Deutsch* 8 (Göttingen: Vandenhoeck and Ruprecht, 1964): 77.

demands; therefore he is just. The ethical rule "whoever treats equals equally is just" is taken for granted in such a context.

To summarize: the Gospel deals with moral goodness insofar as it is already lived out, already a reality. To the extent that the Gospel consists in the action of Jesus Christ, it discloses a moral goodness become reality through consummate obedience, obedience unto the death of the cross. But also as efficaciously granted to Christians, the Gospel means moral goodness brought into being through obedience. For by having died to sin, Christians are what they ought to be; likewise by being charged to serve the cause of justice, they are what they have to be. Gospel is *lex impleta*, the moral demand *fulfilled*, whereas Law is *lex implenda*, the moral demand still to be fulfilled. That, again, makes clear that in proclaiming Gospel and Law one is not engaged in normative ethics, in the specification and establishment of the moral demand.

It is true, for Christians, that God and Christ are models to be imitated. The Christian life is *imitatio Dei* and *imitatio Christi*. But then, these fundamental assertions of Christian faith do not belong to normative ethics. They describe a way of proclaiming Gospel and Law, indubitably the most important and most impressive way. The correlated concepts of model and imitation can be considered as deriving from the first reformulation of the Golden Rule: As Christ has loved us, so we ought to love one another; as God in Christ has forgiven us, so we ought to forgive one another (Eph 4:32; Col 3:13). Both the model and the one called to imitate him are measured with the same standard of moral goodness. The difference between them lies in their existential relationship to this standard. One is a model to the degree that his life comes into harmony with this standard, overcoming the gap between "is" and "ought." The one who has not yet achieved this is called to be the imitator. The model is the Law fulfilled *in concreto*, realized and capable of being experienced *in a person*. In this sense, the model is *normal normata* and not *norma normans*.

This holds for Jesus Christ as model, whenever in the New Testament his life and death are presented as obedience, as fulfillment of the Father's will. In this case the Father's will is clearly *norma normans*. There is a certain difficulty in thinking of God's exemplary activity as *norma normata*. Of course, this is possible only if from a purely noetic standpoint we reconstruct the steps which lead us to the insight into God's activity as model. Only under the condition that we already have experienced the call to be morally good are we in a position to comprehend that God, because the absolute realization of moral goodness, is our model to be imitated unconditionally.

(That God is model and that God is lawgiver are two assertions the sense of which differs remarkably.)

Let us for a moment assume that *imitatio Dei* and *imitatio Christi* are not a special kind of paraenesis, but belong to normative ethics. What would that mean? Presumably this: God's and Christ's activity disclose to us in a logically original way what the difference between good and bad, right and wrong signifies. If so, how would we understand that? Would it not amount to the metaethical thesis, that the expression "to do what is morally good" is logically equivalent to the expression "to do what God and Christ do?" That, it seems to me, would be pure moral positivism. And every form of moral positivism, its theonomous and christonomous variations not excluded, destroys the very basis of morality. There is no need to pursue that line of thought any further.

But it is still worth considering *what exactly* in God's and Christ's behavior the New Testament bids us to imitate. Remarkably enough, to designate this, the New Testament always uses an expression capable of describing moral goodness in general, just like the term "love" = "agape." Therefore Heinz Schürmann can sum up: "The behaviour of Jesus is the example and the standard for serving and self-sacrificing love."[7] Why does Schürmann use the qualifying adjectives "serving" and "self-sacrificing?" What kind of love would be one that refuses to be serving and self-sacrificing? It certainly could not be viewed as the summary of the moral demand. The adjective "serving" explains the moral meaning of the word "love." And if the moral demand is essentially unconditional, then there is only one way to accept it, "with all your heart and all your soul." And if the moral demand implies that it is better to suffer ill than to do ill, then in certain conflict situations it must bid us to sacrifice our own lives. And finally, love of enemy is to moral goodness the criterion of authenticity. For as it says in Luke 6:32: "Even sinners love those who love them in return." So love of enemy, when presented in contrast to love of one's friend *only,* can stand as the embodiment of moral goodness. Therefore it is by loving their enemies that children ought to imitate their Father in heaven (Matt 5:44 ff.).

What the New Testament presents as the specific content of the imitation of God and of Christ describes—point for point—the concept of moral goodness; not for discussion and debate, but rather as an offer, an admonition, and an entreaty: "Follow the way of love!"

---

[7] Heinz Schürmann, "Die frage nach der Verbindlichkeit der neutestamentlichen Wertungen und Weisungen," in Joseph Ratzinger, ed., *Prinzipien christlicher Moral,* p. 18.

Thus I would draw this provisional conclusion: Gospel and Law, Model and Imitation are paraenesis, not normative ethics.

At this point, reformed theologians would say that I have left untouched the most important part of paraenesis as remembrance of the Gospel. The love of God and of Christ is not only the *standard* of our love; it must also be the *ground* of our love. Let me reply to that briefly. If the Gospel as proclaimed to mankind is already the fulfillment of the moral demand, if God has already reconciled the world to himself and therefore mankind *is* reconciled to God, then it seems difficult to see why we still need the admonition that men should reconcile themselves to God. To all appearances we have here a dilemma in the truest sense of the term. *Either* the Indicative of the Gospel is true, in which case the Imperative of the Law is meaningless because it is superfluous; *or* the Imperative of the Law is meaningful, in which case the Indicative of the Gospel can no longer be true. This is the dilemma which underlies the debate between Augustine and Pelagius, between the Reformers and Catholic theology, and even within the Catholic Church in the so-called "grace controversy" between the Dominicans and Jesuits. This dilemma, because the reflection of a mystery of faith, does not admit of a plain rational solution. Yet it is safe to say: Paraenesis, which refers to the Gospel as its ground, gives it to be understood that the fulfillment of the moral demand, even though really the free and responsible act of man, is first of all and above all the gift of God in Jesus Christ. Paraenesis like that follows the paradoxical form of Philippians 2:12-13: ". . . work for your salvation in fear and trembling. (For) it is God, for his own loving purpose, who puts both the will and the action into you."

Paraenesis based on remembrance of the Gospel does not cease to express itself in genuine imperatives. Therefore it can and must move into a second kind of paraenesis—a warning of the coming judgment, of the evaluation based on one's works. This can also be derived from the Golden Rule in its second reformulation: "Do not judge, and you will not be judged. Do not condemn, and you will not be condemned. Pardon, and you shall be pardoned. Give, and it shall be given to you. . . . For the measure you measure with will be measured back to you" (Lk 6:37 f.). The Lord's Prayer connects the petition for God's forgiveness with a commitment to forgive one another. The parable of the unforgiving official in Matthew 18 shows how these two types of paraenesis—remembrance of the Gospel and warning of the coming judgment—work together. After the king has forgiven him his enormous debt, the official meets a fellow servant who owes him a paltry sum. In this situation both forms of paraenesis confront the official: you have been forgiven, so forgive your fellow servant, or the forgiveness you received will be withdrawn.

As you have certainly noted, we have entered that problematic area which dogma treats under the headings of grace and justification. There is no need to go any further in that direction. One insight will suffice. Whenever the Old Testament and the New Testament connect the moral demand with the Gospel and with the coming judgment, we are dealing with paraenesis and not with normative ethics!

Let us now connect this with an old and ecumenically widespread thesis, one which belongs both to metaethics and to normative ethics. Franz Hürth, who was both a professor at the Gregorian University and an influential advisor to Pope Pius XII, formulated it like this: "All the moral commandments of the 'New Law' are also commandments of the natural moral law. Christ did not add to the natural moral law any moral prescriptions of a purely positive type. . . . This is also true of the commandment of love. . . . The moral demand to love God and to love our fellow man for God's sake is a demand of the natural moral law."[8] Rudolf Bultmann shares this opinion. He writes: "With regard to the content of the moral demand, there is no specifically Christian ethic. If one were to offer the commandment of love as specifically Christian, he should remember that Paul called it the summary of the commandments of the Law. One is capable of knowing these even before he hears the Christian message. Each person has a conscience and can know what is good and evil. The authentic Christian message offers no specific demands with regard to ethics."[9] According to Paul Althaus,[10] this was Luther's position; and the position of all the reformers, according to Ernst Troeltsch.[11] Cardinal Newman held this position.[12] In this, he agreed with the two greatest Anglican theologians, Richard Hooker[13] and Bishop Joseph Butler.[14] Another

[8] *De principiis, de virtutibus et praeceptis,* 2 vols. (Rome: In Aedibus Pontificiae Universitatis Gregorianae, 1948), 1:43.

[9] Glauben und Verstehen 3, 3d ed. (Tübingen: Mohr, 1965), p. 125.

[10] Die Ethik Martin Luthers (Gütersloh: G. Mohn, 1965), pp. 32 ff.

[11] "Grundprobleme der Ethik," *Gesammelte Schriften,* 4 vols., reprint of the 2d ed. (Aalen: Scientia, 1962), 2:598 f.

[12] Compare Erwin Bischofsberger, *Die sittlichen Voraussetzungen des Glaubens. Zur Fundamentalethik John Henry Newmans* (Mainz: Matthias-Grünewald, 1974), pp. 144 ff.

[13] *Of the Laws of Ecclesiastical Polity,* Everyman's Library, 201 (London: J. M. Dent, 1969), pp. 199 ff.

[14] *The Analogy of Religion,* in the series Milestones of Thought (New York: F. Ungar: 1961), p. 183; see also Hastings Rashdall, *Conscience and Christ* (London: Duckworth, 1916); Herbert Hensley Henson, *Christian Morality* (Oxford: Clarendon Press, 1936).

Anglican, the famous C. S. Lewis, expressed the same view.[15] On the Catholic side, we find this thesis held by Francisco Suarez,[16] and also by Thomas Aquinas, if we are permitted to rely on Alfons Auer[17] and Jean-Marie Aubert.[18]

How do theologians arrive at this conclusion? Protestant and Anglican theologians primarily hold to a thought which Paul develops in the first chapters of his letter to the Romans. In Christ, each person is offered and granted the forgiveness of his sins. But a person is morally culpable and in need of forgiveness *only* if he has already refused to subject his life to the moral demand. Only insofar as a person already considers himself a moral being is he in the position to understand the meaning of the Christian message and to allow himself to be challenged by it.

The forgiveness of guilt is theologically explained as divine *grace* and thus as the quintessence of the Gospel. It transforms a person into a "new creation" as it changes his disobedience into obedience. And so we can formulate the thoughts we have outlined as follows: Christ is the Gospel, not the Law; or Christ is not the Law but rather the fulfillment of the Law. This, it seems to me, is how we must interpret Saint Thomas: "The New Law is primarily the grace of the Holy Spirit, which manifests itself in faith and realizes itself through love" (S.T. I, II q. 108 a. 1c). The question is, how do we interpret the term "New Law?" If it meant the same as "new moral demand," then this statement would have, to put it mildly, a very strange meaning: "The new moral demand consists primarily of the grace of the Holy Spirit." Grace is something that God grants mankind on his own free initiative. A moral demand is something that God expects from mankind in free obedience. A demand is not a gift, a gift not a demand, neither "primarily" nor in any other way. Whoever maintains the contrary doesn't understand the meaning of the words he is using. So next let us translate *lex nova* as "new covenant." Then the statement reads like a Pauline truth of the faith. "The new covenant is primarily the grace of the Holy Spirit,

---

[15] "On Ethics," in *Christian Reflections,* ed. Walter Hooper (London: Bles, 1967), pp. 44-56.

[16] *De Legibus,* 1, 10c, 2 n. 5-12; compare also Eduard Génicot, *Theologiae Moralis Institutiones* 1, 5th ed. (Lovanii: Polleunis et Ceuterick, 1905); Arthur Vermeersch, *Theologia Moralis,* vol. 1, 4 ed. (Rome: Apud aedes universitatis gregorianae, 1947), number 153; Marcelino Zalba, *Theologiae Moralis Summa* 1 (Matriti: Editorial Catolica, 1952), no. 368.

[17] Klaus Demmer and Bruno Schüller, "Die Autonomie des Sittlichen nach Thomas von Aquin," in *Christlich glauben und handeln,* ed. K. Demmer and B. Schüller (Düsseldorf: Patmos, 1977), pp. 31-54.

[18] "La spécificité de la morale chrétienne selon Thomas," *Le Supplément* 92 (1970): 55-73.

which manifests itself in faith and realizes itself through love." Faith which realizes itself through love is not a moral demand but rather its fulfillment in conviction and action.

Catholic theologians who assign normative ethics to a philosophical reflection are primarily governed by another consideration. They believe that all moral rules of behavior which are commonly regarded as incumbent on Christians can principally be recognized from their inherent ground of validity. To them a moral directive such as the command to love one's neighbor has hardly anything in common with a mystery of faith, which can be known only through trusting in the word of Christ. They hold, for instance, that one who is aware of the human person as a value and an end in itself finds himself called to respect and love a person for the person's own sake. This view hangs together with the well-known fact that Catholic moral theology thoroughly rejects every moral positivism, even in its theonomous form. It argues that, confronted with a commanding will, obedience can be true moral obedience only when in fact it can be shown that it is morally good and right to accept the authority of this commanding will. That is to say, the real meaning of the difference between good and bad, right and wrong, is by logical necessity a matter of immediate insight and not of any belief which bases itself on the authoritative guarantee of another, even if the other is God himself.

This consideration is purely epistemological. It draws its conclusion exclusively from the different epistemological character of reason and faith, immediate insight and belief relying on authority; just as St. Augustine, *De Utilitate Credendi* 11, puts this difference: *"quod intellegimus . . . , debemus rationi, quod credimus, auctoritati."* It does not and need not take into account that reason is *natural* reason, Christian faith *supernatural* faith, the gift of divine grace. The distinction between nature and grace, natural and supernatural has no bearing, if the point to be made is solely that the meaning of good and bad, right and wrong, can be disclosed only to logically immediate insight.

Again, a theologian like Hürth defines the *natural* moral law by contrasting it to a *positive* moral law and *not* to a *supernatural* moral law or a moral law of *grace*. Therefore when asking if there is a specifically Christian moral directive, it does not occur to him to reflect on the relationship of nature and grace. Rather he tries to make out whether the moral demand, incumbent on Christians, contains any rules which are to be interpreted according to the pattern of *positive* law, that is, rules laid down: *"bonum quia praeceptum, malum quia prohibitum."* As a matter of fact, Hürth cannot find any rule of this pattern. And that is the reason why he concludes that the moral demand which Christians are called to fulfill is identical with the *natural* moral law. This makes clear what in this context we have to understand by "natural law." It means the sum total of all those moral rules which are laid down: *"praeceptum quia bonum, prohibitum quia malum."* In other words, the whole question is primarily governed by the classical distinction between *physei dikaion* and *thesei* or *nomo dikaion.*

"An attitude is good or bad by nature," "an action is right or wrong by nature;" these statements mean that an attitude or an action owe their moral character to their own inherent properties, that given these inherent properties an attitude is good or bad *by necessity,* an action right or wrong *by necessity.* If so, then it does not matter who the person is that assumes the attitude or performs the action; the moral character of the attitude and of the action is and remains invariably the same. It does not matter whether the rational agent is an angel or a human being, an archangel or a guardian angel, a Jew, a Christian or a pagan; in making use of Tolkien's marvellous imagination one could go on, nor does it matter whether the person is an orc or a goblin, an elf, a dwarf or a hobbit. In short, moral goodness and moral rightness are constituted by their relationship to personhood as such. Only because this is the case does it make sense for human beings to speak of God's mercy and justice and to believe themselves to be called to imitate Christ's forgiving love. Only because theologians took that for granted could they reasonably attempt to reflect on the fall of angels. Seen in this way, the *natural* moral law comprises moral goodness of attitude and moral rightness of action as concerning simply every personal being, comprehended on the only level of insight that human beings on this earth are given.

Obviously, not every action that a person judges to be morally right is possible for him. Only finite beings can experience the moral good in the structure of a categorical imperative. Only human beings can live out in attitude and in action that virtue which we call *temperantia.* Only one who has children is subject to the demand of parental duties. "Ought" implies "can." Obligation presupposes the corresponding ability. But once we have accepted all of this as a matter of course, it is still worth recalling that moral goodness and moral rightness, when interpreted after the pattern of *physei dikaion,* are constitutively related to every rational and personal agent.

It is a misunderstanding to assume that being Christian would be levelled out and reduced to simply being human, if the moral demand for Christians is nothing more than the natural moral law. One who thinks so ought to ask himself why he does not say of the imitation of God that it is either hybris or blasphemy because it denies the infinite difference between God and mankind, exhorting us to act either as if we were like God, or as if God were like ourselves. Every notion of differences being levelled out is mistaken, since morality, conceived of in the way of natural law, is related to personhood as such, and not to nature as distinct from supernatural grace.

This much explains the old thesis concerning the natural moral law. It is this thesis which of late has become a stumbling block for a number of theologians. But why not? It depends upon the arguments raised against it. What are these arguments? Let me quote word-for-word a thesis apparently meant as antithesis: "Christian ethics must be based upon Jesus Christ himself. As the Father's Son, he has fulfilled for us the entire will of God (every obligation) in this world, so that we could win from him, who is the fulfilled concrete norm of every moral action, the freedom to fulfill God's will and to live out our selection as the Father's free children." This is the fundamental thesis; it is incontestable. De facto I know of no one who would contradict it. But, it is *no* antithesis. It is no part of normative ethics; rather it describes New Testament paraenesis, paraenesis which recalls the Gospel. It is the first of the Nine Theses on Christian Ethics formulated by Hans Urs von Balthasar.[19]

Josef Ratzinger has also found it necessary to argue from the Scriptures with great passion and fervor *against* the thesis that for the Christian the natural moral law and nothing other than the natural moral law is the moral demand. How does his argument go? Mainly it is an exposition of biblical paraenesis. He builds expressly upon Heinrich Schlier's outstanding articles about the quality of the apostolic admonition.[20] But in the very title of the articles stands the word "admonition"—paraenesis. Yet Ratzinger wants to use it as normative ethics.[21]

Strange as it may sound, neither von Balthasar nor Ratzinger have understood that paraenesis is not normative ethics and that normative ethics is not paraenesis. In Ratzinger's case, it can be seen instantaneously in a misunderstanding he slipped into. Somewhere he has come across the two rival theories of normative ethics—the deontological and the teleological theory. Unfortunately he analyses the word "deontological" as consisting of the Latin *de*

---

[19] "Neue Satze zur christlichen Ethik," in Joseph Ratzinger, ed., *Prinzipien christlicher Moral,* p. 71.

[20] "Vom Wesen der apostolischen Ermahnung," *Die Zeit der Kirche,* 4th ed. (Freiburg: Herder, 1966), pp. 74-89; "Die Eigenart der christlichen Mahnung nach dem Apostel Paulus," *Besinnung auf das NT* (Freiburg: Herder, 1964), pp. 340-57.

[21] Ibid.

and the Greek *ontological* and concludes that its meaning is "derived from being." Based on this, he says, "Paul knew the 'teleological motive' (the coming judgment and reward) just as well as he argued 'deontologically' from the implications of being a member of Christh."[22] What is Ratzinger actually referring to? To the two types of New Testament paraenesis—paraenesis which warns of the coming judgment and paraenesis which recalls the Gospel. This has nothing at all to do with normative ethics of the teleological and deontological types—not in the least.

There is a specifically Christian paraenesis, a paraenesis which stands and falls with belief in Christ. This is what von Balthasar and Ratzinger expose and prove, and they do it *brilliantly*. They have a way with words.

But they have so little feeling for the prosaic business of normative ethics that they do not recognize it as something different from paraenesis. And they reproach us moral theologians because instead of preaching Christ the way they do, we busy ourselves with questions like the moral difference between killing and letting die. But enough about the difference between paraenesis and normative ethics and its importance for specifying the proprium of Christian ethics.

Now for our second distinction: the difference between the truth-value of moral insight and its psychogenesis. I must be brief. As I have already pointed out, the natural moral law can be disclosed only to immediate insight; therefore it is related to reason, not to faith (both reason and faith considered as epistemologically different kinds of knowledge). If this is so, how are we to judge the reliability of reason? Quite a few theologians think it necessary to remind us of what seems to be an empirical fact, all too often confirmed, that men who rely on reason alone succumb to all sorts of errors and confusions, especially in the area of morals. They refer to Romans 1, that very chapter in which Paul paints such a vivid picture of this problem. They adduce Aristotle, Epicurus, the Stoics, Hume, Kant and others in order to compare their positions with authentic Christian ethics. All these historical variations of philosophical ethics are supposed amply to prove, by their deficiencies and errors, that faith alone can be trusted, not reason. A plausible argument, no doubt, at least at first glance. But what does it look like when we apply to it the distinction between the truth-value of an assertion and its psychogenesis? Let us see.

When we say "Christian ethics," we usually take it to mean the moral demand as Jesus himself lived and proclaimed it. It is a normative concept of ethics for everyone who believes in Christ. The

---

[22] Ibid., p. 61, footnote.

person of Jesus guarantees the validity or the truth of this understanding of the moral demand. And so we must ask whether what Martin Luther, John Calvin, and Alphonsus Liguori wrote and preached can truly be called "Christian ethics." Obviously this depends upon whether and to what extent they really achieved what they certainly wanted to achieve, namely a correct interpretation of the moral demand as Jesus lived and proclaimed it. Luther would have conceded to Liguori and Liguori to Luther only with substantial limitations that the other presented Christian ethics. Each would have justified his own position against his critics by appealing to the New Testament or to specific texts in the New Testament. Whoever wanted to judge Christian ethics in this normative sense would then have to decide from these texts just how Jesus understood and presented the moral demand. He could turn to Luther, Calvin, or Liguori as commentators, but only insofar as they could help him grasp the fundamental moral message of Jesus.

Now suppose we want to make a comparison between Christian ethics in this sense and the understanding of the moral demand which is accessible through reason—what we might call "natural ethics" or "philosophical ethics." Where have we to look for natural ethics? With the philosophers, one may be inclined to answer, with Aristotle, the Stoics, and Kant; they are to be consulted. Quite so. But this leads immediately to the question of truth-value. Kant, relying on reason alone, presents the moral demand as such and such; but is his position correct? The question is inevitable because Aristotle, the Stoics, and Kant are at least not in perfect agreement about the correct understanding of the moral demand. Apparently these philosophers are related to a correct understanding of natural ethics in the same way as Luther, Calvin and Liguori are related to Christian ethics in its normative sense. They all try hard to use their reason correctly and to present the moral demand correctly. But trying hard and succeeding are by no means one and the same thing. Whoever wants to find out whether the efforts of philosophers were successful has no other choice than to do his own philosophizing and to see which understanding of the moral demand presents itself to his own reason as plausible. If he is smart, he will study Aristotle, Kant, and the others; but it cannot be a mere *jurare in verba magistri*. He must pursue systematic philosophical ethics, which is something different from the history of philosophical ethics.

In addition to this normative concept of Christian and of natural or philosophical ethics, there is another concept, one which can be called "historico-genetic." It is customary to call the ethics of Luther, Calvin, and Liguori "Christian ethics" without any qualifications. How is the adjective "Christian" to be understood in this case? It serves to characterize such ethics according to their "conceivers" and the manner of their "being conceived"—Luther, Calvin, and Liguori were Christians and theologians. It was clearly their intention to understand and to present the ethics of Jesus. They let us know that the final authority for their argumentation is the New Testament. This is reason enough to call them "Christian ethicians" and their ethics "Christian ethics"—leaving open the question to what degree their ethics correspond to the ethics which Jesus himself lived and taught. Likewise we usually speak of "natural" and particularly "philosophical" ethics in this historico-genetic sense. There is hardly any hesitation to call the ethics of both G. E. Moore and of H. A. Pritchard "philosophical ethics" even though they present the moral demand in widely divergent ways, so that at least not both of them can have been successful in finding the one "true" natural ethics.

With these distinctions in mind, let us raise the following question: When theologians, both in exegesis and systematics, compare Christian ethics and natural ethics, what exactly are they referring to by means of the terms "Christian ethics" and "natural ethics?" Almost always they think of and write about Christian ethics in a normative sense. They do not appeal to Augustine, Aquinas, or Luther as if these were their final guarantee, with no possibility of appeal to a higher authority. The same theologians, however, usually speak of natural ethics in a historico-genetic sense. This is perfectly legitimate, especially in exegesis, as long as one follows a predominantly historical purpose. For example, in order to clarify the quality of the early Christian ethos, H. Preisker[23] contrasts it with the Jewish and the pagan ethics of the early Christian world. But one must keep in mind that the possible differences between the early Christian ethos and Stoic ethics cannot simply be taken for the difference between Christian ethics and natural ethics understood normatively. For instance, the term *tapeinophrosyne* is used in the profane Greek idiom only in a negative sense.[24] It appears in the Stoic catalogues of vices. But from this we cannot deduce that the moral attitude which the New Testament calls *tapeinophrosyne* is foreign to a normatively understood natural ethics. It could be that the Stoics did not employ their reason well on this point, just as any Christian and theologian can err in his understanding of the faith. (Incidentally, this example shows that even an historical comparison requires a certain familiarity with systematic ethics.) When the word *tapeinoph-*

---

[23] *Das Ethos des Urchristentums,* 3d ed. (Darmstadt: Wissenschaftliche Buchges, 1968), p. 11.

[24] Wolfgang Schrage, *Die konkreten Einzelgebote in der paulinischen Paränese* (Gütersloh: G. Mohn, 1961), p. 204.

rosyne appears in the Stoics' catalogues of vices, whereas the New Testament uses it as the name of a virtue, the only immediate conclusion is that the Stoics and the New Testament make a contrary use of the term. The Stoics understand by *tapeinophrosyne* meanness of character, the New Testament, humility. This would disclose a contrary moral judgment on an inner attitude *only* if the Stoics and the New Testament, logically preliminary to their value judgment, both characterized this attitude as the same in all relevant descriptive properties.

As I have said, it is perfectly legitimate to compare Christian ethics in a normative sense with Stoic or Epicurean ethics, when one pursues an historical purpose. Yet it is no uncommon occurrence that theologians make use of the same procedure, even though their purpose is obviously a systematic one, namely to determine whether there is agreement or disagreement and to what extent between Christian ethics and natural ethics *as such*. For natural ethics, they take the ethics of certain philosophers—Epictetus, Bentham, Scheler, or Bloch—or else they take whatever philosophical ethics is currently in vogue. And strangely enough, usually they fail to mention any Christians who have distinguished themselves by their philosophical achievements, as if only non-Christians could do genuine philosophy. What is the outcome of this procedure? On one hand we find the *one* Christian ethic, true and certain in itself; on the other hand a seemingly bewildering multitude of philosophers all at variance with each other, from Plato to the latest positivists and linguistic analysts.[25] But this impression is mainly the result of a logical fault or fraud, of a *vitium subreptionis*. It is very easy to produce a similarly bewildering picture of Christian ethics. To do that, we need only take the term "Christian ethics" in a historico-genetic sense, and we are no longer confronted with Jesus alone, but with a multitude of Christians of all ages and denominations who are at variance among themselves.

This same mistake is made quite often when faith and reason, *fides* and *ratio,* are compared. We think of "faith" in a normative sense so that it means *true* faith. This is easy to do because in theological language the word "faith" often stands for "truth of the faith" (*fides quae creditur*). In contrast, we then take the word "reason" in a genetic sense so that we can, without inconsistency, attribute to reason all sorts of self-deceptions, illusions, and errors. This is easy to do because we often think of "reason" as an *ability* or *capacity* of knowing. In this hypothesis it is immediately evident that in its rela-

---

[25] Cf. Robert Spaemann, "Wovon handelt die Moraltheologie?," *Communio* (1977).

tion to reason, faith has the role of a critical defender of the truth, simply because it lies in the nature of truth to reveal error as such. Yet it is no great achievement to relate faith and reason in such a manner that inevitably a change of roles takes place. First, take "faith" in a genetic sense; then it stands also for erroneous faith and superstition. Second, use the word "reason" in a normative sense so that it becomes logically equivalent to "true reason" (reason insofar it recognizes the truth). Given these semantic stipulations, reason, in its relation to faith, by necessity takes on the role of a critical defender of the truth. And indeed, it may happen that a theologian presents as a mystery of faith what on closer inspection turns out to be a mere logical absurdity. Josef Ratzinger is one of those theologians who think it necessary to warn us against the fallacies of reason. He points out: "In every age, we find both false reason and the discovery of truth through reason."[26] Of course; who is so naive as to forget that? But then Ratzinger fails to add: In every age, we also find false faith and the discovery of the Word of God through faith. If we want to compare faith and reason with each other in their epistemological aspect, then we must compare true knowledge of faith with true knowledge of reason, or truths of the faith with truths of reason. Then the relationship becomes: *"fides supponit rationem et transcendit eam."*

Likewise we have to compare the moral demand as Jesus lived and proclaimed it with the moral demand as true reason presents it. Because the Christian believes in Jesus Christ, he is convinced that Jesus has fulfilled the moral demand perfectly in his own life and has presented it authentically through his word. Thus he has every right *in rebus morum* to hold unconditionally to Jesus as an infallible authority. But in no way does this imply that the moral demand as Jesus lived and proclaimed it lies beyond the ability of reason to know. From a theological perspective, the moral demand is the command of the creator, accessible through natural reason. Looking at it this way, we cannot exclude the idea that Jesus may have wished to establish the validity of exactly this command of the creator against any possible misunderstanding. But apart from that, whether and to what extent the moral demand as Jesus lived and interpreted it lies within the realm of the insight of reason can be determined only when we attempt to examine the moral proclamation of Jesus through the very insight of reason. Hence the Christian and the theologian must allow himself to become a philosopher as well. It cannot be objected that because the Christian is a believer, he is

---

[26] "Kirchliches Lehramt-Glaube-Moral," in Joseph Ratzinger, ed., *Prinzipien christlicher Moral,* p. 65.

inept as a philosopher, that he tends to present as rational knowledge what he actually owes to his Christian faith. True, there can be this tendency toward a kind of rationalism; but there is likewise a tendency among some theologians toward a kind of fideism—to restrict reason as much as possible in order to broaden the realm of faith as much as possible. For the fideist, philosophical skepticism and philosophical positivism are the most beloved of all the historical forms of philosophy. But how *else* could anyone err in seeking to compare the realms of faith and reason epistemologically except by thinking either like a rationalist or like a fideist? If a Christian is inept as a philosopher because he is capable of error, then *everyone* is inept as a philosopher because each of us is likewise capable of error.

Whether someone who undertakes systematic philosophical ethics is a Christian or not concerns only the genesis of his ethics, not their truth-value. It is worth recalling a very simple example to see how questions of the genesis and of the truth-value of moral insight (real or merely supposed) must be distinguished. A schoolboy does his arithmetic homework and writes ''2 plus 2 equals 5.'' Now we can ask whether this arithmetic statement is true or false and with what right we can maintain that it is a mistake. This deals with the truth-value of an arithmetic statement. But we can also ask how it happened that the schoolboy made this mistake—whether his mind was wandering or whether he blundered in applying the rules of addition. This deals with the genetic explanation of an erroneous arithmetic statement. One should not object that this is a poor example because there is a fundamental difference between an arithmetic statement and a moral value judgment. We need not contest this difference. Yet provided we admit that moral judgments are also capable of verification—that is, they can be true or false—so it is evident that we must also carefully distinguish between *their* genesis and *their* truth-value or validity.

To all appearances, the genesis of existentially significant insights and errors goes hand in hand with the moral situation of mankind. The one who gives himself over to a life of selfishness can be so cut off from any contact with what he ought to do that he truly doesn't comprehend it. As the Church teaches, human reason is *''primi hominis culpa obtenebrata''* (DZ 1670). The encyclical *Humani Generis* offers an explanation of this. Moral truths are such that they challenge us to a life of selflessness. But as a result of original sin, mankind is influenced by selfish desires. *In rebus morum,* a person can easily persuade himself that something is false or at least dubious which he does not want to be true. This explains why people often have such difficulties in attaining correct moral insights (DZ 2305). In light of this, Vatican I teaches that the Judeo-Christian revelation is necessary so that people as they actually are can know *"expedite, firma certitudine et nullo admixto errore quae in rebus divinis humanae rationi per se impervia non sunt"* (DZ 1786). At the same time, because faith is also obedience, conversion "through the renewal of your mind," it includes in itself an existential susceptibility to "what is God's will, what is good, pleasing and perfect" (Rom 12:2; cf. Phil 1:9 f.). I know of no theologian who would deny any of this. There is an agreement on that point. But then it concerns only the genesis of moral insights and errors. It has no bearing on the epistemological distinction between the realms of faith and reason. Neither the "value-blindness" of a person nor his existential susceptibility to the moral demand makes any difference in the cognitional status of a moral value judgment. Only this cognitional status is the issue when theologians claim that the moral demand incumbent on Christians is identical with the natural moral law.

Whoever wants to falsify this claim is of course permitted to try to adduce his arguments. However, by explaining biblical paraenesis and pronouncing on genetic questions he adduces no argument, but rather misses the point.

A Response to Fr. Schüller

by Rev. Richard Roach, S.J.

Before I could assent to what Father Schüller claims in this provocative paper, I would have to understand better what he means by "normative ethics." It is possible that his understanding of "normative ethics" leaves open the door to the rejection of unexceptional moral laws which enjoin or prohibit specific intentional actions. I believe that such an ethic denies what the paraenesis of faith presumes.

In order to get at what he might mean by normative ethics, permit me to quote from an English digest of an earlier article by Schüller.

> "Some of the natural ethical norms are called by a consensus of Catholic experts 'universally' binding. Of these some are mere tautologies, like, 'Always act justly, never kill unjustly.' Others really say something, like, 'You must always love and hope in God.' But in this group is reckoned also a third class, really 'synthetic' or composite precepts like, 'Every false statement is a lie and thus morally wrong' or 'Every use of artificial means to impede conception is immoral.' Alas, these examples show that the more practically helpful such formulations are in daily life, the more questionable is their speculative justification."[1]

If Schüller does not believe normative ethics includes unexceptional moral laws of the kind he describes as synthetic, then I would find a contradiction between his position and what I believe the gospel paraenesis presumes.

Unfortunately, I am not sure from reading this paper whether or not Schüller has faced the question of unexceptional moral laws *which enjoin or prohibit specific intentional actions.* He would, I believe, accept unexceptional moral laws. It is the adjectival clause "which enjoin . . ." that is at issue, because it is not clear to me that when defining "synthetic" precepts Schüller has in mind an adequate description of an intentional action.

I have thus far raised my questions for Schüller abstractly. Let us turn to an example from his paper.

Do no murder, in my opinion, has more force than Schüller concedes when he says it means killing "wrongfully" or killing "even though one is not allowed to do so." If these were all it meant, I would have to agree with Schüller that the command is something like a tautology. But I would submit that in Roman Catholic moral theology it has not been understood in so impoverished a manner.

---

[1] "What ethical principles are universally valid?" *Theology Digest* 19 (Spring 1971), p. 23.

I believe the point at issue will become clearer if we consider a passage from a chapter Schüller wrote for a book recently published in the U.S. He there says:

> "The executioner cannot dispatch a murderer without intending death as the result of his action. This intention does not impair the rightness of the action. Hence, if intentionally killing an innocent person is said to be invariably wrong, *the wrongness of the action cannot be derived from the intention of causing death, a nonmoral evil.* The proposition: 'It is wrong intentionally to kill an innocent person,' is a synthetic one. Tradition accounts for the wrongness of the action by the attempt to show that it is not authorized by God."[2]

I believe Schüller is right about how tradition accounts for the wrongness of the action. That is not the point. The issue is whether or not he has, at least implicitly, described an intentional action falsely.

If so, I suggest the error would consist in this: it is impossible simply to intend merely to cause death. If an executioner is asked, "why are you hanging that man by the neck?" the answer, "to cause his death," would not satisfy. The form of description of the action as intentional would run something like this: "I am executing the man for capital crime." Even in describing the actions of brute animals we observe this form. If you ask a friend, "why is your cat crouching?" the answer, "to get closer to the floor," will not suffice. But the answer, "he is trying to catch a mouse," explains the action as "intentional" immediately.[3] It is possible that Schüller has described as intentional what is a physical component of an intentional action, but which cannot be intended merely as described physically. It would take a lengthy analysis to establish this point. I intend only to raise the question.

If my questions are to the point, we then may contrast Schüller's understanding of "Do no murder" with the way I believe St. Thomas understands the prohibition: it is impermissible for a private person directly to kill human life. Define private person by contrast with a public official and explain the difference between killing directly and killing indirectly by accurately describing killing as an intentional action, and I submit that you have not a tautology nor an analytically true assertion, but a meaningful rule that is unexceptional. I would further submit that the rule or moral law, "Do no

---

[2] "The Double Effect in Catholic Thought: a Reevaluation," in *Doing Evil to Achieve Good,* ed. R. McCormick and P. Ramsey (Chicago: Loyola University Press, 1978), p. 189.

[3] For an exact description of intentional action, cf. G. E. M. Anacombe, *Intention,* 2d ed. (Cornell University Press, 1976).

murder,'' has been understood in a manner substantially like what I have just described and has been believed to be an unexceptional commandment from God so universally throughout the history of the Church that it would be accurate to speak of it as infallible teaching. I believe the same would be true for a number of other moral precepts which are presumed unexceptional in Christian paraenesis.

If the way Schüller seems to describe intentional actions were adequate—i.e., an agent could intend merely to cause death, a non-moral evil—then "Do no murder" might be unexceptional but it might no longer apply in some cases where the Church has applied it. So, it would no longer be the same "synthetic" precept.

Schüller might consider the inclusion of the adjective "innocent" sufficient to identify his formulation with the traditional prohibition, but I suspect that it is not. Thomas does not use it in the *locus classicus* for the principle of double effect.[4] His approach, which leads to the distinction between direct and indirect killing, has a different conceptual significance from explicitly judging an assailant not "innocent."

Unfortunately, space prohibits developing the different significances. Regarding "murder" the practical differences may not be great. If adultery were handled according to the two different understandings, practical results would vary widely. For, if a person could intend just to have intercourse without intending to fornicate or to commit adultery, one might not violate these prohibitions when having intercourse with someone other than one's spouse.

Therefore, before we assent to the claim Schüller makes in this paper, I think we should know what unexceptional moral laws, particularly what kind of unexceptional moral laws, may be found within his normative ethics.

---

[4] *Summa Theologiae,* II-IIae, q. 64, a. 7.

A Response to Fr. Schüller

by Dr. Mary Rousseau

Fr. Schüller has done an important semantic task well. He shows that the question is whether there are ethical norms generated by correct Christian faith that differ in content from ethical norms generated by correct reasoning. His answer is negative: there is a distinctive paraenesis generated by our faith, an exhortation to observe certain norms, but the norms themselves do not differ from those which prescribe morally good action for anyone who reasons correctly. The moral precepts generated by faith have the same truth-value as those generated by reason. Good Christians, then, differ from other good men not in what they do, but in why and with what urgency they do it.

The question, however, is far from being merely semantic. It is, indeed, the most real of all issues in Christian theology. It is but an aspect of a question that has drawn the recent attention of dogmatic theologians, *viz.,* whether Jesus Christ has any distinctive onto-logical status in comparison to Buddha, Socrates, or anyone else. Those who deny that he does can easily deny any distinctive content to Christian ethics, even while agreeing that the foundation of Chris-tian morality is not a set of abstract precepts but a Person. Jesus can be taken as not just an example of moral goodness, but as the Way, the Truth, and the Life. Then He is Himself our moral norm. But if His being is not distinctive, then neither is the normative content of Christian ethics.

Such a Christological theory rests upon an oversight; it overlooks the nature of the faith which is prior to all theology and to all hermeneutics. The oversight is evident in Paul Knitter's recent arti-cle in *Horizons:* he assumes a commitment to Jesus, to His message, and to the tradition which has interpreted that message, and then asks what, if anything, a person so committed is obliged to believe about the uniqueness of Jesus Christ as a person. He concludes that it is not only unnecessary to attribute to Him any uniqueness at all, but that it is impossible to do so.

The argument is logically and psychologically backwards. We do not, if we are to claim a religious faith, first commit ourselves to Jesus and then begin to wonder about His uniqueness. We first see something in Him which we do not see in others to whom we might commit ourselves, and then choose to be Christians rather than Bud-dhists, Druids, or humanists. In other words, the act of Christian faith is an act of choice; not a leap in the dark, but one that is specified by an intellectually apprehended good, by the judgment that belief in Jesus is better than not believing in Him. Such a judgment can only be made by comparing alternatives. And comparison is an intellectual act, an act of relating one intelligible content to another. The content of Jesus is His ontological status as Son, a status claimed by Him and no other, a status won by His unique dying and rising. Our Christian commitment is not a religious act unless it is an acceptance of this unique ontological status; it may be an act of acculturation, or of social or political affiliation, but it is not Christian faith. And without Christian faith, there is no Christian theology—philosophy of religion, yes; Biblical criticism, yes. But not a study of God as we have access to Him in the Person of the risen Christ.

It is not clear that Fr. Schüller makes this same oversight. He seems to, when he distinguishes paraenesis from normative ethics, locates the distinctiveness of Christian ethics in paraenesis alone, and says that paraenesis exhorts but does not inform. That argument does seem to overlook the choice by which we allow Jesus to be paraenesis for us, the faith by which we take Him as our model instead of someone else. To make that choice, we must compare Him to other models, thus seeing in Him some intelligible content. Paraenesis, in other words, must first be norm in order to be paraenesis. Counsel presupposes precept; otherwise it cannot be recognized as counsel.

Fr. Schüller may allow for this dependence, however, when he asserts that Jesus as our model is *norma normata* rather than *norma normans,* with *norma normans* being for Jesus His Father's will. That will is morally good in the fullest sense. But what is measured by a norm must contain, though in a deficient degree, the same content as the norm. The Father, then, is moral goodness in the fullest sense; Jesus submits to, or is measured by, that will by being deficient in comparison to it, and thus comes under obligation to fulfill what He lacks. Such a relation of *norma* to *normata* is that of one intelligible content to another. Good is convertible with being, and moral goodness is but a kind of ontological goodness, that which belongs to persons as such. And being is intelligible content. Thus two things cannot be compared in their goodness except by one who knows what each one is. Jesus, if He is *normata,* must have, must be, some kind of intelligible content.

Likewise, Jesus as *normata* in relation to the Father's will becomes *norma* for us by our own free choice to accept Him as such. In that acceptance, we submit to Him by comparing our moral goodness to His, by comparing, that is, what we are to what He is—the intellectual process of relating our intelligible content to His. Just as He must have some specific content in order to be subject to the moral demand of His Father's will, so must He have content in order to make a demand on us, to be the *norma* by which we are *normata*.

There is, then, some kind of normative content that is distinctive to Christian ethics. It is content of an odd sort—that of a person rather than that of a set of precepts, concrete rather than abstract, existential rather than essential, specified by personal freedom rather than natural necessity. Yet it is not divorced from the abstract precepts which are the stock in trade of moral theologians and philosophers. Jesus, this man, is *norma normans* for all men of all times and places. Moreover, He resorted to abstract, apparently absolute precepts in explaining His own moral choices. Christian moralists thus have a uniquely complex version of the problem of relating the abstract to the concrete: not just in the application of abstract precepts to concrete actions, but in the use of a norm Who is at once a unique person and a universal norm, and in the relating of this concrete universal norm to the abstract precepts of moral systems. The problem is, indeed, fundamental to any system of Christian morality, for in the final analysis, Christian moral life is not the measuring of actions by precepts, nor even the imitation of a model; it is a participation in the interpersonal life of Father, Son and Spirit. We are baptized into His death, and our moral life is a living out of that baptism, a living and dying in Jesus which draws us into the interior life of the Trinity. That kind of morality is surely unique in its content. Any systematization of moral precepts cannot, if it is to be Christian, overlook the historic events of Easter and Pentecost, events which occurred in no other religion, nor anywhere else in human experience.

Fr. Schüller's motive for denying that there are specifically Christian norms for morality is the laudable desire to avoid moral positivism. The alternative that he points to is intolerable, namely, that certain actions will be right only because commanded and others wrong only because forbidden. Morality would thus become an unintelligible divine whim rather than an intelligible expression of the exigencies of our nature. But such a view is not the only alternative. If the Son is the Father's Word, spoken out of love to us who are constituted hearers of that Word by the same Father's love, we need not fear even a theonomous positivism. In fact, to suggest that any addition to natural law would be positivistic is to imply a voluntaristic notion of God which reduces even the natural law to a positive law. That theory locks us into a rationalism that is a clinging to security instead of the surrender to mystery which alone secures our fulfillment. Such a surrender, however, is not fideism or credulity. It is, indeed, a choice to commit our minds to what we do not, and cannot, fully understand—to the divine mystery as it is revealed in the events recorded in Scripture, pre-eminently in the dying and rising of Jesus. Our acceptance of that revelation does not render the mystery intelligible to us. But neither is the choice to accept it a blind choice. The choice is motivated by an intellectually apprehended good—not an insight into the truth of revelation, but a recognition of the goodness of submitting to it without such insight. We come to recognize the goodness of doing that as Father Muschalek showed us yesterday—by seeing our need for fulfillment in something other than ourselves, something which we can possess only by surrendering ourselves to it.

God, then, can be a mind rather than an arbitrary will, one Whose understanding of our nature exceeds our rational grasp, Who can thus reveal needs and fulfillments of that nature which are not arbitrary, even though they lie beyond the purview of immediate insight. The revelation of those needs would then constitute a law which would be not positive but as natural as any other, an intelligible expression of divine ideas which lie beyond our poor power of insight.

To point the issue more sharply, Fr. Jacques Marquette and Fr. Karl Rahner, the two men whom this occasion honors, both undertook the risky life of the explorer on the assumption that it is better, somehow, to be a professed Christian than an anonymous one. Fr. Marquette came to bring the sacramental life of the Church to America, not just to improve the moral reasoning of the natives. Fr. Rahner has labored, surely, in the hope that we who are partly professed and partly anonymous in our Christianity might become less anonymous and more professed. Now to be better existentially is to be different morally. Every real improvement in a person as such is a moral good, a content, a difference in *what* one does and in *what* one is. Since moral actions are all of a piece, a difference in intention makes a difference in the content of a moral act, even if the outward act is the same in both cases. Thus if Christian morality did no more than to elevate our motives for doing the same things that the pagans do, it would add to the content of moral norms. Giving a cup of water to a thirsty man for humanistic motives and giving a cup of water in order to be an instrument of Trinitarian life are two acts which differ in content, for our intentions are part of the content of what we choose in a moral act.

Fr. Schüller's paper rests, then, on a view of faith which would reduce it to a kind of intellectual laziness that in principle ought not to occur. Faith is the acceptance on authority of what could be known by immediate insight. The norm by which we allow Jesus to be paraenesis for us seems to be reason, that is, we see Him as having fulfilled the natural law better than anyone else. But He did not, apparently, *do* anything more than what natural law prescribes. His life—and all the rest of the experience related in Scripture—tells us nothing that could not, in principle, be discovered by reason. Sacred Scripture as a special revelation in comparison to other religious literature thus disappears.

What is at stake, then, behind the question of the specificity of Christian ethics is the notion of faith as neither credulity nor rationalism but a genuine third alternative. This point could perhaps be clarified by some explication of the Latin phrase which Fr. Schüller quotes at the end of his analysis of the relation between faith and reason. After showing that correct faith and correct reasoning generate propositions which differ not in truth value but only in their psychogenesis, he says, in summary of his argument, *"Fides supponit rationem et transcendat eam."* One wonders about the force of *transcendat*. How does faith transcend reason? Does it yield propositions which exceed those of reason in their truth value, or their certitude? From the preceding argument, one is inclined to say, "No." What, then, is left? If the propositions of faith transcend those of reason in their content, then Christian ethics would have some specific normative content, a content realized supremely in the Person of Jesus. For He must be either a word who has no hearers because no one really needs to hear Him; in that case, He is no word at all. Or else He is our word of exhortation, a word which can only exhort by being first a word, the Word of revelation which we discover, the word of the discovery which is revealed to us. In that case, He says something, and we would do well to try to hear the normative content that He speaks.

Canonical Criticism: A Place on Which to Stand In Doing Theology

by Rev. John F. X. Sheehan, S.J.

I. Introduction

For several decades, the relationship between what a simpler age called "dogmatic" theologians and scholars who devoted themselves to the study of the Bible has been somewhat strained. Growth in each of the two disciplines, systematics and biblical studies, has not really alleviated the strain. The reasons for the strain are many. Systematicians look fondly back to the age when the biblicists acted like the proverbial well-trained Victorian child appearing to be seen and heard only briefly when called on to recite his "proof texts" before an admiring (or patient) audience of grown-ups and then sent back to the nursery where he could play with those toys with which biblicists were rumored to enjoy themselves.

One is tempted to extend this figure by saying that the Bible scholars reached adolescence with all its attendant ills and a strained relationship become a hopeless one. But I am not sure that the figure will continue to support the reality. This much is true. The biblical scholars "grew up" to the extent of realizing that the scriptures were simply too complex to be used the way some systematicians wished to use them.

The problems got worse rather than better. Many biblical scholars began to take refuge in the hidden fine points of their discipline. If they became, correctly, aware that there was far more to the study of scripture than that it should serve somehow as a "handmaiden" of a "real" theology, they fell into other errors. They responded to the arrogance of the systematicians by developing an arrogance of their own. Judging that the systematicians were incapable of the refined language studies, text analysis, and other *arcana* of the biblical discipline, they began secretly (or not so secretly) to despise the systematicians. In fact, they began to have questions about any biblical scholars who thought of themselves as theologians.

All of this would be a reasonable attitude, of course, for anyone who wished to study the biblical texts for some reason or another while not thinking of them as "revealed" or "inspired."

Many years ago, Karl Rahner addressed himself to this unhappy state of affairs.[1] In one address, he lectured both systematicians and

---

[1] Karl Rahner, "Exegese und Dogmatik" in *Schriften zur Theologie* 5 (Einsiedeln: Benziger, 1962): 82-111.

biblical scholars and pointed out wisely that they could not properly live without one another. Perhaps the wisdom of his insight came from his emerging views of inspiration[2] and revelation.[3] It is not certain that his wise words were heeded.

In fact, biblicists went on to make some more serious mistakes all alone without the help of the systematicians. Perhaps the most serious one was that, freed from the demands of providing "proof texts," they proceeded to isolate themselves in their study of Old Testament or New, to a single gospel or epistle and ignored the fact that all of scripture speaks to the *qahal.*

II. Canonical Criticism

The relationship of canonical criticism to these earlier writings of Rahner is something which should be clear at the end of the paper. But first, what is "canonical criticism?" Most broadly defined it is a study of the focus which a given religious community (Hebrew, Jewish, early Christian or other) gave to a particular body of scripture.

This definition is intentionally broad. It can apply to the work of Childs[4] who is more concerned with the end product of canonization, Sanders[5] who is more concerned with the process of canonical formulation, and Blenkinsopp[6] who may be seen to mediate between the opinions of the first two. It is the last who wrote:

> Study of the Canon is not a panacea for Biblical Studies nor can it explain everything. But no historical or theological explanation will be adequate which neglects it.[7]

This paper is a method paper. While it will deal with a number of problems in biblical theology, the foci of the paper will generally begin with the delineation of these problems as treated by Blenkinsopp, Childs, Sanders et. al.

Let me spare the reader some suspense. The materials that follow will be preoccupied with a number of problems not yet resolved, that is: What is the relationship between the authority of the prophet and that of the community? What constitutes the validity of the teaching

---

[2] Karl Rahner, *Über die Schriftinspiration* (Freiburg: Herder, 1961).

[3] Karl Rahner, *Offenbarung und Überlieferung* (Freiburg: Herder, 1965).

[4] Brevard S. Childs, *Biblical Theology in Crisis* (Philadelphia: Westminster, 1970). This is his major work in Canonical Criticism as of this writing.

[5] James A. Sanders, *Torah and Canon* (Philadelphia: Fortress, 1972). This is his major work in Canonical Criticism to date.

[6] Joseph Blenkinsopp, *Prophecy and Canon* (Notre Dame: University of Notre Dame, 1977).

[7] Ibid., p. 17.

that is derivative from a "true" as opposed to that from a "false" prophet? If a contemporary *qahal* is to teach something "new" and insist that this is biblical, is this valid? How is it valid?

All this having been said, the research for the paper began with one question which the writer has answered to his own satisfaction: Is historical criticism, aided by canonical criticism, a valid locus for doing theology? Some are beginning to suspect that it is not.[8] The answer of this paper, however, is emphatically affirmative. It is a valid locus for doing theology. There is some serious question of whether or not there is any other valid locus for doing theology.

It may be useful to cite a passage from Sanders in which he points up the difference between "historical criticism" and "canonical criticism." Writing in 1928, Dodd had said of the "historical method":

> The great positive achievement of the critical method is easily overlooked, namely that it enables us to read the Bible historically as perhaps no preceding generation has been able to read it.[9]

Sanders then explains the difference between mere historical criticism, in the broadest sense, and the emerging discipline of canonical criticism:

> Some . . . material shows up in the Old Testament more than once, and hence is available for tradition-critical work on it. The moment one asks *why* such material bore repeating, however, he is engaged in the question of authority. Such material which met a need in one situation, was apparently now able to meet another need in another situation. And that is precisely the kind of tradition that becomes canonical—material that bears repeating in a later moment both because of the need of the later moment and because of the value or power of the material repeated (the dialogue between them).[10]

And before we are done, we shall discuss problems flowing from the fact that this canonical process does not end with the assembling of the sacred text in printed form. Here let us only note that any "tensions" that may result from the treatment of a tradition now in one scriptural situation and now in another must be retained. An earlier tension cannot be smoothed over in light of the latest biblical treatment of the tension. All polarities must be retained because the

---

[8] Such, at least, was the oral communication of Bernhard Anderson in lectures at the Princeton Seminary.

[9] C. H. Dodd, *Authority of the Bible* (Nisbet: London, 1928), p. 139.

[10] James A. Sanders, "Adaptable for Life: The Nature and Function of Canon," *The Mighty Acts of God,* ed. Cross, et al. (Doubleday: New York, 1976), p. 542.

churches live in any moment with the expectation that they may be given the light to see the interpretation of a polarity lost to an earlier age. Perhaps we can phrase this more simply.

> Yahweh is in the doing
> Yahweh is in the re-telling.
> Yahweh is in the hearing.

The first sentence has long since been accepted by religious men who are scientific students of some of the more empirical aspects of Bible study, e.g. archaeology and history. It was possible to see the Lord at work here. Here we only ask the question, as we read the traditions, is it not possible to see the Lord at work in the shaping of the retelling? Finally, in the contemporary age, as the churches attempt to listen to the voice of scripture, we ask only, is the Lord not at work also in the act of hearing? Blenkinsopp comes close to asking the latter two questions.

> [Canonical Criticism shifts] attention from original meanings and the prehistory of texts to their function within broad contexts of meaning which are themselves part of what Peter Berger calls the social construction of reality.[11]

The validity of what the "canonical critics" sometimes wish to do has been under challenge. But an analogous challenge goes back at least as far as the differences between Augustine and Jerome on the possibility of doing a translation from the original Hebrew that was not "diligently compared" to that of the Septuagint.[12] At least as developed, Augustine's problems were perhaps more political than theological. He was concerned about a loss of unity in the Church which would now be dealing with two principal translations, in two major tongues. But his political reasoning was at least undergirded by a theological view. If there were significant differences between the Greek and the Hebrew, ought not these differences to be attributed to the work of the Spirit? And if the Spirit has so worked, *is it not impossible to go back on what has been already done?*

> In his response Jerome abruptly rejected Augustine's arguments. Among other things he argued for the necessity of clarifying uncertain passages in the Septuagint on the basis of a better understanding of the Hebrew. He insisted that the task of translating from the Hebrew served the same purpose of supporting the faith as had the translation from the Greek.[13]

It would be unwise to attempt simply to see Jerome as the

---

[11] Blenkinsopp, *Prophecy and Canon,* p. 17.

[12] Childs develops this in *Biblical Theology in Crisis,* pp. 106-7.

[13] Ibid.

"protocanonical critic." He is not. There is in his writing, however, material that is seminal for a position already stated in this paper: the listening church(es) must attempt to retain all polarities as it may be given to a contemporary church to hear a nuance that was lost to an earlier age. The above is not a new and radical idea:

> When Jeremiah used the Rechabites as an object lesson for obedience, he did not approve of their static view of it (Jeremiah 35). The Rechabites practiced obedience by attempting to retain earlier nomadic contexts of living: Jeremiah, in contrast, stressed *continually listening* (Jer 35:14).[14]

How compatible is this with any modern theories of inspiration?

> Calvin's doctrine of the Spirit's internal testimony points toward a frequently held theological conviction that a fruitful paradoxical tension must be maintained between a close reading of the biblical text and a logically independent spiritual or existential appropriation of the Divine Word within the text. But Calvin sees no impediment at all where nineteenth- and twentieth-century theologians find the heaviest thickets. A modern commentator on Calvin's principles of exegesis, H. J. Kraus, rightly says that the Bible is, for Calvin, not inspired and hence does not itself in the first place inspire, but communicates and informs. The reader, not the text, is to be illumined by the internal or inspiring testimony of the Spirit so that he may discern the written biblical word to be God's own Word, intended for his own Church's edification.[15]

Rahner has certainly never written that scripture is not inspired. Still, he has insisted that revelation, inspiration, and canon are gifts to the apostolic church.

Before this paper is ended, we shall have suggested that rather they are gifts to the living church(es), that the duty of continually listening which Jeremiah preached to the Rechabites is no less a duty of all contemporary religious communities. Perhaps it should be easier for members of religious orders to grasp this. Granting that the degree of "inspiration" which the boldest of them has been willing to grant to their founders is at a great remove from that attributed to the written word of God, nonetheless, there is an analogy. In our age, the most distinguished of the religious orders have been compelled to make some distinctions: between the layers of their founding documents that are "inspired" in some analogous sense, those which are to be viewed as strongly "culturally condi-

---

[14] James A. Sanders, "Hermeneutics in True and False Prophecy," *Canon and Authority,* ed. Coats and Long (Philadelphia: Fortress, 1977), p. 33. (emphasis added).

[15] Hans W. Frei, *The Eclipse of the Biblical Narrative* (New Haven and London: Yale University, 1974), pp. 21-22.

tioned" by the ethos of the founder, and the layers of contemporary applicability to be found even in those strata which are judged "culturally conditioned."

III. Canonical Criticism and Targumic Interpretation

Sanders has written:

> Why has the Hebrew Bible lasted so long? Surely not only because there have been churches and synagogues to pass it along, but because of its essential diversity, its own inherent refusal to absolutize any single stance as the only place where one might live under the sovereignty of God. There is no position or doctrine which falls outside the challenging judgments of God; that is, there is no creed which out-Gods God. He is here presented as not so much immutable as ever moving, and the record reflects that divine freedom in ways which defy man's attempt to domesticate it.[16]

This eloquent statement offers a major argument for the values of canonical criticism. Less eloquently put, all of the varieties of canonical criticism seem to offer a focus in terms of which we may read the entire Old Testament as "revelation" and not concern ourselves merely with the "pretty parts."

Is canonical criticism something totally new then? Yes and no. The term is of most recent vintage. But like most developments in the history of thought, the movement did not come out of nowhere. It is a commonplace that the Targums felt quite free to recast old material into a theology contemporary with the composition of the Targums. Blenkinsopp follows the work of Vermes in noting:

> Later Jewish interpretations of a more or less official nature highlight the disadvantages of limiting oneself to canonical meanings. Thus the targumic tradition finds in the text (Gen 17:12) an attestation of the vicarious efficacy of sacrifice epitomized in the shedding of blood. As with the Akedah or Binding of Isaac (Gen 22) such a re-reading opens up a richer vein of meaning than is attainable by use of the form critical method.[17]

Canonical criticism stands in a long line of modern theories of exegesis that reaches back at least to Dilthey.[18]

Bernhard Anderson, in his translation *A History of Pentateuchal Traditions* (Prentice-Hall, 1972), attributes to Gunkel and Dilthey

---

[16] Sanders, *Torah and Canon,* p. 116.

[17] Blenkinsopp, *Prophecy and Canon,* p. 10.

[18] Cf. the point as developed by B. Anderson in his introduction to Martin Noth, *A History of Pentateuchal Traditions* (Prentice-Hall: Englewood Cliffs, 1972), p. xviii.

the following view of exegesis: "Exegesis is not a science but an art in which the critic with sensitivity and imagination seeks to 're-create' the situations in life of the people which find expression in literary works."[19] As I have written further:

> In H. A. Hodges' work *Wilhelm Dilthey: An Introduction* (London: 1944), he makes the point that the skilled reader can recreate or experience those very life processes which led to the printed page. "In the operation of understanding itself, the life-process is reversed." A centuries' long progression led to a given text. By contemplating the text long enough we can come not only to know the meaning of these lines, but can reexperience the life-process which produced them.[20]

Can this be pushed a step further? By entering into communion with the life process which produced this given page or stratum, *are we not then in a position to continue the process beyond the point it had reached with the production of the printed page?* In other words, cannot a contemporary community reach conclusions that are organically related to a life-process that was interrupted with the printing of the page? I had earlier justified this through analogies to the philological reasoning of James Barr.[21]

Barr had noted that the analysis of obscure biblical texts through post-biblical texts had much to say for it, perhaps more than many other philological methods, since "the Bible is a very limited segment of all that was said in ancient Hebrew" and clear meanings may well be found in later texts supported through oral tradition.[22]

Perhaps following analogous lines of reasoning, Blenkinsopp notes, "to study the shape of the canon is to be led back to the hermeneutics of the successive ages in which it was formed."[23]

But perhaps the best analogy to the corollary of the Dilthey insight which I have offered above is to be found in the relatively recent writings of J. Weingreen. He started from a totally different perspective. He never used the term "canonical criticism." He had no interest in the topic as such. His was a different thesis, "presenting a case for the continuity of tradition from at least the later historical period of the Old Testament to that of early rabbinic times."[24]

---

[19] Ibid.

[20] John Sheehan, *Let the People Cry Amen* (New York: Paulist, 1977), p. 177.

[21] Ibid., pp. 126-27.

[22] James Barr, *Comparative Philology and the Text of the Old Testament* (Oxford: Clarendon, 1968), pp. 224-25.

[23] Blenkinsopp, *Prophecy and Canon*, p. 16.

[24] J. Weingreen, "Oral Torah and Written Records," in *Holy Book and Holy Tradition*, ed. Bruce and Rupp (Manchester: Erdmans, 1968), p. 54.

Instead of following the conventional practice of moving forward from the Old Testament to a post-biblical literature, I have adopted the method of looking back from the Rabbinic to pre-Rabbinic, i.e. post-exilic times and, on occasion, still further back to pre-exilic times. In this exercise I have come across what I have termed Rabbinic-type situations recorded in the pages of the Old Testament.[25]

IV. Is the Living Community the Canon?

The so-called *Letter of Aristeas* from at least the second century B.C. is an interesting witness to Jewish Theological belief, however admixed it may be with legend. The argument for the role of the community in canonization is often aided by the reference in Aristeas to a remarkable phenomenon. The sacred text is presented to what we may call the assembly, here a gathering of men, women and children, and *only after their approval* is it offered to the leadership.[26] It is true that historically this has been interpreted to refer to a process of canonization as an action of finalization, but could it mean something else: *the living community is the canon?* The scholar cannot pass on the work until it has been approved by the living assembly.

It is difficult not to see some of that in Aristeas. Granting the cultural conditioning of the day, we think it was a far more remarkable statement then than it would be now that a sacred text should be approved by mere women and children before it is handed over to the *Übermensch* of that culture—the scholar. Does this represent considerable progress over Neh 8:7 ff. where the people are given the opportunity to say amen but the official figures, scholars and Levites, "cause them to understand?" Perhaps not. In the Nehemiah passage, beginning with vs. 2, the hearers, men and women, are described as "those that could hear with understanding." Only in vs. 8 are we told that the Levites and scholars "caused them to understand." Has a later hand already begun to scruple at a democratic theology?

This reference and that of Aristeas give us a deeper dimension to the remark of Blenkinsopp that "to study the shape of the canon is to be led back to the hermeneutics of the successive ages in which it was formed."[27]

---

[25] Ibid.

[26] *Lettre d'Aristée a Philocrate,* ed. A. Pelletier (Paris: Cerf, 1962) nos. 308-312. John W. Bowler understands the dichotomy of these texts (of Nehemiah and Aristeas) a bit differently in *The Targums and Rabbinic Literature* (Cambridge: University Press, 1969), pp. 3-4.

[27] Blenkinsopp, *Prophecy and Canon,* p. 16.

It is a firm contention of this paper that it is reasonable to push the "successive ages" back further than any other scholars have done. By the same token, in light of the Dilthey-Barr principle, it is not unreasonable to see the results of the original hermeneutics extending to the present day. (I am calling the Dilthey-Barr principle the conviction that the oral world around the text of the Old Testament is accessible to us.)

Let us argue from analogy.

Stolz[28] and Ruprecht[29] have argued strongly for the origins of Hebrew cult in the world of the Jebusites. But if this was so, there had to be a popular acceptance in which Jebusite worship became "Yahwised." Ahlström has tried to show how that happened.[30] Moreover, the "cult legend" of II Sam 24:10 ff., which rehearses the tale of the threshing floor of Araunah the Jebusite, places Hebrew worship in a long, long continuum. Sanders has much understated the case when he says "there has been through the centuries a remarkable continuity of cultic institutions which have been the vehicles of the Bible's survival: the church and synagogue."[31] Perhaps he has not said the half of it. In the Mishna Sanhedrin iv. 3, which he dates to the third century A.D., it is written:

> The Sanhedrin was arranged like half of a round threshing floor, so that they might all see one another. Before them sat the two scribes of the judges, one to the right and one to the left, and they wrote down the words of them that favored acquittal and the words of them that favored conviction.[32]

There is more here than the statement of a poor simile: "It was shaped somewhat like a barn." Rather, there is reference to judgment in a cultic situation.[33] The antiquity of this can be seen from Gordon's translation of a Nuzu document[34] where Gordon points out that an obscure word is perfectly clear if one sees it as a derivative from the Hebrew *grn*, "threshing floor" and understands

---

[28] Fritz Stolz, *Strukturen und Figuren im Kult von Jerusalem* (Berlin De Gruyter, 1970).

[29] Konrad Ruprecht, *Der Tempel von Jerusalem* (Berlin: de Gruyter, 1977).

[30] Gösta Ahlström, "Der Prophet Nathan und der Tempelbau," *Vetus Testamentum* 11 (1961): 113-27.

[31] Sanders, *Torah and Canon,* p. 5.

[32] Weingreen, "Oral Torah and Written Records," p. 56.

[33] Cf. Sheehan, *Let the People Cry Amen,* p. 102 and Stolz, *Strukturen und Figuren im Kult von Jerusalem,* p. 8.

[34] Cyrus H. Gordon, *Orientalia* 12 (1943): 65 n. 1 cites a Nuzu text *i-na [ma] ag-ra-at-ti us-te-si-wa-ni* (not his own transliteration but one from a previously published text) and translates it: "in the threshing floor, he hailed me to court." The root of *magrattu,* Gordon points out, is *grn* as "threshing floor" in Ugaritic.

it as "law court" which the most ancient of Hebrew threshing floors often was.

In other words, empirical evidences of "continuity" are to be found which bind early Christian times with pre-Hebraic Jerusalem. Consequently, the material in the *Letter of Aristeas* is not to be seen as stray antiquarian witness but as part of a piece that binds early Christian times with ancient Hebrew times and the contemporary era with early Christian times. If this is so, then the remark that Childs has made about the "challenge of our day" has much wider implications than he has stated:

> The challenge of the Christian interpreter in our day is to hear the full range of notes within all of Scripture, to wrestle with the theological implication of this Biblical Witness, and above all, to come to grips with the agony of our age before a living God who still speaks through the prophets and apostles.[35]

To which should be added *in the circle of a believing community.* Although Wilfred Cantwell Smith may be correct when he says:

> All religions are new religions, every morning. For religions do not exist in the sky somewhere elaborated, finished, and static; they exist in men's hearts.[36]

Still the *Letter of Aristeas* and the texts in Nehemiah merely confirm human witness that religious experience is inevitably related to life in the community.

We have already introduced some fundamental conflicts. It is true that theologizing takes place in the community, but the biblical witness has preserved, at least vestigially, a host of conflicts. In fact, as already noted it may be the very diversity at least of the Hebrew Bible, if not of the New Testament, that has enabled it to last so long under such a wide variety of circumstances and meeting such a wide variety of needs.[37]

But if theological reflection, ancient and contemporary, is something that takes place in community, what does this do to the notion of the prophet—often envisaged as the solitary figure standing against mighty hosts though they be drawn in battle array?

This is a good question and it seems that most who have written on our topic have at least occasionally seemed to contradict themselves. Sanders, for example, in a recent article notes that an [authoritative] story is passed on "because it spoke to the majority of the community"[38] but later remarks that "authoritative traditions

---

[35] Childs, *Biblical Theology in Crisis,* p. 163.

[36] So quoted by Bernard J. Lonergan in *The Way to Nicaea,* trans. C. O'Donovan (Philadelphia: Westminster, 1976) p. vii.

[37] Sanders, *Torah and Canon,* p. 116.

[38] Sanders, "Adaptable for Life: The Nature and Function of Canon," p. 538.

were used in particular situations to challenge the way that the majority . . . thought."[39]

When is a majority not a majority?

While the following does not end the discussion of the "true" versus the "false" prophet, it is difficult to improve on McKenzie's opening statement that the true prophet was one that was heard by the community as speaking "with the voice of Yahweh."[40]

Since this correct judgment was not always made by the contemporaries of the prophet, might it be that the true prophet was able to appeal to the majority yet unborn?

For Christianity at least, there is another avenue to the solution. For von Rad, the true prophet is perhaps identified by his access to the divine secret.[41] The Hebrew word *sod* is used among other places in Jer 15:17 and Jer 23:18. The word is best explained in conjunction with Amos 3:7. It has both the meaning of the "Council of the Deity" and "the secret." The latter is that which is discussed in the Council of the Deity. For von Rad, it is the prophet and he alone who has access to the Council, its deliberations, and the results of those deliberations—the secret.

He writes:

> Later Israel knows Yahweh as the one who is ready to speak and even to have questions put to him (Is XLV.11); he does nothing without taking his prophets into confidence. (Am. III.7).[42]

A partial resolution of some of our conflicts can be found for the Christian community in Jn 15:15:

> Henceforth I call you not servants; for the servant knoweth not what his Lord doeth: but I have called you friends; for all things that I have heard of my Father I have made known unto you. (King James Version)

What follows pellucidly then from the juxtaposition of these two texts is this:

V. The Christian Community is a Prophetic Community

As contemporary people, when they hear a purported prophet or the living voice of scripture, they have only to compare it to the *sod*, to which they have easy access, to know whether or not they are in the presence of God's truth.

---

[39] Ibid., p. 544.

[40] John McKenzie, *A Theology of the Old Testament* (New York: Doubleday, 1974), p. 101.

[41] Gerhard von Rad, *Old Testament Theology*, 2 vols., trans. D. Walker (New York: Harper and Row, 1965), 2:359.

[42] Ibid.

But perhaps even the New Testament itself gives witness to an analogous gift of the Old Testament community, that it had access to clear knowledge of what was God's will. Childs has written:

> The biblical tradition stresses the one unchanging will of God. Thus, Jesus argues against the practice of divorce [in one tradition at any rate] on the grounds that God's intent was absolutely unequivocal from the beginning in spite of accommodations to human sinfulness (Cf. Mark 10:2). Nowhere is there a hint of criticism made by the New Testament writers of the Old Testament to suggest that God was unable to make known his clear will to Israel.[43]

By now it should be clear that discussions that begin with the idea that the *Kanon* as "fixed" or "measuring rod" are not only not terribly useful, they are simply wrong. Even G. E. Wright's efforts at finding the "canon within the canon" as he developed them are not totally helpful.[44] Blenkinsopp, for example, saw the efforts as somehow contradicting the "real work" of canonical criticism which is to deal with the actual, historical canon.[45] Rather, the most proper discussion of the "canon within the canon" should cause us to recognize an effort that is common to a contemporary enterprise. By this is meant, a soul searching on the part of a community and the simple putting of the questions:

1. Does this material fit with our present self-identity?
2. Does the standard interpretation of this material fit with our present self-identity or must we search in it for layers of meaning lost to an earlier age but consonant with our grasp of who and what we are?

Before one panics at this as at subjectivity gone riot, one should note that such fears are badly placed, for Christians at any rate.

> What in fact controlled the self-understanding of early Christianity as a Jewish sect was above all an alternative understanding of what Israel was meant to be, an understanding of its own interpretation of certain biblical texts.[46]

Early Christianity was as obliged to the *ascesis* of continually listening as are we.

A good example of the legitimacy of this practice is found in the fact, as Sanders observes, that such an epic as the tradition of the Conquest of Canaan is dropped from the final Torah and reduced to the first book of the prophets.[47] He is annoyed that Blenkinsopp

---

[43] Childs, *Biblical Theology in Crisis*, p. 128.
[44] Cf. Wright cited by Blenkinsopp, p. 13.
[45] Blenkinsopp, *Prophecy and Canon*, p. 13.
[46] Ibid., p. 15.
[47] Sanders, *Torah and Canon*, p. 26.

seems not to have seen how significant this is.[48] Whether or not one is in agreement with Sanders in particulars on this issue, it seems that he has made a strong case for the fact that a community can drop something which does not fit the contemporary scene, provided that there is an authoritative tradition in the community's collective memory to which the community can have reference. For Sanders this is the "Torah story."[49]

All laws are written down in terms of the "Torah story." Pharisaism was wise in that it placed the authority of its teaching back at Sinai, at the origins of the Torah Story.[50] How was this possible? Sanders eventually argues from the strength of oral law in the ancient Near East and the tabu against the writing down of laws.[51] (Yet perhaps this should be read against the backdrop of Weingreen's having noted the tensions between the forbidding of written laws lest the truly uninitiated have access to them and the inevitable pressure to write the down so that students could study them.[52])

Pace Weingreen, though, Sanders adds some strong arguments on oral law from British precedent[53] to which may now be added the work of Klostermann who argued for the strength of oral legal tradition in the Old Testament.[54] His argument does not look so bizarre since the contemporary work of Parry and Lord in the entire matter of oral composition.[55]

Perhaps some of the above is too involuted to be terribly useful. Let me summarize it briefly. It is not simply a subjective feeling in the community that a certain teaching is consonant with the contemporary self-identity and therefore something that can be absorbed or "canonized." Rather, there is a deep conviction that this present self-identity is something with terribly ancient roots. All that is new is absorbed only in terms of the conviction that it is most congruent to that which is old. The community that went to Babylon (or heard about Babylon) absorbed into its mainstream much (e.g. Wisdom materials) that was seen as consonant with what was old, while rejecting other possible adaptations (the use of idols!) that were seen

---

[48] Sanders, "A Review of Prophecy and Canon," in *The Catholic Biblical Quarterly* 40 (1978): 599.

[49] Sanders, *Torah and Canon,* pp. 24-30 *et alibi.*

[50] Ibid., p. 3.

[51] Ibid., p. 31.

[52] Weingreen, *Oral Torah and Written Records,* p. 58.

[53] Sanders, *Torah and Canon,* p. 31.

[54] August Klostermann, *Der Pentateuch* (Leipzig: Deichert, 1907), pp. 348-428.

[55] Albert Bates Lord, *The Singer of Tales* (Cambridge: Harvard, 1960) and the works of his mentor cited therein.

as totally inconsonant with a very new self-identity born of an old, old past.

In this new re-thinking of an ancient past, what do the contemporary churches have as a model? What better than the memory of the Lord himself? So, at least, does Childs read Jn 5:17,[56] "My Father works until now and I am working." So does the Church remember the Lord as dispensing himself from the Sabbath obligation or (better) *as reinterpreting it.* Here too the one unchanging will of God is not seen as altered, but the human condition bathes one aspect of it in a different light. (It is worth pointing out, that in the New Testament examples, Christ is remembered by the early church as calling always to a more lofty ethic.)

> His criticism of the Sadducees is very pointed. "You are mistaken because you know neither the scriptures nor the power of God."—i.e., you are deficient both in the understanding of the tradition and in personal intuition of divine things.[57]

This much is clear from the words of the Jesus whom we see in the New Testament. His presumption is that his hearers (and followers) are ever waiting for a more accurate perception of the divine will, one that will make them more like unto the Father and his perfection. They are not relentless students of the scriptures who are in quest of an easier discipline.

And so Dodd remarks:

> If Jesus was understood [to have said something] all experience shows that it is worthwhile to wait with great humility and patience until the truth in it, or behind it, declares itself and separates itself from any temporary and relative element.[58]

Because of this, there is yet one more polarity to be dealt with in Childs' use of the cliché, "Surely there is something wrong with an interpretation that is no longer concerned *to hear the Old Testament on its own terms.*[59] There is a contradiction or two in this. We all tend to say amen a bit too quickly to the notion of reading a text on its own terms. And yet what does *on its own terms* mean for much of scripture? Childs has been among the most eloquent of the critics who have noted the ambiguity of the relentless quest for the "original meaning" as primary.[60] One is tempted to note that the "truly original" meaning of some of scripture has us in the heart of pre-Hebraic Zadokite theology and few would see that as the truly primary meaning of our sacred texts.

---

[56] Childs, *Biblical Theology in Crisis,* p. 210.

[57] Dodd, *Authority of the Bible,* p. 278.

[58] Ibid., p. 238.

[59] Childs, *Biblical Theology in Crisis,* p. 159 (emphasis added).

[60] Blenkinsopp praises him for this in *Prophecy and Canon,* pp. 14-15.

It is perhaps worth noting here the plethora of unresolved tensions in all that write on this subject, including this writer, between viewing what has been done as model for future doing and the temptation to take the model as frozen and static image for others to comment on. A couple of fine scholars "have taken the easy way out." Stendahl sees biblical theology as historical and descriptive, *simpliciter*. [61] Perhaps there is an analogy between this and Bonhoeffer's "religionless Christianity." [62] Both of these procedures would put a reflective salvation somewhere outside the church, the only place where salvation happens. It does not wash, at least for the thoughtful who would be saved—and saved reflectively.

VI. The Example of Ethics

We have earlier suggested that the notion of canonical criticism has a great deal to say to any world of ethics which would call itself in any way "Christian" or "biblical." Let us return to that notion.

Childs writes that "The Scriptures of the church are not archives of the past but a channel of life for the continuing church through which God instructs and admonishes his people." [63] If Childs has not always been faithful to this insight, nonetheless it is his. How is it to be read?

Dodd is blunt:

> It is high time to insist unambiguously that the Bible contains a good deal which if it is taken out of a temporary historical context and given general and permanent validity is simply pernicious. The old dogmatic view of the Bible therefore is not only open to attack from the standpoint of science and historical criticism, but if taken seriously it becomes a danger to religion and public morals. [64]

There is little British understatement in these words, is there?

In light of all that we have said until this point in the paper, there should be little surprise at Childs' remark that development in "Christian" Ethics were almost unaffected by anything that happened in Biblical Studies. [65] In the first place, this was part of a larger picture and we have already seen some of the causes for lack of dialogue between "biblical" theologians and theologians of any other stripe.

---

[61] Krister Stendahl, "Biblical Theology, Contemporary," *The Interpreter's Dictionary of the Bible 1* (Nashville: Abingdon, 1962): 419.

[62] As cited by Childs, *Biblical Theology in Crisis,* p. 84.

[63] Ibid., p. 59.

[64] Dodd, *Authority of the Bible,* pp. 13-14.

[65] Childs, *Biblical Theology in Crisis,* p. 59.

On the biblical side, there was another problem. Biblical theologians had a fear (founded in their study of some millenia of human activity) that a study of religious matters which allowed a serious focus on human behavior (a reasonable goal some might think) frequently wound up somehow or another in reducing the majesty of God. Historically, of course, the reason is rather simple. Those persons who worked hardest at "being good" throughout most of religious history, seemed always to have the tendency to think that they should be treated far better by events under the divine hand than those who indulged in "being bad." (Do we have here an explanation of the preference which the Jesus of the New Testament seemed to have for sinners?) Some of the other reasons for the lack of mutual influence of course have already been spelled out and perhaps more easily apply to the field of ethics. The ethician too could point over a period of time to an *arcanum* of his own and felt that he was doing well if he called in the biblicist for an appearance at the final curtain or paragraph.

But to return to the way that a focus on human behavior tends to reduce the deity:

> The Hittites, among others, believed that the reason there were ruins of still more ancient cities lying about for the ancient tourist to see was that the gods of those unfortunate cities had been displeased with their subjects.[66]

At least some layers of Deuteronomy "were able to take an ethically oriented religion to the people in their daily lives, insisting that God chose them as a people for no other reason than that he loved them and that as a people they were his sons for no reason other than that he was their father" (Deut 7:7-8; 8:5).[67] Perhaps the human ambivalence on the stern concept of the God Who Cannot be Bought[68] is best indicated by Sanders' juxtaposing of two notions while he is in the process of debunking the "useful god."[69]

> Deuteronomy broke forever the power of the ancient idea of a useful deity obligated to guide and protect his peculiar people [so far so good] by stressing that the sins of God's own people would incur appropriate punishment.[70]

A page later, Sanders says well enough that things happen the way they do, not only because God acts in history, but because of man's

---

[66] Sanders, *Torah and Canon*, p. 84.

[67] Ibid., p. 42.

[68] Cf. Sheehan, *Let the People Cry Amen*, p. 55.

[69] Sanders, *Torah and Canon*, p. 42.

[70] Ibid.

conduct. But then he adds, "Adversity befalls a city because its citizens have displeased their god."[71]

So perhaps ambivalence on the connection between ethical behavior and a relationship to the Divinity is no more biblical than it is human.

Still is it true that there has been a failure on the part of the churches to respond biblically to the demanding pressures of a contemporary society including calls for change in sexual mores and in fact for a social revolution.[72]

Does canonical criticism have something to say to this failure? The answer is emphatically affirmative. It enables the ethician (or better the ethician and biblicist working in concert) to avoid what Sanders considers a primary "abuse" of the Bible[73] and what Childs would call a failure to recognize a peculiar species of biblical authority.[74]

Sanders' "primary abuse" occurs when the believing community reads the Bible to find there "models for its morality" rather than "mirrors for its identity."[75] Childs would phrase it a bit differently. Assuredly the central problems of ethics have been pointed up by the Bible itself.[76] But then he goes on to put the question, "How does the Bible function for the Christian when making ethical decisions?"[77]

Of all the efforts which he makes at the answering of this question, the one that rang most true for me was his noticing that the pious reader is called to recognize "the correct biblical warrant" for a given situation.[78] Bad biblical ethics results when the scholar decides that the proper model is Paul before Agrippa, although the correct warrant called for is that of the compromising sage of Proverbs. An undergraduate suggested the following to me for the title of a chapter on ethics some years ago, "How's a Feller to Know?" First of all,

> The church's prayer for illumination by the Holy Spirit when interpreting Scripture is not a meaningless vestige from a forgotten age of piety, but an acknowledgment of the continuing need for God to make himself known through Scripture to an expectant people.[79]

---

[71] Childs, *Biblical Theology in Crisis*, p. 83.

[72] Ibid.

[73] Sanders, *Torah and Canon*, p. xvi.

[74] Childs, *Biblical Theology in Crisis*, p. 135.

[75] Sanders, *Torah and Canon*, p. xvi.

[76] Childs, *Biblical Theology in Crisis*, p. 126.

[77] Ibid.

[78] Ibid., p. 135.

[79] Ibid., p. 100.

VII. Triadic Discussion

For Roman Catholic readers, I should perhaps stress something else. There is a plethora of warrants available in the Old Testament. We can agree that the Jesus who is Lord and Christ surely embodies all that is good in the Old Testament. Unfortunately, such a Jesus is not easily available to us in the New Testament. We can perceive him only as a variety of early Christian communities perceived him. It is better that we grant to our community the right to read both Old and New Testaments in the light of a contemporary canon. Indeed, it is their duty.

And precisely that canonical context reminds us "that the Bible does not function as Scriptures *apart from the community of believers.*"[80]

The lodestone of that canon is the quest for the perfection which belongs to the Heavenly Father. (Mt 5:48)

Let me defend the above paragraph and indeed democratic theology by a personal experience. While one religious order, the Jesuits, was engaged in the "canonical criticism" of the works done by their founder to which I alluded earlier in the paper, one of the elders complained that too much heed was being paid to the youth in the group by reason of their numbers and their eloquence. Another worthy elder grew forever famous by replying, "I cannot believe that the Holy Spirit is perversely attracting to the Society of Jesus young men who are bent only on her destruction!"

By the same token, I cannot believe that the *pleroma* of the Christian assembly is called to accede to the destruction of the churches, whether theological movement in that direction should come from an "infallible" clergy or an "infallible" theological academy.

But Childs is far braver than I and so he sets out to treat some "practical" matters, among them questions of sexual ethics. (Here is an example, perhaps, of the low stress that he occasionally puts on the canon of the contemporary community.) He seems to read two "layers" of the Old Testament as having been canonized precisely because they are mutually corrective, Proverbs 7 and the Song of Songs.[81]

Similar erotic vocabulary is used in both, but the Song surely does not see sex as a *remedium concupiscentiae*[82] but as "the most valued of all human prizes." This force which can unleash the most cruel of human passions, is—for some translators—still "the flame of God."[83]

---

[80] Ibid., p. 100 (emphasis added).

[81] Ibid., pp. 185-200.

[82] Ibid., p. 193.

[83] Cf. R. Gordis as cited by Haim Cohen, in *The Drunkenness of Noah* (Alabama: University Press, 1974), p. 5.

If Childs has managed to do nothing else in his treatment of sexual ethics from a biblical perspective, he has succeeded in pointing out the number of "ambiguities" that the various biblical warrants present to the ethician who is searching for a solution.

The act of "Moses' slaying of an Egyptian" becomes a classic for Childs because of its wide treatment throughout scripture (Ex 2:11-22, Acts 7:23-29, 35, Heb 11:23-28).[84]

> Our text does not provide one clear answer to the complex problem of using violence for the sake of justice. But it does raise a whole set of issues that are inherent in such action. By uncovering the ambiguities in the act of violence, the reader is forced to confront rather than evade those basic factors which constitute the moral decision.[85]

Childs suggests that even the "theology of liberation" may be illumined by careful study of these passages.[86] With its careful effort not to condemn Moses, the scriptures have made clear how little it is that violence accomplishes, that assuredly no deliverance results from it and finally that the "savior," Moses, must be sent back to Egypt with a new authority and a new mission.[87]

But perhaps Childs has used an unfair example since both Moses and violence play such a large role in the history of the development of scripture. Childs has done extremely well in this passage in his treatment of the "history of interpretation," Jewish and Christian, after the close of the New Testament period.

I would prefer to place the methodological stress somewhere else. A colleague in the discussion of canonical criticism notes that the text of the Scriptures as we have them is an "accidental precipitate" from the dialogue between the *qahal* and its leadership. Since this dialogue was carried on in the rabbinic period[88] the real question as Seeligman puts it was how the materials were allowed to "congeal" in the first place[89] before analogous dialogues in the Christian communities produced another "accidental precipitate" of their own.

With characteristic truculence and courage, Smith says that the problem of "congealing" is soluble simply by recourse to political history.[90] Few would agree with him. He has however made the

---

[84] Childs, *Biblical Theology in Crisis,* pp. 164-83.

[85] Ibid., p. 183.

[86] Ibid., p. 182.

[87] Ibid., p. 183.

[88] As was developed in the works of Weingreen cited in note 24 above.

[89] Isaac Seeligmann, "Voraussetzungen der Midrasch-Exegese," *Supplements to Vetus Testamentum,* ed. Anderson et al. (Leiden: Brill, 1953), pp. 176-77.

[90] Cited by Sanders in "Adaptable for Life: The Nature and Function of Canon," p. 543.

good point that an intrusive force of some kind is required to stabilize a text that would otherwise have continued to float in a sea of dialogue. Sanders praises him for another observation:

> [His other] observation is correct. We should assume that what we inherit in the Old Testament is only a fraction of what had been available, and that they were the needs of the community which shaped the surviving, earlier traditions into the bible as we know it.[91]

Though Childs admits it is valid to begin from the perspective of the modern problem[92] one would have preferred a clear statement of why it is valid.

It is valid because the living communities are the canon, and the Spirit attested to in the *Letter of Aristeas* lives yet in a variety of religious assemblies.

Obviously, that dyadic discussion now is at least triadic, and involves the prior "accidental precipitates," the current living assembly, and its leadership. In this discussion, the communities desperately need historical criticism to counter the temptation to blend or simply to avoid conflict. One would wonder about a theology department that offers no courses in New Testament ethics or theology, for example, but prefers to allow individual professors to work within the comfortable framework of a given gospel or epistle. Such a program avoids the need of the community's confronting the majestic serenity of Christ in the gospel of John with the disturbing problems of the emerging messianic consciousness haltingly expressed by the Synoptics.

VIII. Conclusion: Further Reflections on Authority

What has emerged in our study until now is a concern with three different areas of problems: The historical process which produced the collection of "canonized texts," the tension between the "canonized text" that did result and the "living canon" which is the contemporary community. Finally, there is the way in which we are to view major problems of faith and ethics, bathed now in the light of the canonized text, now in the light of the living canon.

Common to all of these is a concern for the vital question of authority. Where does it come from? What sort of gradations of authority are there and who determines them? Dodd has written:

> The church read as scripture those writings which it felt to be most vitally related to the spiritual impulse that created it. It did

---

[91] Ibid.

[92] Childs, *Biblical Theology in Crisis,* p. 183.

not at first regard these writings as especially authoritative
because they were canonical; they became canonical because
they had already made good their authority.[93]

To which we have already added, of course, the idea that a hidden
level in them was at least authoritative in potency because a later
church was to feel their authority.

Certainly it is advantageous that this concept enables the contemporary religious community to resolve the impossible question of
inerrancy; it is in dialogue between the living church and the written
text that "scripture is inerrant."

But can we ask further questions about the circumstances under
which these texts became "authoritative?" What happened in the
process by which the community which received a variety of texts
began to make selections, at least in the highlighting of one text or
other? Sanders makes the interesting suggestion that "Reforging of
Traditions takes place in the sort of emotional mood that takes place
after the withdrawal of Sennacherib."[94] Many would have some
problems with that. It seems to go against the commonplace, that
texts or doctrines are delineated only under challenge. Reforging of
texts takes place not when the mood is ebullient, but threatened.

But regardless of when the reforging or reforming takes place,
what is the nature of the equation between text and community?
Elsewhere Sanders had written:

> So the study of canon cannot begin with the notion of stability
> and the concept of inclusion. Rather . . . there was a story exist-
> ing in many forms from early days. In all likelihood, there were
> a number of such stories, but the Law and the Prophets as we
> inherit them highlight only two basic themes, those we call the
> Mosaic and the Davidic. Only these survived, other traditions
> adhering to them; and only the Mosaic, less the conquest,
> became the Torah.[95]

Why?

I wonder if the answer to this question is not to be found more in
depth psychology than in any of the areas of the theological enterprise. Here we are dealing with the problems of group identity. If
certain texts, or interpretations of them, are simply not compatible
with the group's identity, can the group not simply change in its
identity? But how much of a change in self-identification is compatible with the group's remaining the group that it was?

---

[93] Dodd, *Authority of the Bible,* p. 196.

[94] Sanders, *Torah and Canon,* p. 30.

[95] Sanders, "Adaptable for Life: The Nature and Function of Canon,"
p. 540.

Blenkinsopp had written of his own efforts:

> In the case of early Israel and early Judaism (as that of early
> Christianity) we will argue that the decisive factor was the need
> to resolve conflicting claims to authority. This may not lead us
> to view writing with Levi-Strauss as an instrument of oppres-
> sion and control, but it should alert us to the possibility that it
> will embody claims of a political and tendentious nature.[96]

What I have insisted upon increasingly throughout this paper is
that the special genius of the scriptures is that those layers which
may have been downgraded by "claims of a political and tenden-
tious nature" remain through the Dilthey-Barr principle accessible
to the later communities. This is especially the case, if the
theological academy remains in steady communion with the people
of God.

> It was not by accident that a working pastor in the forgotten
> Swiss village of Safenwil first discovered what Romans could
> mean to a congregation before dropping his theological bomb
> on the scholarly community.[97]

And yet perhaps this last example makes the resolution of the problem of authority too easy. We have here "charisma," represented in
the modern example by that of great scholarship, in dialogue with a
given community which is then overwhelmed. There are no real
problems of authority here.

But in ancient Israel, the early church(es), or in any contemporary religious community, the problems are far more complex.
First of all, because "the establishment," whatever it may be, has
an interest in shutting off further growth. The Hebrew text (*lo' . . .
'ôd*) is at pains to point out that "never again" has there arisen a
prophet like Moses. The syntax goes out of its way to insist that it is
most unlikely that such a prophet will ever again rise. Moses is
unique.[98]

And yet the shutting off of a canon is not that much easier than the
re-opening of a canon, or the permitting the intrusion of new interpretations into previously canonized materials. How is it done? That
both *can* be done seem universally assumed. Rivkin's work which
attempted to upset a scholarly consensus by attributing authorship
of the Pentateuch to the Aaronides has been widely criticized, but
almost never on the score that it would demand a totally new interpretation and its acceptance by the ancient Hebrew community.[99]

---

[96] Blenkinsopp, *Prophecy and Canon*, p. 4.

[97] Childs, *Biblical Theology in Crisis*, p. 96.

[98] I am following Blenkinsopp, *Prophecy and Canon*, pp. 86 ff. here, although the
uniqueness of Moses is a commonplace.

[99] Ellis Rivkin, *The Shaping of Jewish History* (New York: Scribner, 1971).

Östborn would put the authoritative key in the cult.[100] He is not alone. Reventlow writes of Jeremiah's "official relationship" to God in the cult and claims that the authority which this gave him derived from his ability to preach and pray in a liturgical context.[101] Sanders originally wrote that writings were partially canonized through cultic usage[102] and later suggested that the lectionary was assembled in an effort to confront a contemporary majority.[103] Blenkinsopp brings to our attention the work of von Rad[104] and Kraus[105] who deal with materials that they see refuting the notion of the "uniqueness" of Moses the teacher once-and-for-all and place in some opposition to him the "cultic prophet" who has the authority to "teach with authority" but always in the cultic situation.

Perhaps it is here that we have come to the heart of the question which biblical scholars and systematicians are called to resolve. Is the nature of proximate theological authority definable or is theological life more complex than that? It is a good idea to place a serious stress on genuine dialogue between biblicist and systematician, between "community" and "theological academy," between the two varying anthropologies of Gen 1-3, between the sacramentality of cult in the Hebrew Scriptures and their sacramentality of the word, between a "virgin birth" in Isaiah 7:14 (as Mowinckel long ago found supported by the Ugaritic material[106]) and the normal event of a young woman giving birth.

Still, none of these stresses (not even the first) can be resolved unless we begin with the conclusions of this paper: the Bible must be read for its religious message; the hermeneutic principle applied to the religious person implies that faith (and therefore inspiration) are both objective and subjective, i.e., both in the Bible and in the believing reader; and that this subject-object polarity can be found in the Bible itself, which contains multiple interpretations of one event.

---

[100] Gunnar Östborn, *Cult and Canon: A Study in the Canonization of the Old Testament* (Uppsala: Lundquist, 1950).

[101] Henning Reventlow, *Liturgie und prophetisches Ich bei Jeremie* (Tübingen: Gutersloh Verlagshaus, 1963).

[102] Sanders, *Torah and Canon,* p. 111.

[103] Sanders, "Adaptable for Life: The Nature and Function of Canon," p. 544.

[104] Gerhard von Rad, *The Problem of the Hexateuch and other Essays,* trans. E. Dicken (New York: McGraw-Hill, 1966), p. 30.

[105] Hans-Joachin Kraus, *Worship in Israel,* trans. G. Buswell (Richmond: John Knox Press, 1962), pp. 101-12.

[106] Sigmund Mowinckel, *He that Cometh,* trans. G. Anderson (Nashville: Abingdon, 1954), p. 114.

A Response to Fr. Sheehan

by Ms. Toni Craven

In opening my comments on Fr. Sheehan's paper, let me emphasize its title: "Canonical Criticism: A Place on Which to Stand in Doing Theology." I emphasize the author's claim that this is *a* place on which to stand, not *the* place, because standing before you this morning you have four biblical specialists, each of whom might describe a different place on which to stand in doing biblical theology. Lest you shake your heads in despair at our plurality, let me characterize the four of us in terms which bespeak a unity familiar to all of you: just call us J-E-D-P. In this parody, Fr. Sheehan is the P author, he is the one interested in the process within the believing community in which the *qahal,* the assembly, and its leadership give the canon its shape. Prof. Rylaarsdam is D, he defines the work of the theologian of the Old Testament as that of "an historian and a critic" (". . . of Old Testament Theology," *Criterion,* Autumn 1971, p. 29). Fr. Sklba is the E author, partly by default since I don't know him well, partly because he comes from the north—at least for today, and partly because his comments and mine are united on this occasion to form the JE epic response. I am the J author, the one interested in good story-telling, or as we say today the one who specializes in literary/rhetorical criticism. Each of us interprets the task of the biblical theologian in a distinct yet complementary fashion. All four of us are deeply interested in one body of literature, the Hebrew Scriptures. No one of our positions can or should be absolutized as *the* position from which to understand scripture, and so I open my comments on Fr. Sheehan's paper with an acknowledgment of the wisdom and humility of its title.

Fr. Sheehan defines canonical criticism as the "study of the focus which a given religious community (Hebrew, Jewish, early Christian or other) gave to a particular body of scripture" (p. 338). He affirms that "historical criticism, aided by canonical criticism, [is] a valid locus for doing theology" (p. 339). By invoking what he calls the Dilthey-Barr principle (p. 345), he argues that our study of the process of canonization should be expanded to incorporate stages of development which both precede and follow the establishment of a fixed set of sacred texts. Thus "canon" is broadened to incorporate not only the sacred text in its final form but also the process in the oral world which shaped these texts and the process in the contemporary religious community which uses these texts. The contemporary listening church(es) plays a double role here as both the inheritor of canon and the maker of an ongoing living canon. The "canonized text" and the "living canon" which is the contemporary community in turn affect the way in which we are to view major problems of faith and ethics. The paper is primarily an investigation of the criteria which define canon and its function in contemporary theology. It is an investigation which involves a particular confessional stance. Is it by accident that the paper moves from the Jewish community in the section on "Targumic Interpretation" (p. 342ff) to the Christian community in the section on "The Christian Community is a Prophetic Community" (p. 347ff), to the Roman Catholic community in the section on the "Triadic Discussion" (p. 354ff)?

It is with Section VII, the "Triadic Discussion," that I most strongly agree and disagree. The trialogue is a three-way conversation involving the " 'accidental precipitates,' the current living assembly, and its leadership" (p. 355). While I wholeheartedly endorse Fr. Sheehan's argument that our religious communities have the right and the duty to read both Old and New Testaments in the light of a contemporary canon (p. 354), I deplore the sentiment expressed by the unnamed colleague he quotes as saying that the text of the scriptures as we have them is an "accidental precipitate" from the dialogue between the *qahal* and its leadership. The final text an "accidental precipitate," never. Literary artistry of the quality we find in the Hebrew Scriptures can hardly be the sudden or unexpected result—which is how my dictionary defines a precipitate— of any dialogue. I find myself somewhat assuaged by Prof. Rylaarsdam's comment to me that Fr. Sheehan really meant to say that the final text is a "providential precipitate" of the dialogue between the *qahal* and its leadership.

And so I ask Fr. Sheehan three questions:

(1) What about the individual who is out of step with the *qahal* and its leadership? What place does your view of biblical theology allow one whose *vocation* runs counter to democratic theology?

(2) What about differing definitions of canon? For example, the Book of Judith was obviously widely accepted in its day and afterwards, witness the numerous Greek recensions of the text and the thirteen midrashim. Yet, despite its wide circulation, *Judith* is not part of the Jewish or Protestant canon. It is, however, a deuterocanonical work for both Roman Catholic and Orthodox churches. Does your broadened interpretation of canon help account for this phenomenon?

(3) What about the particularity of the texts themselves and the improvement of our experience of what they say and how they say it? Is there a danger in the methodology you espouse that we will split form and content in the attention you would have us give to

what is said in the contemporary community and to the process in which the group seeks out its religious identity?

Finally, let me share with you the wider audience two passages that struck me in a special way as I prepared this response:

Fr. Sheehan opens his paper with a description of the strained relationship between biblical theologians and systematic theologians. He characterizes the problem in terms of biblical theology as the "hand-maiden" of "real" theology (p. 337). So, too, Prof. Rylaarsdam opens his article ". . . of Old Testament Theology" with a description of biblical theology as a "handmaid" (p. 24).

It is no surprise that biblical theologians find it unacceptable to be "hand-maidens." Since it is sexist language that has been employed to describe the brokenness of the relationship between biblical and dogmatic theologians, perhaps we would do well to meditate on what the creation stories tell us about relationships.

Recall that Gen. 2, the Yahwist story, says, "The Lord God said, 'It is not good that *'adham* should be alone; I will make him a helper fit for him' " (2:18). Then, of course, God made the animals, "but for *'adham* there was not found a helper fit for him" (2:20). Finally, God caused a deep sleep to fall upon *'adham* and when *'adham* is out of it, God fashions the woman. In the Garden, male is different from female, but both are equal acts of divine initiative. As Gen. 1:27, the Priestly account, so powerfully affirms female and male are both in "the image of God."

Perhaps the time is right for us to think about life in the Garden, of life which allows for equality and difference, of a theological relationship between systematic and biblical theologians in which both can serve and be served by the other, in which there is no rigid distinction between hand-maiden and master. Fr. Sheehan's paper on this occasion honoring Karl Rahner invites us to think seriously on our professional relationship and in particular on the legitimacy of canonical criticism as a place on which to stand in doing theology.

A Response to Fr. Sheehan

by Very Rev. Richard J. Sklba

The issue of "Canonical Criticism" selected by Fr. Sheehan for his paper today is most appropriate for this Symposium honoring Karl Rahner, who once accepted as a working definition of dogma that which the community judged "worthy of being remembered."[1] The biblical Canon also contains material judged worthy of remembrance, and the similarities between the process of dogmatic formulation and the canonical legitimation of the Scriptures are very striking indeed!

However it be defined, the concept of Canonical Criticism incorporates the recognition of pluralism within the biblical tradition, as well as the faith of the community which endorses those traditions. Canonical Criticism presumes Revelation as a process beginning with an historical event, but including the inspired interpretation of that event together with the final acceptance of that interpretation by the Church.

Fr. Sheehan's paper, with its exploration of the role of the community in determining the shape and value of the Canon, raises three basic questions for the biblicist who would be both member and servant of the Church: which community is the ultimate human norm of continuity? how does one deal with the expanding limits of the Canon throughout history? what is the enduring validity of any given stage in the evolution of a biblical tradition?

The first question, though initially hermeneutical, is at base clearly ecclesiological. If the living community is the canon as stated by Fr. Sheehan, and I believe it is, it requires a more exact delineation than he was able to give it. Like the human mind of Levi-Strauss' Structuralism, the community is the uninvited guest at every stage in the formation of the Canon, but one cannot judge theological continuity by mere vote or majority, unless the latter be carefully defined and extended to include the consent of faithful still unborn. To invoke the *sensus fidelium,* one must have an accurate perception of what constitutes the genuine *fidelis.* The issue seems an essential component to any discussion of Canonical Criticism.

The second question raised by this paper stems from our realization that the Canon was a constantly expanding reality in the experience of Israel. Canonical Criticism shortly after the common acceptance of the Pentateuch would have been much simpler than at a later date after Judah's adoption of the writings of the Prophets as

---

[1] H. Schlier, cited with approval in Karl Rahner and Karl Lehmann, *Kerygma and Dogma,* trans. W. Glen-Doepel (New York: Herder and Herder, 1969) p. 72.

inspired and normative. How is the critic to deal with this changing size of the Canon? The community's willingness to add the words "and Judah" to Jeremiah's earlier diatribes against the Northern Kingdom (cf. Jer 30:3,4 etc.) recognizes the inner vitality of those traditions. The Christ-event as viewed through the eyes of the people of the New Testament, while placing definitive if elastic limits upon the traditions of Judah, attempts to underscore the deeper significance of those same traditions, and invites new understanding of familiar themes. The critic cannot with equal assurance exclude the possibility of newer material ever being added to the Jewish corpus. Even after the experience of gathering Talmudic literature into a form essentially diverse from that of the Hebrew Scriptures, the restoration of the Jewish state after these many centuries and the trauma of the Holocaust may yet inspire a theological statement within Judaism so poignantly perceptive as to raise the question of canonicity once more. But even without speculating on such provocative *futurabilia,* one must ask if Canonical Criticism can content itself with examining each statement or each thread of tradition in its diachronic formulation, or rather must not the critic study the tradition in tension with the remaining portions of the Canon of that age? Does this not raise the question of a "canon within a canon" once more?

Finally, I am led to affirm the problem of authority as raised by Fr. Sheehan in his conclusions. As a result of our contemporary appreciation for the fruits of historical criticism, we can often disentangle layers in any given biblical tradition or practice. Theological constructs were constantly modified by successive historical experiences or needs. For example, the biblicist perceives vividly if not always clearly that responsibility shifted from a corporate to a more individualized notion after the Exile, or that the theodicy of earlier Deuteronomic formulations was ever after nuanced by Job's more skeptical scrutiny. Yet polarities once refined are still retained within the theological *textus receptus!* What remains normative? At which moment in the evolution of such a concept does a particular vision of reality assume authority and command response from the community of faith? And at which point does such an idea lose that authority to a more carefully nuanced formulation? Can a believer return at whim to an earlier phrase still retained within the body of canonical literature, and even insist on it as an acceptable norm for the community? Can one return to the threshing floor of pre-Hebraic cult with impunity simply because the same is described with approval in the Hebrew Scriptures, or to first century forms of Church order simply because Paul records them in the Corinthian community with apparent approval? Does the fact that the community of faith might retain a literary unit for its inherent polarity invest that unit with enduring value? Careful study shows that an earlier statement such as Isaiah's affirmation in Zion's inviolability (Is 31:4-5) can become itself aberrant and even heretical in the later age of Hananiah (Jer 28:10-17) when shifting circumstances required new solutions from Jeremiah!

As Fr. Sheehan concludes, it is the question of authority which lies at the base of his treatment of Canonical Criticism. Such an issue demands still further criteria for judging the power of a given text to gather the *qahal,* and to speak with God's voice to that community. Fr. Sheehan wisely includes the community in this discussion, but does not tell us what finally constitutes that community, nor has he come to terms with the steadily expanding boundaries of the Canon, nor has he offered the necessary criteria for avoiding the archaicizing regression which inevitably marks genuine heresy. Such questions are obviously too vast for any single presentation, but they are apt and valid for a Symposium of this nature. May their discussion contribute in some small fashion to the stature of the man we honor this week!

Appendix 1

Symposium Schedule

FIRST DAY
Thursday, March 29

10:00 a.m.

Presentation: Rev. William V. Dych, S.J.
"Method in Theology According to Karl Rahner"

Commentators: Rev. Bernard J. F. Lonergan, S.J.
Rev. Walter Stohrer, S.J.

11:00 a.m.

Presentation: Rev. John F. X. Sheehan, S.J.
"The Historical Method and Canonical Criticism:
A place on which to stand in doing Biblical Theology"

Commentators: Very Rev. Richard Sklba
Ms. Toni Craven

2:00 p.m.

Presentation: Rev. Johannes B. Metz
"An Identity Crisis in Christianity?
Transcendental and Political Responses"

Commentators: Rev. David Tracy
Rev. Matthew Lamb

3:30 p.m.

Presentation: Rev. George Muschalek, S.J.
"The Impasse of Ultimate Reassurance and Christian
Certitude"

Commentators: Rev. Ladislas Orsy, S.J.
Rev. Joseph Bracken, S.J.

8:00 p.m.

PUBLIC LECTURE
Rev. Avery Dulles, S.J.
"Revelation and Discovery"

SECOND DAY
Friday, March 30

10:00 a.m.

Presentation: Rev. Avery Dulles, S.J.
"Revelation and Discovery" Summary

Commentators: Dr. Andrew Tallon
Rev. Joseph Lienhard, S.J.

11:00 a.m.

Presentation: Rev. Bruno Sch8uller, S.J.
"Christianity and the New Man:
The Moral Dimension"
Commentators: Dr. Mary Rousseau
Rev. Richard Roach, S.J.

2:00 p.m.

Presentation: Rev. Leo O'Donovan, S.J.
"Making Heaven and Earth: Catholic Theology's
Search for a Unified View of Nature and History"
Commentators: Dr. William O'Brien
Dr. Dean Fowler

3:30 p.m.

Presentation: Dr. Thomas Ommen
"The Pre-Understanding of the Theologian"
Commentators: Rev. Peter Schineller, S.J.
Rev. Roland Teske, S.J.

8:00 p.m.

Presentation: Rev. Jon Sobrino, S.J.
"Current Problems in Christology in Latin American
Theology"
Commentators: Dr. Fernando Segovia
Rev. Joseph Komonchak

THIRD DAY
Saturday, March 31

10:00 a.m.

Presentation: Rev. Harvey Egan, S.J.
"Rahner's Mystical Theology"
Commentators: Rev. Kenneth Baker, S.J.
Dr. Keith Egan

11:00 a.m.

Presentation: Rev. Gerald McCool, S.J.
"Karl Rahner and the Christian Philosophy of
St. Thomas Aquinas"
Commentators: Rev. Robert Kress
Rev. Patrick Burns. S.J.

Appendix 2

Authors

MAJOR PRESENTATIONS

Rev. William Dych, S.J., former Professor of Systematic Theology, Woodstock College.

Rev. Avery Dulles, S.J., Professor of Systematic Theology, Catholic University of America, Washington, D.C.

Rev. Harvey Egan, S.J., Professor of Systematic Theology, Boston College, Chestnut Hill, Massachusetts.

Rev. Gerald McCool, S.J., Professor of Philosophy, Fordham University, Bronx, New York.

Rev. Johannes Metz, Professor of Fundamental Theology, Westfalische Wilhelms-Universität, Münster, West Germany.

Rev. George Muschalek, S.J., Professor of Systematic Theology, Marquette University.

Rev. Leo O'Donovan, S.J., Professor of Systematic Theology, Weston School of Theology, Cambridge, Massachusetts.

Dr. Thomas Ommen, Professor of Systematic Theology, Villanova University, Villanova, Pennsylvania.

Rev. Bruno Schüller, S.J., Professor of Moral Theology, Westfalische Wilhelms-Universität, Münster, West Germany.

Rev. John Sheehan, S.J., Professor of Old Testament, Marquette University.

Rev. Jon Sobrino, S.J., Professor of Systematic Theology, Universidad Centroamericana José Siméon Cañas, San Salvador, El Salvador.

COMMENTATORS

Rev. Kenneth Baker, S.J., Editor, *Homiletic and Pastoral Review*

Rev. Joseph Bracken, S.J., Marquette University

Rev. Patrick Burns, S.J., Marquette University

Ms. Toni Craven, Marquette University

Dr. Keith Egan, Marquette University

Dr. Dean Fowler, Marquette University

Rev. Joseph Komonchak, Catholic University of America

Rev. Robert Kress, University of Evansville

Rev. Matthew Lamb, Marquette University

Rev. Joseph Lienhard, S.J., Marquette University

Rev. Bernard Lonergan, S.J., Boston College

Dr. William O'Brien, University of Notre Dame

Rev. Ladislas Orsy, S.J., Catholic University of America

Rev. Richard Roach, S.J., Marquette University

Dr. Mary Rousseau, Marquette University

Rev. Peter Schineller, S.J., Jesuit School of Theology in Chicago

Dr. Fernando Segovia, Marquette University

Very Rev. Richard Sklba, St. Francis School of Pastoral Ministry

Rev. Walter Stohrer, S.J., Marquette University

Dr. Andrew Tallon, Marquette University

Rev. Roland Teske, S.J., Marquette University

Rev. David Tracy, University of Chicago

INDEX OF NAMES

INDEX OF SCRIPTURE REFERENCES
Old Testament

INDEX OF SCRIPTURE REFERENCES
New Testament

* Spelling according to Goodspeed Bible